ALSO BY SCOTT EYMAN

Charlie Chaplin vs. America: When Art, Sex, and Politics Collided

20th Century-Fox: Darryl F. Zanuck and the Creation of the Modern Film Studio (Turner Classic Movies)

Cary Grant: A Brilliant Disguise

Hank and Jim: The Fifty-Year Friendship of Henry Fonda and James Stewart

John Wayne: The Life and Legend

Empire of Dreams: The Epic Life of Cecil B. DeMille

Lion of Hollywood: The Life and Legend of Louis B. Mayer

John Ford: The Searcher, 1894–1973

Print the Legend: The Life and Times of John Ford

The Speed of Sound: Hollywood and the Talkie Revolution, 1927–1930

Ernst Lubitsch: Laughter in Paradise

Mary Pickford, America's Sweetheart

Five American Cinematographers

WITH LOUIS GIANNETTI

Flashback: A Brief History of Film

WITH ROBERT WAGNER

Pieces of My Heart: A Life

You Must Remember This: Life and Style in Hollywood's Golden Age

I Loved Her in the Movies: Memories of Hollywood's Legendary Actresses

JOAN CRAWFORD

A WOMAN'S FACE

SCOTT EYMAN

SIMON & SCHUSTER
New York   Amsterdam/Antwerp   London
Toronto   Sydney/Melbourne   New Delhi

Simon and Schuster
1230 Avenue of the Americas
New York, NY 10020

For more than 100 years, Simon & Schuster has championed authors and the stories they create. By respecting the copyright of an author's intellectual property, you enable Simon & Schuster and the author to continue publishing exceptional books for years to come. We thank you for supporting the author's copyright by purchasing an authorized edition of this book.

No amount of this book may be reproduced or stored in any format, nor may it be uploaded to any website, database, language-learning model, or other repository, retrieval, or artificial intelligence system without express permission. All rights reserved. Inquiries may be directed to Simon & Schuster, 1230 Avenue of the Americas, New York, NY 10020 or permissions@simonandschuster.com.

Copyright © 2025 by Paladin Literature, Inc.

All rights reserved, including the right to reproduce this book or portions thereof in any form whatsoever. For information, address Simon & Schuster Subsidiary Rights Department, 1230 Avenue of the Americas, New York, NY 10020.

First Simon & Schuster hardcover edition November 2025

SIMON & SCHUSTER and colophon are registered trademarks of Simon & Schuster, LLC

Simon & Schuster strongly believes in freedom of expression and stands against censorship in all its forms. For more information, visit BooksBelong.com.

For information about special discounts for bulk purchases, please contact Simon & Schuster Special Sales at 1-866-506-1949 or business@simonandschuster.com.

The Simon & Schuster Speakers Bureau can bring authors to your live event. For more information or to book an event, contact the Simon & Schuster Speakers Bureau at 1-866-248-3049 or visit our website at www.simonspeakers.com.

Interior design by Wendy Blum

Manufactured in the United States of America

10 9 8 7 6 5 4 3 2 1

Library of Congress Cataloging-in-Publication Data

ISBN 978-1-6680-4730-9
ISBN 978-1-6680-4732-3 (ebook)

Frontispiece photo: Lucille LeSueur, circa 1924.

Naturally, for Bob Bender

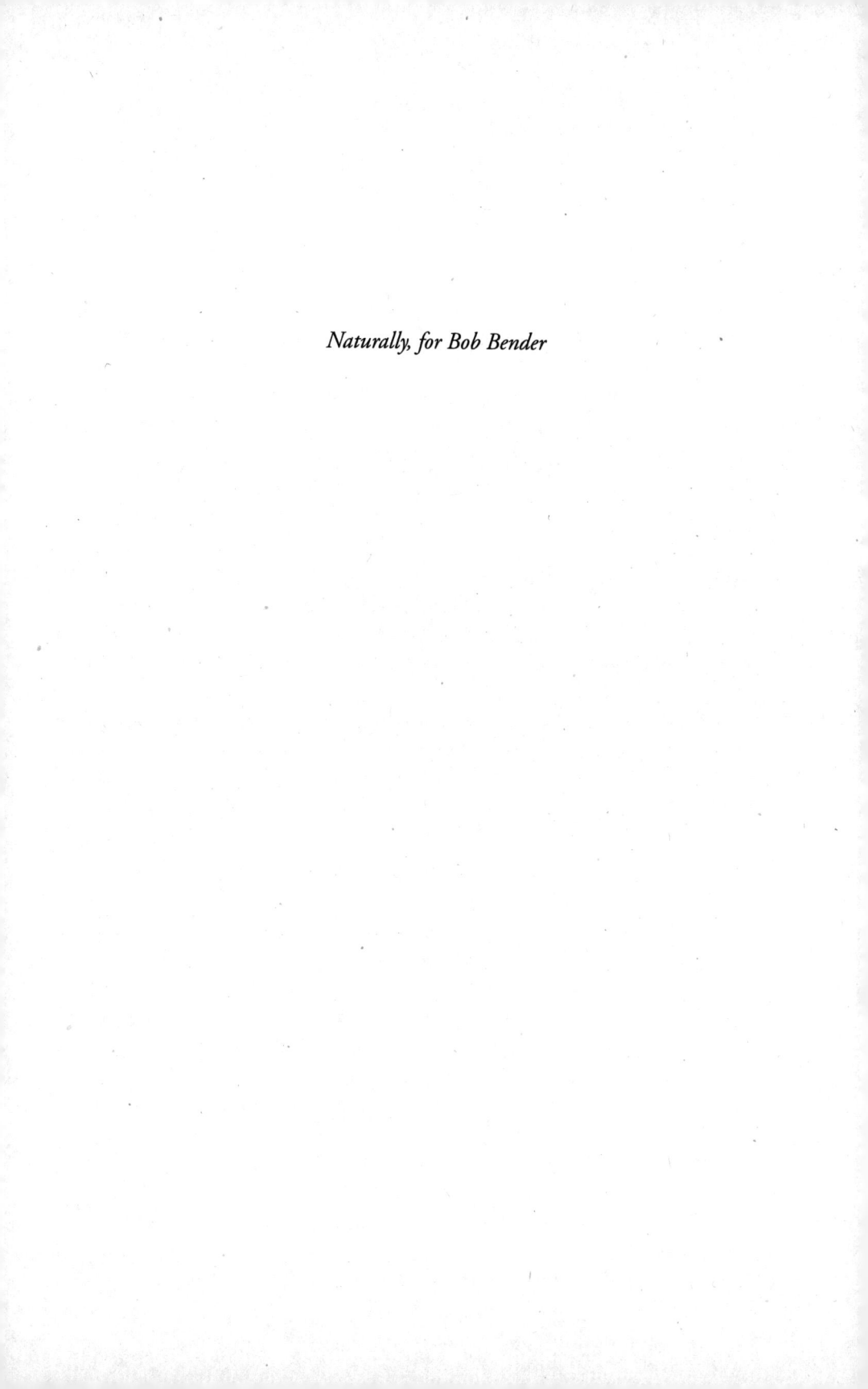

"My beauties line the tables and shelves in my mind. I don't want objects lining my home. I'd rather look at Joan Crawford on a big screen. She was the ultimate work of art, crafted for us all."

—Tennessee Williams

*"Writing the story of Joan Crawford?
Isn't that something like rewriting the Lord's Prayer?"*

—William Haines

CONTENTS

Prologue	3
Part One	7
Part Two	143
Part Three	223
Acknowledgments	387
Bibliography	391
Source Notes	397
Index	429

JOAN CRAWFORD

PROLOGUE

THE FILM IS 16MM Kodachrome, so it has those "nice, bright colors" Paul Simon sang about. The cans were stacked in the back of Joan Crawford's closet when she moved back to New York in 1955. After she died in 1977 they sat in the closets of her daughter Cathy, and of Casey LaLonde, her grandson.

The expectations were that they would be the usual movie star home movies—birthday parties with the kids in Brentwood, some behind-the-scenes shots from the studio, etc. There was some of that, but there were also several cans sealed with masking tape on which was written "Charles and Me."

They were Joan Crawford home movies all right, but they weren't what anybody had expected. From her look, and from the cars on view, the bulk of them were made in 1939 or 1940 outside New York City. There are shots of the Dakota apartment building, of Central Park in the winter as well as the spring, but mostly the atmosphere is country—a glamorous movie star on strangely unglamorous vacations: trudging through the woods, lugging a rifle on a hunt for pheasant, having a cigarette by a dying campfire.

The Kodachrome reveals Crawford's russet hair, her freckles, even her impromptu dance moves, as she does an enchanting little sideways shuffle while playing with her dachshund. She's relaxed, coquettish, glowing, completely unguarded. In one shot, she's sunbathing nude.

There are two startling factors revealed by the footage. Most obviously, there is the way Crawford pops through the screen without the intervention of a script, editing, or even rudimentary lighting. She loves the camera and the favor is returned—she was born to be captured on film, any film, under any conditions. And the rifle, the earnest trooping through the woods, means she's obviously shaping herself to fit in with her man's predispositions.

Despite her reputation as an imperious diva, this was always Crawford's pattern. When she was married to Douglas Fairbanks Jr., she immersed herself in fiction and philosophers, albeit with a singular lack of enjoyment, while her marriage to Franchot Tone meant a conversion to the gospel of Stanislavsky.

The man behind the camera some of the time, in front of the camera most of the time, is pushing middle age, has a widow's peak, and sports a Bertie Wooster-ish set of hunting togs indicating a charge account with Hammacher Schlemmer. From Crawford's body language and the intimacy of the footage it was obvious they were a couple.

Casey LaLonde asked me if I had any idea about the man's identity, but I was stumped. He wasn't a director, although he could have been a producer. But why meet up outside New York City when Palm Springs was only a few hours away from Crawford's home in Brentwood?

I turned to *A Portrait of Joan*, Crawford's autobiography, published in 1962. I didn't expect much, but I found something dating to shortly after her divorce from Franchot Tone in April 1939: "In New York, I had met a marvelously mature man, one of the best people I've ever known. This man must be nameless because he was never able to get a divorce. He is a business executive, and I respect him thoroughly. Again I had to settle for a long and lovely friendship. He taught me to hunt and fish, we used to go on these expeditions with a whole group of men. The first time, I'm sure, their reaction was, Oh No, not a dame tagging along! Carried my own gun and my own camera, waded through streams in the vanguard, and at noon when we'd camp, I'd help fix lunch and surprise them with all sorts of snacks packed away in my knapsack just in case they didn't catch any fish. This friend introduced me to politics, to banking, big business and public affairs.

"He says I taught him to be brave, to stand up for what he thought was right, to be considerate of other human beings, especially those with whom he was working, and to be generous in giving of himself. I didn't teach him. Those were his instincts. He merely needed someone gently to remind him."

That told us some of what the film had already told us, but it didn't offer any hints about Charles's last name. That came through the back door—an item in a Hedda Hopper column from 1940 that carried a whiff of sulfur, as many Hopper columns did. Hopper included the name of Charles McCabe in the cast list of an upcoming Crawford movie. Charles McCabe? Who the hell was Charles McCabe?

There were no actors in Hollywood with that name. Perhaps a New York actor? Nope. A quick glance at Wikipedia, and there he was—the same man with Crawford in the footage. Charles McCabe was the publisher of the New York *Daily Mirror*, a Hearst paper that Woody Allen called "a sparse rag that would have gone out of business were it not for the fact it housed Walter Winchell's column." Unfortunately, irrelevance can only be withstood for so long—the *Daily Mirror* died in October 1963.

Hedda Hopper had found out about the affair and wanted Crawford to know she knew.

Casey LaLonde called one of McCabe's surviving sons, who told him that after their father's death in 1970, his sons had gone through his papers and found letters from Crawford that made the relationship obvious. McCabe's wife hadn't known about the affair, or about any of McCabe's numerous extramarital entanglements. In any case, McCabe had never asked his wife for a divorce. McCabe's sons didn't want their mother to find out about the affair, so they burned Crawford's letters.

Joan Crawford died seven years after Charles McCabe; there were no letters from him in her papers.

A relationship with a public figure such as Crawford must have been risky for McCabe, but the footage clearly indicates neither of them cared, while the fact that Crawford kept the movies for the rest of her life indicates the affair was far more than a passing fling.

The home movies are a glimpse into the unexpected emotional accessibility of a woman often regarded as ferocious even by other ferocious movie stars. How did Crawford and McCabe meet? How long did the affair last? We can't be sure, because Joan Crawford could keep a secret.

But not all of them.

PART ONE

"*I think most of our fears are developed in childhood. . . . All mine came out of childhood.*"

—Joan Crawford

"*I was born working.*"

—Joan Crawford

Left: The teenage Lucille LeSueur with her mother and her brother Hal.

CHAPTER ONE

ALMOST ALL STAR BIOGRAPHIES issued by movie studios glossed, elided, or lied, but very few managed to cram more concentrated disinformation into two brief paragraphs than MGM's 1939 biography of Joan Crawford:

"Joan Crawford was born in San Antonio, Texas on March 23. She was baptized Lucille LeSueur Cassin.

"Her father, Henry Cassin, was a theater owner, and her mother, Anna LeSueur Cassin, a housewife."

None of these assertions was true.

Her father was not Henry Cassin, Anna's third husband, but Thomas LeSueur, Anna's second husband. Henry Cassin took on the role of husband and father after LeSueur disappeared from the family residence without leaving a forwarding address just before or after Lucille Fay LeSueur was born.

As far as being born in San Antonio, no birth certificate exists for Lucille in San Antonio, or, as far as can be determined through an assiduous search, anyplace else in Texas. This makes her an outlier in the family—her brother Hal was born in Bexar County, Texas, in September 1903, as is proven by both a birth certificate and a newspaper announcement.

There are several possible explanations. The most obvious one is that circumstances were too ragged for her mother to hire a midwife or doctor to attend to her daughter's birth and file a birth certificate. Another possibility is that Lucille wasn't actually born in San Antonio but in some small town on the periphery, but a check of those small towns also fails to turn anything up. Clearly, the family was nomadic—Tom LeSueur met Crawford's mother in Texarkana, married her in San Angelo, and by the time she bore Hal they were living in a shack in San Antonio.

The lack of a birth certificate is not particularly suspicious; by the late 1920s, only about 80 percent of Texas births were recorded; for births twenty years earlier, the percentage would have been lower.

At various times, 1904 and 1908 were put forth as her birth year. The latter year became the official year and was cited by Crawford herself later in life. In 1922, when Lucille LeSueur—or Billie Cassin—registered for her only semester of college, she said that she was born in 1906. It's possible—why lie about her birth at such an early age?

What is certain is that in the 1910 census for Lawton, Oklahoma, taken in April, Lucille is listed as being five years old, with her place of birth listed only as Texas. So: almost certainly 1905. Maybe: 1906.

The woman the world would come to know as Joan Crawford was descended from a French Huguenot colony established in Virginia in the early eighteenth century. Her paternal ancestor was David LeSueur, born in 1703 in London. David settled in King William Parish in Goochland, Virginia, marrying one Elizabeth Chastain in 1730. David had twelve children and died in 1772 in Cumberland, Virginia.

James LeSueur, David's grandson, Joan Crawford's grandfather, was still in Virginia when the 1840 census lists him as an apparently prosperous slaveowner—two male slaves under the age of ten, three male slaves between the ages of ten and twenty-four, and two female slaves between the ages of ten and twenty-four—seven in all.

By the 1850 census, the family real estate is valued at $800, about $31,000 in modern money. By 1860, the real estate is valued at $3,000 ($110,000 in modern money), and the family's personal estate is valued at $2,000.

In 1861, James LeSueur was mustered into the Confederacy, to be specific the 2nd Regiment of the Tennessee Infantry, Company H, which was part of Walker's Legion, later known as Robison's Legion.

It was at this point that everything went to hell, because the Civil War ruined the LeSueurs. By 1870, James is in Sumner County, Tennessee. That year's census lists Joan's father Thomas as being four years old while the family property is now valued at only $800. The space for "value of real estate" is left blank.

By 1880, nothing much had changed, although Thomas is now living in Dixon Springs, Tennessee, with his father, who probably taught Thomas the craft of plastering, which became his primary occupation. In 1897, Tom LeSueur was still in Tennessee, then began working his way west.

All this contrasts with Lucille's maternal great-grandfather, William Johnson, who fought for the Union in the 99th Indiana Infantry, Company G, and died of wounds received at the Battle of Atlanta on August 9, 1864.

To recap: Lucille's maternal great-grandfather fought for the Union and died, while her paternal grandfather fought for the Confederacy and became poor.

Lucille always remembered her childhood in tones of gray, with a prevailing absence of joy. There were father figures who came and went, a mother she tolerated but never seems to have loved, and a brother she disliked. She would only rarely be able to escape this dissonant familial environment.

"I've never admired perfect beauty," she told a friend when she was an old woman. "I like flawed beauty. I always had to work like hell to be beautiful."

The hardscrabble life of her paternal ancestors was replicated in her own childhood, which was invariably flavored with a seasoning of bitters. Her memories of her mother's lessons were all along the lines of grim wisdom: "'Everything comes out in the wash . . .' 'Make your own bed and lie in it.' All those laws of—what's it called?—yeah, retribution."

The documentary record for her mother is sparse but intriguing. Anna could fairly be said to be a woman with issues.

According to her death certificate and the dates on her tombstone, Anna was born in 1884, but the 1900 census lists her as being born in 1881 in Arkansas. She refuses to state where her parents were from, but she can read and write. In 1900 she was living with her husband Ed McConnell at 324 State Street in Texarkana, Texas. Her husband is twenty-six years old and his occupation is "newspaper reporter." For someone in the information business he's shy—he also refuses to say where his parents were from, although he does go so far as to say he's from Kansas.

Anna married McConnell in January 1898, when he was already the city editor of the Texarkana *Morning Call* and Anna Johnson was the seventeen-year-old daughter of a Salvation Army captain. Sylvester Johnson tried mightily to keep his daughter out of the hands of a lowly journalist. One wry newspaper report said that McConnell was prone to hanging around the Salvation Army "when they were on the streets battling against Satan, and the boys who knew 'Ed' best thought he was there to have the devil purged from his soul, but such was not the case."

"Captain Johnson is a man of great pride and strong determination," said another report. "He was a soldier in the southern cause and the event [of his daughter's marriage] has worked his mind up to a pitch of revenge. The young people were not unmindful of these possible effects and, in anticipation of such results, they planned well their programme for a total disappearance. The wrath of the commander is great. He declares that he will not relent in his determination to prosecute young McConnell for kidnapping."

That threat came to nothing, but luck was not with Anna and her husband. Edgar McConnell died in Texarkana on November 2, 1902, "after a long illness" that might have been cancer. McConnell left his wife with a daughter named Daisy, whom Crawford was aware of, but who she seems to have believed was from her mother's marriage to Tom LeSueur. Daisy McConnell was born in San Antonio in January 1901 and died in November 1904 in Fort Smith, Arkansas. The cause of death was listed as "congestion," and her funeral was paid for by her grandfather in the Salvation Army. The funeral home charged $29.50 for the funeral, while Daisy's grave is in a section of the cemetery that was a potter's field.

Anna was not one to grieve her husband. Precisely eight days after Ed McConnell's death, she filed a new marriage license. Her intended was the aforementioned Thomas LeSueur, who would become Joan Crawford's father. Slightly more than three weeks later she married LeSueur in San Angelo, Texas.

Anna's surviving daughter never mentioned the late Mr. McConnell, and it's entirely possible she knew nothing of her mother's initial marital go-round. By the time Lucille began to walk and talk, Anna was a divorced Catholic, and could have simply expunged McConnell in order to save embarrassing explanations about multiple husbands.

The marriage to Tom LeSueur lasted just long enough to produce Hal in 1903 and Lucille a few years later. The 1902 marriage license and a 1908 listing in the San Angelo city directory lists Anna and her brood as living at 204 Second Street in a house owned by a relative. After Tom LeSueur disappeared, Anna appears to have depended on the kindness of family; for a time she also lived in a house owned by her mother on West First Street. They moved to Lawton, Oklahoma, in 1909, where they stayed until 1917.

Tom LeSueur would meet his adult daughter precisely once, in a meeting stage-managed by MGM for the still cameras in 1934. He wrote her after she became famous, and she began sending him a stipend. The few surviving pictures of him indicate he was responsible for his daughter's large eyes and the definitive cheekbones that made her so remarkably photogenic.

None of this made any difference in Tom LeSueur's own life. In 1938 he died broke in Abilene, which sounds like a Hank Williams song. His daughter sent a check for $558 to cover the cost of the funeral in Abilene's Independent Order of Odd Fellows Cemetery. She did not attend the funeral.

After Tom LeSueur disappeared, Anna dealt with her shaky status by portraying herself as a widow, which was only true if you were speaking of Ed McConnell. She was listed that way in the city directory for San Angelo in 1908, where she and her children were living in the home of her father, the irate Captain Johnson of the Salvation Army, who was now listed as a "Reverend."

The next phase of Lucille's life began in 1909, when "Anna Leseur" married Henry Cassin in Fort Worth on July 13. Cassin was managing the Opera House in Lawton, Oklahoma, which presented acts such as "The SheathGown Girls" in *A Trip to Zulu*.

They set up housekeeping in the Cassin residence in the 800 block of Lawton's D Avenue. The new Mrs. Cassin had been a saleslady at Simpson's "and was highly esteemed and popular."

Henry Cassin was regarded around Lawton as a serious man who could be trusted—in 1907 he served on the committee to write a new commission-based charter for the town. A year or so later, Cassin changed the name of the Opera House to the Cassin Airdrome, which continued "all-star vaudeville," offering acts in transit between Dallas and Oklahoma City. The local newspaper enthused that "Lawton is entitled to just as good amusement as the larger cities.

Mr. Cassin is sparing no expense to get the best that money can procure. . . . Two shows will be given each evening. First show at 8:15, second show 9:15."

In March 1910, Henry Cassin announced that he was running as a Democrat for the Registrar of Deeds in Temple, Oklahoma. The local newspaper gave him a hearty endorsement: "He is especially qualified for this position and should be successful in receiving the nomination and in election, he will make the people of Comanche county a good register."

Cassin was clearly industrious, but Lucille remembered hearing quarrels in the night. He was certainly an improvement on Lucille's father in that he was actually there. He dressed with a flair befitting a showman. He also drank, but he always treated Lucille with affection. He didn't care for her name, so he called her "Billie," a name she used for years.

Lawton was the scene of an early childhood catastrophe—Lucille was playing on damp grass one day when she stepped on a broken bottle, which slashed her foot. A boy named Don Blanding, later to become a poet, picked her up and carried her home. Billie believed that Blanding's action prevented her from bleeding to death. Blanding would later write a poem titled "The Little Girl Across the Street":

She was just the little girl who lived across the street:
All legs and curls and great big eyes and restless, dancing feet.
As vivid as a hummingbird, as bright and swift and gay.
A child who played at make believe . . .

As an adult, Crawford believed that the event "taught me at a very early age the meaning of pain, and the strength to endure it." This emphasis on her childhood as a series of brutal episodes never wavered: "It seemed to me that I was always blamed, not my brother, not Hal," she would assert. One day another boy threw a ball into their yard, and Hal ran to get it and trampled her mother's nasturtiums. Anna assumed Lucille was the guilty party, took a switch to her, then stuck her in a corner. Lucille was furious and began muttering that she didn't do it, which made her mother switch her yet again.

The only outings she remembered from this period involved her brother taking her to the Electric Park in Kansas City. The dancer Sally Rand was appearing, and Lucille wandered around scared to death while Hal ogled Rand.

It was in Lawton that Lucille fell in love with the movies—their romance, their scenes of exotic adventure that reflected nothing of the cow town ambience surrounding her. The vaudeville acts were almost as entrancing. "I inhaled the smell of greasepaint, the musty scent of scenery, the dancers flying about, light dazzling in their spangled skirts."

Lawton natives remembered her as "skinny and under-sized—they call it malnutrition now." She did not have the slightest semblance of prettiness. Her face was freckled and her hair was stringy, of a color grudgingly referred to as "towhead." When she wasn't making mud pies in the gutter she was climbing trees. When she wasn't racing through the house, she was chasing some playmate with a sizable stick.

Money was always a problem. "I did eat ice cream once," she remembered. "When I was a kid I used to run out at the first fresh snow and get cups, let it snow into the cups, then bring them in and eat the snow with sugar and cream on it. That was my ice cream."

Until she was about eleven years old, Lucille was just one of the neighborhood kids, albeit one who was nervous, quick-tempered, restless. According to the people who grew up with her, "In all the Big Pasture town of Lawton there was no more complete tomboy." One time she organized an "Indian parade" for the neighborhood children in which they all painted themselves and marched through the streets making what they imagined to be war cries.

Children who ran with her in those days remembered a child whose family was regarded as faintly disreputable. "I remember when Garvene Gooch and I attended a birthday party for 'Little Billie' even though our mothers did not like for us to play with her," said Christina Swanson, who became a teacher. "A funny thing that has stuck with me through all the years was that a little kid in the neighborhood brought her a toothbrush as a birthday present."

Another woman, Ruth Clifford Melton, remembered how Billie would stand in front of the movie theater in Lawton and beg the manager for the photographs of movie stars that decorated the lobby. "My picture will be up there one day," she told her friends.

While Crawford's memories of Henry Cassin were always positive, the citizens of Lawton began to think otherwise—her stepfather became involved in an embezzlement scam, and things slowly devolved. In August 1915 a legal notice appeared in the Lawton newspaper announcing that Cassin, along with his wife and one J. S. Hixon, were being sued for $3,414.03 plus interest. In 1916, a legal notice appeared announcing the foreclosure of several lots co-owned by Cassin, his wife, and four other people to satisfy a debt of $681.65 plus $500, not counting attorney's fees.

It appears that Anna was co-signing her husband's legal papers, and they were being dunned for an inability to pay their debts. Depending on what story you believe, the vaudeville house either failed on its own, or Cassin nudged things along by dipping into the till. After the vaudeville house crashed, Cassin's occupation was listed as the Cassin Abstract Company.

All this didn't mitigate against Lucille being part of the community; they were still in Lawton three months after the foreclosure, as a notice about a Halloween party included both Lucille and her brother Hal, who won a prize for Best Costume. Lucille didn't hold any of the financial shortfalls against her stepfather. To the end of her life she considered him the only meaningful paternal figure she ever had.

It was Henry Cassin who encouraged her to think about a career in dancing, which angered Anna, because she didn't think it was a reputable undertaking. As far as Lucille was concerned, it was one more strike against her mother.

In late 1916 or early 1917, Cassin and family took off for Kansas City, where he managed a hotel. Anna got a job at a department store, and Lucille was placed in St. Agnes Academy, where she paid for her tuition by doing housework, cooking, and cleaning up after the well-to-do girls. She liked the school well enough, but she hated being relegated to the position of someone bartering labor for education. "The minute I started serving at table, it was a step down into the menial class." The religious environment left her unmoved—the only religion she would ever follow was an erratic interest in Christian Science, a belief system that emphasizes optimism and refuses to acknowledge evil.

The 1918 Kansas City Directory lists Henry and Anna as living together at the same address (403 East Ninth Street). There is no employment listed for Cassin, while Anna is working at the Gate City Laundry, as is one Henry

Hough, who would soon become Lucille's unofficial "stepdad," coolly referred to as "Mr. Hough" in her memoir.

After St. Agnes (1916 to 1919) there was Rockingham Academy (1919 to 1922). While Lucille was theoretically getting an education, as she described her environment she was in fact working full-time, cooking and cleaning for the owners and the students of the schools and picking up whatever shards of education she could manage on the margins of her employment. The Rockingham Academy, so-called because it was on Rockingham Road, was for children from well-off families. To earn her tuition, she got up at dawn and cooked for and cleaned up after more than thirty other children, this at a time when she was only fourteen or fifteen herself.

"I did not have time to enter a classroom because I was cooking for 30 people . . . teaching the little ones to make their bed, wash all the dishes, prepare the next meal and also three meals a day for the Stuttles who owned the school."

All this formed the relentless work ethic that would dominate her life. If she wasn't working, the water was at her chin; if she wasn't working, she wasn't earning. Hollywood would be full of girls like Lucille, and a surprising number of them became stars—dispossessed, damaged women for whom work was simultaneously definition, salvation, and burden. The problem was that work is never enough. "Hollywood is like life," she would say. "You face it with the sum total of your equipment. And mine was meager."

Henry Cassin vanishes from the Kansas City Directory in 1919 and 1920, while Anna continues to manage the Gate City Laundry. "Mr. Hough" had moved in, and Anna was hoping he would marry her. Lucille left Rockingham and went back home to help her mother in the laundry.

Nineteen twenty-one brought more of the same, as Anna's father died in Phoenix at the age of sixty-five of a liver ailment. His obituary in *The Arizona Republic* paid tribute to his habit of gathering "cast-off clothing and distributing it to the needy of the community."

Henry Cassin makes his final appearance in Kansas City in 1922. He and Anna are now living about a twenty-minute walk from each other. Hal is living with his mother and working at Wolferman's bakery. Lucille is still living at 309 East Ninth Street, a block away from her mother. There would be no listing for her in 1923 because she was enrolled at Stephens College in Columbia, Missouri.

What all these wanderings meant was that an increasingly resentful child was dragged through a succession of cow towns and surrogate fathers. Anna was a working-class woman with children but without education, physical or social graces, and her daughter would find no sympathy for her, not then, not ever.

It was a childhood and adolescence not so much of abject poverty as of poverty of outlook, of ambition. Anna McConnell LeSeuer Cassin had that unerring combination of bad luck and bad judgment that foretells romantic catastrophe, which, for working-class women in the early twentieth century, invariably meant economic catastrophe as well. Anna did not lift her daughter up so much as ladle out a portion of her own troubles for the child to share.

Her beginnings left Lucille with a free-floating grudge about her childhood and, beyond that, about her family. She regarded her brother Hal with cold disdain, which didn't stop her from supporting him for the better part of his life, for most of which he was a drunk and layabout burdened by what she believed to be an outrageously outsized ego.

When her mother and brother moved to Hollywood, Hal would borrow his sister's car and demonstrate a tendency toward drunken accidents, while her mother would run up bills in department stores. The practical and emotional transaction never really changed—Lucille would give her mother and brother money, but she drew the line at giving them time or affection. That would always be saved for those who gave her their affection—her coworkers, a few close friends, and, above all, her audience.

The only positive aspect of Lucille's childhood was that it instilled in her a determination to better herself by any means necessary. Self-pity was irrelevant; survival was all.

Her luck began to change as she became less of a girl and more of a young woman. Boys suddenly began paying attention to her, which was a first, and she discovered that she had a knack for dancing.

In the fall of 1922, Lucille registered at Stephens College —a women's college. When Lucille had been attending school in Kansas City, the principal was a man named H. S. Walter. Walter had become the secretary at Stephens and finagled a job for Lucille at the school. Once again she bartered her labor for education—in return for Lucille waiting on tables in the cafeteria, the school would waive her tuition. These years of domestic labor formed what would be a lifelong passion for privileging grim reality over fantasy, a passion that would be reflected in her movies, which tended to center on matters of class, sex, and money—the true engines of democracy.

Lucille received a different variety of attention at Stephens than in Kansas City. Dr. James Wood, the president of the school, told one reporter that she was surrounded by "Boys, boys and more boys." Supposedly, the son of a wealthy man from St. Louis wanted to marry her, but Wood managed to convince her to stay in school.

Socially, she felt like an outcast and probably was. One girl suggested Lucille would make a welcome addition to her sorority, but the other girls wouldn't accept "a waitress." When it came time for midterms, Lucille began to panic because "college was only comprehensible when I was dancing."

She always spoke of Wood as a wise father figure, saying he gave her three rules for life that stood her in good stead:

Never quit a job until it's finished.

The world isn't interested in your problems.

If you can find you can do a job, move on, because you're already bigger than the job. If the job is impossible, stick with it. You may never accomplish it, but you'll grow in the trying.

Although Lucille said she attended Stephens for a year, the college's records indicate it was only one semester. According to a letter from the registrar, she "took a few courses and did receive grades, which cannot be revealed." Despite what the paperwork says, as late as April 1923, "Lucille Cassin," along with twelve other girls, attended a steak roast thrown by the Sigma Nu fraternity.

According to Crawford's retrospective comments, her stay at Stephens was hampered by the cruel fact that she simply didn't have the academic capabilities to do the work because she hadn't really had much primary education beyond the ability to read and write. Study habits were a mystery, and she was soon in over her head.

She felt out of place, knew that the other girls made fun of her and didn't take her seriously because she had to wait on them in the dining room. When it came to academics, she remembered, "I didn't understand a damn thing they were talking about. Not a bloody thing." She would elaborate that "I was in dire need.... I longed to stay... but the classes were Greek to me." One alumna, who considered Lucille a "residence hall friend," said that she was "a very attractive girl" and the best Charleston dancer in Columbia, Missouri. "She was popular with University of Missouri boys, which aroused the jealousy and teasing of other Stephens College women. She did not enjoy school and felt unprepared for college... and also tried to return to Kansas City, her home, several times."

An administrative staff member at the college said that Lucille was "a girl with real pretty eyes, carriage and teeth, who kept up with fashions and had nice hair. She didn't like it here. She wasn't used to having restrictions placed on her. She liked to date, and she liked the men a lot." Another classmate said that she would "dance all the time on the tables in the dining room and do the Charleston in the kitchen. Billie would bring me whole cream instead of milk because I was so skinny. She'd say, 'Now, don't let [dining room supervisor] Miss Newton see this.'"

Finally, she gave up. She packed her suitcase, left the dorm, and walked to the railroad station. James Wood came after her. "You're not a quitter," he told her. "Don't behave like one. Do this properly." He took her hand and walked her back to school, where he phoned Anna and told her that her daughter was coming home—her "education was too sketchy for college at this point."

Wood would say that "She was extraordinary. Her work was original. All alone, working her way through, I tried to persuade her to stay, but—other girls can be cruel. She had no preparation in deportment, the girls didn't understand her and she didn't understand them."

She would tell this story for the rest of her life as a tribute to the kindness of Dr. Wood, but it sounds like a hard reckoning. The main lesson was that she tried never to run away from anything ever again. She didn't hold a grudge, at least not against Wood. She would host him whenever he came to Los Angeles, and she came back to Stephens in 1970 as a distinguished alum... even if she had only been there for a single semester.

BY 1923, LUCILLE WAS a teenager who felt out of place in every environment she had experienced. Added to her lack of social graces was what she believed were the flaws of her appearance. Her mother had always made most of her clothes, and she didn't think her mother had much talent as a seamstress, or, for that matter, anything else. She would give chapter and verse about all the ways in which she fell short as young girl, but the masochistic litany was over-the-top. Her picture in the Stephens yearbook shows a very attractive girl—the cheekbones and the smile that would become world-famous were already present.

Her attempt at college failed, but it's still indicative. By both heredity and parental influence, Lucille should have been headed for a blue-collar job, but she clearly had ambitions larger than her surroundings. She also had energy—spectacular, almost demonic energy, and a willingness to outwork anybody else. Fame seemed impossible, but success wasn't. The question was, what could she be successful at?

CHAPTER TWO

AFTER LEAVING STEPHENS, LUCILLE returned to Kansas City and a department store, where she wrapped packages for people who had more money than she did. "I hated the job," she would remember forty years later, "so I saved every penny I could and then took off. $46 got me from Kansas City to Chicago, and that's when life began."

It was actually a little more complicated than that. She remembered that the man who hired her for her first job in the chorus called her "the little fat girl with blue eyes." She weighed 145 pounds—a lot for a young woman who was 5-4. She took the remark as an order. "I [had to] reshape myself. I was very stupid in the way I dieted. I lived on crackers and mustard and black coffee. Luckily I was young and healthy. I survived."

The intriguing thing about her at this stage was that she didn't have any ambition to act. The very idea made her freeze, but when she danced she was totally at ease, at least partially because she wasn't as good as the other girls, so there was nothing to lose. As she would remember in 1970, "I didn't even make the first line of the chorus. I could only make the second."

In her autobiography, she stated that precisely twelve weeks after leaving Kansas City, she was on Broadway. Amazingly, she doesn't seem to have been exaggerating, at least not by much.

The chronology: around January 1924, Lucille got a job in a "little review" starring Katherine (sometimes Catherine) Emerine that started in Kansas City at the Hotel Baltimore. Emerine appraised the young girl as a talented dancer and asked if she had any stage experience. Not really, Lucille said, but Emerine said that she was taking a dance act to Springfield, Missouri, and Lucille could go if she wanted.

Ads in the Kansas City paper announced it as "A happy, snappy syncopated revue" featuring "8 girls of Syncopation and the La Petite Ballet . . . Note: Critics have proclaimed this to be the most attractive and fastest floor show in America." The nights were long—the revue and dancing went from 6:45 p.m. to 9 and from 10:45 to 1 a.m. nightly—but second line or not, Lucille was in show business.

The Kansas City Times appraised the show as introducing "some new faces. The old ones are still pretty, too. . . . The chorus and ballet numbers are well handled." After the show closed in Springfield, Lucille trooped back home to her job at Kline's department store.

After a quarrel with her mother—she had come home late from a dance—Lucille packed her bag, stormed out of the house, and took a train to Chicago. The plan was to look up Emerine, who had told her, "Any of you kids come to Chicago, look me up. I know a producer, Ernie Young, he'll get you a job."

Emerine was touring, so Lucille went to see Ernie Young in room 910 of the Capitol Building. "I went to his office and found it crowded with beautiful, well-dressed girls," she remembered in 1929, "whereas my clothes were shabby and I looked tacky. I don't know what impulse seized me, but I rushed into his private office and shouted in his face, 'Mister, I gotta have a job.' He looked up with a smile and asked, 'Is that any reason to come bustin' into my office like this?'"

Young asked her if she could dance. "A little," she said. He took her one floor up where there was a Victrola and ordered her to "Hop to it." She danced. He hired her for a job at a mob hangout called the Friar's, where the bootleg booze flowed like the Rio Grande at flood tide—a good place to try out a dancer. By her own account, Lucille was no more than adequate, and probably still in the second line, but she was good enough to keep getting work.

After that, Ernie Young slotted her into a job in Oklahoma City. *The Passing Parade of 1924* played at the Shrine Auditorium from March 17 to the 24th. *The Passing Parade* was meant to coast on the momentum of the Shuberts' similarly named *Passing Show*. *The Daily Oklahoman* ran a story headlined "This Lawton Girl Hunts Her Daddy." Underneath a fetching picture of "Miss Billie Cassin," the story rhapsodized:

> Down the rainbow pathway of the stage she trips, hoping to find at the end of her journey a father she has neither seen nor heard from for five years. And underneath the sparkle of her eyes, and the wit of her repartee to her fellows, is a serious wistfulness that is hidden when she steps brightly into the 'spots' colored glare. . . .
>
> Years ago, her father . . . was a theater owner in Lawton. When he sold out, Billie left school and went with him to Kansas City. So she secured an engagement with a vaudeville act, and then her father disappeared.
>
> Three months ago, she received a letter from a friend in Oklahoma telling her that her father was here. So she joined "The Passing Parade" and has come to search for him.

Lucille had been misinformed. Henry Cassin had died in Nashville of heart failure in October 1922 at the age of fifty-four, after which he was buried in an unmarked grave in Lawton. His death certificate lists his marital status as "Devorded" and his occupation as "hotel keeper," while his obituary in the Lawton newspaper said he was in the oil business.

Her yearning for Henry Cassin, or, more precisely, the acceptance and affection that Cassin represented, was authentic and it never abated. Sometimes she would find that acceptance from a man, but more reliably she would get it from the public.

After the booking in Oklahoma City, Ernie Young sent Lucille to Detroit for a revue at the Oriole Terrace café—thirty-two women, eight dances per night. An ad for Young's *Marvelous Revue* appears in the *Detroit Free Press* on April 26, 1924—the same week a Shubert musical called *Innocent Eyes* was playing in Detroit.

Innocent Eyes starred the French chanteuse Mistinguett and was trying out before heading for New York. Compared to Ernie Young's catch-as-catch-can revues, it was high-end. The music was by Sigmund Romberg, the choreography by Seymour Felix. Three chorus girls had just left the show, and the stage manager,

Zeke Colvin by name, grabbed one of the chorus boys, a young man named Jack Oakie, and said they were going to see an Ernie Young revue to find replacements.

That night in Detroit, Oakie pointed out three girls he thought could do the job. Colvin objected to one of them. "Look at those eyes! They're so big they look like they're going to pop right out of her head." Oakie managed to change Colvin's mind, and all three girls were hired for *Innocent Eyes*. Because of the strict Shubert rules against fraternizing, Oakie didn't talk to the girl with the big eyes until they were on the train to New York.

Give or take a few weeks, it wasn't much more than three months since Lucille had stormed out of her mother's house and out of Kansas City. And now she was headed for New York.

———◆◇◆———

"SHE WAS SO EASY to talk to," Jack Oakie remembered. "It seemed we both had been dreaming about the same things all our lives. We both wanted to be great dancers."

"I want to be the most famous ballroom dancer in the world," Lucille told him. "I don't know how, but I dream about it all the time."

He countered with, "Someday I'm going to be a big musical-comedy star. I want to sing and dance and have a style all my own. You know, like Harry Richman!" Oakie told her he was nineteen, Lucille told him she was sixteen. They were both lying.

Innocent Eyes opened at the Winter Garden on May 20, 1924, and Lucille and Oakie, outfitted in white tie and tails, had a number together called "Organdy Days."

Lucille adored New York. She and four other chorus girls lived in one room in a brownstone on 50th Street just off Fifth Avenue. "Our beds stood in a row like the dwarfs in *Snow White*. You could tell which corner was mine—the window was plastered with my hankies, panties and stockings (I had two pairs). When it was cold enough, they froze."

Lucille thought Mistinguett was magical and had "the most beautiful legs in the world. That's all I ever saw, dancing behind her, or peering from the wings, the lady of the fabled legs."

She became friends with Ruby Stevens, another chorus girl who was dancing for Ziegfeld. They had a lot in common—Ruby was an orphan literally, while Lucille was an orphan psychologically, and they were both terribly insecure. They would be friends for the rest of their lives, after Lucille became Joan Crawford, after Ruby became Barbara Stanwyck.

Lucille and Jack Oakie would sneak meetings at the barns in back of the Winter Garden that were used for the storage and repairing of trolley cars. "We'd sit and talk and dream and try out new dance steps," Oakie remembered. Unfortunately, *Innocent Eyes* closed after only three months, which meant Lucille and Oakie were right back where they started, and winter wasn't far away.

Lucille had been making $35 a week, with an extra $4.50 for matinees—more money than she had ever seen in her life. There was enough left over at the end of the month to buy some nice clothes. The men she dated expected to spend money on a woman, which was certainly a switch from her dating experiences in Texas and Oklahoma. Less than a week after the Shubert show closed, Lucille picked up a job in the chorus of *The Passing Show of 1924*.

The Shuberts scheduled a tour of *Innocent Eyes* and offered Oakie a specialty number. Lucille decided to stick with *The Passing Show*, but that only ran from September 3 to November 22, 1924. Just as Oakie was about to leave New York City, Lucille called him and told him to meet her at Penn Station.

"I'm going to be tested for the movies!" she told him.

"Who says so?"

"MGM! Harry Rapf from MGM!"

"Are you sure? Remember you have those great big pop eyes. What if you don't photograph? You'll be giving up a good job."

She waved him off. "I'm going to take the chance."

At long last, her luck was about to change. It seemed that after performances she would head to speakeasies, including one run by the singer Harry Richman, where she would do specialty dances. Nils Granlund, a publicist for Marcus Loew and producer of revues for Loew's theaters, had mentioned her to Richman.

Granlund had a good eye for gorgeous. He had cast Ruby Stevens in a play and remembered Lucille as "a gorgeous girl, with huge blue eyes, perfect features, and ripe, voluptuous lips."

Lucille came to him crying one day. It seemed that she wanted to get back to Kansas City for Christmas but was short of cash. Granlund called Harry Richman and told him he had a likely candidate for his nightclub revue. "I don't need a girl in my act," Richman complained.

"Just let her sit on a piano or dance a Charleston or something. Give her $50 a week and don't give me any argument."

That should have been the end of it, but it wasn't. Richman wanted her to wear an evening gown, and she didn't have an evening gown. Granlund gave her a blank check and sent her to a dress shop, where he told the proprietor he would stop payment on anything over $20. The evening gown cost $14. Granlund was taken with the girl and suggested to his friend Marcus Loew that he knew a girl who might have some possibilities for MGM.

Lucille's own version of her discovery prominently mentioned Granlund and his kindness, but never went into details about him fronting money for an evening gown. Rather than Granlund mentioning her to Marcus Loew, her version had him mentioning her to Harry Rapf.

What is certain is that Rapf had her, along with about eighteen other women, make a basic screen test in New York City consisting of full-face, profile, and a few primary expressions—sad, coy, wistful. It only took about fifteen minutes, but they called Lucille back for a second test, after which an employment offer was made. A telegram was sent to Anna's house in Kansas City over Christmas of 1924, where Lucille was spending the holidays: LUCILLE LESUEUR YOU HAVE BEEN PLACED UNDER CONTRACT MGM STUDIO STOP SIX MONTH OPTION STOP SEVENTY FIVE DOLLARS A WEEK STOP LEAVE IMMEDIATELY FOR CALIFORNIA STOP.

The offer was the standard MGM beginner's contract, with the options all on the studio's side. That said, the salary was nearly twice what Lucille was making as a dancer. She took the job. The first memo in her MGM employment file informs her that she has to provide her own underwear and silk stockings for any parts she might play. Years later, she asked Harry Rapf what on earth he had seen in her. "Structure and vitality," he answered.

On New Year's Day 1925, Lucille left for Hollywood. Many young women would have been homesick, but she wasn't, mostly because at bottom she felt she had never had a home to miss. "I'd been on my own since I was nine," she asserted.

The formative years she had spent in the barren reaches of the Plains had been a comprehensive education in all the things she didn't want: debt, drudgery, a life remotely like her mother's. What she did want may have been ill-defined, but California was sure to bring things into sharp focus.

As for Jack Oakie, he toured with *Innocent Eyes*, then went back to New York with a show called *Artists and Models* that opened in June 1925 and ran for a healthy eleven months. After that came vaudeville. In 1927, Jack Oakie went to Hollywood, where he spent the rest of his life playing bumptious comic sidekicks in the movies and earning an Oscar nomination for his hilariously vulgar replica of Mussolini in Charlie Chaplin's *The Great Dictator*.

In 1929, Oakie was all dolled up in a tux attending the premiere of the all-star musical *Paramount on Parade* when he heard a voice behind him: "I ain't seen ya looking like that since 'Organdy Days.'" And then the girl he had known as Lucille LeSueur walked right past him. "Don't you wish that we could get into a chorus today?" she said.

CHAPTER THREE

IN 1925, ADELA ROGERS St. Johns wrote a novel called *The Skyrocket* that was serialized in *Cosmopolitan* magazine. It concerns an ambitious young woman named Sharon Kimm who comes to Hollywood, begins as an extra, and has a slow but steady rise to the height of Hollywood fame. "Sharon belonged to Hollywood," wrote St. Johns. "She had given herself to Hollywood . . . and in return Hollywood was to give her many things, not all of them good. But the two of them were bound together so close that the history of Sharon Kimm is almost the heart-history of Hollywood."

Sharon has endured a poverty-stricken childhood as the only daughter of a woman trapped in a bad marriage with a man who's unable to support his family. She is haunted by her mother's misery and her own deprived childhood—years spent yearning for beautiful things she couldn't afford.

This grinding poverty propels Sharon to pursue a career in the movies, where she indulges her need for notice, expensive clothes, and a lifestyle denied her mother. The price turns out to be high—higher than Sharon ever dreamed, as her demands for sexual and economic independence make her a symbol for an entire generation spurning the conventions of nurturing motherhood.

Nothing is enough for Sharon. Her arrival as a movie star ignites "a raging fire of desire, a small blaze that was to be fed continually with the tinsel of Hollywood success." Sharon vows that "I want to be a star and have money and beautiful things and diamonds and dresses and be somebody."

In the end, Sharon pulls back from the abyss by marrying a moderately successful actor and settling into the role of wife and homemaker. St. Johns has it both ways—titillating the reader with conspicuous consumption and sexual degradation, while allowing that same reader to pat their sweaty brows in satisfaction about the value of their own plebeian choices.

The Skyrocket began running in *Cosmopolitan* in January and continued through April. This meant that St. Johns was writing it in the latter part of 1924, when Lucille LeSueur was still hoofing in New York City. Yet until the conventional ending, the story is an eerily accurate emotional X-ray of Lucille, as well as dozens of other women who rose to fame in Hollywood in the 1920s and afterward—women who were running away from a life far more defined than the goal they were pursuing.

IN 1925, HOLLYWOOD WAS the New Jerusalem, the spiritual as well as the production center for a world ravenous for movies. In 1911, the population of Hollywood was 5,000. Ten years later, it was 60,000. And the year Lucille came to Hollywood, it was 130,000.

This boom town supplied the product for about 20,000 movie theaters in American towns and cities and countless more overseas. Within ten years, the Hollywood press corps would be the third largest in the country, behind only New York and Washington.

From the beginning, Lucille liked Hollywood. It was physically attractive and didn't have frigid winters. In the Plains the houses were mostly basic frame and plaster, while Hollywood offered Spanish, Moorish, Italian, and everything in between.

Lucille wasn't in Kansas anymore.

As for Metro-Goldwyn-Mayer, Lucille had arrived at a movie studio that was less than two years old but was already competing with Famous Players-Lasky—soon to be renamed Paramount—for the title of the biggest, the grandest, the most successful studio in Hollywood.

MGM was the production arm of Loew's theaters, a combination of three different but equally unsuccessful studios: Metro had been purchased by Marcus

Loew because it had an excellent distribution system struggling beneath ineffective management. How ineffective? Metro had made Rudolph Valentino a huge star in Rex Ingram's *The Four Horsemen of the Apocalypse*, after which Famous Players-Lasky spirited him away.

Then there was Goldwyn, which had a solid roster of actors and a superb physical plant stretching over forty-six acres on Washington Boulevard in Culver City. Bringing up the rear was Louis B. Mayer Productions, a small company on Mission Road in Los Angeles that was making good money off well-engineered commercial movies under the direction of Mayer and his creative vice president, the twenty-four-year-old Irving Thalberg. Also on Mayer's staff was Harry Rapf, whom Mayer had recently brought over from Warner Bros. Marcus Loew had correctly gauged Mayer as a brilliant manager with a flair for organization and a strong business sense.

Mayer had been a successful New England exhibitor who struck it rich when he hocked his wife's jewelry to purchase the New England rights to *The Birth of a Nation*. The result was a clear profit of $500,000. Irving Thalberg, who had run production at Universal before joining forces with Mayer in 1923, was generally regarded as a genius in the making whose only limitations were physical—he had a rheumatic heart. In 1925, MGM made forty-six motion pictures and earned a net profit of $4.7 million—about $80 million in modern money.

"Irving was (basically) an invalid," said Sam Marx, who would become MGM's story editor as well as the producer of, among others, *Lassie Come Home*. "He spent most of his early school days in bed. He was an avid reader with a dominating mother. He never went further than Bushwick High in Brooklyn. He learned speed typing. He had three secretaries at the studio and saw them all typing madly. 'Hold everything,' he said, and he got another typewriter and beat them all."

MGM functioned as "a walled city in the middle of Culver City," as Marx put it. The studio had both dentists and barbers in-house, while the commissary served excellent food and was run as a nonprofit. In short, there was no need to go anyplace else. "When Culver City wanted to raise their water fees, MGM promptly got their own water," said Sam Marx. "The studio was superb in their departments. If the producer was smart, all he had to do was make a great picture."

The environment was plush and proud. Sam Marx told a story about the director Victor Seastrom, who tried and failed to have a conference with an overbooked Irving Thalberg for several weeks. Seastrom then took a month off to go home to Sweden for Christmas. On Seastrom's first day back at the studio he ran into Thalberg's secretary. "I think Thalberg can see you this afternoon," the secretary said.

Foremost among the departments was the art department, headed by Cedric Gibbons, a proponent of Art Deco who was, remembered Marx, "erudite, charming and addicted to beautiful things, including women." As for Mayer and Thalberg, they were a highly effective team. "Mayer had a marvelous eye for talent. Thalberg didn't, but could develop talent." Both men shared one essential belief that permeated the studio: a theoretically paternal sense of control. "Actors are waiters delivering the dinner," said Sam Marx. "They're not in the kitchen."

As far as MGM was concerned Lucille LeSueur was just contract flesh, and a lot of it. Her face was round, and covered with freckles, which she hated. Worse, she had never acted in her life. Nevertheless, promoting contract flesh was what MGM did, so they began running her through the generic publicity mill.

By the spring of 1925, random publicity pictures began appearing in the Los Angeles newspapers. In May 1925, the *Los Angeles Daily News* ran a picture of "Lucille Le Sueur" and one Paul Ellis "of Metro-Goldwyn-Mayer studios" sitting on a couch in Brent's department store. The same two kids appeared in the same paper two days later, but this time they were in A.M. Smith's South Broadway furniture store checking out baby beds for the children they didn't have. Two days after that, there was yet another photo of Lucille trying on hats in a store on South Broadway while Paul Ellis pretended to sleep.

Paul Ellis soon disappeared, never to be seen again. Lucille was another matter entirely. There was only one problem. Both the names Lucille LeSueur and Billie Cassin were regarded as nonstarters. Especially the former—it was a mouthful and sounded too much like "sewer."

Harry Rapf ordered a new name for her, so the publicist Pete Smith ginned up a name-that-actress contest in a magazine called *Movie Weekly*. Whoever came up with a new name that was redolent of an "energetic, ambitious and typically American personality" would get a prize of $500. The contest was to close on May 2, 1925—a week before MGM cast Lucille in a story about showgirls titled *Sally, Irene and Mary*.

The winning name was "Joan Arden," suggested by Mrs. Louise Artisdale of Rochester, New York. Unfortunately, "Joan Arden" had also been suggested by two other contestants. "Essential to change name," cabled MGM's publicity chief Howard Strickling, "or it will cost about $1,500 extra total prizes. Same thing applies runner-up names Diana Gray, Joan Gray, Ann Morgan, Peggy Shaw."

One of the few public signs of Joan Arden was a brief item in the *Los Angeles Times* in July announcing that "Joan Arden, along with Sally O'Neill, Estelle Clark," and a woman supposedly named Rose Blossom "would form the Metro-Goldwyn-Mayer quartette of girls . . . receiving their initial screen opportunity at that studio." The studio even managed to place a still of Harry Rapf handing Lucille a nameplate bearing the name "Joan Arden" in the *Daily News*. Harry Rapf's son Maurice would be the proud possessor of a true collector's item: a portrait still bearing the inscription "To the sweetest little boy in the world," from "Joan Arden."

The name "Joan Crawford" was chosen by Adele Whitely Fletcher, who would become a fan magazine writer with a career that stretched from 1931 to 1972 but in 1925 just happened to be the editor of *Movie Weekly*. "There was a . . . showgirl, Lucille LeSueur," she remembered. "Harry Rapf of Metro was very interested in her, and he offered a $500 prize for a name. He had very prestigious judges—oh my—but when it came time to judge they were all very busy and some of them were not available, and they said to me, go ahead, any name you choose is all right with us.

"And Joan hated the name at first—hated it."

A name, like a specific identity, had always been a fungible asset for the young woman. Lucille LeSueur had been informally replaced by Lucille Cassin or Billie Cassin at school in Lawton and at Stephens College. Indeed, she had been Lucille Cassin as late as 1923, shortly before her dancing career took off. Reverting to her official birth name only occurred when she was working for the Shuberts in New York. Her dislike of "Joan Crawford" might just have been because of the clash of consonants.

Lucille's new name was announced on August 20, 1925, via a brief item in the *Los Angeles Daily News*: "She was formally rechristened yesterday by Harry Rapf, associate executive at the Metro-Goldwyn-Mayer studios." The *Los Angeles Times* ran a photo of the girl looking virginal along with an explanation of the name change. "The old name, it was said, was considered too difficult. Very few knew how to spell it and even fewer how to pronounce it, and it was felt it was an obstacle to her success."

She never liked the name the studio gave her, but the studio had invested money in it and her, which meant that she was probably not going to be dumped anytime soon.

Under any name, Joan Crawford was adrift in an environment unlike any she had experienced. MGM had signed a bunch of other young women at the same time they signed her: Dorothy Sebastian, Carmel Myers, Gertrude Olmstead, Renee Adorée, Gwen Lee, a few others. Some of them would become demi-stars, some would marry well or badly, and some would disappear. But as the publicist Pete Smith wrote, "Of all the girls at MGM in that period, only Joan Crawford actually attained the very top billing to give serious box-office competition to the studio's leading stars."

As would be her lifelong pattern, the newly christened employee dove in. She walked all over the lot, made friends wherever she could, made herself available for anything and everything the studio asked, from idiot cheesecake stills to doubling for Norma Shearer in a dual role.

Don Gillum, a still photographer at the studio, told Pete Smith he needed to pay attention to Crawford. As Pete Smith remembered, "Gillum was especially proficient in snapping our starlets in mid-air as they gracefully leaped about the sands of Santa Monica beaches attired in fetching bathing suits or high-jumped over a tape in track shorts and tight-fitting T-shirts. With an enthusiasm seldom displayed by Gillum, he dumped a batch of photos on my desk. In those still pictures—and at the peril of still sounding like Joan's press agent—[she] displayed a wild youthful abandon—among other things—and leaped higher and more gracefully than any of the others. She was a perfect subject for 'Action pictures.'"

So she became what the publicity department called "the Action queen," the focus of pictures that were easy to plant in newspapers and magazines. Similarly, her skill at the Charleston and the Black Bottom meant that MGM could publicize her as the symbol of a jazz-mad epoch. "When Joan entered a dance contest others lost heart," wrote Pete Smith. "She had more cups than the Brown Derby."

Smith noticed that Crawford had a vague resemblance to Pauline Frederick, a noted stage and film actress of the period. They took a profile shot of her that synced up with a similar shot of Frederick and that got a lot of play in the papers as well. Crawford was already an admirer of Frederick and the young ingenue went backstage at the El Capitan Theatre in Hollywood to meet the star. Frederick took Crawford's face in her hands and said, "You're far more beautiful than I ever was at your age, dear. You should go far."

Carey Wilson, who spent his career at MGM as both writer and producer, became an early fan as well. "You weren't like the others," he told Crawford years later. "You were just plain scared to death." As well she might have been. If MGM didn't pan out, she would be back dodging handsy Stage Door Johnnies in New York or, worse, Kansas City.

The only way out was forward, relentlessly forward.

———◆———

THE STANDING JOKE ABOUT Harry Rapf was that you could turn him upside down and use him to plow a field. Another line, credited to the screenwriter Robert Hopkins, had him bidding Rapf bon voyage as he left on an ocean voyage: "Don't stick your head out the porthole, or the boat will turn around."

In other words, Harry Rapf had a huge nose. Other than that, he was well liked, an unpretentious workhorse whose pictures (*Min and Bill*, *The Champ*, *Tugboat Annie*) would keep the MGM lights on during the worst days of the Depression.

Rapf introduced Crawford to his son Maurice. The boy was only eleven years old, but precocious—Maurice immediately began fantasizing about her. "She was a bit plump with a face that was much rounder than the one we are familiar with, and the famous Crawford eyes had not yet exploded into those big saucers that we know so well. . . . She was a very attractive girl."

The word around the lot was that Joan was sleeping with Rapf. Maurice Rapf would be asked about this near the end of his long life. "I can't tell you if my father had an affair with Joan Crawford," he said. "What I can tell you is that my mother devoutly believed he did."

Put it this way: Joan Crawford had the knack of making the right friends. John Arnold was an expert cameraman at MGM who took a liking to her. Contracts for young players were provisional, with options every six months, which meant they had to make some sort of impact quickly.

"I was terrified the day I made [a] test," said Crawford. "I had to read lines from a play, go through some light comedy movements. Johnny saw how scared I was. 'Don't be afraid of that thing,' he said, pointing to the camera. 'It's only got one eye, it can't talk back to you.'"

Crawford never saw the test, but Arnold told her that she was "quite different," this at a time when the girls were trying to look alike in order to fit with prevailing tastes. Arnold told her she had an athletic quality and her face was "built."

"Johnny used to talk to me like a Dutch uncle. He's seen so many hopefuls come and go. When he'd hear people on the set inviting me to go here or there he'd take me to one side. 'Hey, wait a minute. Don't pay any attention to these good-time Charlies. You've got something on the ball. You can't stay out late and get up early and you have to be careful whom you go with.'"

John Arnold was an MGM lifer—he would become head of the camera department, in charge of assigning cinematographers and much else, and he remembered Crawford with affection. "Viola Dana and Joan were the only two actresses I ever sort of took under my wing. They were both just kids when they started at the studio. Joan had a freshness and a sincerity. You had to believe in her and she never let you down."

Joan's first job at MGM involved the back of her head. The picture in question was called *Lady of the Night* and featured Norma Shearer in a dual role. When the two characters Shearer played were in the same scene, director Monta Bell placed Joan in the foreground while the camera focused over her shoulder on Shearer's face.

It was an ignominious beginning. Then and for the rest of her life Crawford was unimpressed by Shearer and what she called "her three expressions." She was not alone. The actress Mrs. Patrick Campbell worked with Shearer and announced in a too-loud voice, "Look at that Shearer person. Her eyes are so far apart you'd have to get a taxi between them."

Crawford's childhood had produced a young adult whom one writer called "ravenous for attention," and here she was subsuming herself to an actress she neither liked nor respected.

Writing in 1955, Shearer thought the young girl had "the most beautiful eyes. They were the biggest eyes I had ever seen. But they didn't trust me. I could see that. They never have." For a brief time, they were friendly. "I saw her crying up on the balcony outside the dressing rooms," continued Shearer. "I stopped and asked her what was troubling her. She told me that she didn't like the dress the wardrobe department had given her. I tried to console her by telling her it looked lovely."

Joan would remember that she watched everything Shearer did, if only because Shearer was dating Irving Thalberg, who was clearly brilliant and oddly compelling as well. Thalberg was compact, studious, and looked slightly consumptive. He had a habit of dropping by the sets and watching intently while flipping a coin in the air—his primary nervous habit, like a character in a gangster movie. Joan couldn't work up the courage to speak to him.

The newly christened would-be actress wandered around the studio soaking up atmosphere and, when she could get it, advice. Eleanor Boardman, a superb actress who was married to the director King Vidor, allowed Crawford to watch her on the set for days and occasionally invited her to her home. Not everybody was so welcoming. Mae Murray, who was working for Erich von Stroheim in *The Merry Widow*, saw Crawford chewing gum and snapped, "Spit it out. Never chew gum." Murray then swept past, never deigning to speak to Crawford again until nearly ten years had passed. Crawford paid attention to Boardman's advice, ignored Murray's.

While Joan was getting her sea legs, it was apparent that the right hand of studio publicity couldn't be bothered to tell the left hand of production what was going on. A week after the *Los Angeles Times* announced the name "Joan Crawford," MGM's *Pretty Ladies* was released featuring "Lucille LeSueur" billed eighth.

Pretty Ladies is sharply directed by Monta Bell, a former newspaperman who ghosted Charlie Chaplin's 1921 book *My Trip Abroad*, after which Chaplin took him on as an assistant director. Bell quickly graduated to directing his own pictures at MGM and proved more than adept—his best movie is *Man, Woman and Sin* starring John Gilbert and the fascinating, doomed Jeanne Eagels.

Pretty Ladies is a drama about the *Ziegfeld Follies*, the showgirls who populated it and the wealthy roués who tried to seduce the showgirls. The stars are Zasu Pitts as a comedienne who yearns to be a dramatic actress and Tom Moore as her drummer boyfriend. Lucille is billed below special guest appearances by Conrad Nagel and Norma Shearer, below look-alike actors impersonating Ziegfeld and stars such as Will Rogers and Eddie Cantor.

She's on the periphery, parading around in a costume and white wig that suggest Marie Antoinette, necking in a corner with a playboy, but she does it well, and she's clearly attractive.

Pretty Ladies was shot in the spring, which means the studio would have had plenty of time to change her billing to Joan Crawford, and they undoubtedly would have if they had known what her future at the studio was going to be. As it was, they let the film go out with her real name—the first and last time it would be seen on a movie screen. At least she got billing. Myrna Loy, also playing one of the chorus girls, labored in anonymity. The two young actresses quickly bonded and remained close for the rest of their lives.

Anonymity was every young contract performer's perennial peril, as was proven by an unbilled semi-appearance that same year. In Frank Borzage's film of Somerset Maugham's *The Circle*, a rotund sixty-ish matron is sobbing over her failing marriage, when a beautiful young woman (Eleanor Boardman) idly picks up a photo album and sees a photograph of the matron as a young girl. The young girl in the photograph is Joan Crawford.

She also shows up in an equally unbilled but less ignominious part in *Graustark*, a 1925 Norma Talmadge vehicle made for First National but shot on the MGM lot. Crawford plays a lady-in-waiting to Talmadge in reel six, and adjusts the star's veil in reel seven, where she can be seen for the next minute or so, including something of a close-up. She's easily identifiable but the film has never appeared in her list of credits, probably because it's not technically an MGM picture, so nobody ever looked for her. In any case, she's just filler in the frame.

Whether under her old name or her new name, whether in a part that was billed or unbilled, the newly christened actress was miserable—she thought her name sounded too much like "Crawfish," and, more importantly, she felt like she was flying blind. She knew her eyes were startlingly beautiful and her legs were excellent. Other than that, she believed she was playing a bad hand.

She was talked off the ledge by a young actor named William Haines, whom she had met on the set of a film called *Memory Lane*. "She was bovine," remembered Haines nearly thirty years later, "very pretty, very alive. Her hair was parted in the middle and she had enormous eyes."

"'Crawford' is not so bad," he told her. "They might have called you Cranberry and served you every Thanksgiving with the turkey." For the rest of an intimate friendship that extended for just under fifty years, Crawford would be "Cranberry," a name she delighted in.

Haines had never met anyone quite like her, and he never would again. "What was I? An office boy. An office boy who'd won a contest, Eleanor Boardman and I. I'd only been in pictures three years."

Haines observed Crawford closely, as if she was the sole representative of a vanished species. He told her that the camera was a "one-eyed monster," which was undoubtedly counterproductive. He remembered that "She dieted viciously. There was a long period of black coffee, gallons of black coffee. You admired her for this as you admired her for everything."

But if Joan had been unlucky for the first twenty years of her life, her luck was finally changing, both in her friends and in her opportunities. There would be other gay men who became close friends—George Cukor, Cesar Romero. But William Haines would be her best friend as well as spirit guide to the mores of Hollywood, which he instinctively understood.

Billy Haines could always make her laugh. Whenever somebody else answered the phone at her house, he would ask, "Is the movie star there?" She trusted him absolutely, and it went both ways. They both had a knack for friendship, and both valued loyalty, if only because neither of them ever received much of it—Haines because he was gay and saw no reason to lie about it, which made him an outlier in the early twentieth century, while Joan was working-class with no education to speak of but plenty of vaulting ambition and saw no reason to lie about either.

Haines explained that it wasn't enough to be talented; it wasn't even strictly necessary. What was necessary was a persona that struck a chord with the audience. It helped if that persona was visible off-screen as well as on: "You've got to draw attention to yourself. There are fifty other girls trying to get roles in pictures, and the producers don't know one pretty face from another. You've got to make yourself *known*. Get yourself some *publicity*. Go to dances and premieres. Let people know that Joan Crawford is *somebody*."

Her timing was excellent. Only ten years before, Hollywood nightlife had been severely limited. The best restaurant was called the Oasis, and you could always tell who was working because that was the person who got the check whether they wanted it or not. "The Oasis was on Hollywood Boulevard near the Taft building," remembered Mary Ford, the wife of John Ford. "Then we had one nightclub called John's, and it was a place where you'd go downstairs on Hollywood Boulevard but nobody went there. They had the Hollywood Hotel Thursday night dances—that was the thing! And if you wanted to go slumming, you went to Vernon. There was a nightclub there, and you could get liquor under the table. Leo McCarey was the bouncer out there before he became a director."

But 1925 Hollywood was a boom town, and Crawford soon became the Belle of that particular Ball. She became a regular at the Montmartre on Hollywood Boulevard, the Cocoanut Grove at the Ambassador Hotel, and Eddie Brandstatter's Sunset Inn in Santa Monica, which had a $5 cover charge to keep the trash out. Crawford dined and danced the Charleston, squired by a succession of young men.

In particular, the dance floor at the Cocoanut Grove was the place to be. "I couldn't keep up with her," said William Haines. "She wore out dozens of dance partners. An evening at the Grove and you had a hernia for life."

The Cocoanut Grove charged $1.25 for the tea dance, which included a cucumber sandwich and some cheese. Women would order some punch, into which they poured bootleg gin. (Crawford was a very light drinker in this period.) Failing that there was always champagne. Since Prohibition was the ostensible law of the land, the code for champagne was "ginger ale." The Montmartre on Hollywood Boulevard had lunch dances on Wednesdays and Saturdays, and Joan and her friends were regulars. Crawford developed a circle of friends: Polly Ann Young, Sally Blane, and the fan magazine writer Dorothy Manners.

Polly Ann Young's mother, Mrs. Belzer, told Crawford that she had to take Polly Ann's sister Gretchen out with them. But Gretchen was just encountering puberty and Crawford thought a thirteen-year-old would be a buzzkill. Mrs. Belzer upped the ante by saying if Gretchen didn't go, neither could Polly Ann. As it turned out, Gretchen took the Cocoanut Grove by storm, which sent Crawford into a snit. "That's the last trip for Gretchen!" she told her friends. She didn't hold it against the child, who would soon change her name to Loretta Young. Crawford and Young would always be friends.

The town was full of rich young men, foremost among them Mike Cudahy, the heir to a meatpacking fortune. Cudahy would take Crawford for long drives along the coast. She would pour out her heart to him, but he seemed insufficiently serious and insufficiently interested, or, to put it more accurately, interested in only one thing.

Cudahy was Joan's favorite dance partner, while her main competition on the dance floor was a young actress named Jane Peters, who would change her name to Carole Lombard. "Joan had great body tension," Lombard remembered. "She was better than I, but she seemed to be working at it. And for me it was all play. It was a thrill to beat her, and she liked to beat me, too. But that wasn't the big thing with her. She didn't just want to get a start in pictures, she kept talking about reaching the top."

Crawford found that she liked the spotlight, both literally and figuratively. "My skirts were a little too short, my heels a little too high, and my hair a little too frizzy and a little too bright. I wore brilliant red nail polish when everybody else wore pink, and when it was the thing to be fair I got a deep suntan. I loved being in the vanguard—and I was. They all followed along behind."

"[Joan] had as much love of life as anyone I knew," said the writer Adela Rogers St. Johns. "She loved life, loved living it, a triple-A heartbeat. She wanted respectability; she always wanted to be respectable, [but] Joan had a simplicity that was moving. When she didn't know which fork to use she said so."

Crawford told St. Johns about her time at Stephens College and how kind Dr. Wood had been to her. "I'd like to have a little veneer so I won't look like I came from nowhere," she said with more than a touch of wistfulness.

Mike Cudahy lived in a big house on Franklin Avenue, and attendees of the Cocoanut Grove grew used to seeing Crawford pull up in Cudahy's white

Cadillac convertible. Adela Rogers St. Johns said Cudahy "was out of his mind" about her, but his mother didn't approve. "There was a confrontation at the Cudahy house and Joan told her where she could go." The relationship ended.

Not everybody at the studio was as enthralled with Crawford as Billy Haines. For some she came on too strong, sold it too hard. The MGM screenwriter Frederica Sagor Maas described her as "a gum-chewing dame, heavily made up . . . [with] wildly frizzed hair. An obvious strumpet. Crude as she was, everything about her seemed to say, 'Look out. I'm in a hurry. Make room.'"

But for the first time in her life, Joan had excellent timing. Mayer and Thalberg had been charged by Marcus Loew with supplying Loew's theaters with a stream of commercial product. The production line they established was enterprising, aggressive, and immediately successful. In 1925 alone, MGM's output included such major critical and commercial successes as King Vidor's *The Big Parade*, Erich von Stroheim's *The Merry Widow*, and the silent version of *Ben-Hur*.

Crawford may have been a stranger in a definitively strange land, but her instincts were excellent. She didn't just sit waiting for fate to tap her on the shoulder. She hung around sets watching how actors acted, how they worked camera angles to their advantage. And she made friends on the crews by asking questions. Despite all this, she was, she remembered, cripplingly shy. "I lived in a little room a few blocks from the studio so that I could walk back and forth. I never talked to anyone. When I worked as an extra . . . I wouldn't even eat in the studio commissary for fear someone might talk to me. One day I peeped in trying to get my nerve to go in and have lunch there. Jack Gilbert passed me and said 'Hulloa.' I fled from the place and ran down the street to Mother's Café, where a few chauffeurs and extra people lunched on stools in front of a counter. I ate there every day for six months."

Since she didn't have any particular performing identity, MGM threw her in a variety of bread-and-butter pictures in which she played a series of ingenues: supporting America's favorite waif Jackie Coogan in *Old Clothes*; uncredited in an Elinor Glyn concoction called *The Only Thing*; as one of the title characters in *Sally, Irene and Mary*. The latter picture teamed her with the skilled Edmund Goulding, who wrote and directed and would play a crucial role in Crawford's 1930s roster of successes.

Sally, Irene and Mary is a rough draft of *Valley of the Dolls*—three girls on the road to varying show business fates. One lives, one dies, one gets married. At bottom, it's one of the flapper movies that would catapult Crawford to stardom, but it's exceedingly well shot. The camera never moves, but every shot is perfectly framed, and Cedric Gibbons's set designs are on the fringe of Art Nouveau rather than Art Deco.

Crawford plays Irene, who comes to a bad end. What's striking about her is how she holds the screen even though she doesn't really have much to do—the movie belongs to Constance Bennett, already a reserved, controlled presence at only twenty-one years old, and Sally O'Neil, whose vogue ended with silent movies.

Crawford does a good Charleston and projects a vibrant presence. She looks more like Joan Crawford's slightly homelier sister than she does *Joan Crawford*—her hair style is unflattering and she wears so much eye shadow that her greatest physical attributes—her eyes—are almost negated.

What all this meant was that she was uncomfortable. In rehearsal she was giving it all she had, and John Arnold, the cameraman, took her aside and told her, "Pretend that the news you hear in this scene concerns someone close to you and you've just heard it for the first time. No matter how many times you've rehearsed it, hear it now for the first time."

"I think it was on this scene that Johnny tried something new," remembered Crawford. "He shot it two ways, one shot showing me full length and another shot close up so that my face filled the whole screen. The shot was used this second, more dramatic way. A face up close like that has such strength."

The underlying problem was that she hadn't quite found her look. Crawford was still in her chrysalis stage, but she was lucky in that she was working with a couple of actresses who didn't really have much more experience than she did. *Variety* didn't like the picture, calling it "rather trashy chorus-girl stuff that the 'sticks' may eat up. It's not a good picture." Nevertheless, it made a profit of $141,000.

The most important thing about *Sally, Irene and Mary* was that it converted Edmund Goulding into a Crawford fan. Louise Brooks remembered a night at the producer Walter Wanger's apartment in New York City when Goulding came in "like an enthusiastic lion about to eat us up. He had just finished directing *Sally, Irene and Mary*. It was a big hit, but he didn't talk about that, nor did he talk about Constance Bennett and Sally O'Neil, who were also big hits in the picture. He talked exclusively about Joan Crawford. 'She's the find of the year, Walter—the greatest find of the year! Beautiful, wonderful emotional quality—bound for stardom.'"

Brooks had been the flavor of the month until being supplanted by Crawford. Brooks was frankly jealous, and she stayed that way. She went to see *Sally, Irene and Mary*. "She was beautiful, all right, in spite of her hair parted in the middle to give her a madonna look. And her legs were beautiful even though she used them to dance the Charleston like a lady wrestler. But she played her part like a chocolate-covered cherry—hard outside and breaking up all gooey with a sticky center. I didn't care for her."

Brooks's jealousy led her to see things that weren't there. Crawford's Irene is the least delineated of the three girls—she's cute, ambitious, and that's about it. Crawford's own estimation of her performance was that "Eddie Goulding started teaching me how to act. . . . That picture told me I was doing the right thing, that I might just last."

Goulding wasn't blind to her shortcomings; he said that she "had a habit of overacting to compensate for her lack of dramatic training." Still, they kept an eye out for each other, and the friendship would yield great benefits. "I would still be dancing the Charleston on table tops if it weren't for Eddie," was Crawford's summation of their collaboration.

After a film that was two steps forward, it was two steps back with *The Boob*, a film that director William Wellman boasted was "the worst picture Miss Crawford ever made—a great distinction." Wellman wasn't far wrong. *The Boob* is stocked with comedians (Charlie Murray, Hank Mann, Babe London) from Keystone who (over)act as if they're still working for Mack Sennett. The film seems to have been intended as a parody of the Charles Ray local-yokel-makes-good movies that had burned out by the early 1920s. Crawford gets third billing but only appears in a couple of scenes as an unlikely federal Prohibition agent. *The Boob* didn't do her any good, but it didn't do her any harm either. After Louis B. Mayer and Irving Thalberg watched the picture, Wellman was immediately fired, but recovered nicely when he directed the epic war film *Wings* for Paramount, which won the first Academy Award for Best Picture.

NINETEEN TWENTY-SIX BROUGHT SOME recognition when Crawford was named one of the Wampas Baby Stars, an annual publicity stunt singling out promising young actors and actresses. It was a good year for young actresses—besides Crawford, the roster included Fay Wray, Mary Astor, Dolores Costello, and Dolores Del Rio.

Crawford was loaned out to First National for Harry Langdon's *Tramp, Tramp, Tramp*, then came back to MGM for *Paris* and *The Taxi Dancer*—cumulatively a regression from the vaguely promising 1925 pictures.

In *Tramp, Tramp, Tramp* Crawford is blandly decorative and still in search of a performing personality. Like most comedians, Langdon made sure to keep the focus on the comedian. In a 1929 interview, after Crawford had become a star, Langdon complained about her lack of discipline, saying she laughed so hard they had to retake her scenes, which might be the reason she seems slightly at sea—stiff and unsure of herself.

Crawford complained about the lack of fun involved in working with Langdon. She particularly hated being locked in a manhole for a scene centering on a hurricane. It brought back childhood claustrophobia stimulated by her brother locking her in a closet. One semi-unpleasant experience and Crawford began to rethink her career choice. "I wasn't so sure I wanted to be in the movies."

After the loan-out to Langdon, she was slotted into a series of profoundly unimportant pictures opposite has-beens (Charles Ray) or never-wases (Douglas Gilmore, Francis X. Bushman Jr.), more or less to see if she held the screen without any help from writers or costars.

Paris reunited her with Edmund Goulding, who continued to make creative demands on her. One day on the set he suddenly said, "Take off your shoes. Now . . . stand with your feet apart and grip the earth firmly with your feet. Draw the strength of the earth right into you!"

Photoplay said that she played the girl in *Paris* "exquisitely," while *Variety* had their doubts: "Advance information on Miss Crawford among the 'picture mob' had her strongly heralded as a 'comer.' Undoubtedly a 'looker' . . . Miss Crawford will nevertheless have to show more talent than in this instance."

When it came to *The Taxi Dancer*, *Photoplay* insisted she had what it takes: "Joan Crawford . . . rides high over the inferior material. Here is a girl of singular beauty and promise. And she certainly has IT."

She remained a good soldier, going to work on *Winners of the Wilderness*, a Tim McCoy Western. McCoy had a ranch in Wyoming adjacent to the Sioux reservation and had served as an Indian agent. He came to Hollywood to put on a prologue at Grauman's Egyptian for *The Covered Wagon*, the first epic Western. Irving Thalberg thought McCoy looked like a movie hero, ordered a screen test, and asked McCoy to watch it with him. "I wouldn't pay a dime to cross the street and look at that fellow," said McCoy. Thalberg had a different point of view and signed McCoy to a contract.

Nobody at MGM had much experience with Westerns, so McCoy and W. S. Van Dyke, a recently hired director, were left alone. (Van Dyke would spend the rest of his life at MGM as the primary studio workhorse.) The McCoy Westerns started making profits for the studio and, as McCoy remembered it, "Joan was getting uppity so they decided to put her over in our unit as punishment."

It seemed that Joan had committed a faux pas: asking Irving Thalberg why Norma Shearer was getting all the good parts. "Joan, your career is coming along nicely," Thalberg replied with his usual cool condescension. "You still have much to learn. If you tried something too ambitious, it might be disastrous. You wouldn't want to be laughed at, would you?"

As punishment for her audacity, Crawford was handed off to the McCoy unit for two pictures. Unfortunately, she had a good deal of fun working on location with McCoy's unit, primarily because she didn't have to ride a horse. "She was a great gal on the set," McCoy said.

What Joan liked about McCoy was that while he played cowboys and actually was a cowboy, that wasn't all he was. His best friends were elegant gentlemen: Ronald Colman, William Powell, and Richard Barthelmess. He was the first actor she knew who somehow contrived to have the best of both worlds. And despite Crawford's insecurity, you can see her improving on a picture-by-picture basis—progress that was incremental but real.

And then, after barely two years, the ice broke.

Lon Chaney had already established himself as the great interpreter of horror and Grand Guignol in pictures such as *The Hunchback of Notre Dame* and *The Phantom of the Opera* when Crawford was assigned to work with him in *The Unknown*. Chaney scared her, but in a good way, for it was Chaney who taught her to act by both example and osmosis.

The Unknown is a spectacularly twisted tale about Alonzo, a knife-thrower in a Spanish circus who pretends to be a double amputee so he can demonstrate his specialty of throwing knives with his feet. If that isn't sufficiently outré, he also has two thumbs on one of his hands. Alonzo is obsessed with a young girl who can't stand to be embraced, so he has his arms amputated.

After that, things get weird.

Chaney was not handsome, not romantic, not in it for the money or the women or the fan mail. The scripts for his pictures could be ridiculous, the direction nominal, but with or without startling makeup transformations he was always compelling because of the physical and psychological pain he endured and communicated.

"Here was the most tense, exciting individual I'd ever met," Crawford recalled, "a man mesmerized into this part. Between pictures when you met him on the lot you saw a grave, mild-mannered man with laughing black eyes who seldom laughed but when he did, his laughter was irresistible."

When it came time to go to work, Chaney transformed. "His concentration, the complete absorption he gave to his character, filled all of us with such awe we never even considered addressing him with the usual pleasantries until he became aware of and addressed us. He was armless in this picture—his arms strapped to his sides. . . . Mr. Chaney could have unstrapped his arms between scenes. He did not. He kept them strapped one day for five hours, enduring such numbness, such torture, that . . . he was able to convey, not just realism, but such emotional agony that it was shocking . . . and fascinating.

"When he worked, it was as if God were working, he had such profound concentration. It was then I became aware for the first time of the difference between standing in front of a camera and acting."

As far as the studio was concerned, Chaney was a gem in that he saved the drama for his performances. He showed up on time, did his job, and went home. His films were shot economically—*The Unknown* was made in a little more than five weeks by Tod Browning, Chaney's favorite director—and they reliably made a lot of money. *The Unknown* returned a profit of nearly $400,000 on a modest cost of $217,000. Chaney made at least three pictures a year, which meant that all by himself he was usually responsible for a million dollars a year in profit for MGM.

As Chaney's biographer Michael Blake would write, typically "Browning took a lifelike character, possibly displaying a physical or emotional deformity, and placed him in believable surroundings. From that point, Browning wove a tale that took the character to extremes."

The critic Michael Dempsey said that "Chaney's films, at their individual best . . . evoke a sense of human fineness that, impenetrably masked by deforming flesh, finally dies alone and unseen, never achieving, or achieving only in flashes, the release of fulfilled love."

Crawford's part in *The Unknown* is nothing special—she's still basically The Girl. But given the plot and Chaney's charisma, just being noticed was a triumph. Crawford's beauty, energy, and increasing confidence hold the screen, helped by her noticeably skimpy wardrobe. As Jeanine Basinger wrote, "Crawford is a tremendous plus in the movie because somehow she seems worth it all. At this point in her career she's totally unaffected, very natural in her acting and inherently sexy. Yet she has a sweet shyness to her."

For the first time she ramps up her own intensity to successfully compete with the performance of a great movie star. It's the first film where she transcends the category of the nominal leading lady. *Photoplay* noticed: "It has the merit of possessing a finely sinister plot, some moments with a real shock, and Lon Chaney. Besides, Joan Crawford is an optical tonic as Estrellita."

Chaney posed for a lot of informal stills off-screen with Crawford, implicitly lending her a portion of his celebrity. Michael Blake believes that "He admired her seriousness when it came to acting. Lon would gladly spend time sharing his experience and advice with any young performer who showed a seriousness in their work."

Chaney meant to take his audience into the dark places that lurk within the soul, and his example taught Crawford to commit to her characters, to give the audience a window into the deepest part of their pain. His influence shadowed her throughout her career. Her unrelenting focus, her willingness to empathize, to absorb and reflect pain translated to an intensity that could overwhelm mediocre material and make her seem out of key with a trivial picture. But when she played a character of an equivalent size to her emotional fury—or vulnerability—the results would be astonishing.

After the Chaney picture, MGM paired her with John Gilbert, the studio's biggest romantic leading man, in a movie about bootleggers called *Twelve Miles Out*. It was a programmer and nothing special, but the fact that she was playing opposite a huge star meant that the studio was taking her seriously. Gilbert was highly attractive to Crawford, but he was consumed by his affair with Greta Garbo, so nothing happened.

Joan Crawford was a rising star at the most successful movie studio in the business. She had been an actress for less than three years.

CHAPTER FOUR

CRAWFORD'S RAPIDLY ACCRUING STATUS was made clear in an MGM memo of July 1, 1927, concerning her purchase of a house at 513 North Roxbury Drive in Beverly Hills. The house cost $28,000 fully furnished, and the studio guaranteed the down payment of $6,000. Crawford ended up with a mortgage of $10,000, while MGM held the deed in the amount of $12,500. Crawford was to repay the loan at the rate of nearly $500 a month deducted from her salary of $500 a week. Clearly, she was residing in the studio's good graces—her salary had increased by a factor of seven in only two years.

This sort of largesse became the norm at MGM. It cost the studio trouble and a lot of paperwork, but it earned them gratitude from actors who might otherwise have been fractious. Generosity on the one hand resulted in obedience on the other—as Louis B. Mayer undoubtedly observed, a fair exchange is no robbery.

Crawford was assigned to what amounted to a paid vacation: two consecutive pictures with her pal Billy Haines, one about golf (*Spring Fever*) and one about West Point called, unsurprisingly, *West Point*. Haines remembered a priceless moment on the set of *West Point*, which shot for five weeks on location at the military academy.

"The cadets were putting on a dress parade," he said. "Crawford who been delayed on the Coast, was due at any moment. Then I suddenly saw her in the distance. As she walked toward the rows of cadets standing at rigid attention,

I saw that she was wearing a huge picture hat, a slipper with enormous pompons, a dress that didn't quite meet the dimples on her knees, and she was carrying a chiffon parasol. As she swayed past the cadets, the . . . line made a serpentine turn and there was a wild look in their eyes. You could hear them thinking: *Wow!*"

The overall impression of a luscious female cat set among gaping pigeons was confirmed by costar William Bakewell, who called Crawford "a hyper-sexy, provocative redhead [who was] a living symbol of the jazz age."

Bakewell's mother had accompanied him to West Point, and he remembered her scathing disapproval when Crawford appeared in the Thayer Hotel dining room without stockings. "For the duration of our stay on the Military Reservation, her full-blown figure and animal magnetism had the effect of an aphrodisiac on the esprit de corps around the Quadrangle. One hapless cadet was reported to have been sacked from the Academy for skipping classes just to keep a date with Joan."

In fact, the location shoot resulted in some unpleasant publicity when an actor named Edgar Neely told his wife he had an affair with Crawford while on location, information that was repeated in the wife's divorce complaint and picked up by the newspapers.

West Point isn't much of a movie, although the location photography certainly helps. It ends with a blatant rip-off of Harold Lloyd's *The Freshman*, as Haines single-handedly wins the Army-Navy football game, thus proving his manly mettle. Crawford doesn't really have much to do, but she's beginning to come into her looks, and she's relaxed, vivacious, and clearly having a wonderful time working with her pal.

Next up was a silent version of the operetta *Rose-Marie*, opposite James Murray, who was about to make a big splash in King Vidor's masterpiece *The Crowd*. A silent version of an Oscar Hammerstein II/Rudolf Friml operetta sounds counterproductive, but stranger things have happened in the movie business. It was a problem picture, starting out as a starring vehicle for Renée Adorée, the female lead of *The Big Parade*, but after two weeks of shooting in Yosemite, MGM yanked Adorée, fired director William Nigh, and had Edmund Goulding take over the direction. Goulding promptly slotted Crawford into the title role and switched out most of the supporting cast as well, with Lucien

Hubbard writing a new script. Although Goulding was credited as director throughout the production in the trade papers, when the film was released Hubbard was credited on screen as the director. The picture sounds like a train wreck, but we can't be sure because it's lost.

James Murray was a belligerent alcoholic in need of frequent hospitalization. After many failed attempts to help him and large amounts of money expended in paying off police, not to mention sanitariums, MGM finally cut Murray loose in 1929. After that it was a fast trip to Poverty Row, where he worked for various independent companies until his death in 1936, when he fell—or jumped—into the Hudson River.

Murray was a classic Hollywood cautionary tale, one that Crawford undoubtedly stored away. A movie studio would be an indulgent corporate organism for only so long.

ON OCTOBER 17, 1927, Crawford and MGM producer Paul Bern went to see John Van Druten's play *Young Woodley* at the Vine Street Theatre. The star was Douglas Fairbanks Jr., and the evening would constitute the pivot point of his young life. As the curtain fell and the audience rose to its feet to applaud, the cool, determined star stepped to the stage apron to accept his due.

For all of his eighteen years he had been treated dismissively, as a genetic adjunct to his legendary father. Douglas Fairbanks Sr. was already a movie star in 1918 when he fell in love with Mary Pickford, and the resulting divorce from his wife was accompanied by a settlement of nearly $500,000. Attempting to increase her settlement, the former Mrs. Fairbanks blew it all in the stock market. Young Fairbanks thus had to go to work as an actor to support his mother, which provoked his father's anger.

"Father didn't know why I was going to work because my mother made a great effort to make sure he didn't know the whole story. They didn't want him to know we were broke. He, quite rightly, felt I should go on with my education." Dinner invitations to Pickfair, the baronial home of Pickford and Fairbanks Sr., were rare, and the father ignored his son's seventeenth and eighteenth birthdays.

Standing there taking his bow onstage, Doug Jr. remembered that he was "Rather smug, as if to say, 'Well, it's about time you all treated me as something more than a shadow.'"

That night changed everything. Fairbanks Sr. went around town asking people if they had seen Junior's play. The father even gave his son a copy of Henry Irving's *The Art of Acting* and inscribed it, "To Junior: Let your own discretion be your tutor. Dad, 1927."

Crawford went backstage to congratulate the young actor on his performance and, as she put it, "fell in love at once. Immediately." It made perfect sense: Junior had only a portion of his father's charisma, but was taller, better looking, and less egocentric.

Fairbanks remembered meeting Crawford after the show, but it wasn't as memorable for him as Charlie Chaplin sitting with him on the curb in front of the theater after everyone else had gone home. Chaplin took "enormous pains to give minor but helpful criticisms. Most important, he gave me a long and encouraging lecture about my future, about what I should do and how. . . . No other friend or relative took so much time or trouble as did Charlie that late night."

The play was a hit, a palpable hit, and the next day Fairbanks got a note from Crawford asking for a signed photograph and, if he was so inclined, a phone call.

He went to her house with the photograph. The meeting was nervous, but after an hour it was time to go and he asked her to return the favor and give him a signed photograph. "To Douglas," she wrote. "May this be the start of a beautiful friendship. Joan."

Fairbanks believed her to be about four years older than he was, which he found "quite in accordance with my preference for older women." Within a few weeks they were besotted by each other. "The total effect was magnetic," he recalled. "Hers was less a talent than a distinctive gift that inclined her to 'perform' her passing thoughts as if she were going through a repertoire of characters at an audition. . . . Her figure was beautiful . . . fine-trained by years of dancing and continuing devotion to keeping fit." Fairbanks realized that her looks were not actually her strongest feature. Rather, it was her "true magnetism superimposed over her striking appearance."

As the relationship grew more serious, she asked Fairbanks not to call her Joan. That was a name that MGM had foisted on her. She much preferred "Billie," the name she reserved for close friends. For the rest of their lives, both together and apart, he called her "Billie."

They played together, they worked together. "Such fun. Such fun," she sighed decades later. "We played at keeping house. Baby talk, our own language, 'I love you' across the table."

Both of them were nervous about meeting his father and stepmother, and the first meeting was even more problematic than they had imagined. After dinner, everybody settled in to watch a movie. Fairbanks Jr. and Crawford were in a chaise lounge for two, and in that stage of infatuation when they couldn't keep their hands off each other. After the lights went down they started necking. This went on until Senior grew angry and gave Junior a dressing-down for his lack of decorum, ending with, "Don't you blame Joan now! It was all *your* fault!"

The episode did not fill Senior with happy thoughts, confirming in his mind the belief that they were both too young, a feeling that was not shared by Junior. The young man came to believe that Joan was more experienced in the erotic arts than he was, but that was just fine with him.

CRAWFORD MIGHT HAVE BEEN too moonstruck about the younger Fairbanks to notice that MGM was engaged in career-building on a high level. The studio had come to the realization that she possessed something valuable—an electric charge that made an audience sit up and take notice. As a result, they didn't rush her. They tried her in various genres, opposite leading men both high-end and low-end. When she had a costar and a story that amounted to something, she didn't disappear—she more than held her own. Crawford had a legible vibrance similar to that of Clara Bow, but with the additive of a certain elegance. The two young women had similarly compromised childhoods, but Crawford was better able to cope with the emotional problems that destroyed Bow's career.

The beauty part was that Crawford's needs and MGM's coincided. She needed security, and the studio provided it; she needed a sense of mission, and the studio provided it. She needed a sense of family to fill the yawning void that had been her lot since birth, and the studio provided it. In return, MGM got a hard worker who wanted to please the company, or at least wanted to please Louis B. Mayer, which was really the same thing. In short, she was a committed novitiate in the church of MGM.

Nearly fifty years later, Crawford was asked what happened if a star was late for work at MGM. She looked astonished and did a double take. "I can't remember anyone ever being late," she said. When she was pressed, she got stern: "No one was *ever* late."

"But what if they were?"

"They were *not*."

In fact, showing up *was* crucial. Actors who made a habit of not showing up—Errol Flynn, Marilyn Monroe—were demonstrating a psychological resistance to their craft that eventually led to unemployment and early death.

So Joan Crawford kept showing up, in a lavish picture with Ramon Novarro about clipper ships called *Across to Singapore*, in another Western with Tim McCoy, and still another picture with John Gilbert called *Four Walls* in which Gilbert played a mobster named Benny Horowitz. Whatever the studio asked her to do, she did rather well.

The important thing about *Across to Singapore* is that the great John Seitz was the cameraman, and every close-up of Crawford amounts to a caress. It's a bipolar picture with stock characters in an unstock period melodrama marked by casting lunacy—the tiny, beautiful Ramon Novarro plays the brother of craggy Ernest Torrence, who's six inches taller and about twenty-five years older.

Novarro had become a star in Rex Ingram's vibrant swashbuckler *Scaramouche*, followed by the spectacular silent version of *Ben-Hur* and Ernst Lubitsch's *The Student Prince*. He was dreamily handsome and capable of filling the screen despite his small physical stature. Sound reduced Novarro—he had a light, inexpressive voice—but his radiant looks and likable personality made him perfect for silent movies, and he and Crawford mesh very well as lovers.

Novarro was deeply religious—he had two sisters who were nuns—as well as gay. Unlike William Haines, he was closeted. He and Crawford never became particularly close, but Novarro was willing to play go-between for Fairbanks and Crawford.

During Christmas of 1927, they were on a boat off the California coast shooting location footage for *Across to Singapore*. Fairbanks Jr. had given Novarro a package to give to Crawford on Christmas morning. Novarro told her, "Billie, Doug feels terrible about not spending this holy day with you, but he hopes that this little token of his affection will be of some consolation." The box contained a pair of beautiful jade earrings, and Crawford cried in delight. When the ship docked in Long Beach on New Year's Eve, Doug was there to meet her. That night he proposed.

THE SMOOTH MELDING BETWEEN the studio's needs and Crawford's provided the primary reason why she worked at MGM for nearly twenty years. "I remember every one of my important roles the way I remember a part of my life, because at the time I did them, I *was* the role and it *was* my life for 14 hours a day."

The transition from promising young actress to star was specific, and it had nothing to do with an individual movie. "I really knew I was a star when Mayer ordered the publicity department to . . . accompany my every personal appearance and make sure I said the right things . . . make sure I dated the right men." In other words, the setting of her screen personality had already been accomplished; the task became emphasizing that personality at every off-screen opportunity. Nothing could be left to chance.

To the end of her life, Crawford had nothing but positive things to say about Louis B. Mayer. "He knew how to build and protect his properties and he had considerable regard for them as people," was the way she put it.

Even F. Scott Fitzgerald noticed the thriving young ingenue. In a discursive interview he gave to *Motion Picture* magazine, he opined on Clara Bow ("the quintessence of what the term 'flapper' signifies as a definite description. Pretty, impudent, superbly assured, as worldly wise, briefly clad and 'hardberled' as possible"); Colleen Moore ("the carefree, lovable child who rules bewildered but adoring parents with an iron hand . . . dances like a professional and has infallible methods for getting her own way"); Constance Talmadge ("the epitome of young sophistication . . . Fifth Avenue and diamonds and Catalya orchids and Europe every year").

And then he got down to cases with Crawford: "Joan Crawford is doubtless the best example of the flapper, the girl you see at smart night clubs—gowned to the apex of sophistication—toying iced glasses, with a remote, faintly bitter expression, dancing deliciously, laughing a great deal, with wide, hurt eyes. . . . Their one common trait being that they are young things with a splendid talent for life."

This interview appeared in July 1927, and given the lead time of the fan magazines, took place in March or April. Which means that Crawford was drawing serious attention when she was still on the ingenue fringe. The obvious next step for MGM was to design a movie around her, a movie that would proclaim her stardom.

That movie was *Our Dancing Daughters*. Anchored by eye-popping Deco sets courtesy of Cedric Gibbons and supporting actors (Johnny Mack Brown and Nils Asther) who complemented her without overwhelming her, this Fitzgeraldesque story of flappers glamorously slamming into their fates at 90 miles an hour struck a nerve, not to mention making a great deal of money on a nominal budget.

The story was clearly written and structured around Crawford's off-screen personality. The first line of Josephine Lovett's story, fifteen pages originally titled "The Dancing Girl," reads thusly: "Diana's personality is described by a picture of her feet—dainty, capable, flashing, irresistibly reckless—encased in ultra smart slippers, topped with glittering winged ornaments."

"I would have to say that Joan had more ambition than most actresses I worked with," said her costar Anita Page. "We made three pictures together . . . [and] I found her to be a very hard worker, always professional and dedicated to being a star. In those days, we knew how to be a *star*."

The screenwriter Frederica Sagor Maas put it another way: "No one decided to make Joan Crawford a star. Joan Crawford became a star because Joan Crawford decided to become a star." More accurately, MGM decided that Joan Crawford was a star and the public agreed.

Most stars want it, but only some of them need it with a hunger approaching the feral. For Crawford, it was march or die. It wasn't about the money—she would spend most of it as fast as she made it—and it wasn't even about acting per se. It was about finding and receiving the attention and love she had always hungered for and never had.

Crawford knew *Our Dancing Daughters* was special while she was making it, and the confidence the studio had in her shows. For the first time Crawford has top billing, and she deserves it. The story is similar to *Sally, Irene and Mary*—three flapper girlfriends, one of whom dies as retribution for betraying a trust. Anita Page's character has been inculcated by her mother with the lofty dating guideline "Beauty—and purity," but she decides to trim back the purity component when she seduces and marries the boyfriend of Crawford's character.

This time Crawford is not peripheral to the narrative but front and center, and she confidently holds the screen. You can feel her maturity as an actress arriving with each vivid close-up reflecting her command of shifting emotions. Despite Gibbons's knockout sets and some serious competition from Page, it's Crawford's movie.

The critics took notice. "Joan Crawford . . . does the greatest work of her career," wrote the critic of the New York *Mirror*. "She has a typical Clara Bow role and she gives Clara a lively run around for first honors as a modern flap. Joan has beauty, charm, and more refinement than the trim-legged Bow." The *New York World* wrote, "She has good looks, sprightliness, intelligence and a good sense of humor. She dances with great grace and versatility and she knows when—and how—to call a halt." The public took notice too. *Our Dancing Daughters* cost a modest $178,000 and returned rentals of more than a million dollars.

Before *Our Dancing Daughters*, Crawford was residing in the gray area between featured player and star. Afterward, she was a star, period, and both MGM and Crawford knew it. Her response was to take her box camera and drive around Los Angeles taking pictures of theater marquees that featured her name in lights.

Lucille LeSueur and Billie Cassin had languished in obscurity. Joan Crawford was about to flourish with fame, but the cost would be high. "I think from this time on my life was never again carefree," she would say thirty years later. "Before, I'd been absolutely sure of myself in a brash and very young way. Now I began to study and observe myself. I was immersed with myself and enchanted with myself on the screen (that will show you how immature I was). But I did have sense enough to know I must work and work hard. I kept setting the goal higher and higher."

Crawford was not like Garbo, not even like Shearer, both of whom aspired to high-toned elegance. Crawford would be frisky and down-to-earth, a striver with a sardonic knowledge of the world, her place in it, and how sex can occasionally come in handy. In other words, MGM took what Crawford was, enlarged it, then polished it—but not too much.

Crawford would be an approachable star, an actress whose fans saw themselves reflected in her performances. They believed she was one of them, and, assuming they had a roaring engine of need and a modicum of luck, they were right.

———◆◇◆———

JOAN CRAWFORD AND DOUGLAS Fairbanks Jr. married on June 3, 1929, at St. Malachy's Catholic Church in New York City—the "Actor's Church." The groom's mother attended; his father did not. Mary Pickford had tried to intercede with her husband on his son's behalf while simultaneously suggesting that perhaps the young lovers should wait six months or a year.

They honeymooned at the Algonquin, and Fairbanks Sr. relented to the extent of sending a long congratulatory telegram to his son that was both charming and (apparently) sincere. The newlyweds spoke briefly to reporters. Fairbanks told one that "Marriage is a wonderful thing, but it certainly scares you."

Crawford wired MGM, "If I have worked hard in the past, just watch me now." Joan had sold the house on Roxbury and bought another at 426 North Bristol in Brentwood that cost $57,000—double the cost of the Roxbury house. The newlyweds moved in without furniture and slept on a pallet on the floor with an apple box for a table. Her black maid Bessie slept in a bed that Crawford bought for her. "I had my first house," she remembered. "A real movie star house." The new house had ten rooms, with Spanish tile and iron-grille windows in the dining room.

She would live there for twenty-five years, own it for more than thirty years, through numerous expansions and redesigns. After the Spanish style was banished, it became French, then Venetian, then Early American. She would buy a lot in back of the house and build a movie theater, a garden, a pool, and bathhouses.

Her neighbors included her old friend from the New York chorus line Barbara Stanwyck, who lived with her husband Frank Fay in a walled mansion. Stanwyck would become a star working for Frank Capra, but she was laboring beneath a disastrous marriage. Fay was a drunk and all-around nasty piece of work. After one bruising encounter with her husband, Stanwyck ran across the street to Joan's house for shelter. Fay knew better than to try to strong-arm Crawford and stayed away. The two women became even closer.

Once they settled in, a reporter for *Photoplay* took a partial inventory of Joan's clothes closet: "Forty dresses, thirty street hats, five dinner hats, sixteen pairs of sports shoes, eighteen pairs of evening shoes."

The sunporch was a particular *bête noir* of Doug's—shelves stacked with dozens of dolls, not to mention mechanical pigs and hens, as well as Doug's electric train set, which probably ended up on the sunporch because there was no other place to put it. There were portraits by Erik Haupt and Beltran-Masses, who had done a full-length portrait of Marion Davies that Crawford had admired. She promptly commissioned a full-length portrait of her and her husband. She was holding gardenias while Douglas wore a pea jacket.

In retrospect, Crawford understood the dolls: "I was subconsciously collecting them for [my] children and because I had none in my own childhood."

The August 1929 issue of *Photoplay* rhapsodized over both Joan and her collection. "You never saw such a wonderful collection of toys. One precious doll, with lovely long hair used to belong to Joan's grandmother—but most of the toys are modern, diabolically clever, irresistibly funny. A life-sized hen that cackles and lays an egg! A life-size baby pig, that walks and grunts! Teddy bears of every shape and size—with provocative expressions! Rag dolls, gorgeous lady dolls, clowns that sing—and at the end of the porch, a little table about two feet high, with four chairs, and four funny dolls seated in them—with the table laid for dinner."

There were also black-velvet paintings of dancing girls with real blond hair and rhinestones. "I thought them beautiful," said Joan. Her husband thought them hideous.

Nineteen twenty-nine would be a crucial year in terms of Crawford's stardom as well as in the shaping of her narrative. It was, for instance, the last year she told reporters she was born in 1906. That same year, the date was magically moved up to 1908, where it stayed for the rest of her life.

ADELA ROGERS ST. JOHNS placed herself at every important event of the twentieth century save Pearl Harbor, and she always implied that she and Crawford went way back: "I taught at Stephens . . . [Lucille] was working as a chambermaid." In fact, St. Johns was writing for *Photoplay* in 1922, and her stint at Stephens was as a guest lecturer in 1939. She didn't actually meet the woman she would write about incessantly until Crawford arrived at MGM. Nevertheless, she managed to imply that they knew each other when Lucille was running around Kansas City.

As one reporter noted of St. Johns with a touch of well-deserved suspicion, "She dramatizes everything from a recipe for squash to an acquaintance with a street cleaner."

What is certain is that St. Johns knew Crawford by 1929 and "admired her inordinately. She fought her way to the top. She wasn't the world's greatest actress, but she made the best of what she had."

St. Johns was at Pickfair for one of the uneasy meetings between Crawford and her in-laws. "Mary was in white and had what looked like a crown on her hair." According to St. Johns, Pickford was eager to make an accomplice of Doug Jr., because she thought her husband might have been losing interest in her.

Crawford had to make an entrance down what St. Johns said was "an exquisite staircase," which propelled the young star into a nervous state. "You know I'm going to fall down and my skirts will fly up and I'll show I've got the wrong panties on," she told St. Johns. "You'll do all right," St. Johns told her, and she did. As St. Johns noted, "She showed on the screen the warmth of life that other stars didn't have," and she could project that same warmth in life as well.

Despite Crawford's best efforts, she and Pickford never quite hit it off, although Fairbanks Sr. won her heart. "It took me years to call her 'Mary,'" Crawford admitted. "We were there every Sunday, an ordeal I dreaded at first. But it was very necessary. . . . We'd usually go to lunch, then the Douglas's [sic] would go over to United Artists for steam baths and I'd sit and do needle point or knit." She talked with Pickford's nieces Verna or Gwynn more than she talked to Pickford. During dinner, she kept an eye on Pickford to see which fork she used. "I never picked anything until I saw what she did." Eventually it would be time for dinner and then a movie.

All this plus a burgeoning career was a lot for a young wife to handle. Fairbanks Sr. and Pickford were entering a period of difficulty that would result in mutual infidelities and ultimately divorce. A lower-middle-class (at best) interloper was not what they had in mind for a daughter-in-law, a classification that made them feel definitively middle-aged—not a category movie stars wish to inhabit.

That said, Fairbanks Sr. liked his daughter-in-law and she liked him in return. For one thing, he was fun, with a penchant for practical jokes. "In front of people like the Mountbattens, he'd ask me, 'Billie, tell them which of my pictures you liked the best.' He got a boot out of kidding me, and of course, I hadn't seen [his] movies."

Then there were the practical jokes that lurched into the juvenile. Knives and forks could be breakaways. Dining room chairs were wired to give electrical charges, and some of the chairs were designed to collapse when someone sat down. One time Fairbanks signaled his butler to hit the juice and give a dignified lady guest a shock. Nothing happened. Fairbanks again gave the signal. Still nothing.

Finally he asked her to stand up and step aside. Fairbanks sat down in her chair, got the hot shot, and jumped up. "Didn't you feel anything?" he asked.

"Well, yes," she said. "I just thought that's how you feel when meeting a movie star."

But Crawford had little emotional contact with Pickford. She would tell friends that Mary's primary concern was that Crawford would get pregnant and make Pickford a stepgrandmother. "Mary always asked her about it, and kept looking at Crawford's stomach," said Crawford's publicist Walter Seltzer. According to Crawford, "Weekends at Pickfair were excruciating."

Fairbanks Jr. said that Crawford got it wrong. "Dad—or 'Pete,' as I always called him—took pity on her. She came from the poorest circumstances. Mary recognized herself in Joan. Mary went out of her way to make Joan feel acceptable at Pickfair. We'd go there every Sunday afternoon [but] Joan complained how dull it was."

While all this was going on, Crawford's husband wrote an analysis of his wife's character for *Vanity Fair*:

> She has the most remarkable power of concentration of anyone I have ever known. Under any circumstance this tremendous faculty is at her very fingertips. She is consumed with an overwhelming ambition. . . .
>
> She is not easily influenced and must be thoroughly convinced before she will waver in her opinion on any point. She must always feel herself moving forward, and when anything tends to arrest that progress she sulks mentally. She will stand by a belief with a Trojan ferocity. . . . When she meets with disappointment she has a tendency toward bitterness rather than remorse, which no doubt, is a throwback from an acute memory of less happy days. . . .
>
> When she is depressed she falls into an all-consuming depth of melancholy out of which it is practically impossible to recover her. At these times she has long crying spells. When it is over she is like a flower that has had a sprinkling of rain and then blossoms out in brighter colors. She is extraordinarily nervous. She is frightened out of her wits to be left alone in the dark. She has a secret desire to eat everything with a spoon as a small child would. . . .
>
> She is a ten-year-old girl who has put on her mother's dress—and has done it convincingly.

As metaphorical character sketches go, there have been far worse. Fairbanks understood her fear, as well as her ferocious will to succeed, if only to put her past behind her. All these qualities were largely alien to his own character, which was blithe and optimistic.

As far as Pickfair was concerned, Crawford was intimidated and stayed that way. The decorum was stifling. What you wore had to be right, what you said had to be right, and you had to know how to use a finger bowl, which was a lot for a woman who had probably never seen one before.

There were occasional flares of light. One night at Pickfair she was sitting next to Irving Berlin and asked him about the meaning of a word. He replied, "You're the only person I know, except me, who's not ashamed to admit they haven't had an education."

Crawford's husband was aware that the Pickfair invitations were made out of obligation rather than genuine interest or affection. "Usually our conversation was limited to sports and the news," remembered young Doug of his father. "He tried hard to be a conventional father, but just couldn't quite bring it off." But there was never any overt unpleasantness.

When Crawford and Doug Jr. weren't struggling to make conversation at Pickfair, they would frequently be the guests of William Randolph Hearst and Marion Davies at San Simeon, which Crawford greatly preferred to Pickfair. As she told Jeanine Basinger, "Marion Davies was always just one of the gals, and Hearst put catsup bottles on the table, but Mary was a Queen and everybody knew it." Davies was always very sweet to Crawford, there as well as at Marion's beach house at Santa Monica, which was only slightly smaller than Buckingham Palace.

William Haines observed all this with the eye of a discerning reporter. He noticed how Davies, a generous comic in life, tended to congeal on-screen in everything except comedy because of what Haines called "the ever-watching eye of the hawk—better known as Mr. Hearst . . . that most likely made her freeze." At MGM, Irving Thalberg recognized Davies's talent, while Louis B. Mayer placed greater emphasis on her connections: the Hearst press gave incessant attention to MGM pictures because Davies worked there.

Haines was one of the court jesters at San Simeon, along with Charlie Chaplin's assistant Harry Crocker, Davies's nephew Charlie Lederer—later a prominent screenwriter—and Chaplin himself. "Charlie Chaplin was the head jester and there was a great deal of jealousy among the lesser ones," said Haines. "Of course, Mr. Chaplin used to get on and never get off."

What Crawford found at San Simeon was something like Paradise. The ranch around San Simeon amounted to 365,000 acres, mostly virgin land encompassing everything from redwood groves to twisted pines. "There were parts of deserts," said Haines. "There was . . . 50 miles of seashore. . . . There was never a dead flower. I had never seen a dead flower at San Simeon. All of them were removed at night. All the gardens were done at night."

The basis for all this was Hearst's joy in beauty. Haines remembered one morning when he was awakened by the sound of a ringing bell. He went out to find Hearst looking like an enormous Roman senator incongruously ringing a cowbell. It had snowed during the night and the camellias were covered with snow. "It was the most beautiful sight you had ever seen. And he . . . wanted to share this with everyone else. It was this sort of sensitivity with the man about beauty."

The other side of Hearst and Davies could be seen in Marion's mansion on Santa Monica beach, which featured Howard Chandler Christy portraits of Marion as she appeared in all of her generally dull costume pictures: *Yolanda, Little Old New York*, etc.

The only negative side of the San Simeon experience involved Marion's stashing her booze in the toilet reservoir in the lady's powder room. Hearst was a teetotaler, Marion liked to drink, and Crawford was her front. Crawford drank sparingly, which left Marion free to knock them back and quickly hand her glass to Crawford if Hearst came in the room.

"I've never seen you take a drink before, Joan," Hearst said.

"I thought I'd try it."

"Well, try it!" So Crawford had to pretend she liked the taste of Marion's drink.

For all his personal generosity, Hearst was on the wrong side of every social and political wave of the twentieth century, and he was quite capable of abusing his considerable power. Fairbanks Sr. once asked him why he didn't concentrate more on movies than on journalism. "Movies aren't that powerful, really," Hearst replied. "Why, you know you can crush a man with journalism but you can't with motion pictures." But you can try, as Orson Welles would find out.

Years later, Crawford would talk enthusiastically about the lavish accoutrements at San Simeon—the private zoo, the projection room, the way each bungalow was decorated in a different style. But at the time she seemed overwhelmed. "I enjoy it in retrospect," she would say in the early 1950s. "Right there, I was too awed, like my children on [our] trip last summer. They couldn't wait to tell the kids at school about the giant redwoods and the salmon run in Oregon, but they were restless and fidgety most of the time they were seeing it."

Faced with the regal, somewhat impersonal splendor of Pickfair and the more individualized splendor of San Simeon, Crawford realized she had to make a transition. The house on North Bristol had to be upgraded. She appealed to the most stylish man she knew to help her out. When Cranberry called, William Haines answered.

He threw out the black-velvet paintings and the dolls. He painted the living room white and bought white sofas and carpeting. He furnished it with antique chairs and tables that he brought from the shop he had recently opened as a hedge against the vagaries of the movie business. For color accents, he used Wedgwood blue.

When he was finished, the house had been upgraded, but at something of a cost. It looked beautiful, but the white carpeting and furniture that Haines favored were completely impractical. In a pattern that would be present for the rest of her life, Joan would insist that guests take their shoes off when they came into the house. When plastic slipcovers were invented, she promptly put them on her couches. She insisted that they were easy to take off when visitors came, but they didn't always come off. The result was a subtle conflict between the pristine beauty of her surroundings, the profusion of beautiful flowers that Crawford personally arranged, and the antiseptic environment that was a by-product of her growing passion for perfection.

For Billy Haines, the experience—and the favorable response the house got from visitors—confirmed him in the career he would eventually follow for the rest of his life. He would effortlessly mimic period styles such as English Tudor, adding his own particular touches to enliven the designs. Mostly, though, his was a theatrical style that came to be known as Hollywood Regency. One historian called it "a stage set . . . [an] architecture of glamour [that] required the seemingly effortless balancing between the formal and the casual, as well as for well-placed exaggeration and well-chosen omission."

Haines would decorate Crawford's houses through successive, often radically different transformations. Crawford would remember that "We'd fight like cats and dogs over some of his ideas. He always won because of his excellent taste and knowledge and my lack of both. . . . We went through periods the way some women go through wardrobes."

Haines also served as spirit guide to the social niceties. Once, when Crawford was throwing a party for more than a hundred people, she said she didn't think she could handle it. "I think I'll have them here for cocktails and then take them to Chasen's, where I'll have a private room prepared for us."

"Never move your party," Haines snapped, "except from one area to another in your own home."

When Billy Haines did a house, he hovered over it like an anxious parent, and the sky-high bill usually reflected all his relentless focus. Over the years he would spend many hours fussing over details at the house on Bristol, installing new carpets or switching out toilet seats. In the process he would also reliably give Cranberry a hard time with jokes about her overly fastidious need for control—jokes she always accepted because they came from Billy.

Haines's career transition from acting to decorating was forced. For years, MGM had slotted him as one kind of character—a variation on George Minafer in *The Magnificent Ambersons*. Typically, Haines played an entitled brat convinced of his own adorableness who gets his comeuppance in the sixth reel and becomes a chastened, decent human being in the seventh. Haines played that part twenty times, and he wasn't always subtle about it. The sameness and the mugging cumulatively wore out his welcome. By 1932, his box office fell off, and then there was a (probably false) scandal about an underage boy that MGM managed to hush up.

In short, Louis B. Mayer had his fill of Mr. Haines. MGM cut him loose, and the only studio that picked him up was the small independent Mascot, a clear indication that he had been blackballed. After two films at Mascot, Haines quit acting and, with the help of Crawford and a few other loyal friends, became one of Hollywood's primary interior decorators. He was extremely expensive, continually delightful, and remained a go-to talent for the rest of his life.

FIFTY YEARS LATER, DOUGLAS Fairbanks Jr. had nothing but kind things to say about his first wife. "I can honestly say I never saw her in a temper. She was, I would say, over-ambitious, but more than anything else, it was our extreme youth that killed the marriage."

Fairbanks was always indebted to Crawford for her insistence that he begin breaking away from his mother's, Anna Beth Fairbanks, incessant demands for money and attention. Crawford had erected a psychological barrier that protected her from needy relatives, and she knew it was vital that her new husband do the same.

That said, because Fairbanks Jr. had been born into status, he never quite became acclimated to Crawford's compulsive striving. "Billie had a different set of values than I. Hers were based on the belief that success was the alpha and omega of life. . . . Her horizons, her standards, her interests and enthusiasms were limited to her own professional world. . . . All this effort was directed at leaving nothing to chance in her campaign to win the public's adulation."

For entertainment, they played tennis and swam, but he remembered that her favorite time killer was competing to see who could flip the most playing cards into a wastebasket from six feet. Their sex life was clearly vigorous, but, as Fairbanks delicately phrased it, "She did worry about ever having a child lest it somehow ruin her figure and she saw to it that she had none."

In later years, Crawford would assert that she had several miscarriages with Fairbanks, but in his memoirs he wrote that "I had done some medical snooping that indicated nothing of the sort had happened." Privately, Crawford would indicate to her friend and ghostwriter Jane Kesner Ardmore that the miscarriages were actually abortions.

Crawford's husband was a star in both name and attitude. "He was smart, but he was also clever and talented," said his lifelong friend Herbert Swope Jr. "He was, for instance, a good artist." Fairbanks's knowledge and horizons were broader than his wife's, which would eventually prove to be a problem.

Fairbanks and Crawford had been together for two years by the time they got married, but Fairbanks still found her an object of study. "Never before or since, have I known any other professional who expended more personal energy on self-improvement courses and on her relations with her fans and the press. . . . If she decided that some particular fan was consistently ardent and devoted enough, or if someone in the studio made a voluntary slave of himself for her (as some certainly did) they were favored by her frequent thoughtfulness and extravagant generosity."

He wondered about her insistence on projecting actual moods rather than acting them. "She could not believe that Lynn Fontanne might feel physically dreadful yet be able to perform high comedy with supreme and subtle wit. Nor could she believe that a great actress like Helen Hayes could consciously reduce audiences to uncontrollable tears while she thought about having a juicy steak sandwich after the performance." A happy scene meant that Joan had to find something that made her happy beforehand, and the reverse was true with a sad scene. She would always be an actress of emotion rather than technique.

She also developed a private vocabulary of something approaching baby talk to avoid crudities of speech she found unnecessary. "Making love" was converted to "They went to heaven." Breasts were "ninny-pies." A kiss was a "goober."

———◇◇———

FROM THE BEGINNING OF her career in Hollywood, there were rumors about Crawford having appeared in a stag film. These shadowy stories followed her for the rest of her life, fueled by people who insisted that they had seen the film, despite the fact that nobody ever produced said film.

Crawford knew about the rumors and laughed them off. She would tell Jane Kesner Ardmore,

> The first I ever heard of such a movie was when I was honeymooning with Douglas. We were at the Algonquin in New York when an urgent stranger phoned and left a message that he had information pertaining to my career and my future. It was scary and I phoned the number he'd left. What he wanted was a sizeable sum of money for which he'd give me the reel of film.
>
> "What reel?" I said.
>
> He described it. I almost wish I'd had some money to have bought the thing and burned it, whatever it was. Douglas said that I had nothing to be afraid of.
>
> I never heard of the film again until my wedding night with Franchot

[Tone] at the Waldorf Astoria Towers. This time I had the call traced. They had threatened to show the film to MGM. That's just what I wanted them to do. Stop the nonsense. Show it to the MGM executives.

Mr. Mayer, Mr. Rubin and Mr. Rapf saw the film and did not pay the blackmail. The girl was not identifiable. My appearance had changed, of course, but she wasn't identifiable either with the youngster Mr. Rapf had signed.

Almost twenty years later, the rumor persists. But have you ever met anyone who actually has seen the film? I haven't, except the three men I mentioned. Almost everyone knows someone who knows someone who in Washington or Pittsburgh or Kokomo [has seen the film]. Bunk. I have nothing to be ashamed of except my own limitations, my moments of self-pity.

Years later, she told her publicist Henry Rogers a story that roughly corresponds to her comments to Ardmore. She told Rogers that in her early days at MGM, Louis B. Mayer had called her into his office and told her a man was trying to blackmail MGM with a stag reel. "I want you to be aware of it," he told her.

Mayer told her that he had looked at the film and knew immediately it wasn't Crawford. He then took Crawford to the projection room and showed it to her. She agreed that it obviously wasn't her, and all talk of paying blackmail ceased.

What didn't cease were the rumors, which gradually assumed the status of the second shooter in the JFK assassination. Depending on whom you talked to, MGM bought the film and A. kept it locked in a vault to ensure Crawford's obedience, or, B. burned it. Some invariably anonymous people even claimed to have seen the film. Decades later the FBI would get involved in a serious attempt to establish the truth in a prime example of J. Edgar Hoover's obsession with what he was convinced were Hollywood degenerates.

HOWARD STRICKLING BELIEVED THAT on Joan's part the romance and marriage to Doug Jr. was a simple calculation. "She decided she wanted stature and social standing, so she married Doug Jr."

William Haines saw it differently. He thought that the ambition might have been there, but so was the desire to become a functioning adult instead of a wounded child. "The big change took place with the challenge of marrying Douglas and having the Fairbanks's as in-laws. . . .

"In the early days she had the complete abandon of youth. . . . [Then] fear and insecurity crept in and she began slowly taking inventory. She wanted to know about human behavior. She observed. She became so quiet she was a bore because she was afraid to open her mouth for fear she wouldn't say the right thing. And out of that came the great lady with the broad A's and the pear-shaped tones."

Increasing stature brought increasing confidence. "It was about this time that I began to have difficulties with Crawford," remembered Pete Smith. Part of the problem was that she was being rushed from one movie to another and began to neglect her publicity. Smith talked to her about the importance of publicity and the equivalent danger of a bad press. She would listen, nod attentively, and then show up late or not at all for her next publicity appointment.

After Smith would point out her failure, Crawford would invariably be "sweetly repentant," promise to change her errant ways, and send an armful of roses to Smith as an indication of her overwhelming grief. She would then ignore yet another appointment. Smith decided to fight fire with fire. He told everyone in the publicity department to stop giving Crawford any of their time. Soon, Crawford realized that her phone had stopped ringing. She once again became the most cooperative star on the lot and stayed that way. As Pete Smith put it, "Joan Crawford had grown up."

AS CRAWFORD'S STAR ROSE, even Oklahoma noticed. The Muskogee *Daily Phoenix and Times-Democrat* ran a story quoting James Wood, the president of Stephens College, regaling a group of alumni about "Lucille Cassin" and how she was "forced to work her way through school by waiting on tables in the dining hall of the school." Wood said that she "was one of the most popular students of the school by merit of her personality, ambition, brains and 'simple, downright grit,'" qualities he regarded as basic qualifications for success.

Dr. Wood came out to California for a visit and accompanied Crawford to a dance at the Biltmore Hotel. He spoke of the many dozens of admirers who came up to their table and asked her to dance. "I noticed a big change in Billie," he reminisced. "She is more serious now, more interested in life, and tall and slender."

Success brought increasing responsibilities that Joan hadn't asked for. Mrs. Anna McConnell LeSueur Cassin left her job managing the laundry in Kansas City and moved to Hollywood to be with her daughter. Brother Hal soon followed. Once again, Joan was hemmed in by her family.

"Hal was always broke and in trouble," was the way Pete Smith put it. "He used to sleep under the pier at Malibu." Joan's publicist Walter Seltzer would put it another way: "He was a drunk and a gambler, which may have been part of her revulsion of drink."

Crawford used her position to keep her family at arm's length. She would give them money, but she would not give them her time.

AFTER TWO PROGRAMMERS, ONE with Nils Asther (*Dream of Love*) and another with Billy Haines (*The Duke Steps Out*), Crawford's reckoning with sound couldn't be postponed any longer. By early 1929, all the MGM stars had taken voice tests. Crawford recollected that "Some stars panicked, among them Lon Chaney and John Gilbert. I didn't panic. I didn't have enough sense." For those actors with problematic voices, MGM hired a voice coach named Oliver Hinsdell, who found William Haines's voice iffy. Hinsdell accused Haines of being "lip lazy."

"I've had no complaints," replied Haines.

Crawford had no stage experience, so was every bit as stunned as most people are when they first hear their own voice. "That's a *man*!" she said about her deepish contralto.

When MGM made *The Hollywood Revue of 1929*, one of the many all-singing, all-dancing musicals of the early sound era that are such a trial to sit through a hundred years later, she was billed third, beneath only John Gilbert and Norma Shearer. Gilbert would soon experience a precipitous career decline, based mostly on the fact that he didn't sound like what audiences thought he should sound like.

Conrad Nagel introduces Crawford in *The Hollywood Revue* by saying, "She's the personification of youth and beauty and joy and happiness," which segues into her singing "I've Got a Feeling for You" (not bad), after which she breaks into a solo dance (she does the steps, but her line is shaky).

What obliterates the indifferent quality of the scene is her joy in performance. She radiates her specific star quality as a young woman—a gung ho attitude projected through abundant sexuality.

Some idea of the chaotic nature of the changeover to sound can be gauged by the fact that after Crawford's first sound film, her next movie was silent, with a musical soundtrack. *Our Modern Maidens* involved the same writer as *Our Daring Daughters*, but despite the similar title, a different plot and characters. There's also a different leading man, undoubtedly chosen for the sake of publicity: Douglas Fairbanks Jr., who was nearly as striking as his wife even if he was only twenty years old.

This time nobody dies, but the off-screen couple don't end up together—a preview of coming attractions. Rather, the two-timing Fairbanks gets Anita Page pregnant, a plot point nicely communicated by an appointment slip at a doctor's office. Crawford saves her friend's reputation by telling everybody her boyfriend broke off their engagement because his parents found out something scandalous about her. She ends up with Rod La Rocque in Argentina, where nobody cares about her past.

What's clear is that MGM was taking pains with Crawford, nudging her forward in terms of both characterization and settings that clearly indicate the studio saw her as a long-term asset, especially when compared with the meatgrinder of mediocrity Clara Bow was enduring at Paramount.

Our Modern Maidens offers all sorts of lagniappe above and beyond the narrative —Fairbanks Jr. stops the show with an entertaining group of impressions that include John Barrymore, John Gilbert, and Fairbanks Sr. Cedric Gibbons again surpasses his achievements in Deco, while director Jack Conway shows off the sets with a series of slow zoom-outs designed to demonstrate the possibilities of the lens. A lot of plot, a lot of star power, a lot of production value, and it's all crammed into seventy-five minutes.

Crawford extends her franchise by extending her performance. Her growing confidence is obvious, as is her physical and emotional strength—her jaw could shatter an iceberg. As Jeanine Basinger wrote, "she's a vision of female power unleashed," which undoubtedly explains why she would always be a slightly threatening figure for those who preferred softer, more compliant female role models.

Judged in terms of story, *Our Modern Maidens* is nothing special, but it's a masterpiece compared to Crawford's first all-talking starring picture. *Untamed* is fairly typical of early sound movies, which amounted to a very expensive game of 52 pickup. Crawford, laboring beneath the unlikely nickname of Bingo, plays the daughter of an oil prospector in South America. After her father dies and she becomes an heiress, the plot moves to New York, where she meets Robert Montgomery, who seems to have been only recently weaned.

Crawford is radiantly beautiful, sings in her wavering but not unattractive voice, and dances. When she gets angry she clenches her fists and holds them rigid at her side like a thwarted four-year-old. For the climax, she shoots her boyfriend instead of a more appropriate target: the screenwriters.

Untamed was and is a shambles, but nobody cared. All that really mattered was that it featured Joan Crawford talking, singing, dancing, and being wildly dramatic. In retrospect, she was aware of at least one of the problems: "I was awful," she would say. Nevertheless, *Untamed* made a profit of half a million dollars. MGM could relax—in sound as in silence, Crawford was a star, which is to say an actor with the ability to transcend bad pictures.

She was also lucky. Most of the limited roster of silent stars who sailed into sound without problems were either young—Crawford, Garbo, Gary Cooper, Norma Shearer, Janet Gaynor—or had only recently become popular—Stan Laurel and Oliver Hardy.

Crawford would remain a star for the rest of her life, through many different phases, but one thing never changed: her relentless focus on her image, on her face and how it could be presented so that the attention and love she had always craved would keep flowing toward her.

MGM continued to respond to their new star with generosity. As of November 1928, her salary was $1,000 a week, and after *Our Dancing Daughters* she got a $500-a-week raise. Not only that, she was given that salary fifty-two weeks a year, without the standard twelve weeks a year of layoff at the studio's discretion. In February 1929, the head of accounts asked MGM attorney Floyd Hendrickson, "Is Joan Crawford to be considered a star and is all her accumulated salary to be charged to the pictures in which she works?"

Hendrickson responded with a ringing "Yes."

Four years before, Lucille LeSueur had considered herself lucky to be making $75 a week. As sound rolled over Hollywood, Joan Crawford was a movie star, and not just a garden-variety movie star, but a primary building block of the most successful movie studio in Hollywood.

CHAPTER FIVE

AFTER *MONTANA MOON*, WHERE she endured the inert Johnny Mack Brown as her costar, Crawford and Robert Montgomery were reunited in *Our Blushing Brides*, a second semi-sequel to *Our Dancing Daughters*. The characters are not repeated, but the format is—three young women in an urban environment finding out hard truths about men and life. Crawford, Anita Page, and Dorothy Sebastian are the Blushing Brides, and Montgomery is Crawford's spoiled rich boy love interest. The film has the added attraction of casting Crawford as a model in a luxe department store, so the story can pause for fashion shows, including some eye-popping lingerie that would soon be forbidden by the Production Code. Unlike *Untamed* and *Montana Moon*, the film moves fast and remains quite watchable.

After that, she was slotted into a musical called *Great Day!* with music by Vincent Youmans. Crawford didn't want to make it, and after two weeks of work she really didn't want to make it. She went to Louis B. Mayer and said the film was dreadful and so was she. He looked at the footage and must have agreed with her, because he shut the picture down at a cost of $280,000.

Paid is less than memorable, mainly because of the archaic dramatics of Bayard Veiller's 1912 play *Within the Law* on which the movie is based. The plot: a department store clerk is jailed for a theft she didn't commit, and after she's released she takes revenge by marrying the boss's son. Complications ensue.

If Crawford is trapped by the story and a dreary supporting cast, she still stands out because of her body language. All the other actors are physically stiff, standing and declaiming their lines as if they're animatronic, but Crawford enters a room as if she's just arrived from the beach at Malibu—casual, full of life, arms swinging from her shoulders. It's her way of letting us know not just that she's the star, but that her character will survive the antediluvian plot. Of more marginal interest is the appearance of the silent star Marie Prevost, whose performance demonstrates why her sound career was so spasmodic: the poor woman sounded like Olive Oyl.

Paid proved to be a prophetic title. The film returned a profit to MGM of $415,000. The studio responded accordingly—a bonus check of $10,000 accompanied by an obsequious note thanking Crawford in "appreciation of the co-operation and excellent services rendered by you, we take great pleasure in handing you your check made payable to your order."

Dance, Fools, Dance is an entertaining conglomeration devised by screenwriter Aurania Rouverol, who would make a great deal of money for MGM by creating Andy Hardy. We begin with Crawford as Bonnie Jordan, a bored socialite who has to get a job after the stock market crash decimates the family fortune, kills off her father, and leaves her namby-pamby brother adrift.

She promptly becomes a newspaper reporter, as is common with busted heiresses. She becomes friends with a hard-bitten reporter played by Cliff Edwards, who is soon bumped off by bootleggers. Bonnie goes undercover to bring down said bootleggers, who are led by a brusquely nasty Clark Gable without either mustache or leading man status. Gable has previously hired Bonnie's feckless brother to sell bootleg hooch.

All this gives Bonnie the chance to go to work as a chorus girl in Gable's speakeasy and perform a dance number. Order is restored when her brother suddenly develops a backbone and kills Gable at the considerable cost of being killed in return. Bonnie returns to the newspaper to be hailed as a journalistic titan and promptly reconciles with a dreary boyfriend she had discarded in the second reel.

Complaints about credibility are pointless when confronted with such exuberantly plotted melodrama. Along with the plethora of story, the film manages to squeeze in two musical numbers in which Crawford again demonstrates the sheer joy she found in dancing. Cameraman Charles Rosher photographs his star with the same glowing attentiveness he once lavished on Mary Pickford.

Gable had previously made a brief appearance in an MGM movie called *The Easiest Way*, where he had made the audience sit up and take notice. As the MGM story editor Sam Marx recounted, "Every time Gable came on the screen, the audience got interested." Afterward, Irving Thalberg stopped people in the lobby and asked them what they thought of the actor. He gathered the studio executives into the parking lot and told them, "We've got ourselves a new star!"

Gable was quickly slotted into movies opposite Shearer, opposite Garbo, opposite Crawford—actresses who were already stars. He held the screen with all of them and became the resident bull in the MGM china shop. He was brusque, decisive, innately masculine. Gable's arrival at MGM in 1931 immediately made every other leading man at MGM either second-string or irrelevant, especially John Gilbert.

Norma Shearer was extremely married, but she was not immune to Gable's sexual charge: "He was beautiful from his head to his feet. He was rhythmic, unconsciously alive with powerful grace. Like a jungle animal."

Dance, Fools, Dance cost less than $300,000 and made a profit of more than $900,000. Mayer quickly ordered that Crawford reshoot her love scenes in a currently shooting film called *Laughing Sinners*. The hapless Johnny Mack Brown was fired and replaced with Gable.

The result was another $10,000 bonus for Crawford and a lengthy series of hardball negotiations over a new contract. The end result was $3,000 a week, with four one-year options that would eventually result in her earning $5,000 a week by 1936. There were only two actresses at MGM who made more money: Garbo, who got $250,000 a picture, and Norma Shearer, who got $110,000 a picture.

Gable's working-class sensuality matched up well with Crawford's female version of the same quality. *Laughing Sinners* is a remarkably sleazy (for MGM) pre-Code film in which Crawford plays a nightclub entertainer who's been having an affair with a traveling salesman (Neil Hamilton). He decides to go off the road and marry an heiress in Cleveland, which leads Crawford to consider a swan dive off a bridge. She's saved by Gable playing the least likely

Salvation Army officer in movie history. He first talks her out of suicide, then falls in love with her. Enter the traveling salesman again, who has grown bored with Cleveland and gone back on the road. Crawford spends the night with him, narrowly avoids being raped by his drunken pals, until Gable once again comes to the rescue and restores her self-respect, if not her virtue.

MGM would figure out more plausible screen occupations for Gable sooner rather than later. The point was not dramatic verisimilitude; the point was the way the audience stopped rustling and started focusing whenever Gable came on-screen.

Gable was a better actor than he was ever given credit for—watch him in a scene, notice how he really listens to the other actor—and he always converted the rare challenging parts he got to play—*It Happened One Night*, *Gone with the Wind*, *The Misfits*, etc.

Crawford and Gable would soon establish an off-screen relationship that went on for several years. Like Crawford he had been dirt-poor and was more or less a castoff from his family; like Crawford, his early marriages were simultaneously aspirational and safe: a couple of older women, then a movie star (Carole Lombard) who reliably called him on his bullshit. Psychologically, Gable and Crawford were mutts who regarded themselves as lucky to have been adopted out of the pound by MGM.

Luckily, they never married—the proximity of their shared insecurities would have killed off the passion.

NINETEEN THIRTY-ONE PROVED IMPORTANT for all sorts of reasons. Beth Fairbanks, Crawford's mother-in-law, had been getting her hair done at Saks in New York by a man named Sydney Guilaroff, who was slowly building a reputation among the ladies who lunched. Beth raved about "Mr. Sydney" to Crawford, who booked an appointment on her next trip to New York. He asked if there was any particular style she wanted. "Please do whatever you think would be becoming on me," she replied. "I would like to know how you think I should look."

She was extremely polite while Guilaroff worked, always adding "Thank you" to every question he answered. He parted her hair on the left and made a single wave on the side, then brushed it back behind her ear so it fell in flowing waves. The right side he brushed into a similar single wave, leaving the top of her head sleek and smooth. When he was finished, she said, "I love it! Thank you, Mr. Sydney. I never looked like this before." She asked if he had any time available the next day, because she wanted to return with a still photographer and publicity man so the hairstyle could be preserved for her next film. And then she asked Guilaroff to come to California.

That didn't happen for a few more years, but in the meantime there were two or three yearly trips to New York where Guilaroff, having relocated to Bonwit's, continued to style Crawford's hair until in 1934 she finally convinced him to work at MGM.

Unfortunately, Irving Thalberg told him that under no circumstances should he join the Make-Up Artists and Hair Stylists Guild because "union membership could stifle your creativity." (Thalberg and Mayer were militantly anti-union.) The result was that while his paychecks arrived regularly, Guilaroff was a man in corporate limbo.

Crawford heard about Guilaroff's predicament and stormed into Thalberg's office. "I brought him out here," she said, "and I plan to use him. You'll have to work something out."

Thalberg's solution was to have Guilaroff work away from prying union eyes. He would slip into Crawford's dressing room before any of the other hairstylists arrived for work and arrange her hair, then go back to limbo. But his work was noticed by Jeanette MacDonald and Norma Shearer, who both demanded he work for them as well. Thalberg might have been able to dodge MacDonald's wrath, but not his wife's, and Guilaroff gradually emerged from the union-mandated closet. By 1938, he began receiving screen credit for his work at MGM.

IN THOSE FIRST YEARS at MGM, Crawford made friends that lasted the rest of her life. She attached herself to Paul Bern, part of Irving Thalberg's inner circle of bright, artistic young men who took care of the aesthetics while the more clinical Thalberg tended to the box office. Bern, Albert Lewin, Lawrence Weingarten, Bernie Hyman, and Hunt Stromberg had all been to college and were happy to sublimate their egos to Thalberg's precise instincts. All of them became successful producers, and the ambitious Lewin would direct some haunting films: *The Portrait of Dorian Gray* and *Pandora and the Flying Dutchman*.

Paul Bern was born in Germany in 1889 and came to America at the age of nine. He studied at the American Academy of Dramatic Arts, did some acting and directing in the theater, directed some movies, and wrote the script for Lubitsch's *The Marriage Circle*. He was liked as well as respected around MGM, but had a strange emotional need to involve himself with actresses whose tempestuous private lives led them to an early demise—Barbara La Marr and Mabel Normand among them. Bern gave Crawford a black fan that had belonged to La Marr, telling her, "Barbara would want you to have it." It became a treasured possession.

Crawford saw Bern as something more than an ally. He was a mentor, an extension of Fairbanks Jr., someone who could tell her what to read and explain why it was important. Years later she would tell her secretary Betty Barker that Bern had "practically begged" her to marry him. Joan's reaction to the diminutive, nondescript man's ardor was laughter, a response she always regretted.

Bern functioned as the line producer on Crawford vehicles such as *Our Dancing Daughters* and *Grand Hotel*, until his life ended violently in 1932, shortly after he married Jean Harlow. He was a suicide, or, depending on another reading of the evidence, a murder victim. (Crawford seems to have come down on the side of suicide.)

Crawford continued to be close to Billy Haines and Myrna Loy. Loy was from Montana, devastatingly beautiful, with an internal serenity Crawford didn't share but envied. "We'd meet on the run at the studio or chat at parties," Loy remembered, "We were always friends; it was the kind of friendship, set in the early years, that stayed."

More than most people, more than most stars, Crawford needed friends for ballast. The studio was quickly moving her from movie to movie in order to maximize profits; the merry-go-round was spinning faster and faster, and friends assumed outsize importance.

Crawford was in her obsessively absorbent mode. Even the usually dreary task of posing for publicity pictures served as a way of figuring out her physical strengths and weaknesses. "Lots of newcomers to film undoubtedly think that posing for photos is a waste of time," she said. "It doesn't need to be. I have made a careful study of every single still picture that was ever shot of me. I wanted these stills to teach me what not to do on the screen. I scrutinized the grin on my face, my hair-do, my posture, my make-up, the size of my feet."

What comes across in these early pictures, both the still and moving variety, is Crawford's sense of her own possibilities. She's onto something and she knows it.

CHAPTER SIX

THE FIRST STARS TO welcome Crawford to their inner circle were Gloria Swanson, Corinne Griffith, and Ruth Chatterton. Crawford admired them all, and for a similar reason: they were all comfortable in their own skin.

> Gloria has never changed an iota. She has the same flair for living now as she had then. Fabulously wealthy or broke, she remains intact. If she's upset you'd never know it. Corinne Griffith was married to Walter Morosco. They were charming and I always learned by listening.
>
> Ruth Chatterton . . . what a brilliant woman she was. There are brilliant women who are not articulate, but she was and she had such ease and originality. At all the other homes, the service was quite formal. Ruth's dinners were divine and they were formal certainly, the butlers in white ties—but [afterward] people sat on the floor around the fireplace with their coffee. It was the first time I'd ever seen this, people in evening clothes sitting on the floor quite at ease and so charming. Ruth always sat on the floor at a low coffee table and poured. I don't know that I dreamed of being a great lady like Swanson, Griffith or Chatterton, but I certainly was going to sit on the floor and pour coffee and have a big house.

ONE COLUMNIST HAD LUNCH with Crawford early in her career at MGM and told a story about her table manners. The salad "consisted of chopped vegetables nicely laid on large lettuce leaves. She didn't want the lettuce, so she picked them out of the salad and tossed them over her shoulder onto a tray on a table behind her. I admired her marksmanship, but not her manners."

A few years later, he interviewed her again and found "a charming hostess and a gracious lady and one of the best interview subjects I ever encountered. She not only had the desire to improve herself, but the ability."

Crawford's gradual transition from cheerfully vulgar ingenue to youthful mistress of her domain struck many as an excessively artificial construct. "Tallulah Bankhead thought I was stuffy," said Crawford. "We met on a train. 'Dahlings, come into my drawing room.'

"Thank you Miss Bankhead," said Crawford. "I must rest." Crawford said she'd come by later. When she did stop by, she brought her knitting needles. "If you don't put down those knitting needles, I shall die," said Bankhead. "Please, I don't drink or smoke," Crawford responded. "I don't put on a performance. Please let me do what I like: listen."

Out of this Bankhead devised a reputedly devastating imitation of Crawford being frantically domestic while continuously knitting. William Haines said it was "Hi-larious." One evening Bankhead did her routine for a party including a young actor named Franchot Tone, who said, "That woman is impossible." Haines rose to defend his friend. "Listen you, do you know Miss Crawford? Well, I do. I'm not speaking to her at the moment but she is my dearest friend and no one can criticize her but me. That's my privilege. I won't tolerate it from anyone else. Now you never say another word until you meet Joan Crawford and when you do you know what? You'll not only like her, you'll fall in love with her."

MOST OF FAIRBANKS'S AND Crawford's friends were from the English colony, to which he was always drawn, although there were times Crawford found them slightly dull. In the summer of 1931, Laurence Olivier and his wife Jill Esmond arrived in Hollywood for a foray into the movies. Fairbanks and Olivier would be friends for the rest of their lives.

For a time, the four of them were the Bright Young Things of the town; Olivier would remember that "I needed the lick of luxury in those lush valleys," although in retrospect he admitted that he found the parties, particularly the grand ones, "a sheer joy if you were in the mocking vein. Those glorious creatures, with their entrances and their descents down the staircase, were quite magnificent in their grace and stateliness and their confident composure—so soon to disappear without trace. After a couple of bootleg shots, and in as many minutes, all that majesty was sprawling and rolling about unable to utter a sentence that could be understood."

Fairbanks was churning out pictures for Warner Bros., and Crawford was churning out pictures for MGM. Olivier and Esmond saw no reason why they couldn't do the same. James Whale wanted Esmond for the female lead in *Frankenstein*, and she tested with wig and without. (Mae Clarke got the part.) Olivier went into *The Yellow Ticket*, then tested opposite Pola Negri. "Poor Larry was very disillusioned," wrote Esmond to her mother, "as he had always loved [Negri] on the screen, but she has become ham and rather fat." None of that mattered, because, continued Esmond, Olivier "is so thrilled with himself that he decided that it would be wiser to make a name here and get a definite position before going back to the stage."

"It was a wild, wild place in those days," Olivier said about Hollywood, "and Bob Montgomery, Doug Fairbanks and I were the wildest." One of the wild situations involved Olivier's strayings from his marriage, with the assistance of his friend Doug.

Olivier confided to Fairbanks that he had enjoyed the company of both Lili Damita and Elissa Landi, so Fairbanks took it upon himself to arrange a practical joke involving a supposedly rich woman who had fallen head over heels with Olivier on the screen and wanted to meet him. She was actually a studio extra, but willing to play along. As it happened, she and Olivier began a real affair, which led Fairbanks to up the ante and borrow his uncle Robert Fairbanks's apartment as a trysting place for the ardent lovers. He also hired a burly stuntman to break down the door and bellow, "What are you doing with my wife?" According to Fairbanks, Olivier fainted.

All these hijinks came to an end when Olivier was fired as Garbo's leading man in *Queen Christina* because A. He was in over his head, and, B. Garbo wanted John Gilbert to play the part. Olivier had to wait for *Wuthering Heights* in 1939 to become an authentic American movie star.

It's doubtful if Crawford knew about all this. For one thing, it wouldn't have amused her—she liked Jill Esmond. For another she was increasingly preoccupied by her affair with Clark Gable.

It's hard to know who strayed first. Herbert Swope Jr. said that "Doug was always a good husband, until he wasn't. He was faithful in between bouts of being unfaithful." Much the same could be said of Crawford. There were no fights, barely any disagreements. They had settled into a smooth marital groove, or, to put it another way, the doldrums.

Crawford's tells were changes in her schedule. She would head for MGM an hour earlier than usual and stay later. She even went to work on what was supposed to be her day off.

"With Douglas I played the part of a girl in love and lived it. With Gable, I really felt it, but was afraid to live it. . . . Were we good friends? If you can call goose flesh up and down your spine friends. [Gable] was very sure of himself, had an electric something."

Crawford's portrait of Gable syncs up with that of most people who knew him: a decent, straightforward, charismatic man deeply insecure about his acting skills.

In other words, he had some of the same issues that Crawford had. And they had other similarities as well—sex was a currency with which they were comfortable. "When a man asked her to bed," said Adela Rogers St. Johns, "she felt, 'I suppose I should.'"

It was a case of like gravitating to like. Both Gable and Crawford had an internal insecurity that worldly success never quite dispelled. Each of them possessed the electric hum of sex and, as Crawford put it, they were both "peasants by nature, not too well educated, and so frightened and insecure we felt sort of safe and home again when we could get together." She summarized their relationship as "a glorious affair, and it went on a lot longer than anybody knows. Even though we usually knew our marriages wouldn't last, we were awfully skittish about making any more commitments."

The affair wasn't exactly a secret—they rarely are. Howard Strickling said that "Joan was a pal to male stars. They were always glad to see her. She may have laid them, but it was nothing serious to her. . . . I don't think that Joan was very interested in sex. She used it only as a weapon."

As for Gable, his politics were Republican but his attitude toward women was highly democratic. Strickling said that at the end of the day Gable was often seen leaving the lot with a secretary or an extra. As Gable explained to Strickling, "Actresses are not good lays; they're too busy thinking about themselves." Adela Rogers St. Johns once asked Gable why he bothered patronizing the girls at Lee Francis', a famous Hollywood bordello. "Because I can send a girl from Lee Francis's home," he replied.

As to what was going on at the house on North Bristol, Douglas Fairbanks Jr. would say, "I suppose there were some career conflicts between us. There's bound to be that sort of thing, particularly with the kind of spotlight that was centered on everybody out here. It was a largely artificial spotlight ignited by the big studios, who would build things up out of all proportion or even invent interviews. I have looked recently at interviews I allegedly gave. I know perfectly well those interviews never took place. I didn't even know who the writers were, and they quoted me as saying things I never would have dreamed of saying. They were simply churned out by the publicity department of the studio.

"So Joan and I couldn't have had a conventionally normal life with all the nonsense that was written about us, with two careers and two spotlights going."

As far as Crawford was concerned, the marriage to Fairbanks was an object lesson in what can happen when you dive into the deep end of the pool. She elected to keep her head down and make the movies L. B. Mayer wanted her to make.

CRAWFORD WAS STILL A sponge, soaking up attitudes and technique on the way to developing a personal style. When she was making a movie, she inhabited the character to such an extent that she would reflect some of the character's qualities as much as her own. When a script arrived, she would read it quickly and absorb the story, as well as her character's movement or lack of movement. Then she'd read it again specifically for her character and begin to figure out how to play it. If the script was terrible, she would rarely complain but would try to figure out a way to make it better. If the script was good she would be excited by the challenge. In short, she was a worker bee.

In all sorts of ways, she was something unusual for the movie business. For one thing, she was all alone. Early Hollywood tended toward the matriarchal—the town was full of powerful mothers pushing their daughters toward stardom, toward financial security for themselves and, not coincidentally, for the rest of the family: Mary Pickford, Lillian Gish, the Talmadge sisters, Norma Shearer, and Mary Miles Minter were all in thrall to their mothers, and in most cases their careers went off the rails after their mothers died.

But Crawford was out there all by herself, personally providing all of her propulsion. Her ambition was all-encompassing, but it could be randomly applied. All this made her a particularly apt pupil for the studio head. "Mayer's school couldn't succeed unless the actress really wanted it," was the way Howard Strickling put it.

Joan really wanted it.

It was easy to gauge what most men wanted—Preston Sturges called it "Subject A." What Mayer wanted was different. He didn't want sex. He wanted—*needed*—respectability. *Status.* As a result, Joan made it a habit to drop in at Mayer's lunches for visiting VIPs and play up to him. "Of course, this impressed the visitors and made Mayer seem important," said Strickling.

And Strickling noticed something else. "She woke up in the morning wanting to live life to the fullest. She wanted to be a star; she loved being a star."

Mayer had all sorts of rules for his actresses. One of them was that no actress could come onto the lot in slacks. An MGM actress had to look like a star even if she was only grabbing lunch in the commissary. His overriding theory was actually very simple: he wanted the best in everything, but that best had to accommodate itself to the MGM style, the MGM ethos.

Crawford thrived on all this, if only to put as much space between Lucille LeSueur and Joan Crawford as possible. She wanted to be the best Joan Crawford she could be and worked relentlessly to get there. And there was another attribute that was uncommon: Crawford was quickly becoming extremely discerning about the business and her place within it.

Crawford's dynamism implied she set her own course, which was not really true. MGM was essentially a huge service organization for stars, but it was organized in a rigorously top-down fashion in which all the power rested with producers rather than directors or actors, as opposed to a studio like Paramount, which granted more autonomy to directors and even actors.

A big plus was that Mayer made sure that the casting couch was not a condition of employment around MGM, as opposed to Fox or Columbia, where Darryl Zanuck and Harry Cohn thought actresses owed them a lot more than a good performance.

MGM would bend to please a star, but only up to a point. Both Mayer and Thalberg believed in control, but Mayer had a more diplomatic approach. Publicist Pete Smith remembered a conversation with Mayer in which he referred to a disagreement between Crawford and Thalberg. "She didn't know what her part was about," noted Smith. "[Thalberg] just told her to do what the director wanted—walk, sit, stand, kiss, etc." In other words, be a puppet. Mayer had to step in and smooth things over while maintaining Crawford's ambition and dignity.

The result of this daily work environment meant that Crawford had little respect for most of the directors she worked with—journeymen such as W. S. Van Dyke, Jack Conway, or Richard Thorpe. She thought the cameraman was more important than most directors, singling out only Edmund Goulding, Clarence Brown, and George Cukor as first-rate, Cukor most of all.

In sum, the only real downside to life at MGM was that you had to do what the studio wanted you to do. And there was something else: when the studio's attention was diverted to someone younger, things could get shaky fast.

In many respects, it was a strange environment, but Crawford was young, her star was rising, and she had no worries.

Yet.

CRAWFORD'S PERSONALITY WAS EMPHASIZED and dramatized by the costume designer Adrian. Born Adrian Adolph Greenburg in 1903 to a mother who was a graphic designer and a furrier father, Adrian came to MGM as part of Cecil B. DeMille's retinue in 1928. His salary was $450 a week, which was adjusted to $500 a week within a month. DeMille's sojourn at MGM was brief and unsuccessful, but Adrian stayed for thirteen years and in the process revolutionized screen glamour. Beginning in 1929, when he became Crawford's exclusive designer, he helped create the Joan Crawford style that has rippled down through the succeeding century.

Crawford said that the first time they met Adrian told her, "You are a female Johnny Weissmuller," referring to her hips and shoulders. "Well," he sighed, "we can't cut 'em off, so we'll make them wider."

What that meant was that Adrian focused on what was striking and de-emphasized what was ordinary or bad. When Crawford had a dramatic scene to play, he used dark colors that emphasized her startlingly large blue eyes and avoided any distracting jewelry. For a light or comic scene, he'd abandon the stark look and go a little crazy.

Decades later, shortly before his death, Adrian would talk about dressing Crawford in what amounted to a personal manifesto:

> Joan was athletic, she had broad shoulders. The only thing to do was to find something becoming to those shoulders. The classically tailored suit was naturally becoming to her. I didn't emphasize the shoulders, those shoulders were Joan's. But the broad-shouldered look became almost an overnight style.
>
> In the first place, the wide shoulders made hips look smaller. The style was good for women who didn't have perfect figures as well as those who did. From then on, everything Joan wore was closely watched and everything was copied.
>
> Joan had a very quick feeling for drama. She could wear anything. She trusted me. Clothes should be simple so that a woman shines out of them. And the effect should be all at one, not diminish the center of interest by many centers of interest. The woman herself is the center.

What Adrian generally did was give Crawford a sleek, pantherish aura, emphasizing her natural features with equivalent stark lines of fabric that at times approached geometry. As the costume historian Howard Gutner observed, "Adrian reserved many of his most extreme fashion statements for Crawford, whose visual appearance was an overstatement all by itself—enormous eyes, a jutting, defiant jaw, and a large mouth made larger through a generous application of lipstick. Her long waist, short legs, and broad shoulders would have been a challenge to any designer, but these physical characteristics, when coupled with the often fierce intensity of her characterizations, tended to overwhelm conventional clothes."

As far as Adrian was concerned, Crawford simply gave him an opportunity to put his ideas to their ultimate test: "Every costume should have one note," he said. "Concentration on that one note emphasizes it and makes it interesting. When you start to concentrate on more than one note, then you detract from the main idea and merely have a conglomeration. Sound one note truly; then it will have a definite value."

Adrian took extraordinary pains with his costumes. After a sketch was approved by an actress, Adrian did another sketch in watercolors. Fabrics were attached to the sketch to better visualize texture and color. Then the dress was created by one of the cutters in unbleached muslin, after which the star came in for a fitting. Any alterations were made on the muslin, after which the dress itself was made with the fabric and colors deemed appropriate for the film. At the final fitting, Adrian would often photograph the actress wearing the dress with a 16mm movie camera in order to study the movement of the fabric on film.

The result of all this was a perfect amalgam of style and construction. Edith Head, who knew something about clothes and actresses, said that watching Adrian's costumes on the screen gave her "pangs of inadequacy." The look Adrian gave Crawford in the 1930s was Hollywood's single most important influence on American fashion.

Crawford appreciated Adrian because his clothes were stunning, but she also appreciated the fact that she never felt that the dress was giving the performance.

"Adrian always played down the designs for the big scenes," said Crawford. "For the lighter scenes he'd create a 'big' dress. His theory, of course, was that an absolutely stunning outfit would distract the viewer from the highly emotional thing that was going on. There should be just the actress, her face registering her emotions, the body moving to express her reactions—the dress is only the background. But in the next scene, where she goes to the races and cheers for her horse, the costume would be just absolutely smashing."

It wasn't really that easy. Sheila O'Brien worked with Adrian at MGM and worked with Crawford one-on-one as late as *Johnny Guitar* and *Female on the Beach*. "If she was dedicated to an idea, she was never halfway about it. She had to have the highest heels, the biggest bows, the most lipstick. It wasn't easy for her to change.

"I did her plain. Adrian was right."

O'Brien said Crawford was 5-4 1/2. She was very long-waisted, with broad shoulders and back, and a slim hip line. "Her torso was too long for her legs, which made her look tall, and she had big chest expansion. She had a slim waist and good hips."

Adrian worked with dispatch and could produce up to seventy-five drawings in a single day, a necessary pace because he designed every costume on an assignment, even mammoth productions such as *The Wizard of Oz* and *Marie Antoinette*.

He was a coherent personality—calm, self-possessed, with a playful sense of humor that emerged at odd moments. He would sometimes assume a Chinese accent on the telephone in order to inveigle friends into wild stories of smuggled Oriental jewelry.

At work, he emphasized the theatrical aspects of the women he dressed for a good reason. "I found that meeting with a star was like conducting a session in psychoanalysis. In order to create my designs for an actress, I had to see the direction of her drive. I studied her, deciding how I would fire her imagination, and knowing that I could only do it from the plateau of her own comprehension. To watch the unfurling of each woman's emotions was part of my job."

Despite the undeniable power of their collaboration, there was never a personal simpatico between designer and actress. "I felt the fitting [should] be private," he wrote years later. "I would ask (Crawford) not to bring friends. She invariably arrived at these first fittings with a producer, a hairdresser, a fan magazine writer, and a dear friend, singly or in a group. It was like doing a fashion sitting in Grand Central Station."

It got worse. "The first thing Joan would do would be to whirl her arms about like windmills, ripping seams and bursting armholes until the poor tailor would look at his ruined work in despair. 'Can't move,' she would say, her mouth squared with determination. Just why she needed so much room only she knew. Her gyrations were suitable for a gymnasium."

Adrian took the presence of a retinue as Crawford being rude. In fact, she was obeying a deeper psychological imperative. As Tennessee Williams would write, "Every film star I ever met, particularly those of the female persuasion . . . has a core of obsessive connection, by which I mean a craving to connect with each and every person upon contact. . . . There is a ravenous quality to film stars that is deeply sexual, deeply disturbing. I don't think that a person acquires this quality through training: I think it lodges within the system of a person through experience and expression, and I think it begins in childhood, with the development of multiple lacunas that must be filled. Hungers that must be sated."

As with any long-term creative collaboration, Crawford and Adrian were essentially having a conversation, and each of them was competing for dominance. Adrian had a suspicion he was losing. Shortly before he left MGM in 1941, he groused, "Who would have thought that my entire reputation as a designer would rest on Joan Crawford's shoulders!"

If Adrian was ambivalent about the collaboration, Louis B. Mayer was not. Mayer allowed Crawford to keep the clothes from her movies so she could look like a star at all times, and on the studio's dime.

Adrian's co-conspirator in creating and promoting the Crawford image was George Hurrell, the still photographer who eroticized Crawford even more than nature already had. Hurrell became chief portrait photographer at MGM in 1930 and would describe Crawford as "the most decorative subject I have ever photographed. . . . If I were a sculptor, I would be satisfied with just doing Joan Crawford all the time."

It didn't start out that way. Crawford was Hurrell's first star assignment at MGM. She had been used to working with the photographer Clarence Bull, who was serious and quiet. The studio wanted Hurrell to get some shots of Crawford at her favorite off-screen hobby: knitting. When they started working, Hurrell didn't like her poses and she didn't like Hurrell, finding him entirely too bossy.

"I kept telling her how to pose. She finally got so upset about it that she went into the dressing room and said, 'I'm not going to pose anymore.'" Crawford had no way of knowing that Edward Steichen had once told Hurrell, "Never let the subject know you are baffled. Shoot the film anyway [but] . . . be the master of the situation at all costs." This brought the publicity department into it. A publicist told Hurrell, "You can't talk to her like that. She knows how to pose and she doesn't want you telling her how to pose."

That immediately got Hurrell's Irish up—by his own estimation, he was an "arrogant, egotistical bastard. . . . What the hell am I doing here, then? She doesn't want me to tell her how to pose? Pack it up. . . . Let's get out of here."

Crawford realized she had gone too far, so she ran after Hurrell and lured him back to the studio. Two days later, Hurrell was eating lunch in the MGM commissary when Crawford came up to his table, knelt, and kissed his hand. "Please forgive me, Mr. Hurrell. I've just seen the proofs. They are so very, very lovely."

In all, Hurrell and Crawford collaborated on thirty sittings, each of which exhausted the photographer. Most actors regarded shooting stills as contractual drudgery, but Crawford went at it with the same avidity with which she approached a challenging film.

"Crawford was a natural at posing," said Hurrell.

> She had an instinctive sense of design and of herself. . . . Each sitting was a new experience for both of us . . . she constantly altered her appearance, the color of her hair, eye makeup, eyebrows, mouth. Yet with all the changes there was a classic beauty, a weird kind of spirituality. . . .
>
> She'd put Bing Crosby records on and go from one pose to another. Practically everything she did was a picture. She loved to be photographed. I think she'd rather do that than work in movies!
>
> She would work at it. She'd spend a whole day, changing maybe into twenty different gowns, different hairdos, changing her makeup, changing everything. She'd spend maybe an hour between changes just getting herself ready for the next attire. In a sense she used this opportunity to try to present a new image that might possibly work for her whole screen personality.

"His camera was on wheels," remembered Crawford. "How he used to move that camera, shoot the picture, and move the key light with it, I'll never know. He looked like an octopus! But it all got there!"

By four o'clock in the afternoon, Hurrell would be dragging, but Crawford would nudge him to keep going for another hour or so. By the end of the day they would have about 150 negatives.

She went on to say that "George Hurrell used to give me just one key light, and for him I never wore makeup. Just a scrubbed face. . . . I'd scrub my skin until it shone. . . . Hurrell loved photographing me without makeup—except for my eyes and lips, of course." Retouching would take care of Crawford's freckles and any other problem areas, which were minimal. Like Crawford's directors and cameramen, Hurrell raved about the perfection of her face, how there was nothing to work around. In his old age, Hurrell always referred to Crawford as "the dear girl."

The author David Stenn had his portrait made by Hurrell late in his life, and he noticed how Hurrell couldn't be swayed by mere sexuality. "He shot [Marilyn] Monroe and he saw a void. 'I would never have expected her to become anything,' he said. And Rita Hayworth had 'Nothing in her head. I couldn't figure out what to do with her. Lie down. Prop yourself up on your elbow.' He wasn't after intelligence, he was after an inner spark."

Hurrell's essential tactic was to give actors what they didn't already have. Hurrell worked with Norma Shearer until she looked sexy, a queen of the hot sheets. In the process he gave Irving Thalberg a woman he probably hadn't known in his own bedroom. Because Crawford already radiated sex, Hurrell had an easier time of it. Hurrell's photographs were nearly as important as Crawford's movies in establishing her as a star with a brave new look and, more importantly, a new attitude—appraising, startlingly sensual.

ADRIAN'S SLIGHTING MENTION OF "fan magazine writers" marked a difference between his temperament and Crawford's. Many stars regarded the fan magazines with open disdain if only because their interviews were usually done with at least two studio functionaries present to guide the conversation. After that, nothing could be printed without approval by the studio publicity department. All the would-be MGM stars were given Howard Strickling's Publicity 101 lecture: "Don't let them interview you. You interview them. Find out what they're interested in and ask them about it. Then you can direct the interview in the direction you want."

Strickling's people knew which columnists were good for specific story angles—the heartbreak of divorce might mandate a different writer, say, than a freshly minted star struggling with fame. Crawford would always go over the studio's notes on a specific writer and be ready for the interview.

Crawford openly courted the writers and photographers who were dependent on studio goodwill, and some of them regarded her as a personal friend. "Joan was the queen and we were her ladies-in-waiting," said Dorothy Manners, who wrote more than a dozen articles about Crawford for the fan magazines.

Manners remembered that Crawford was remarkably open; the only thing she didn't want printed was her weight. "She was always eating steak and tomatoes. She put on a show everywhere she went. She was the bride at every wedding, the corpse at every funeral."

Crawford went out of her way to become friends with gay male publicists such as Norbert Lusk and Jerry Asher, who often doubled as writers for the fan magazines. When times were tough, she'd find jobs for them. Similarly, Crawford arranged and probably paid for a deluxe wedding for a photographer named Hymie Fink at the upscale Victor Hugo restaurant.

AROUND THE MGM LOT, Crawford had earned a reputation as a compleat professional. "Joan Crawford was a real star," said cameraman George Folsey. "She was very obedient, very cooperative, a good coworker, very capable and very knowledgeable about the business. She was the opposite of what some people think. Evidently she was a great actress, because people believe she was the roles she played."

Crawford had developed a ritual for the first day of every picture. She'd arrive early and individually welcome every crew member as they showed up on the set. It went beyond just saying hello. She'd inquire about their wife by name, ask after the health of any family members who had been sick. "It was uncanny," said MGM publicist James Merrick. "We all appreciated it, even though it shot two hours to hell, and to this day I don't know if it was something she did out of genuine kindness or a desire to be liked. Anyway, it worked."

It might have been about currying favor—she understood that the crew would be more likely to work harder for stars with whom they had a relationship—but part of it could have been an entirely sincere signaling that she was one of them—just another a working stiff, albeit one making $3,000 a week.

There were other anomalous traits, redolent of an obsessive-compulsive temperament, a need to create order in a life where order had been in short supply. Her need for the soundstage to be kept around 58 degrees Fahrenheit, no matter how uncomfortable it might be for everybody else; her nervous habit of knitting to pass the time between takes or, sometimes, in social situations that didn't particularly interest her.

Vincent Sherman, who would direct her at Warner Bros., said that "She was very good in script conferences. She knew instinctively the things that she could do well. She was a collaborator in working to achieve a total effect. She was the kind of person that you could talk to about the way you wanted to shoot the thing, the background, the cutting. She was conscious of everything that went on set. . . . Her whole life was dedicated to making pictures. She had some outside interests but I would say that 95% of her life was involved in making films. . . . She was an indefatigable worker."

Crawford developed a symbiotic relationship—and not necessarily a healthy one—with her fans. She would read many fan letters, and cumulatively their effect was one of constraint. The letters were predominantly from women who told Crawford how much her pictures meant to them, how much they reflected their own lives and dreams. Crawford's response was to make a concerted effort not to disappoint what Norma Desmond called "those wonderful people out there in the dark."

What all this meant in practice was that there were precious few opportunities for either Crawford or the people around her to escape from Joan Crawford.

CRAWFORD FINALLY GOT A chance to work with her idol Pauline Frederick in *This Modern Age*, a pleasant sixty-eight minutes of restrained melodrama involving Crawford as Valentine, the child of divorced parents. Valentine goes to Paris to spend time with the mother she hasn't seen since she was a little girl. She finds Mom happily ensconced as the mistress of a wealthy

Frenchman, which upsets Val's morality. Complicating things is the fact that the girl is torn between two suitors—a former star on the Harvard football team (Neil Hamilton) as opposed to a Fitzgeraldesque boozer living off a trust fund (Monroe Owsley).

Pauline Frederick and Crawford actually resemble each other, so the parental connection is easily accepted. Frederick was a stately, well-spoken actress with an aura of command, all of which works to the picture's benefit.

It's the only movie in which Crawford has blond hair, and it's surprisingly attractive. This is one of the pictures in which Crawford's growing sense of command is communicated through her confident body language.

After *This Modern Age*, Crawford and Clark Gable were reteamed in *Possessed*, which remains a pure example of the potency of movie stars. *Possessed* was sharply directed by Clarence Brown, probably the best director at MGM at the time. "I want everything an actor knows," Brown said. "If it's a woman, she'll know more about playing a woman than I know. I want to get her angle on the picture. So I always rehearse without giving a word of direction. I follow them around and watch, and listen, and I get their interpretation first. If their interpretation doesn't agree with the one I have in mind, then we begin to talk. A little shading here, a little shading there, a few quiet directions."

The picture begins with Crawford as a young woman named Marian exiting a paper factory somewhere in the Northeast. "What do you want, anyway?" asks her boyfriend. "I don't know," she replies. "I only know I won't find it here." She's fully aware of both her situation and her problem: "All I've got are my looks and my youth and whatever it is about me that fellas like."

On Marian's first day in the city, she meets Gable playing a lawyer named Mark. He promptly accesses what it is about her that fellas like. There's a surprisingly brutal scene where one of Mark's married cronies brings an inappropriately low-rent girl to Mark's apartment and he orders them both out. Marian recognizes that there but for the grace of God goes Marian, and she offers the girl her kindness. Eventually the second-tier relationship drags her down and gets in the way of his political career. She offers to leave if it will simplify his life. In the end they reunite on a stairway to an elevated train in a driving rainstorm. Maybe they'll get married, maybe they won't, but either way they'll be together.

It's a surprisingly adult script by Lenore Coffee, and the movie is simultaneously realistic and romantic—the definitive example of Crawford and Gable's mutual sexual clarity, not to mention Irving Thalberg's grasp of the expedient nature of working-class morality. It made a profit of $600,000. As Alexander Walker wrote, "One doesn't need to believe in the story of *Possessed*. All that's needed is for one to believe in Crawford and Gable. . . . It is not just a case of good casting. It is an *attachment* to each other."

Possessed is a fascinating movie both for what it is and what it isn't. Gable helps, of course. In laborer's clothes he looked like a member of the working class; in a tux he looks like a painting by Leyendecker. But the other key ingredient is Crawford. Other films emphasized her youth, her vigor, her sexuality, or some combination of all three, but *Possessed* tapped into the very specific mixture of resentment and longing that would become her dominant projection in the next phase of her career. No other actress at MGM could have played the part so effectively, or made quite so much money for the studio. (Crawford's films were average in cost but consistently ranked among the top ten earners of their season.)

Possessed once again emphasized the proximity of Crawford's actual character with that of the characters she was playing—a gambit that would continue to pay dividends all the way through *Mildred Pierce* and beyond.

Clarence Brown and Crawford would make four more pictures together (*Letty Lynton, Sadie McKee, Chained,* and *The Gorgeous Hussy*) not counting Brown's four weeks of retakes on the stillborn *Love on the Run*, a Gable/Crawford vehicle sloughed off in eighteen days by the hit-and-run artist W. S. Van Dyke. Crawford believed that Brown was on the same level as George Cukor, but more self-effacing.

Brown came to deeply respect Crawford for her ambition and was moved by her insecurity, her drive, and for the reality she brought to stories of women who implicitly understand that a lousy education and no connections aren't going to get you what you want, let alone what you need.

For her part, Crawford saw Brown as the patient father figure she had never had but always needed. "Clarence Brown was very firm . . . but very gentle and very quiet; no yelling. No screaming. You see, Clarence Brown started out as an engineer, and I always said he could engineer more people together to make a good picture. But he didn't disturb us too much. He let us rehearse, find our way, and gave us a couple of suggestions. . . . He knew that we had studied what we were doing, we knew our craft."

Crawford made four pictures in 1931: *Dance, Fools, Dance, Laughing Sinners, This Modern Age*, and *Possessed*. Their cumulative profits totaled $985,000.

And then Thalberg cast her in *Grand Hotel*.

CHAPTER SEVEN

GRAND HOTEL CONSTITUTES MGM'S ultimate triumph over the Depression. Even *Fortune* magazine chimed in with a lengthy piece about the studio that seamlessly combined anti-Semitism with homophobia. Adrian was described as a "tall, twittering hunchback," while Thalberg was characterized as "a small, finely-made Jew of about thirty-three. . . . He is five and one half feet tall, and weighs a hundred and twenty two pounds after a good night's sleep. This lightness, in calm moments, is all feline grace and poise. . . . He speaks with a curiously calm, soft voice, as if his words were a sort of poetry."

Grand Hotel was gilt-edged, an all-star film with exquisite art direction and equally exquisite stars. As *Fortune* noted, "Mr. Thalberg assembled the Barrymore brothers, Greta Garbo and Joan Crawford, a quartette no movie addict could resist if they were playing 'Charlie's Aunt.'"

Crawford was third-billed, behind Garbo and John Barrymore. Fair enough, although she's better than Garbo, who plays her familiar wounded swan and dials the performance up to ten. John Barrymore projects the ravaged elegance he would perfect in *Dinner at Eight*, while Wallace Beery and Lionel Barrymore slice thick slabs of ham.

This profusion of theatrical radiance was an innovation of Thalberg's. Traditionally, movie studios rationed just one or two stars per film, which made it easier to fill out a year's roster of product. But MGM was top-heavy with stars and made extravagance a primary selling point. Extravagance in stars, in settings, in overall presentation became the dominant MGM studio theme for another twenty years.

Guiding this assemblage of divas of both sexes was Crawford's acolyte, the gifted Edmund Goulding. Anybody who could direct posh, definitive star vehicles such as *Grand Hotel* and *The Razor's Edge* as well as the scabrous *Nightmare Alley* possessed an unusually broad skill set.

Irving Thalberg did most of the preparation before handing the shooting off to Paul Bern. Thalberg addressed what he believed to be shortfalls in the script in a story conference with the director:

> I felt a certain something in this play, which may or may not be important, but I think it's lacking in your treatment. . . . A group of men and women having problems: Preysing and his lie about the merger, the Baron not able to steal the ballerina's pearls, etc.
>
> Then we come down to a music-filled room in which these characters are enjoying life. They make light of their problems. The Baron, who has a terrific problem, makes a joke of it. He is amused by Kringelein, but is kind to him. He takes the time to be nice to him, in spite of his own problems. He dances with Flaemmchen, tells her he's found love with the ballerina, and to be nice to his little friend Kringelein. She dances with him. In the background is Preysing. They laugh at him. Kringelein tries to be nice to him. Preysing rebuffs him . . . Kringelein . . . tells Preysing what the hell he thinks of him, tells him where to get off, in the best way he can. You get that marvelous feeling of underdogs defying overlords. . . .
>
> But we see that in spite of all that Kringelein said, Preysing will get Flaemmchen to go with him. In the last analysis, Flaemmchen has to have clothes and a living. She has to accede to Preysing. And the Baron can't postpone his own business any longer. . . .
>
> Here you get the profound philosophy of the lower classes. No matter how they fight . . . in the end they have to succumb to money, and they do.

In another meeting a few days later, Thalberg went further: "The thing that is most important is this: that audiences love our characters. They must say, 'Aha! This is like my life.' . . . To me this is a lousy play that only succeeded because it is lousy, [but] it's full of life—a painted carpet upon which the figures walk—audiences love those damn things, if they are properly done."

Thalberg was acutely conscious of stars and how their personalities impact a character's reception. "I think Kringelein's speech can be cut," he said. "If Lionel plays this, it will take six reels." He played with Crawford's dialogue to make it more rhythmic. As written, one of her lines went, "Caviar for me? No, it tastes like herring." He changed it to "Have caviar if you like, but it tastes like herring to me."

"I've come to the realization that you have to endow a character with greater complexity than you ever had to in silent pictures," Thalberg told Goulding. "There's nothing new about a man trying to make a girl. But if he starts by pretending that he's a family man, then that's something else again. And that's what talking pictures have given us."

Thalberg believed that if the picture was going to work it had to be cast with huge stars. Garbo and Crawford were locked in early, but every other actor was negotiable. Thalberg gave some thought to Clark Gable or Robert Montgomery for the part of Garbo's lover, while the star lobbied for her old flame John Gilbert, a suggestion quickly vetoed by Louis B. Mayer, who wasn't going to cast an obviously falling star in such an important picture. Gable was also considered for Preysing, the crude industrialist eventually played by Wallace Beery, while Lewis Stone was cast as the rigid doctor, face scarred by war, who portentously intones "Grand Hotel—always the same. People come, people go. Nothing ever happens."

Crawford and Beery had to shoot their scenes at night, from 5 p.m. to midnight, while Garbo and John Barrymore worked conventional hours. Crawford delighted in telling the story of the one time she and Garbo actually interacted. It was on the steps of the women's dressing rooms, where Garbo's dressing room was to the left of Crawford's.

In spite of the fact that they had never actually met, it was Crawford's habit to call out "Good morning, Miss Garbo," and then run down the staircase. Garbo had never replied until one day during *Grand Hotel.* Crawford was in a hurry and didn't call out "Good morning," which led Garbo to open the door and call, "Aloo!" Crawford froze. Garbo walked toward her and took Crawford's face in her hands and said, "You have such a beautiful face. I am so sorry we have no scenes together."

Crawford would complete the scene by saying, "And my knees turned to water and I almost fell on the flight of the stairs. I was transfixed, really. That was the most glorious face, and to be close to it! Eyes, eye lids, bones. I just didn't think anything could be that beautiful and have that perfection. Her skin was alabaster!"

Crawford was petrified at the prospect of working with such a roster of heavyweights. Goulding spent a few days rehearsing with her, going over her scenes so she would be able to integrate her performance with her costars. She decided to accept the rampant competition as potential camouflage rather than potential embarrassment. "If I fall flat on my can in this picture," she told Goulding, "few will notice if Lionel and John are on the screen."

As it turned out, both she and Goulding remembered the picture as a comparative breeze. "Six years before, [Goulding] had to tell me so much, now he told me so little. . . . He told me how much I'd changed. 'You've grown quiet, you've gained strength, Joan.'"

Perhaps to compensate for Lionel Barrymore's typically insufferable grandstanding, his brother works beautifully with his costars. Wallace Beery was Wallace Beery—gross and temperamental, a ham addicted to upstaging. When Beery would lurch out of control, Crawford would appeal to Goulding, who managed to bring him to heel. Between shots, Crawford stayed close to cameraman William Daniels or chatted with the script girl over a Coke. "She was interested in everything that happened around her," said Goulding. The picture cost only $695,341 and earned a clear profit of nearly a million dollars.

As Mick LaSalle writes in his invaluable book *Complicated Women*, "There are two ways to watch and experience *Grand Hotel*, as a Crawford film or as a Garbo film. To Crawford's credit, both ways are equally good.

"For those who receive *Grand Hotel* as a Crawford film, Garbo's performance looks like something from Neptune—histrionic, operatic and bizarre. Yet those who experience it as a Garbo movie will still find much to enjoy in Crawford. She is perhaps a bit lip-quivery and insincere in emotional moments. But for the most part, she is a pleasure to watch and she brings to the film welcome humor and a light touch."

The difference is that most of the film's acting is presentational, theatrical, but Crawford is *real*, even though her character isn't—we're supposed to like Flaemmchen even though she willingly allies herself with three different men within twenty-four hours, which seems excessively enthusiastic. On the other hand, in a tough world a woman has to do what a woman has to do—Flaemmchen has what the twenty-first century calls agency. Ethan Mordden put it well: "Garbo invents her own genre, John Barrymore is high comedy, Lionel is weepie, Beery . . . is blood and thunder melodrama, Stone is austere and military, and Crawford, in superb Adrian outfits, is from life."

In a sense Flaemmchen is a riff on Crawford's struggling proletarian heroine of *Possessed*, but the writing and the context are stronger, as is the competition from the other actors, so the performance benefits. In contrast to Crawford, the ethereal Garbo is utterly removed from the other characters except Barrymore's Baron, even removed from the exigencies of the plot.

The key point about Crawford's breakthrough in 1931–32 is that maturity for an actor usually involves a combination of personality, growing professional assurance meshing with public taste, and a great part. With Crawford it went deeper than that. As LaSalle notes, "Crawford had trouble coming into her *authenticity*." She became a considerable actress and a great star because she learned to use her own frustrations and emotions as foundations for performance. In other words, she was acting only up to a point.

Crawford loved the experience of making *Grand Hotel* and she loved the result, as she should have. The film is a full-blooded story of the intersection of disaster, desire, and ambition, beautifully produced and, for the most part, beautifully acted.

With *Possessed* and *Grand Hotel*, Crawford taps into her own obstinance, insecurity, and bravery. She had arrived as a star a few years earlier; in 1931 and 1932 she arrived as an actress, and MGM being MGM, the pictures were still made expeditiously—*Possessed* was shot in twenty-six days, *Grand Hotel* in forty-nine.

For all of Crawford's competitiveness with Norma Shearer, they really weren't the same kind of talent. Shearer was a nice Canadian girl who generally radiated a *soigné* upper-crust demeanor. She had a slender body made for sleek satin dresses. Thalberg saw her as capable of devastating sexual power, and in movies such as *The Divorcee*, *Strangers May Kiss*, and *A Free Soul*, she commands men as varied as Robert Montgomery, Chester Morris, and Clark Gable.

Shearer was almost certainly a loyal wife to Thalberg, although the screenwriter John Lee Mahin once surreptitiously observed Fredric March and Shearer in a passionate offstage embrace, when Shearer broke away and exclaimed that she was "married to the most wonderful man in the world!"

A more objective appraisal of Shearer than Thalberg's will point out her variable talent. In some of her films she plays parts far beyond her range and is simply embarrassing: *Idiot's Delight, Romeo and Juliet*. She is moving in *Marie Antoinette* when her character slowly loses everything she cares about, including her head, but that movie came after the death of Thalberg, when loss had become real to her.

As Jeanine Basinger wrote, "her role models were clearly the great dames of her day, the Lynn Fontannes and the Katharine Cornells. Her performance style emulates what would be great theatrical playing of the day—graceful arm movements, little twirls about, delightful little laughs, and head movements that telegraphed emotions. Her line delivery was light and arch, from an era that is gone."

In contrast, Crawford had no theatrical debts and was a pure creature of the movies, living and dying by her close-ups and her ability to reflect life as she had lived it. She had a better voice than Shearer and a lot more sex, but a different range—she would have been ludicrous in *The Barretts of Wimpole Street*.

Thalberg cast his wife as a member of the upper class, while Crawford was positioned as a girl from the wrong side of the tracks who nevertheless has everything necessary for success except money and position. As Howard Gutner noted, the unspoken message was "*we* (the working class) are as good as *them* (the rich) if only we can obtain the right clothes."

Comparing Crawford and Shearer performances from the early 1930s is instructive. Shearer is occasionally playful and projects a domesticated attractiveness. When she has to project extreme emotion she gets shrill. She has none of Crawford's visceral class-based resentment or innate sexual power.

Shearer might have thought Crawford's animus was personal, but it was mostly professional. As Crawford told Louis B. Mayer, "Mr. Hearst looks after Marion. Irving looks after Norma. Who will look after me?"

After *Marie Antoinette*, Shearer mostly focused on sophisticated comedies, but even successful ones like *The Women* didn't really answer the question of what Norma Shearer would do in middle age. It turned out to be quitting movies. MGM could not have been sad to see her go. Of her last seven movies, only one (*Escape*, with Robert Taylor) turned a profit.

Crawford was also competitive with Jean Harlow, whom she disliked, which left her an odd woman out—everybody at MGM adored Harlow. As one publicist said, Harlow "was like a soft kitten," but if Harlow was on the cover of a magazine it was a bad idea to show it to Crawford.

"They were never unpleasant [to each other]," said publicist Kay Mulvey, "they were like school queens. They weren't competitive for jobs, but for position. Joan didn't want to be sexy, she wanted to be on a pedestal.

"Joan always had to improve herself; she didn't read trashy novels, she read biographies. She wouldn't do anything mediocre, and she had to have her hands busy. She exercised religiously, and she disciplined herself more than she disciplined others."

Unfortunately, the competitiveness could shade over into meanness. When Harlow died in 1937 publicist Maxine Thomas called Crawford to give her the news. Thomas said that "her reaction was not one of sadness."

———◆◇◆———

CRAWFORD WAS NO LONGER a star on the rise. She had arrived at her destination, and when that happened a specific cameraman was generally assigned to a star in order to bolster their sense of security. Crawford's cameraman for a number of years had alternated between Charles Rosher, the co-winner of the first Academy Award for Cinematography, and Oliver Marsh, but Marsh would be replaced by George Folsey.

"Marsh was an extremely capable cameraman—when he wanted to be," said Folsey. "He'd been in the business a long time and had become, I think, a little jaded. He'd lost the drive and ambition he should have had. He'd find the easiest way to light a scene—everything came out kind of one tone—and Crawford needed *dynamic* lighting."

Folsey stumbled on the way Crawford needed to be lit.

There was a scene which called for her to sit at a table alone and drink a sherry flip. We were rehearsing this scene and all the stage lights were on, but ours went off—and way up on a catwalk was a little light that came down and hit Crawford absolutely beautifully. As you know, she used to wear those Adrian costumes with big white collars. The little light hit the collar and bounced up on her face. It was beautiful. . . .

When I came to light the scene, I took a spotlight and ran it up in line with that other light—keeping it very soft. The spot hit the white collar and bounced up on her face, just the way I wanted it to. I put an optical disc on the lens and she looked like she hadn't looked in years. Well, she was so ecstatically happy with the results that from then on I could do no wrong.

Folsey shot Crawford's films until he was replaced by Robert Planck for her last few years at MGM.

WHILE AMERICA WAS STILL languishing in the Depression, Hollywood was surviving and MGM was thriving. Every other major studio was bathed in red ink, but MGM continually showed a profit. Crawford was given to flamboyant statements asserting her particular brand of capitalist joy. She gave an interview to *Photoplay* titled "Spend!" where she asserted that the high salaries paid in Hollywood were essential not just for the industry, but for America itself. "I, Joan Crawford, believe in the dollar. Everything I earn, I spend!"

Crawford's career was a runaway train, a nonstop succession of hits since *Our Dancing Daughters*. Attention had to be paid, and it was. In an interview with *Variety* in July 1932, she said, "I want to do some really fine things to be remembered by, and then I shall say goodbye, thanks a lot, it was lovely. But how to know it when the time comes?

"That's why I'm always groping, seeking to learn, to improve myself. I want so much to fight off conceit. I must never allow myself to become self-satisfied. But I don't think I ever will. My ambition is too driving—too relentless to permit me to grow complacent. I would never, for instance, talk over the radio—'When I did this, when I did that'—those silly, stupid interviews all about oneself. Who cares? If you're important enough, people will talk about you. You don't have to do it yourself."

CHAPTER EIGHT

LETTY LYNTON HAS BEEN generally unviewable for nearly ninety years because of legal issues, but it remains famous for the ruffled dress Adrian created for Crawford that reputedly sold 500,000 copies. Part of the reason the dress created a sensation was that it was 180 degrees from the stark lines that Adrian had been using for her. It was constructed out of starched chiffon organdy with a rounded neck and large, poufy sleeves that obliterated the famous Crawford shoulders. To modern eyes, it looks like a fairly conventional 1930s ball gown, but that was only because there were so many knockoffs in its wake.

Adrian was as surprised as everybody else. "I [only] became conscious of the terrific power of the movies some months after *Letty Lynton* was released. I came to New York and found that everyone was talking about the *Letty Lynton* dress. In the studio we thought the dress was amusing but a trifle extreme . . . which proves a fact I have long suspected, namely that the movies are giving the American woman much more courage in her dress and a much more dramatic approach to the whole subject of clothes."

Letty Lynton was loosely based on the famous case of Madeleine Smith, a wealthy young woman prosecuted for the murder of her gardener lover in Glasgow in 1857. Although she was almost certainly guilty, the verdict rendered was "not proven." The story was used as the basis of a hit play in 1930 that starred Katharine Cornell, and in 1950 David Lean made a movie based on the same case.

MGM thought the play was too expensive, so they bought a cheaper novel with the same story. Crawford was initially unhappy because she had been hoping for Clark Gable as her costar but instead got the chilly and supercilious Robert Montgomery.

Unfortunately, the writers of the play that MGM refused to buy sued, claiming that the film had used material from their play. The case dragged on for five years, with MGM winning some appeals and the playwrights winning some. In 1937, MGM finally threw in the towel and pulled the picture from distribution rather than pay damages. The picture still rests in legal limbo, which is a loss because it's a vibrant, beautifully shot melodrama whose DNA was replicated in a couple of fine romances that followed in its wake: *History Is Made at Night* and *Now, Voyager*.

Letty Lynton has several problems. She's pursued by both a vain, possessive, psychotic lover (Nils Asther) and a charming, romantic Park Avenue socialite (Robert Montgomery), whom she meets cute on an ocean voyage. She is also burdened by a cold, domineering mother (May Robson) who seems to despise her daughter despite the child's attempts at rapprochement. The denouement is rushed, but effectively managed by Clarence Brown.

Like all Crawford pictures of this period, it was quite successful.

GLORIA SWANSON HAD MADE a silent adaptation of *Rain* retitled *Sadie Thompson* that followed John Colton's theatrical adaptation of Somerset Maugham's short story. The play made a star of Jeanne Eagels and led to Swanson's film in 1928. Only four years later Joe Schenck at United Artists thought a sound remake was a capital idea. He borrowed Crawford from MGM, hired Maxwell Anderson to write the screenplay, and brought on Lewis Milestone, fresh from *All Quiet on the Western Front* and *The Front Page*, to direct.

It was a good deal for MGM, if not for Crawford; United Artists paid MGM $12,500 plus $3,500 a week for ten weeks of Crawford's services. UA also agreed to pay MGM a share of the film's profits. Unfortunately, there weren't any.

It was a film that pleased no one. Not Crawford, who thought both the film and her performance terrible, and certainly not United Artists, who saw the picture lose hundreds of thousands of dollars on a fairly modest investment.

Lewis Milestone believed that Crawford was uncomfortable from the beginning, possibly upset by her increasingly rocky marriage, possibly because it was her first starring picture away from MGM. Crawford had never seen Eagels onstage or the Swanson picture but was scared of comparisons, which she typically thought would favor the other actresses.

Censorship demanded that the Reverend Davidson not be a reverend, which Milestone felt "weakened the structure considerably." Besides that, "after seeing [Jeanne] Eagels, I don't know why anyone [else] would try to do Sadie." Milestone felt Crawford's performance was "surface because of [her] looks and costumes.... You could never get inside."

Although it was widely panned by critics and its star, today *Rain* looks far more audacious than Raoul Walsh's silent version. The incessant sound of rain really does create cabin fever for the audience as well as the characters, and the supporting cast (Guy Kibbee, Beulah Bondi, and Matt Moore) is quite good. Walter Huston plays Mr. Davidson—denatured because a reverend who rapes a prostitute and then slits his throat was a bridge too far in 1932—as an encore of his obsessively fierce patriarch onstage in Eugene O'Neill's *Desire Under the Elms* a few years before.

And then there's Crawford. Milestone constructs her entrance in component body parts, just as a rampant male might observe her. A quick close-up of her hands festooned with bangle bracelets as they steady themselves on a doorway; a shot of her ankle-strap shoes; finally, a close-up of her face—a wide gash of lipstick . . . and those huge eyes.

At first there's a dramatic disconnect. Maxwell Anderson's adaptation is full of lush dialogue, and Crawford was always more comfortable with colloquial dialogue. Experienced character actors such as Guy Kibbee and William Gargan manage without difficulty, but Crawford had never dealt with dialogue like Anderson's and her audacious physical transformation seems overwhelmed by her struggle with the rhythm of the lines.

A little more than halfway through the picture Sadie has been brought to her knees—literally—by Jesus. The makeup and jewelry disappear. Her hair is pulled back, exposing that face. Sadie is chastened, her defiance leached away, and Crawford has a chance to lower the verbal temperature and play scenes with her face. The effect is startling . . . and dramatic. At the same time, Huston's character expresses his arousal, suggesting the erotic desperation his religiosity conceals. At that point the film careens to a successful conclusion. Ultimately, *Rain* is a far more courageous adaptation than either the Swanson or the later Rita Hayworth versions.

After *Rain* was completed, Crawford took a week off *sans* husband, probably with Gable. When she came back she seemed somewhat interested in Fairbanks's idea of taking their long-delayed honeymoon to Europe—a romantic Hail Mary if ever there was one.

Their traveling companions were Laurence Olivier and Jill Esmond. On the ship to London they engaged in marathon games of ping-pong. Crawford would accuse her husband of muffing shots on purpose to make her look good. Finally, Olivier snapped, "For Christ's sake, Joan, shut up and play!"

In Southampton they were all startled to see Noel Coward on the pier to greet them. They spent their first night in London in the Royal Box at the Theatre Royal in Drury Lane to see Coward's *Cavalcade*, his paean to England's generational indomitability. The next day brought the Changing of the Guard at Buckingham Palace, then Westminster Abbey, the Tower of London, and St. Paul's.

They divided one weekend between the houses of Ivor Novello and Noel Coward, then made their way to Paris. Throughout all this, Crawford smiled, said all the right things, but was clearly uncomfortable. She told her husband that she felt like a fish gasping for breath outside its bowl. It became clear that she wanted to get home as quickly as possible—home being the MGM studio in Culver City.

"She hated it," Fairbanks said, "hated every moment of being in London and Paris, where she'd never been before, because she felt insecure away from the movie studio. She was the hardest worker I ever saw. Her only excess I can remember was an excess of ambition. She was completely absorbed with her career and with work, and intensely jealous of her competitors at MGM."

The delayed honeymoon was officially a flamboyant failure. They left for America days ahead of schedule. When they got back to California, they resumed their increasingly separate lives as what Fairbanks called "familiar strangers." On those increasingly rare occasions when they had guests at the house, they gave "a passable performance of a civilized couple." Crawford rented a small hideaway out past Laguna. When Fairbanks offered to come for a visit, she threatened to leave him on the spot.

Crawford went to her father-in-law to tell him of the breakdown of her marriage. Douglas Fairbanks Sr. listened attentively to her over lunch at the Brown Derby. "I told him the truth, that Douglas and I weren't getting on and he listened, then said, 'Billie, I know you're asking for advice. And I must tell you, my son or not, two people who are unhappy should not stay together.'"

Fairbanks Sr. paid attention to his own advice. In July 1933, he and Mary Pickford would separate, although they wouldn't divorce until a torturous series of failed reconciliations a few years later.

In the second week of January 1933, Crawford denied that she and Fairbanks were on the verge of divorce. "It's absurd—no, wait, till I find a better word! It's preposterous, ridiculous, unthinkable." It was also imminent. The breakup finally came through Mike Levee, Fairbanks's agent, who appeared in his client's dressing room at Warner Bros. to tell him that his wife had told Levee to move her husband's possessions out of the house. Fairbanks's new home was the Beverly Wilshire Hotel. "Don't bother to call her," Levee told his client. "She's cut off her phone and arranged a new private number. Even I don't know it."

The next day Fairbanks woke up in his hotel suite to find news of the "amicable separation" in Louella Parsons's column. Crawford filed suit for divorce on April 29. Crawford gave the story to her old friend Katherine Albert, who had graduated from an MGM publicist to a writer for the fan magazines. Given the fan magazine's three-month lead time, Albert knew about the divorce before Fairbanks did.

The divorce decree was handed down in May and would be final in a year. By September there were stories about a new relationship between Crawford and the young leading man Franchot Tone. In November she and Tone boarded the Santa Fe Chief for Chicago for a two-week vacation.

Before getting on the train, Tone grew irritated at the cameras. "You can't take my picture with Miss Crawford," he said. "It isn't exactly proper." He stalked away but returned when Crawford told him to. A few days later, they were in New York and Tone told reporters he had asked Crawford to marry him.

In spite of the way the marriage ended, Crawford and Fairbanks stayed friendly for the rest of their lives—Fairbanks sent lovely condolences when her fourth husband, Alfred Steele, died of a heart attack in 1959, and he was always courtly when speaking of her, ascribing the divorce to her preference for work and his for a more relaxed lifestyle: "[It was] a very satisfactory friendship after the marriage as such," said Fairbanks. "I loved traveling, and people and going back to New York, going over to London and Paris. And she just liked to be, naturally, back at work. . . . She was only happy when she was at MGM, which was fine for her, but not for me."

TODAY WE LIVE MARKED Crawford's return to MGM and proved to be another disappointment. It had been designed by Howard Hawks and William Faulkner as a Lost Generation story about two English brothers and an American in England during World War I. It was written as an all-male picture starring Gary Cooper on loan from Paramount and two recent arrivals to MGM: Robert Young and Franchot Tone.

And then Hawks was informed that the script would have to be rewritten to allow for the presence of Joan Crawford, presumably for box-office insurance. It was not a suggestion, it was an order, so Hawks and Faulkner did their best to accommodate a love story in a movie that had been expressly designed as a war story made up of equal parts camaraderie and gloom. Their solution was to make Crawford a nurse in the ambulance corps.

According to Hawks, Crawford wasn't any happier about her casting than he was. "Are they kidding, Howard?" she asked him, then started to cry. "Now look," he said. "You have to do it, and I have to do it. If you're gonna make drama out of it, it'll all be hell. If we decide to have fun and do it, we'll have a nice time. What do you want to do?"

"We'll have fun," she said.

But the picture was and remains an overlong slog, and nobody had any fun. Hawks was doing time at MGM mostly because he was (temporarily) married to Norma Shearer's sister. The marriage and Hawks's MGM career were doomed by his wife's mental illness, problems on Hawks's production of *Viva Villa!*, and, less obviously, Hawks's chronic inconstancy regarding his wife—not a good idea when you're married to a relative of the man who runs the studio. *Today We Live* lost slightly more than $23,000, which was nothing compared to what it would have lost had Crawford not been in the picture.

Today We Live was and is terrible, unrecognizable as a Hawks picture. As far as Crawford was concerned, the only important thing about *Today We Live* was Franchot Tone.

IT BEGAN ONE DAY when her costar told her, "Gee, you're a nice dame." Crawford was insulted, but Franchot Tone explained that it was the finest compliment a woman could receive because it meant she was unpretentious and had a sense of humor about herself.

As Crawford explained, "I was in love with Clark when I met Franchot, but Franchot had a quiet way of looking at me across a room, across a set, a way of giving more than the scene required. He lived with a fellow named Ernest Thompson—we called him Tommy. Tommy, Franchot, and I had dinner together several times. That's how it started."

Stanislaus Pascal Franchot Tone was twenty-eight years old, sprung from money—his father was president of the Carborundum Company—with an education courtesy of Cornell and the University of Rennes. Along with Lee Strasberg, Cheryl Crawford, Clifford Odets, and Harold Clurman, Tone helped found the Group Theatre, and his money helped finance it.

Elia Kazan observed Tone at close range during the summer of 1932, when the Group was forming. Tone was tall, handsome, and it was clear that the Group needed him more than he needed the Group. Not just because of his money, or because he was a good actor, but because he was an authentic leading man in a troupe overrun with character actors.

"He's taken no part in the experimental work in [Harold Clurman's] classes," wrote Kazan to his future wife. "He read a mystery story all through the rehearsals of *Big Night* and Cheryl Crawford, who's directing that play, doesn't want him in her cast now. He has a car, a red roadster, and leaves camp every chance he gets. And he drinks. A lot. At the same time he's wonderful in his role in *Success Story*. . . . I imagine that Lee Strasberg, who has someone else reading Tone's part now, will be very glad to see him back."

Strasberg believed Tone was potentially the best actor in America, but he didn't want him in the Group because his behavior "undermined the spirit of commitment and devotion that was necessary for the company's continuance."

Despite all this, Kazan admired Tone. "He's better educated, just plain smarter than most of the others and has greater curiosity about life and boldness in dealing with his desires. I like him. . . . I've been wondering if they are, finally, jealous of his talent, his looks, his Hollywood offers, and his money?"

The answer was almost certainly yes. As Kazan realized, "He's the only really top-grade actor here."

Tone seemed perfectly cast as one of the slender, charming boulevardiers popular in that era such as Robert Montgomery and Melvyn Douglas. MGM saw him as a means of keeping Robert Montgomery in line, but as it turned out Tone was at least as fractious as Montgomery.

Tone had more aspects than he let on, a secret self he only showed to intimate friends. By trade he was an actor, but by inclination he was an outdoorsman, with a hunting and fishing lodge in Quebec that had been built by his grandfather and where he returned at every opportunity. Tone delighted in donning fishing pants, a lumberman's jacket, and what he called his "lucky hat," carrying his own canoe and preparing a campfire to cook the trout he had caught a few hours before. The woods full of deer, moose, and beaver gave him the ballast he needed to survive show business.

He was also a fine actor who would prove more than capable of holding the screen opposite charismatic competitors such as Clark Gable and Charles Laughton. Tone's left-wing politics made him stand out at the politically conservative MGM, and the actress he had once thought an empty-headed *soubrette* turned out to be hardworking and serious about being the best actress she could possibly be. They may have fallen into bed before falling in love, but they had one thing in common: they were both serious people who wanted serious careers.

BUDD SCHULBERG WOULD WRITE *What Makes Sammy Run*, a scabrous primary contender for the Great Hollywood Novel, as well as the screenplay for *On the Waterfront*. But in the early 1930s he was doing time writing for *The Hollywood Reporter*.

He interviewed Crawford for the *Reporter* and came away impressed by her personality as well as stimulated by her sexual charisma. Schulberg wrote in his memoir,

> She was mastering the art of big-studio success. It involved much more than sleeping with Harry Rapf or other MGM producers. We could see how hard she worked at stardom, in front of the camera, between takes, in her dressing room, and away from the studio. The commissary, the main studio street, the Vendome, her limousine—these all became sets where the driven Lucille LeSueur acted out the fantasy that had become Miss Joan Crawford. . . .
>
> Joan Crawford was sex at the ready, her dancer's figure threatening—promising—to burst from the tight silk that barely held it in. . . .
>
> And yet when one talked with Joan, it was not the physical but the mental power that came through, the mind of the superachiever. *No matter where you think I came from*, her will imposed itself on you. *I recreate my life story as I live it.* . . .
>
> If movie fans escaped into their tinseled dreams, why shouldn't the movie stars who floated through those dreams?

AFTER *TODAY WE LIVE*, MGM slotted Crawford into David O. Selznick's production of *Dancing Lady*, opposite Gable again, featuring Franchot Tone and a young Broadway star named Fred Astaire playing himself in his first film.

Mayer asked Crawford as a personal favor to make the musical, and Selznick closed the deal by telling her that he didn't know if the character was appropriate for her because "it's kind of tarty. I think it's more Jean Harlow's style."

Mentioning Harlow to Crawford was akin to mentioning Norma Shearer. "Look, Mr. Selznick, I was playing hookers before Harlow knew what they were, so let's not hear any talk about style because I know more about that than she ever will."

One of the songwriters on the film was Burton Lane, later to write the scores for *Finian's Rainbow* and *On a Clear Day You Can See Forever*. Lane was in the projection room watching Astaire's screen test when a couple of MGM executives came in and sat down. They watched the test in silence and afterward one said to the other, "I can walk down the hall and get dancers like this for $75 a week."

While Crawford had made a living as a chorus girl, her dancing could generally be categorized as picking 'em up and laying 'em down. That said, she knew a great dancer when she saw him. As George Balanchine said of Astaire, "He is the most interesting, the most inventive, the most elegant dancer of our times. . . . Astaire has [the] concentration of genius." As a matter of fact, Crawford holds her own with Astaire, largely because the choreography of *Dancing Lady* is directed toward her abilities rather than his.

Crawford must have seen Astaire onstage, because she went out of her way to treat him as an artist. Astaire had just married his wife Phyllis, and while he was making *Dancing Lady* they lived in a suite at the Beverly Wilshire that was inundated with flowers from Crawford.

The dance director on the picture was Sammy Lee, who took Astaire aside and informed him that "This girl you're working with—you know she's a big star?" Astaire replied that he was quite aware of Crawford's status, and the two became friends. Astaire and his wife became regulars at Crawford's dinner parties.

She treated him with something approaching awe, perhaps because she realized that for the first time she was working with one of Hollywood's few geniuses, and an unassuming genius at that. She thought the reason might have been his completely successful marriage. "I've never known him to be rude and never have seen him make a pass at a girl. Pleasant he is to everyone, and invites pleasantness, but no one moves in on Fred Astaire. He's kept himself intact and he could because he's been a fulfilled man in his personal life."

Astaire and Crawford have the film's finale to themselves. They pair off to "Heigh-Ho, the Gang's All Here." At the midpoint of the number, they move onto a platform that moves them up and away to a Bavarian scene where they segue into "Let's Go Bavarian." Astaire is in lederhosen, Crawford a dirndl and blond braids—not a good look for either of them.

This prologue to a nonpareil career would be soon forgotten when Astaire was teamed with Ginger Rogers a few years later, but the number asserts Crawford's fearlessness. The great choreographer Jack Cole didn't think Crawford was a particularly good dancer, but he respected her nonetheless. "Baby, she may be a big, unpleasant, aggressive broad, but, my God, she was in there working. She wanted it and she deserved it. She made a lot of very good actors look like they were standing still. *Dancing Lady*, she was absolutely marvelous, she *acted* dancing."

In the still of the night, Crawford just might have agreed with Cole about her dancing. When Eleanor Powell arrived at MGM a few years after *Dancing Lady* and quickly came to be regarded as the best female tap dancer in the world, Crawford would lie down on the stage floor for hours to watch Powell rehearse.

Next up was *Sadie McKee*, a romantic picaresque with Crawford playing a bedraggled cook's daughter trying to find true love as she moves from Franchot Tone to Gene Raymond to Edward Arnold before finally returning to Tone. The mood shifts radically depending on the leading man of the moment—Raymond plays an irresolute charmer, Arnold a violent alcoholic. The tonal shifts may have been what interested director Clarence Brown, because he creates a different ambience for each of them.

What binds the slightly improbable film together is Crawford's hopeful sincerity during Sadie's search for a love she can trust, and Brown's typical generosity of spirit. There's a lovely farewell scene when one of Sadie's lovers dies in a sanitarium, while snow gently falls outside a wall-sized window. MGM always had the best movie snow—soft and dry, never slushy.

CRAWFORD SEEMS TO HAVE believed that the divorce from Fairbanks damaged her social position within Hollywood, which only increased her paranoia about Norma Shearer. The paranoia ramped up when she invited the Thalbergs to a party at her house and they politely declined.

"I was much too easily hurt," she would say. "I'd wondered if they liked me." "Why Norma and Joan were at odds, I wasn't sure," remembered Helen Hayes, who was close to both of them. "Surely they couldn't have been rivals for the same roles."

Au contraire. Crawford would say that "There were several roles I wanted very badly. One was *A Free Soul*. I was dying to do it. And [author] Adela [Rogers St. Johns] wanted me to. But Norma got it anyway." In spite of what St. Johns thought was an atrocious performance, Shearer got an Academy Award for *A Free Soul*, while Crawford had to wait fifteen years to win her Oscar, as she would undoubtedly have been the first to tell you.

Her number finally came up when she was invited to the Thalberg house along with regulars such as the Charles Laughtons, the Clark Gables, and the Leslie Howards.

Crawford got through it, but as with weekends at Pickfair, she seems to have been terrified. "I don't know who was more frightened, Joan or me," recalled Shearer. "People said that I was inviting a friendly enemy to dinner. Joan proved them wrong by being a most delightful guest."

CHAINED WAS ANOTHER ROMANCE with Clark Gable, this time on shipboard, during which Gable offers Crawford an alternative to the much older Otto Kruger. A few years later, Scott Fitzgerald watched the film in preparation for writing a script for Crawford. "Why do her lips have to be glistening wet?" he grumbled in his notebook. "Don't like her smiling to herself. . . . Cynical accepting smile has gotten a little tired. . . . She cannot fake her bluff." He came to the conclusion that it was "absolutely necessary that she feel her lines. Must be serious from first. So much better when she is serious.

Must have direct, consuming purpose in mind at all points of the story, never anything vague or blurred."

He would write his friend Gerald Murphy of his difficulty: "She can't change her emotions in the middle of a scene without going through a sort of Jekyll-Hyde contortion of the face, so that when one wants to indicate she is going from joy to sorrow, one must cut away and then back. Also, you can never give her such a stage direction as 'telling a lie' because if you did she would practically give a representation of Benedict Arnold selling West Point to the British."

Fitzgerald only came to Crawford's house once, accompanied by Helen Hayes and Charles MacArthur. "All he did was stand in my kitchen near where the liquor was and get very drunk," Crawford remembered.

Fitzgerald's frustration with his lack of success in Hollywood led him to much grinding of teeth, much overstatement, and much drinking, but he wasn't completely wrong about Crawford. She had the flair and intensity of a natural star, but she had to learn to be an actress. Her reliance on emotion meant that on occasion she lacked nuance, but she never lacked energy or, more importantly, power. She didn't have the finesse that matched up with the delicate emotional filigree of Fitzgerald's prose, but then neither did anybody else.

MGM obviously felt that the poor girl searching for love formula was getting shopworn, so they began to make tentative moves toward something different. *Forsaking All Others* is an unexpected delight, a simultaneously rowdy and Coward-esque semi-screwball comedy written by Joseph L. Mankiewicz about a woman who can't make up her mind between two men in open competition for her.

Jeff is a reporter while Dill is a charming drunk who has trouble keeping his pants on. Since Jeff is played by Clark Gable shortly after *It Happened One Night*, and Dill is played by Robert Montgomery, there isn't much doubt about who is going to win Mary. Gable always brought out the best in Crawford, and he does it again here. She's light, charming, and effervescent, qualities that would gradually vanish from a screen character that became increasingly grim by the 1940s.

The director was W. S. Van Dyke, whose only directorial mantra was "Get in close and keep it moving." He was as sloppy as he was fast, and MGM often had to bring in other directors to shoot the close-ups Van Dyke neglected in his rush to the finish line. That said, *Forsaking All Others* has much of the same breezy charm Van Dyke brought to *The Thin Man*.

Unjustly forgotten today, the film was a model of filmmaking efficiency. Showcasing three major stars, it was made for only $392,000 and returned a profit of $1.2 million.

It would seem to have been a carefree production, but it had a serious problem: timing. When the studio bought the play that had starred Tallulah Bankhead, it was the summer of 1933. By the time the picture went into production in the late summer of 1934, the Production Code had been given a set of gleaming teeth in order to forestall censorship being instituted by dozens of states. A lightly suggestive comedy about a woman ricocheting between two attractive men was now deeply problematic.

It was a radical change from just a few years before. When MGM made *Possessed* in 1931, the Production Code office was concerned about the openly mercantile nature of the sexual relationships portrayed in the film. But they were blindsided because they never saw the script, while the film was already in rough-cut form. Lamar Trotti, later to be a successful writer/producer, was working for the Code at the time and called Irving Thalberg for a discussion about the picture.

As Trotti wrote in a telegram, HE APPRECIATED OUR FEARS AND ADMITS HE IS SOMEWHAT WORRIED BUT INSISTS THAT BECAUSE PICTURE HAS BEEN HANDLED IN SUCH GOOD TASTE WITHOUT SEX SCENES IT IS PROPER STOP I AM NOT SURE IT DOES. HE HOLDS COMPANY HAD PERFECT RIGHT TO USE SUCH MATERIAL AND THINKS OUR OFFICE EXPECTS TOO MUCH ON THAT SCORE.

In other words, Thalberg believed that moviemaking was the studio's prerogative. Later that day, Harry Rapf called to say that MGM would voluntarily shoot an additional scene indicating that Crawford's character had earned only unhappiness by being a mistress.

A meeting was then held at Thalberg's office in which he again expressed his opinion that "this theme is usable when handled in good taste, which unquestionably it is in this picture, which hasn't any sex scenes in it." No argument could be made about the care with which *Possessed* had been made. The Code office, though, was worried that "the grave danger lies in what other companies will attempt to do as a result."

Possessed was released later that year to superb box office, excellent reviews, and letters of protest from one or two censors south of the Mason-Dixon line.

The point of all this is that until 1934 everything depended on the goodwill of the parties involved. The Code office had no actual policing authority, only moral suasion, to which Thalberg and many other producers paid as little attention as possible. As the Code's Jason Joy wrote Joe Breen, *Possessed* became "the chief reason the Code was amended making submission of scripts mandatory rather than optional."

All this led to an agonizing series of rewrites on *Forsaking All Others*. In June 1934, Louis B. Mayer received a three-page letter from the Production Code office outlining dozens of strenuous objections to such incendiary lines as "Tell me, what has marriage got that a good massage can't give you?"

Rewrites met with a stentorian response: "The adaptation and treatment . . . has made use of a number of objectionable, dangerous and questionable lines and situations which are not acceptable."

More rewrites ensued while the picture was being shot in October and November, with alternate script pages being overnighted back and forth between the Code office and the studio. MGM considered the picture finished when Breen watched it twice in the last week of November. This was followed by a letter from Breen stating, "We are gravely concerned about it. In its present form, the picture is definitely and specifically a violation of our Code, because of its general low moral tone and specifically because of its very definite wrong reflection upon the institution of marriage. . . . The triangle of this story is not carefully handled."

This was followed by six pages of suggested changes, including cutting every instance of physical contact between Montgomery and Crawford. "The constant kissing and hugging which we now have definitely points up the loose conduct on the part of both." Although many of these objections were typically couched as suggestions, the picture couldn't be released without implementing them.

On December 1, MGM agreed to make all the requested changes. On

December 6, W. S. Van Dyke wrote Breen, "I just want to say that I am heartily in accord with the [retakes] and that this present lineup can do the picture nothing but good." On December 8, Joe Breen wrote to Will Hays, the chief of the Code office, "After a great deal of time and energy had been spent we finally convinced the studio that they should make necessary retakes, which they are now doing."

Peace—and, presumably, morality—were once again in the ascendance. The exhausting effect of this perpetual nannyish interference with a modestly risqué comedy—given Mayer's and Thalberg's belief systems, the only kind MGM made—can only be imagined.

AFTER *FORSAKING ALL OTHERS* finally finished shooting, Crawford and Franchot Tone headed for New York, where he took her to the opening of the Group Theatre's production of Sidney Kingsley's *Men in White*. As the audience was applauding the final curtain, Tone leaned over and told her, "This is where we'll be some day, you and I, in the theater—where you belong."

"Yes, of course," she replied. It never happened—Crawford was calm on a film set, but had crippling stage fright in front of any live audience. Robert Young remembered doing a radio show with Crawford where she was so terrified that the audience had to be removed before she could go on with the performance.

"With a camera . . . it's different," she said. "The camera is mother to me; if I'm nice to it, it'll be nice to me." The problem was that theater and radio were live, and mistakes leading to embarrassment and chaos were always a possibility. By contrast, a movie was—is—a controlled dance. A scene can be shot and reshot until it's right. Radio panic was not unusual; although Clark Gable had stage experience before he got into the movies, he was also noticeably nervous about radio performances.

All this meant that the Theatre Guild's offer to Tone and Crawford to costar in a stage adaptation of *The Postman Always Rings Twice* was certainly interesting conceptually, but a nonstarter.

OFF-SCREEN, CRAWFORD WAS TRYING to make up for lost time and lost childhood by rapidly assuming all the social conditioning that most people experience in their first twenty-five years. She was still circling Christian Science, which led people inquiring about her health during a cold to be met with "What cold?"

As the screenwriter Leonard Spigelgass noted, "She had accepted the role of a movie star, but she played it differently." She was not cool, aloof, and slightly bored, as Garbo and Dietrich were, but "warm and friendly."

Spigelgass, who would achieve a measure of anonymous fame as the all-knowing "Wise Old Hack" in Gore Vidal's tales of Hollywood, was a junior writer at RKO when he was invited to one of Crawford's parties. He had never met her, didn't know anybody else at the party, but was told that "Miss Crawford needs another man." In short, he was drafted. He donned his black tie and showed up.

Billy Haines was among the guests, so there was much laughter. Crawford took a shine to Spigelgass and when he was served a leafy vegetable with which he was completely unfamiliar, he looked at her questioningly. She nodded slightly, shifted her eyes downward to the object on the plate, and proceeded to disassemble it. Spigelgass watched and imitated her. It was his first experience with the arcane mysteries of the artichoke.

After an appropriate pause after dinner, Crawford called out, "Anyone for a swim?" Since she had suits in every conceivable size in her bathhouse, anybody who felt like a dip in the pool could partake. In due time she appeared in a bathing suit bottom but no top. Spigelgass was a gay man from Brooklyn, where people only swam between July Fourth and Labor Day and where nobody went swimming at night. And here it was off-season, with a topless host.

Spigelgass estimated that he was invited to her house more than a hundred times over the years, although he was never entirely sure that Crawford knew who he was, only that he was good in mixed company and she liked him.

Even friends of friends became friends. In 1935, Vincent Price made a hit playing Prince Albert onstage opposite Helen Hayes in *Victoria Regina*. Hayes gave Price a letter of introduction to Crawford before he made his first trip to Hollywood. Hayes told him, "There is nobody in Hollywood more glamorous or more fun to be with." Price mailed Hayes's letter to Crawford fully expecting no response, but on Sunday morning the phone rang in Price's hotel room. "Hello, Vincent. This is Joanie!" Crawford invited him to her house that night for potluck.

Price was from Missouri, where potluck meant leftovers. Joan Crawford's potluck was different: a sit-down dinner for twenty, but before that there was frolicking in the pool with twenty other guests. After that she slipped into a spectacular outfit covered with star sapphires and glided down the staircase looking just like Joan Crawford.

"She was a star without trying," Price remembered. "She just was. And her promise of an informal afternoon somehow also was. Other famous people arrived informally and Joan just welcomed them. It did not matter if she was dressed to kill or swim. She was glamorously informal. After dinner, we were locked into a theater and had to watch two Spencer Tracy films, who she thought was the best actor in the business. That was how Joan entertained her guests."

JOAN CRAWFORD AND FRANCHOT Tone married on October 11, 1935. The wedding was officiated by the mayor of Englewood Cliffs, New Jersey, and the witness was Nick Schenck, chairman of Loew's Incorporated. They honeymooned at the Waldorf-Astoria.

For a while they were happy. Tone moved into her house, which now sheltered one husband, three dachshunds, and several servants. Before her marriage to Tone, Crawford's working-class background led her to distrust movie stars who dabbled in politics, but now North Bristol became a hive of liberalism. Melvyn Douglas and his wife Helen Gahagan Douglas were frequent guests, as was Stella Adler. A woman who had never had a word to say about politics stayed in her dressing room rather than meet Benito Mussolini's son Vittorio when he visited MGM.

Barbara Stanwyck had divorced Frank Fay and took up with Robert Taylor, a young male ingenue at MGM. Joan had long kept a small hand-tinted photograph of Stanwyck in her Ruby Stevens phase in her house, and soon there was a picture of Joan in Barbara's bedroom, alongside those of Robert

Taylor, her son Dion, and Marion Marx, the wife of Zeppo Marx, her other best friend.

Joan's only problem with Barbara's new relationship was that she didn't see what Stanwyck and Taylor had in common. He was a kind young man from a small town in Nebraska, puppyish, eager to please and obviously smitten with Stanwyck, but he had no edge, lacked her great talent and, equally as important, her ambition.

Nevertheless, Taylor and Stanwyck became part of Joan's social circle, along with the Fred Astaires, the Clarence Browns, the Gary Coopers, Clifford Odets and Luise Rainer, the press agent Jerry Asher and Jean Muir, Cesar Romero and Sally Blane, Ray Milland and his wife Mal. After dinner they would play ping-pong, backgammon, or word games until it was time to watch a movie.

Tone brought Crawford to the Group Theatre's summer camp to meet his old friends. Elia Kazan remembered that Crawford sat at a party, knitting with two long white needles, hardly ever looking up. "There was something predatory about her, I thought. But Tone said she was impressed. With what? I don't know."

Back at the studio, Crawford remained basically docile, rarely throwing a fit. She had been slotted for *Reckless*, a musical that had been designed for her. Instead, she was removed about a week before shooting and replaced by Jean Harlow, who had never been in a musical before and, given the results, never would be again. *Reckless* was a hit anyway.

Life at MGM.

The issues that led to the eventual failure of the marriage were there from the beginning, and Crawford was helpless to change them. To begin with, there was competition: "There wasn't the slightest doubt in my mind that Franchot was by far the finer actor, but he was only getting 'good' parts. I was getting stardom. . . . I got the juiciest parts and the biggest build-ups—not to mention the highest salaries. Franchot's roles, especially in my pictures, were secondary ones." The professional imbalance couldn't help but affect the ego of the man in the marriage.

On the flip side, there were strong elements of life coach in Tone's relationship with his wife. They had leather-bound librettos of operas that would never have existed in any previous Crawford household, and he taught her how to play chess and bridge.

Years later, Franchot's son Pat asked his father what the marriage had been like. Tone answered the question in roundabout terms that emphasized perpetual exhaustion. "The limo would pick us up at 7 a.m.," he told his son. "We'd get to the studio, go through makeup and costume and be on the set by 8:30. We'd have a half-hour for lunch. At 6 p.m. we'd watch the rushes, and if we were lucky we'd get home by 8 p.m.

"Three nights a week, a car would pick us up and take us to Ciro's and the Mocambo so we could have our picture taken for the newspapers and magazines. On Sundays we'd sleep till noon and try to get our energy back."

One of the ways Crawford coped with this high-end hamster wheel was through generosity that verged on philanthropy. Using her money to help other people became a watchword. As one writer put it, "Anyone who had a sick cat, an injured dog, a molting canary, or a visiting uncle who broke a leg could call Joan Crawford on the telephone and tell her about it. After that, she took care of the lame, the halt and the blind at her own expense and in luxury—with the best doctors and veterinarians that could be mustered. She never could say no."

Accompanying this was a perpetual insecurity. She knew she was a star and gloried in it, but she was never sure how good she really was. MGM publicist Maxine Thomas remembered a radio broadcast with Spencer Tracy when he somehow managed to hurt Crawford's feelings. She stormed out of the theater. Joe Mankiewicz was there and told Maxine to follow her and make sure she got home safely.

Thomas overtook her and found Crawford with tears streaming down her face. Just before they got to North Bristol Crawford said, "Stay all night." Thomas noticed that all the bathtubs had been removed from the house—Crawford thought baths were unsanitary. Thomas was shy and modest, so she jumped in the shower. Crawford offered her a shower cap, but Thomas turned it down. They slept together in a king-size bed while Crawford complained about her husband's gambling.

The next day Thomas was having breakfast in bed when Crawford told her she had the day off. Crawford had called the studio and told them Thomas had pulled an all-nighter.

After that, Thomas became part of Crawford's retinue, regularly accompanying her to New York. Thomas noticed the servitude of some of the people assigned to Crawford by the studio. The publicist Jerry Asher would put out his hand for her used chewing gum. Asher was gay, extremely shy and withdrawn, with a high-pitched voice. Crawford understood all about the life of the runt of the litter, and took Asher aside. She told him she knew a voice coach who could help him and paid for the voice coach herself. Asher's voice improved, as did his confidence.

Crawford also took Maxine Thomas under her wing. After Thomas had surgery to remove her appendix, she expected to get a bill but was told it had been taken care of. She later found out Crawford paid for the surgery. Once, Crawford called Thomas when she was at her mother's apartment and kept her on the phone for two hours talking about nothing in particular. "It was a sign of how lonely she was."

Part of the relationship involved acquiescence. When Thomas set up some publicity for Rosalind Russell, Crawford demanded Thomas come to her house, where she told Thomas she objected to her working with other stars.

Most of Crawford's fears involved control. Besides her fear of appearing in front of an audience, there was a terrible fear of flying and of elevators. "I used to walk up 14 flights to avoid elevators. Any fear you have thru intuition should be listened to." In later years, the Los Angeles freeways gave her the willies. "You get on a middle lane and if you haven't studied the map, you can't get off. Out in the middle of flying traffic, Melrose looms up and you can't get into the right lane to turn. One day coming from the dentist and heading for lunch at the Beachcomber's, I went all the way to Warner Bros. in Burbank, 15 miles from the Beachcombers."

Conversely, anybody who could make her feel secure was to be cherished. Crawford's first encounter with George Cukor came when he directed retakes on a film she made with Franchot Tone and Robert Montgomery called *No More Ladies*. Woody Van Dyke or Richard Thorpe would have slammed the retakes through in a few days, but Cukor took the job seriously. "He took me over the coals until I gave every word meaning," Crawford said. "It was illuminating to watch [Tone] work with Cukor, both of them from the theater, speaking the same language."

Franchot Tone's influence was felt on the margins, but there was a perceptible touch of Henry Higgins and Eliza Doolittle in the relationship. He managed to get her through a radio broadcast of Maxwell Anderson's *Elizabeth the Queen*, with Tone playing Essex. After that, he developed a passion for her singing. She started singing lessons and had MGM make test pressings of the songs she had sung in their films, as well as various and sundry opera arias.

MGM didn't mind. In December 1934, the studio had renegotiated Crawford's contract. The new deal was for three years and paid her $7,500 a week, rising to $9,500 in the third year. If she completed more than nine films within the three years, she would get a bonus of $50,000.

IN 1936, LOUIS B. Mayer asked Joseph L. Mankiewicz to take over production duties on Crawford's movies. Mayer's tactic involved abject flattery: "You're the only one on the lot who knows what to do with her."

Mankiewicz wanted to be a director but Mayer saw him as a producer, possibly because he smoked a pipe. To prepare Mankiewicz for his new career, Mayer apprenticed him to the highly successful Bernard Hyman. Mankiewicz would say that the job of producing at MGM was like being a jockey—if you won the race, you were a hero; if you lost, it was the horse's fault.

Producers were the creative agents at MGM. With one or two exceptions, directors didn't matter, because they were interchangeable. Jack Conway shot retakes for W. S. Van Dyke and Robert Z. Leonard, and vice versa. Mankiewicz remembered a conversation he had with Hyman and Louis B. Mayer that defined the star system at MGM.

"Why does Clark Gable fall in love with Joan Crawford?" Hyman asked during a script conference.

"That's not important," replied Mankiewicz.

"Yes, it is," said Hyman.

Mankiewicz summoned logic. "The scene is New Year's Eve in Times Square and there's a shot of Joan Crawford at 50th and Broadway going left to right, and we cut to a shot of Clark Gable at 39th St. and Broadway going right to left. The only question is How, not Why. The motivation is on the marquee: Clark Gable and Joan Crawford in _____."

Mayer was impressed. "Bernie, he's got nuts."

Questions of motivation declined.

Over the next six years, Mankiewicz produced seven of Crawford's thirteen films. His opinion of his star had a certain dismissive clarity: "She woke up like a movie star, she went to the john like a movie star. She had a special outfit for answering fan mail. She put on another outfit to have lunch."

As the relationship with Franchot Tone eventually deteriorated, the relationship with Mankiewicz became more than professional. "I was madly in love with him," Crawford said. "At one time or another, all the ladies at MGM were in love with him, I'm sure. . . . He gave me such a feeling of security I felt I could do anything in the world once I got on that stage. . . . He relaxed me, teaching me to have fun in my work. I'd had joy, but not fun. He brought that out of me, frothy or not."

Mankiewicz was talented, attractive, and egocentric, with a college education, which meant that he regarded the citizens of Hollywood much as an anthropologist does a primitive tribe. For the rest of his life he would analyze the character and motives of actors and actresses with an acuity he studiously refused to turn on himself.

Joan was the essential movie star. She had no sponsor of great power, no staff finding properties, no sensational private life. Shearer had [Thalberg] do it for her; Garbo didn't care. Joan Crawford had to do it all herself; Joan Crawford was smoke rings in the air.

She was the bread and butter star at MGM. The public said she was a star, just as they did Marilyn Monroe. Among the producers of MGM she wasn't considered important because she was a chorus girl brought out by Harry Rapf, and you couldn't have a less important sponsor. . . . The only time I knew her to go to Mayer was for *The Gorgeous Hussy* because she wanted a costume picture, probably because Shearer had *Romeo and Juliet* and *Marie Antoinette*.

She never stormed off a set like Maggie Sullavan; she never blew up. Joan was never a pampered star. She would mark up lines in a script that she thought were problematic and come in before the film started to discuss any changes. If she played records in her dressing room, they were her own records, unlike Lana Turner, who would have the sound department set up a record player for her.

I only saw Joan explode once. . . . She went to her dressing room for a change. The assistant director came up to me and said, "Mr. Mankiewicz, we're in trouble. Miss Shearer needs the stage to shoot a wardrobe test." I took him to Joan's dressing room door and said, "You tell her."

Thirty seconds later Joan was standing in the doorway in her underwear. She was livid. "And you can tell Miss Shearer that I got where I am on my own ass! I didn't marry to get where I am!!"

Mankiewicz came to admire Crawford and her sense of control. He remembered a love scene she played with Robert Montgomery when Montgomery slid his tongue into her mouth. Crawford first bit down on his tongue, then inquired sweetly about Montgomery's wife: "How is dear Betty and when is the baby due?"

"What she had was a solid connection with the great mass audience. The essence of old movies is that they gave the mass audience a chance to visualize second-class fantasies. Those fantasies were not about murdering someone, but about wearing a nice dress and marrying a rich guy."

What set Crawford apart from her peers was that she had the same fantasies as the audience. While fulfilling them for her audience, she was also fulfilling them for herself.

"Her motivation was different than Bette Davis's. Bette wanted to be a star actress; Joan wanted to get out of the hash joint. Bette was a star of performance; Joan was a star of identification. . . .

"What set Joan apart was that she was on the level. She was the definitive star from the advent of sound through the war."

Crawford's core problem as Mankiewicz saw it, was her constant need to create and promote an identity. Doug Fairbanks Jr. constituted the Royal Princess phase, while Franchot Tone signified an Intellectual period.

The void she must have had! Spencer Tracy and Joan had a good thing for a while. He had to keep busy because he was an alcoholic and she had to keep busy because she was looking for a proxy identity. He took her riding, she watched him play polo.

She never had an impromptu moment, never had an unconscious moment in her life. She believed stardom might not be permanent; she never felt she had permanent possession of the trophy.

One night when she was married to Franchot Tone I went to dinner at her house. It was just the three of us, but it was black tie and she was magnificently gowned. The menu was written, gardenias all over the place. The butler entered with the wine and Joan said, "Are you sure this is room temperature?" The line sounded familiar, and I realized it was from a picture and the line had been spoken by William Powell's wife.

Mankiewicz quickly learned to hit the ball where Crawford pitched it. "Joan played different roles when she arrived at my office. My secretary, Addie, would say, 'Miss Crawford is here.' And I never knew what role she would be playing.

"If she came through the door in sables and emeralds, I'd get up from my desk and say, 'Joan, darling!' kiss her on the cheek and say, 'Addie, some sherry for Miss Crawford.' If she strode in wearing slacks, I'd slap her on the ass and say, 'Getting much, kid?' I had to know what she was playing and give her the right dialogue. You were in her fantasy of the moment. I always thought she went to bed differently with each man."

In due course, Crawford and Mankiewicz developed a Same-Time-Next-Year relationship, although she seems to have been more devoted to him than he was to her. There is a Mankiewicz family legend to the effect that when Crawford came to visit Mankiewicz's baby son Tom in 1942, she looked down at the child and told Joe, "This should have been mine."

Despite Mankiewicz's understanding of her character and needs, his scripts and productions for her are by no means her best. Mankiewicz's script for a romantic comedy called *I Live My Life* managed to expose many of Crawford's weaknesses rather than her strengths. Romantic comedies about archaeology are few and far between, and *I Live My Life* shows why. Crawford plays an heiress, and Brian Aherne is an archaeologist who wants her to get serious about life and help him dig up statues in Greece. Aherne is handsome but essentially a void, and doesn't provide the charge of Gable, who could always energize Crawford.

Besides that, Adrian's costumes are all visually striking, but one of them has so much fabric it rustles whenever Crawford walks. It sounds like a forest fire.

It's right about here that MGM begins to lose its grip on Crawford's star narrative. After the damp squib of *I Live My Life*, Crawford made one of the worst pictures of her career. David O. Selznick told Crawford *The Gorgeous Hussy* was a bad idea, if only because it was a period film and, as he told Crawford, "You're too modern." Selznick was right. Among other things, cascading ringlets and bows were not flattering to Crawford's face and unnecessarily emphasized the set of her jaw.

Although Crawford plays the title character, she's actually peripheral to the main narrative, which involves Andrew Jackson and what the film strenuously characterizes as a nonscandal. Crawford balances a revolving door of suitors beginning with Robert Taylor, proceeding with Melvyn Douglas, pausing briefly for a brief flirtation with a moonstruck James Stewart, before ending with Franchot Tone, who shows up at the end of the picture and has about two dozen lines. "Franchot hated his part, loathed it," remembered Crawford. "He didn't complain, he just closed up like a clam."

It was an unpleasant shoot. Clarence Brown developed a dislike for Tone because of what he believed was his condescending attitude toward movies. Melvyn Douglas was a young pro on his way to being an old pro, and he was initially put off by Crawford's *noblesse oblige*. "I'd watch in amazement as Joan would arrive with a long retinue of servants, hairdressers, maids, personal assistants, even her chauffeur. So next day I asked my brother, my chauffeur, and whoever else I could dig up and we went in in a single line. Joan was not amused and I got chewed out by director Clarence Brown, who told me he was having enough problems with Joan before this calumny!"

When Crawford had trouble summoning the proper emotion, a record player would be brought out to play "None but the Lonely Heart." Clarence Brown "would then step forward, and taking Joan by the hand, stand with his head close to hers and wait dreamily until she had achieved whatever emotional pitch she was seeking, after which he would signal for the cameras to begin.

The record player's work and Mr. Brown's handling may have been my first exposure to 'method' preparation. At any rate, it was effective."

It's an unusually lifeless picture, and the entire movie is held hostage by Lionel Barrymore's hambone turn as Andrew Jackson. Outfitted with a headpiece and white wig that make him look like Exeter in *This Island Earth*, Barrymore plays Andrew Jackson the same way he played everything—bombastically, with little regard for behavioral reality. Nevertheless, the picture made money.

Crawford and her husband were reunited on *Love on the Run*, sloughed off by W. S. Van Dyke with reshoots by Clarence Brown. It's a comedy, more in theory than in practice. Frantic without ever being funny, the story involves two competing reporters (Gable and Tone) chasing a runaway bride through Europe, and it's the longest eighty-one minutes you'll ever spend. Crawford was still making money for the studio—the profit on the picture exceeded $1 million—but at the considerable cost of a loss of dramatic immediacy, of Crawford failing to inhabit anything larger than the latest indifferent effort of a movie queen.

Joe Mankiewicz liked Franchot Tone, but only up to a point. "He was intelligent, a good actor, but he never could be a star and he was bitter because of it. He had a slightly aloof air; he felt as if he were slumming. On-screen, he always lost out to Gable. He was destined to play the one who ruefully surrenders the girl to the other man. That's a tough position for a man to be in. Tone lost the girl in the movie, but he went home to her. Something's wrong—he or the public.

"Tone was her wedge into the intellectual world. That was when she began reading Edna St. Vincent Millay with a great sense of discovery—glorious, self-pitying poetry. 'This woman has been writing me!'"

Ultimately, Mankiewicz believed that Crawford could not help growing slightly restless with and about Franchot Tone. He was one thing, and she wanted to be many things. It was time to plug into a different identity.

MILTON WEISS WAS A young MGM publicist who regularly worked with Crawford. His estimation of her was that "When she walked in a room, the silverware shined, the crystal sparkled, the champagne tasted better."

In those days she would go to New York twice a year, and part of the drill was that Weiss meet her at Grand Central Terminal, where he and Mel Heyman would meet her train. Heyman was Weiss's boss. More importantly, he was Irving Thalberg's nephew.

They would tip off the papers about Crawford's arrival so that there would be photographers from the New York papers present, not to mention at least fifty fans. Weiss would accompany her to the hotel and watch her put her hair in curlers as they ran down her schedule for the next couple of days.

They would often dine at "21"—to her dying day her favorite New York restaurant. One night at 10:30, there were about thirty fans outside. "Milton," she announced, "I want to take all of them to ice cream on Fifth Avenue." Crawford led everybody over to Fifth Avenue and sat on a stool while thirty fans devoured ice cream on Crawford's—or MGM's—tab.

Even at 10:30 p.m. she was impeccably turned out. "You owe your public," she told Weiss. "They see you on screen, they want to see you in person the same way."

Franchot Tone wasn't with her on that particular trip, although he usually accompanied her. Weiss remembered passing Tone on the street walking Crawford's dachshunds. Tone nodded hello and said, "I married two dogs and a movie star," a statement that could probably stand as a verbal epitaph for the marriage.

———◇———

MGM WAS CLEARLY TRYING to evolve from the standard Crawford working girl-makes-good narrative, and was failing miserably. *The Last of Mrs. Cheyney* began as a 1925 play by Frederick Lonsdale and was made into a movie starring Norma Shearer in 1929. Recognizing that the story was nearing the end of its life expectancy, MGM did a light retooling for Crawford only eight years after the Shearer version.

It's an archaic wheeze about a female con artist who travels with a retinue of assistants, including a butler who doubles as a jewel thief. They move from country house to country house, stealing jewels from a procession of oblivious owners. Robert Montgomery played the designated victim, while William Powell was assigned the butler part for the second time in a year that also included the far superior *My Man Godfrey*.

Ernst Lubitsch might have done something with the premise, except *Trouble in Paradise* works some of the same territory, and Lubitsch wasn't at MGM in 1937. It was a picture that seemed to be born under a dark star. Richard Boleslawski was assigned the direction but died of a heart attack about halfway through the picture. George Fitzmaurice took over briefly, then also fell ill. The picture was finally completed by an uncredited Dorothy Arzner, who had been the only woman director in Hollywood for more than ten years.

Arzner's films were well shot and intelligent, the rough equivalent of George Cukor's except with less dramatic power. She was an out lesbian who dressed in butch twills and tweed. Crawford liked her and years later would hire her to direct commercials for Pepsi-Cola, but the film itself was dull. Whoever was responsible for the bulk of the footage, there are some badly mismatched edits in the last part of the film, which indicates that the normally OCD production system at MGM gave the film up as a bad job.

The problem is not Crawford—she's quite good in a part that's not remotely in her wheelhouse. The problem is that MGM was losing the thread. From Crawford's tentative beginnings in 1925, MGM stumbled on a star who had a primal connection with her audience and her time. She told the story of young women who were up against it, whether "it" was parental expectations, their class, their opportunities, their immaturity, or some combination of all four. MGM customized the pictures to match up with the skill set of the star, and the audience responded accordingly.

But now MGM was casting her in nominal genre pieces, or in glamour vehicles that lacked any connection to star or audience. Part of the drift undoubtedly derived from Crawford herself—the spiritual autobiography might have gotten a little monotonous, as well as claustrophobic.

The gradual shift of narratives didn't necessarily make an immediate difference at the box office—*The Last of Mrs. Cheyney* made a profit of nearly $500,000. But the creative stasis would become the norm for Crawford at MGM, and its impact would gradually be felt at the box office. With a few exceptions (*The Women, A Woman's Face*), every part Crawford got in these last years at MGM could have been played by some other female star on the roster. It was a problem that would only be solved by another studio, and other filmmakers.

The Bride Wore Red was an adaptation of a Ferenc Molnár play that Joe Mankiewicz picked off a shelf and assigned Dorothy Arzner to direct. It concerned a bedraggled nightclub singer in Trieste who is gifted a vacation at a luxury hotel complete with a stunning wardrobe by Adrian. While on her busman's holiday she is attracted to a Count (Robert Young) who's already engaged, as well as a poor but charming postman (Franchot Tone). The script firmly returns Cinderella to its Mitteleuropa roots, which helps, and neither Crawford nor Arzner oversells the charm until a third act that drags on far too long for a conclusion that is obvious about thirty minutes in.

It's one of Crawford's best light performances—she looks happy and doesn't belabor the emotion. Overall, it's an effective star vehicle, except for the fact that it didn't make any money. The days when MGM could manufacture a Crawford picture for $300,000 were gone. *The Bride Wore Red* came in at just under a million and didn't make much more than that at the box office.

It was Crawford's first picture opposite Robert Young, and he was struck by her personal generosity and perfectionism. "Joan wanted take after take," he remembered. "She was always seeking something better." Young thought she was actually confident in herself as an actress, much like an athlete who knows they're good enough to compete. "But she was not confident in herself as a person. She could not overcome her beginnings. I never met anyone so completely dedicated to the unattainable. A perfectionist in everything she undertook."

Young liked to do his own makeup, which he carried in a beat-up bag. After the picture was finished, he received a package from Crawford. "It was a full make-up kit in imitation alligator with my initials in gold." Similarly, when he got married against L. B. Mayer's wishes—"We were warned that having children was bad for your image. If you did have children, you should hide them"—he and his bride received a massive bouquet of six dozen roses from Crawford.

Over time they became friends. She introduced Young and his wife to Kahlil Gibran's *The Prophet*, which became Young's favorite book. They had what Robert Young called "a special relationship"—often separated by the exigencies of show business, but always attentive. But Young was concerned about her close relationship with her fans. "99.9 percent of the adulation is transitory," said Young. "If you believe it, it's a mistake. When it's gone, you will turn inward and there's nothing there, and then you start to fret. 'Why don't people call me?'"

Young's wife Betty put it more succinctly. "I think she was very lonely."

NOW THAT SHE WAS a star, Joan Crawford was a combination of the usual—drive—with the unusual—the Christian Science phase, which went hand in hand with a relentless focus on self-improvement. The columnist Dorothy Manners understood.

> Christian Science fit her philosophy. She was very positive, and an extremely healthy person. She never complained about headaches, never had colds. She exercised, she swam, she danced.
>
> She showed no interest in athletics, but she was athletic in her own training. She insisted on a male masseuse because she argued that a woman masseuse could not give her deep enough rubs.
>
> She was very generous. She liked to share what she had—on her terms. If she lost her temper, she was almost childlike in wanting to make up. . . . But Joan could be overpowering.

Manners remembered Crawford's linen closet. All the sheets were tied with satin ribbons, and each sheet had to be aired out before it was put on the bed.

Just because she was a movie star didn't mean she wasn't a movie fan. When Manners would run a blind item, Crawford would immediately call her and say, "You can't do that to me. Who is it?" Manners felt that Crawford was unusually docile for a movie star. "She never complained at MGM, never refused roles. She was the most tractable of stars, always cooperative."

Manners and her husband once went to Crawford's house for dinner. Afterward they went into the den, where Crawford told Franchot Tone, "Put on some music, darling." Tone put on a complete recording of *Die Fledermaus*, during which he explained the libretto.

One day Dorothy Manners called Crawford with an idea for a magazine piece.

"What angle?" asked Crawford.

Manners explained that it would concern itself with Franchot coming from a well-to-do background, having an upscale education, etc., while Joan was a chorus girl from Texas. Two different worlds.

Long pause.

"I got a better angle for you."

"What's that?"

"I'm divorcing him."

It was indeed a better story, and she ran with it. Crawford and Tone separated in June 1938 after slightly less than three years of marriage. This provoked Adrian to utter the consummately bitchy line, "Well, she'll be footloose and Franchot-free!" thereby indicating that the couture world's gain was the theater world's loss.

Louella Parsons breathlessly informed her readers that "[Crawford] made herself over completely to fulfill Tone's ideals, patronizing grand operas and entertaining only the friends that he liked. But her work in motion pictures has been very dear to her, and she could not withdraw entirely from the career in which she had won such triumphs." Also mentioned was "Tone's disdain of Hollywood and his eagerness to return to the stage."

The divorce was final in April of 1939.

After the divorce, Tone remained a leading man in films both good (*Five Graves to Cairo, Phantom Lady*) and atrocious (*Trail of the Vigilantes*) for ten more years. As long as the Group was alive Tone was always available for money to keep it going, although Elia Kazan thought Tone's primary motivation was guilt.

Both of Crawford's first marriages were clearly aspirational, obvious attempts to plug into a higher social class. The problem was that both men were born into the class Crawford aspired to and therefore lacked her avidity for success. Fairbanks Jr. had a famous name and an inherent sense of belonging, while Tone had money and an equivalent bespoke attitude. Crawford's hunger overwhelmed them and probably exhausted them as well.

The question of what kind of career and, for that matter, what kind of life Joan Crawford would have in her thirties remained open.

PROD 638
194
PICTURE HOUSE
NAME JOAN CRAWFORD
CHARACTER — MILDRED
WARDROBE CHANGE HOUSE DRESS #1
SET WORN IN PIERCE HOME
SCENES
DATE TESTED
CURTIZ-MARLEY-EVANS
REMARKS S.E.
8A-1

PART TWO

"I've been told I was through many times,
but I'm a very dedicated human being."

—Joan Crawford

Left: Costume test for Mildred Pierce.

CHAPTER NINE

AFTER MORE THAN TEN years of stardom, Crawford was a known quantity. Lots of people viewed her with trace amounts of condescension, although she also had a surprising number of partisans. One was the great French actress Arletty, who admired Crawford for her "intelligence and acting."

Others were less enthralled. On May 8, 1938, Harry Brandt, president of the Independent Theater Owners Association, placed an advertisement in the trade papers labeling a group of stars as box-office poison. Among the stars thus categorized were Crawford, Marlene Dietrich, Katharine Hepburn, Fred Astaire, and Greta Garbo. Brandt's opinion was clearly premature, but his primary target in the ad was actually block-booking, by which exhibitors were obligated to take the entire output of a given studio and couldn't choose between obvious winners.

MGM's response was to sign Crawford to a new contract running five years and ten weeks, specifying a salary of $330,000 a year. She would make a limit of fifteen pictures, no more than six of them during the first two years and nine during the last three. "We cannot require her to appear in more than four pictures during any contract year," Benny Thau wrote in his deal memo. "She is to have full radio rights during the life of the contract. During such years as she elects to do a stage play, she has to have a vacation period of twelve weeks. During any year in which we require her to render her services in excess of forty weeks, she is to be paid additional compensation at the rate of $8,250 per week."

So much for box-office poison.

Crawford got everything she asked for except a request to end her shooting day at 5 p.m. so she could take singing lessons. To that, Louis B. Mayer said a firm No Way.

MANNEQUIN WAS A PARTIAL recovery from Crawford's recent run of mediocre pictures, and a better movie than its synopsis would indicate. A girl from a family of bedraggled Irish layabouts in New York City—the squalor is so extreme that Crawford's brother is played by Leo Gorcey—hooks up with a crafty hustler, who suggests she divorce him so she can marry a shipping magnate who loves her. Put a few months in, grab a hefty settlement, and she can come back to the hustler. The only problem is that she falls in love with the shipping magnate, who proceeds to go broke. What's a girl to do?

The shipping magnate is played by Spencer Tracy, who was one of the worst alcoholics in the business but left all that behind when he was in front of the camera, where he invariably underplayed every other actor in the picture. Crawford keys her performance on the same plane as Tracy—honest, real. Frank Borzage has gone down in posterity as a great director of ethereal love stories—*7th Heaven, Man's Castle*—but his specialty was less marital love than tenderness, the delicate ballet of a man and woman warily circling each other while moving toward emotional commitment.

Besides the performances, the residual pleasures include a dry run of the Adrian fashion show in *The Women*. Since Crawford's character is working in a glam Fifth Avenue shop, it's marginally less arbitrary than in the later picture.

SEX WAS A PHYSICAL and emotional reality that Crawford recognized and enjoyed without guilt. Her attitude seems to have been basically utilitarian. Sometimes sex was a straight physical transaction devoid of romance. Other times it verged on the sacramental.

She had affairs with actors on her own level—Spencer Tracy, who she said was "a real son of a bitch when he drank, and he drank all the time," and the intermittent relationship with Clark Gable. She also enjoyed flings with character actors who caught her fancy—among others there was Don "Red" Barry, a diminutive, volatile actor who made B Westerns at Republic as a sort of James Cagney on horseback.

She liked them age appropriate and she also liked them young, as with a teenaged Jackie Cooper. Cooper was seventeen when he and Crawford had a fling in 1938.

Crawford was a friend of Cooper's mother, and he had an open invitation to use her badminton court. One day she got him a Coke after a strenuous hour of batting the shuttlecock, when she noticed him looking down the front of her dress.

"You're growing up, aren't you?" she said. "You had better get out of here, young man."

Instead, Cooper made a move toward her. Crawford stood up, looked at him carefully, and then closed the drapes. "And I made love to Joan Crawford," recalled Cooper. "Or, rather, she made love to me."

They got together eight or nine times over the next six months. It was Pygmalion in reverse—she taught him that sex was more than grab and grope. In fact, it could be a multicourse *cordon bleu* feast. Cooper would remember her with awe and abject gratitude as an expert guide to a sexual version of the Arabian Nights: "She was a very erudite professor of love . . . a wild woman. She would bathe me, powder me, cologne me. Then she would do it over again. She would put on high heels, a garter belt and a large hat and pose in front of the mirror, turning this way and that way. . . .

"I recognized that she was an extraordinary performer, that I was learning things that most men don't learn until they are much older—if at all. There was never any drinking or drugs with her. It was all business. She was very organized. When I left, she would put me on her calendar for the next visit. I could hardly wait."

Finally, Crawford called a halt. After one last session, she said it was over and told Cooper not to call her again. "And put it all out of your mind. It never happened." Then she kissed him and said, "But we'll always be friends." And they were. In later years, they corresponded about his career successes, including winning Emmys for television direction.

DESPITE HER PLUSH CONTRACT, Crawford's professional problems continued to expand, as MGM settled on a pattern of casting her as a slightly bored society creature picking and choosing from a roster of male escorts, which had the effect of robbing her character of urgency, as well as the sexuality that had galvanized audiences. Most Crawford vehicles of the late 1930s are the equivalent of a Broadway musical without an "I Want" song, which is to say that they're stock screen merchandise.

Case in point: *The Shining Hour*, a turgid melodrama about a nightclub dancer who marries a gentleman farmer, after which she has to cope with his obnoxious mother and her brother-in-law, the latter of whom is attracted to her.

Joe Mankiewicz appreciated Crawford's work ethic. "On *The Shining Hour*, she worked with Tony DeMarco for a four piano number by Franz Waxman. She worked her ass off to do that dance!

"Margaret Sullavan was a highly neurotic, brilliant actress. When she and Joan worked together, Joan was not going toe-to-toe in acting. She had top billing and she knew she could only win if Maggie was good. So she wasn't intimidated by Maggie."

MGM had devised a screen character for Crawford that worked brilliantly for phase one, but they clearly had little idea what to do for phase two. For that, she would have to leave MGM and go to Warner Bros. and producer Jerry Wald, who would understand that the middle-aged Crawford needed to be a creative extension of the youthful Crawford—Mildred Pierce is every bit as hungry for money, for status, as Marian in *Possessed*.

But that was in the future. After *The Shining Hour*, MGM gave her *The Ice Follies of 1939* despite the fact that there were alternatives. In the latter part of 1938, the buzz from both the public and the industry was focused on who was going to play Scarlett O'Hara in *Gone with the Wind*. MGM had already agreed to loan $1.2 million and Clark Gable to David O. Selznick in return for distribution rights. MGM held Selznick's feet to the fire, charging him 20 percent of the gross for distribution, with profits to be split 50-50. Crawford had been in the back of Selznick's mind since the book was published—in May 1936, he had mentioned that if he was still at MGM he would buy it for "some such combination as Gable and Joan Crawford."

By 1938, the tally being kept by David Selznick counted 300 letters from the public imploring him to cast Ann Sheridan, 228 asking for Miriam Hopkins, and 58 for Joan Crawford. By then, Selznick's thinking had undergone a shift—Crawford was never even tested for the part.

MGM suggested Selznick get the picture off his plate as quickly as possible. Selznick claimed they told him to fill out the rest of the cast strictly from MGM: Crawford as Scarlett, Maureen O'Sullivan as Melanie, and Melvyn Douglas as Ashley Wilkes.

Instead of being miscast as Scarlett, Crawford was miscast in the misbegotten *The Ice Follies of 1939*. Crawford worked opposite the equally forlorn James Stewart and Lew Ayres, and was still taking voice lessons on the side. "She came to the studio at 4:30 or 5 a.m. to practice opera," remembered Stewart.

In the original script, Stewart was to play a figure skater, except that when he was outfitted in a pair of dashing tights the studio realized that a costume like that on Stewart was fit only for a slapstick comedy. It was back to the drawing board, and it was decided that Stewart would play a comic ice skater, complete with baggy pants, a large bow tie, and white gloves like Mickey Mouse.

"That didn't work either," Stewart said. Finally, Stewart avoided skates altogether, as did Crawford and Ayres. The film was a shambles, but Crawford's professionalism never wavered as she gritted her teeth and tried to make the best of an imposed disaster. "She herself was so disciplined," said Lew Ayres. "She knew inwardly how that discipline gave her the strength and power, and gave her the career, too."

Until the mid-1960s, *The Ice Follies of 1939* was the nadir of Crawford's career. The film is not quite as dire as its title indicates—it's basically a story of striving young people trying to make it, and Crawford, Stewart, and Ayres all give it more energy than it deserves, but it still stops dead several times for stupefying sequences featuring the frozen hellscape of mid-century theatrical ice skating.

After *The Ice Follies of 1939*, Mayer must have felt he owed Crawford, so he grudgingly gave her *The Women*, a project that involved the Production Code in a Hollywood version of the Punic Wars.

Joseph Breen and company began the long march by informing movie studios that Clare Boothe's hit play could not be made into a movie. "If made into a picture, we would have to reject [because] the material submitted seems to be largely a discussion of a number of marital infidelities. . . . These adulteries seem to be taken more or less as a matter of course, and to be presented without the necessary moral values which the Production Code requires." Despite the ominous tone, director Gregory La Cava had some preliminary meetings about how to film the project.

By February 1938, the property was in MGM's court, with Louis B. Mayer and Eddie Mannix, MGM's general manager, heading up a meeting with Breen, where he reiterated that the play as written was impossible. Evidently MGM gave some thought to retitling the property *The Case for Chastity*, which was still impossible as far as Breen was concerned.

Despite Breen's stalwart resistance, MGM moved forward. Crawford's justified discontent with what MGM was handing her was the reason she went after the role of Crystal, but producer Hunt Stromberg and Louis B. Mayer were both wary. Mayer regarded her as his "youngest daughter," which is why he was appalled by her eagerness to play a conniving seductress with a specialty in married men. "The role is that of an outright bitch," he told her. "It could hurt your career."

She countered with, "The woman who steals Norma Shearer's husband, Mr. Mayer, can't be played by a nobody." She got the part.

From the beginning, the picture was a minefield of scene-stealing, status-mongering, and directorial musical chairs. David Selznick had fired George Cukor from *Gone with the Wind*, and he had returned to MGM with his tail between his legs. Ernst Lubitsch had been scheduled to direct *The Women*, but that was given to Cukor as a make-good, while Lubitsch was switched to *Ninotchka*.

Stromberg was playing at being a trusted friend of Shearer's, but at the same time he was maneuvering to make the best picture he could. *The Women* was initially designed by MGM as a vehicle for Shearer, but after Cukor came on board there was general agreement between him and Stromberg about casting Crawford and Rosalind Russell, which inevitably watered down Shearer's dominance.

"George said to go for the broadest comedy," remembered Russell. "I dressed Sylvia horridly . . . with more than a little help from Adrian. We first glimpse her at Mary's house, and I wore an awful blouse with a great big bulging Picasso-like face staring back. Norma [Shearer] took one look and protested to George, 'She's not going to wear that, is she?'"

The first casting problem arose because both Shearer's and Crawford's contracts guaranteed them top billing. Shearer owned a large amount of Loew's stock courtesy of Irving Thalberg, who had died in 1936. The Loew's stock gave her leverage Crawford didn't have, but Crawford was desperate to play Crystal. Shearer yielded—sort of. Crawford got costar billing, but in second position: "Notwithstanding the provision of paragraph 18 of my contract . . . Miss Joan Crawford may be given co-star credit with my name. The waiver to apply only to *The Women*."

Since Crawford had gotten costar billing, Rosalind Russell went after it as well, which meant Shearer had to give up yet more ground: "I now agree that both Miss Joan Crawford and Miss Rosalind Russell may be given co-star credit with my name; provided however, that in no event shall Miss Russell's name appear in size of any type larger than 50% of the size used to display my name."

In October 1938, MGM sent a copy of their prospective screenplay to Breen. A few days later the Code office began its tactical retreat. "We feel that it is possible to develop this story along lines which would be acceptable both from the standpoint of the Production Code and of political censorship." The letter continued for six single-spaced pages documenting scenes and lines that were out of bounds.

Producer Hunt Stromberg took the lead position in dealing with Breen. On April 19, 1939, Stromberg wrote Breen a "Dear Joe" letter informing him that they started shooting in a week and needed an immediate response about the latest version of the script, which had gone through the typewriters of, among others, F. Scott Fitzgerald, Jane Murfin, and Anita Loos.

A day later, the studio was informed that the script was unacceptable "because of the wholesale characterization of so many of the characters as being either adulterous, or engaged in illicit sex affairs—all this without sufficient compensating moral values."

Despite the ominous tone, MGM elected to plunge in.

On April 24, they sent Breen rewrites of the offending passages beginning on page 8 and continuing through page 36. Still no go. Breen now became an uncredited screenwriter and began suggesting alternative dialogue; the line "Stephen Haines is cheating on Mary!" could, he thought, be changed to "Stephen Haines is stepping out on Mary!"

New dialogue was written for scenes between Shearer's character and her mother, which the Breen office thought overly indulgent toward male adultery. Breen approved of the changes and didn't think they would encounter any political difficulty from other countries, as in Ireland's prohibition against the depiction of pregnant women or scenes of bathing.

Nothing got easier when the picture started shooting. On Shearer's first day, she arrived to find three star trailers arranged outside the soundstage. One of them extended about a foot in front of the other two. It was Crawford's, and Shearer promptly ordered them lined up with geometric equivalence.

Oliver Marsh had been the cameraman when the picture started, but he was soon replaced by Joe Ruttenberg. "Shearer wasn't satisfied with the way she looked, so she brought me in," explained Ruttenberg. "It was a college course in one-upsmanship. If I was setting the lights for a close-up of one actress, another actress would come over, plot where the lights were in her head and demand the same positioning when it came time to do her close-ups. You had to be very diplomatic. They were all paranoid about each other and George [Cukor] had to really lace into them a couple of times just to stay even."

Crawford and Shearer had only one scene together, which threatened to turn into a duel to the death. Cukor got his master shot without much difficulty, then moved into close-ups. At that point, Shearer announced that she wasn't going to do the off-camera lines for Crawford's reaction shots. Crawford was infuriated but nevertheless said that she was willing to read her off-camera lines for Shearer's reaction shots. She did so while knitting, with the needles clacking so as to completely distract Shearer.

Shearer lost her concentration and broke off, then asked Crawford to stop knitting. Crawford kept knitting, and at that point, Shearer turned to the director. "Mr. Cukor, I think Miss Crawford can go home now and you can give me her lines." Cukor told Crawford to apologize. She refused and walked off the set and off the lot.

That night Crawford sent a telegram to Shearer's house at 707 Ocean Front that Shearer characterized as making her "hair curl." Crawford would later note that no one had ever been bothered by her knitting before, which was not strictly true. Shearer didn't acknowledge the telegram, but reports that the two never spoke again are clearly false—pictures exist of them embracing at parties fifteen or so years later.

Crawford was almost always rigorously professional, so her behavior has to be considered a function of her long-simmering resentment of Shearer's place as the queen of MGM, a position that Crawford believed was solely because of her husband, a status that his death had done nothing to dislodge. And there was something else: other than *Grand Hotel*, Thalberg had never been a fan of Crawford's, probably because she didn't interest him as an actress. She sensed his indifference and reacted accordingly.

Despite all the backstage politics and onstage tension, Crawford responded with one of her drollest, most sexually enticing performances as, first, the mistress of Norma Shearer's unseen husband, then his wife. The glint in Crystal's eye tells us she knows precisely what men want and is more than happy to give it to them, especially if their wives won't. Crawford, along with rowdy turns from Rosalind Russell and Paulette Goddard, easily steals the movie from Shearer, who was stuck playing the noble wife.

All the squabbling over status was an appropriate preliminary to the behind-the-scenes maneuvering that went on over the picture's climax. Adrian had designed a costume for Crawford with gold sequins and a sliver of bare midriff. When Louis B. Mayer saw the rushes, he went into apoplectic shock at what he regarded as a sleazy presentation and demanded the scene be reshot with a different costume.

It made perfect sense. Since Thalberg's death, the MGM output was gradually but inexorably shifting from Crawford—and Shearer—dealing with adultery, death, class warfare, and errant husbands to Mickey and Judy putting on a show. Worse: the glacial perfection of Hedy Lamarr, or the pious lectures of Lionel Barrymore to Dr. Kildare or Lewis Stone to Andy Hardy.

Adrian had zero interest in Mickey and Judy, whom he regarded as two stumpy midgets. He flatly refused to change Crawford's dress. Hunt Stromberg told Adrian he needed to rethink his position, if only for reasons of house politics. Crawford backed Adrian and fought for her character's autonomy, not to mention her own. If the costume was going to be changed, she demanded final approval of any alterations.

Stromberg was in the middle of a particularly nasty family quarrel and didn't like it. At one point he was scheduled to meet with Crawford and Adrian to go over replacement ideas, but he was a no-show and sent a telegram to Crawford's house: "Must stay home today on account of severe cold. Will see you and Adrian tomorrow 12:30. Have talked with Adrian regarding general treatment. He will try to have something to show us tomorrow."

Adrian thought a dress he had designed but not used for the fashion show sequence might work, but it was very similar to a costume Shearer was wearing in the scene that now featured Crawford and her stomach. The problem was that the new dress would completely negate the lushly erotic/sleazy point his original design had made.

Finally, the creative team of *The Women* trooped into Mayer's office to make a last stand. Crawford, Cukor, Adrian, and Stromberg all made their pitch. Surprisingly, Mayer capitulated and Crawford showed some stomach. (What's surprising is that both Mayer and the Breen office ignored the obvious fact that Paulette Goddard made most of the picture *sans* bra.)

Crawford and Adrian got their way, but the cost must have been considerable. A few years before, it wouldn't have been necessary for them to fight tooth and claw for a costume so perfectly indicative of character, something they both knew in their hearts was right. The environment at MGM was changing to something approaching middle-class, and they didn't like it.

Script revisions continued on specific isolated pages and lines into the first three weeks of May, which were quickly approved, including a new opening scene. On June 6, Hunt Stromberg wrote Breen that "the picture looks magnificent, with everything done in the best of taste and with no offense in any direction. . . . I think we'll all be glad we made it when the final bell is rung. Kindest personal regards and again my thanks for your continued splendid cooperation."

The maneuvering continued even after the film finished shooting. The cast had been scheduled to come to the portrait studio to have group stills done, but on the appointed day and time of 10 a.m., tumbleweeds were blowing through the studio.

"Nobody," remembered photographer Laszlo Willinger. "10:30 a.m., nobody. 11 a.m., nobody still. Finally, Roz Russell walked in and said, 'Sorry I'm late.' I said, 'You're not late, you're the first one here.' She said, 'Jesus, where are the others?'

"I walked outside the stage, and I saw Norma Shearer driving by, looking out of her car window, and then driving on. And right behind her was Joan Crawford, also driving by the stage, looking out and then driving on."

Willinger was desperate and called Howard Strickling: "There are two stars out here driving around the stage and not coming in."

Strickling sighed and explained that Shearer was obviously not going to come in before Crawford, and Crawford was obviously not going to come in before Shearer.

Willinger asked Strickling what he could do, and he replied, "The only thing I can do is to stand in the middle of the street and stop them." Which is what Strickling did, after which he ushered them into the portrait studio.

Once all the actresses were in their dressing rooms to get changed, nobody came out. Russell finally appeared in a clingy evening gown. Willinger knocked on Shearer's door and told her Russell was ready. Shearer stuck her head out the door, saw what Russell was wearing, and announced, "I'll come out when Miss Russell is dressed."

"What do you mean?" asked Willinger. "She is dressed."

"She's not dressed. She's in her slip."

Again Howard Strickling was called, and this time he stayed at the photo studio. Russell changed her dress but put on high heels and a hat with feathers. Since Russell was about 5-6 and Shearer was about 5-2, she now towered over the picture's star. In a stage whisper, Shearer asked Willinger, "Don't you think it's about time you started working with the stars and sent Miss Russell home?"

Willinger said that he ended up shooting about three exposures, "not that we didn't shoot more. And Crawford sort of enjoyed this thing between Shearer and Russell." According to Willinger, the only actresses who were easy to work with on *The Women* were Paulette Goddard and Rosalind Russell, the former "because she was ambitious," the latter "because she didn't give a damn."

Crawford was also a no-show for another day of stills. Willinger called her secretary, asking after Miss Crawford's whereabouts. Her dressing room, after all, was right across the street from the portrait studio.

"We're waiting," said Willinger. "We're over an hour late. What's the problem?"

"The limousine isn't here. It's in her contract to have a limousine."

"I'm only across the street!"

"Miss Crawford has [it] in her contract that she have a limousine."

After another half hour, the limousine showed. It picked up Crawford, made a U-turn, and dropped her off across the street.

On July 19, Joe Breen sent a telegram to Nicholas Schenck, chairman of Loew's Incorporated: WE SAW THE WOMEN THIS AFTERNOON AND I AM SENDING THIS TO TELL YOU THAT IN OUR JUDGMENT IT IS QUITE THE BEST PICTURE WE HAVE SEEN IN A YEAR STOP IT IS REALLY SENSATIONAL AND OUGHT TO BE A SMASH BOXOFFICE HIT MY HEARTIEST CONGRATULATIONS TO YOU.

On the day after the film was sneak previewed, Hunt Stromberg sent a chummy telegram to Breen: DEAR JOE KNOW YOU WILL BE PLEASED TO HEAR THE WOMEN IN ITS FIRST SNEAK PREVIEW LAST NIGHT MORE THAN JUSTIFIED YOUR HIGH OPINION OF IT STOP HAVE NEVER IN MY ENTIRE CAREER EXPERIENCED SUCH TREMENDOUSLY ENTHUSIASTIC REACTION AS WE RECEIVED STOP YOUR OPINION THAT PICTURE WAS NOT LONG DESPITE ITS TWELVE THOUSAND FEET ALSO CONFIRMED AS THERE IS HARDLY A CUT OR CHANGE TO BE MADE STOP THANK YOU AGAIN FOR YOUR ENCOURAGEMENT AND ASSISTANCE ALL DOWN LINE AND I HOPE YOU DON'T HANG ON THE NECKTIES YOU WILL RECEIVE.

The reviews in both the trade papers and the newspapers ranged from solid to spectacular. Frank Nugent in *The New York Times* thought that the industry should compete by making "at least one thoroughly nasty picture a year."

The Women emerged as something of a triumph for all concerned, a story of the ladies who lunch and thus have nothing else to do but primp, dress, and spread vile, factual gossip about their dearest friends. Cukor gives the proceedings energy and style, and the actresses transcend the brilliant central gimmick of an all-female cast.

The only problem was that *The Women* didn't make any money. The clothes budget alone must have been staggering, and the film ended up costing $1.6 million, a very pricey figure for a movie that's almost all interiors. It grossed well but not well enough, losing about $250,000, although it went into profit with a reissue years later.

On the plus side, *The Women* cemented the creative synchronicity between Crawford and George Cukor. She analyzed his specific gift from the inside: "George simply has an uncanny ability to define the character of a woman, any type of woman, and how she should react to any given situation. This is what made the screen version of *The Women* better than the play. It could have been played strictly as farce, and still have been a good picture, but George picked up on so many subtle things that each character had a reason to be and do and say. . . . I don't think any other director could have established the characters I [later] played in *A Woman's Face* and *Susan and God*. He made me *be* those women."

AFTER FINAL MAJOR ACCOMPLISHMENTS with *The Wizard of Oz* and *The Philadelphia Story*, Adrian would leave MGM in July 1941 to devote himself to *haute couture*, which the fashion sequence in *The Women* indicated was becoming his true passion.

That same year, he gave an interview that didn't conceal his growing distaste for the movie business: "Who would have thought," he said, "that my entire reputation as a designer would rest on Joan Crawford's shoulders." He would occasionally come back to movies for one-offs, designing some outfits for Crawford in *Humoresque* and *Possessed*.

The asserted cause for Adrian's leaving MGM was his fury over the studio's bowdlerization of Garbo in *Two-Faced Woman*. He seethed because the studio ignored his designs for her costumes and instead altered existing costumes.

Garbo's words of farewell made his loyalty seem foolish: "I am sorry you are going, but I must say I never did like very much the clothes you made me wear in my pictures." Whatever Adrian thought of Crawford, she understood that his designs had helped create her identity, not just as an actress, but as a woman.

AFTER THE TRIUMPH OF *The Women*, it was back to the salt mines.

From Louis B. Mayer's perspective, movies were a combination of the fresh and the familiar, which in practice meant that the product, not to mention the people fronting the product, needed to be revamped on a regular basis. Norma Shearer and Crawford had been stars in silent pictures. It was in MGM's interest to have an assembly line of future possibilities, and Lana Turner, Hedy Lamarr, Judy Garland, and Greer Garson were all in the ascendance.

Crawford began to have unexplained absences. In November 1939, on location in Pismo Beach for *Strange Cargo*, she was "depressed" for three days and didn't report to the set. In February 1940, she was "unable to rehearse" for *Susan and God*; for several days in March, she had a bad cold and "was unable to work"; on the third and fourth of April 1940, she was "depressed and ill." In October, she was granted a leave of absence "provided [she would return] not later than 11 December." The latter was almost certainly because of her affair with Charles McCabe of the New York *Daily Mirror*, but most of the other absences couldn't be so easily explained.

Strange Cargo provoked yet more *Sturm und Drang* when she saw it at a preview and noted Clark Gable's top billing—a violation of Crawford's contract, which guaranteed her first position. There was a flurry of interoffice panic over Crawford's anger. Eddie Mannix, MGM's general manager, telegraphed Crawford's agent, "Know of no promises regarding billing on *Strange Cargo*. However Mr. Mayer returning to Los Angeles tomorrow and will discuss it with him. Know of no better billing than 'Gable and Crawford' especially taking into consideration Gable's tremendous hit and publicity after *Gone with the Wind*. Am at a loss for you to have any reason for complaining of co-star billing Gable first, as this is not unusual with us with Gable in any of our pictures in which he appears. Only time this has been different was *Idiot's Delight*."

As Mannix well knew, *Idiot's Delight* had paired Norma Shearer with Gable and she was contractually guaranteed top billing, a fact that only would have strengthened Crawford's insistence on the same thing, which she finally got—the last time Clark Gable took second billing.

Another complicating factor was that Crawford had lusted after the female lead in *Idiot's Delight*, in which a tacky showgirl masquerades as a countess—a part Crawford would have understood on the cellular level. Thalberg had been in his cold marble tomb at Forest Lawn for years, but his widow was still the queen of the lot.

Strange Cargo is an odd, haunting picture, far more spiritually oriented than most MGM pictures, which tend to be about June/Moon/Croon rather than metaphysical connection. Gable and Crawford hadn't worked together for a few years, and he remained insecure about his skill set. Crawford remembered that he told her she had grown as an actress while he was still tied to his old tricks.

He was right. In *Strange Cargo*, Gable is the same old cocksure Gable, in command of all situations, hair perpetually dangling rakishly over his forehead. Crawford might be a trifle old to play yet another damaged dance hall girl, this time in the French Guianas stuck with the members of a prison break, but she brings a sense of moral exhaustion and, in one monologue, authentic emotional drift. It's a fine performance in a picture that producer Joe Mankiewicz correctly called "almost a good movie." It's ultimately too gassy, but it does showcase Frank Borzage's bent for spiritual rebirth in extreme circumstances.

It was followed by *Susan and God*, a ghastly picture that Norma Shearer wisely turned down. It's a stage-bound—Gertrude Lawrence starred on Broadway—period piece about a vacuous society dame who bounces back and forth between Sands Point, Newport, and Europe. She comes back home on fire with a passion for a new variety of religious uplift that seems to be Moral Rearmament but that the film avoids defining. In practice it means she ignores her husband and daughter. It's as if Billie Burke's scatty status-obsessed party giver in *Dinner at Eight* has been handed center stage.

Crawford has too much dramatic weight to get away with two hours of twittering artificiality, and she gets no help from the rest of the cast, led by Fredric March encoring his apologetic alcoholic from *A Star Is Born*. Other than the tangential presence of the young, ravishing Rita Hayworth, the rest of the cast is made up entirely of second- and third- stringers: John Carroll, Ruth Hussey, Bruce Cabot. All of George Cukor's dexterity and insight into character prove useless. Despite a late third-act conversion to something approaching common sense, the impression left is of Susan as a deluded prig. Moreover, the part manages to obliterate the sensuality that was one of Crawford's primary attributes.

Susan and God lost more than $400,000. More importantly, it cost Crawford the momentum she had earned with *The Women* and her honorable effort in *Strange Cargo*. MGM must have realized they had blundered, and instead of returning Crawford to one of her several formulas in the hope of recouping, they took a deep dive into the unexpected. This time, they succeeded, and Crawford would come to believe that her performance in *A Woman's Face* gave her the credibility within the movie industry to enable her to win her Oscar for *Mildred Pierce*.

Several writers, Marc Connelly and Christopher Isherwood among them, worked on the script before producer Victor Saville took over the project. Saville turned to Elliot Paul, who had written *The Last Time I Saw Paris*, a *roman à clef* about his time as a journalist in the last days of literary Paris in the 1920s. (MGM would eventually make a soggy soap out of it in the 1950s with Elizabeth Taylor and Van Johnson.) Paul did enough work to get a credit on *A Woman's Face*, but the bulk of it seems to have been written by Donald Ogden Stewart, normally a writer of sophisticated comedy (*Dinner at Eight*, *The Philadelphia Story*) who was also capable of desperate romantic melodrama (*Love Affair*).

The movie begins with a courtroom sequence in which the Crawford character is standing trial for murder, followed by a flashback that leads to her trial. The film cuts back and forth between the trial and the circumstances that led up to it before both narratives reach a simultaneous climax.

It was a nervy project for an actress coming off a ridiculous flop, because two consecutive flops could endanger even a solid career. Crawford was up for the challenge. Saville remembered her sailing into his office saying, "This one has got to be good, and I'll do anything you want me to do." Throughout the picture Saville remembered that "She was a good sport" and was willing to work without the makeup she had been using. According to Saville, she used a light lipstick "and a little gold dust on her skin."

Although it's a remake of a 1938 Swedish film starring Ingrid Bergman,

A Woman's Face plays as a backdoor return to the Lon Chaney films of the 1920s. In Chaney's films, physical disfigurement provokes damage to the soul. If the disfigurement is corrected, the soul can begin to heal. In the case of Crawford's character, she's running a loosely knit group of crooks specializing in blackmail because of a burn scar from a childhood accident that covers almost half her face.

It's a fully thought-out performance. George Cukor directs Crawford to avoid looking directly at other people in order to have them avoid looking at her, part of a consistent push-pull dynamic throughout the picture. Although the makeup is suitably grotesque, Crawford is at her peak of physical beauty.

Her performance is immeasurably aided by the serpentine elegance of Conrad Veidt. Technically he's the heavy, but he's far more sexually suggestive and compelling than Melvyn Douglas, who's stuck playing straight man to both of them. Veidt consistently underplays in his intense confrontations with Crawford, which forces Crawford to underplay as well, and their low-pitched murmuring voices coalesce in what amount to perversely masochistic love scenes—dark sexual chamber music.

There is too much melodrama in the picture's finale—endangered children, a long sleigh chase through snow, falls from great heights—but what lingers is Crawford's grasp of human damage, the way she incarnates a woman whose best instincts have been derailed by circumstance and bitterness.

Crawford had portrayed her own nervy strivings in the blue-collar movies she had made ten years earlier and she would do so again, but she was never braver—or more beautiful—than in *A Woman's Face*.

A Woman's Face made a profit of several hundred thousand dollars, but it seems to have been perceived as a desperation move. Would MGM have allowed Greer Garson to play such a part, even in the unlikely event of her taking leave of her senses and playing something so far outside her skill set?

Crawford's experiences with Cukor on *The Women, Susan and God,* and *A Woman's Face* sealed a friendship that lasted the rest of their lives. With the exception of *Susan and God*, he stripped her of affectation, gave her performances clarity, energy, and clean lines, and in the process earned her undying gratitude. Among Cukor's large collection of signed photographs of stars was one of Crawford, on which she wrote, "To a great actor and a better director, George. Love, Joan. P.S. The marriage offer still stands."

Other than *A Woman's Face*, Crawford would obliquely refer to this period as one of her life's low points without quite specifying any cause, and it's probable that the reason was the affair with Charles McCabe. She would speak of him circumspectly to friends she trusted, and once or twice blurted out his name to her friend Jane Kesner Ardmore without realizing she was giving the game away:

> He lives his newspaper the way I've lived my acting; he thinks, eats, breathes newspaper business and he's good. This man has to be nameless because he has a family. He can't get a divorce. If he could, he's the one man in the world for who I'd give up my career in a minute.
>
> There are men who want to change women. He's not one of them. We've been friends for years. He discusses business with me. He taught me about politics, banking and public affairs; he discusses them and he discusses business with me. He taught me to hunt and fish. I taught him to relax, not to be ashamed of his emotions. . . .
>
> He has been with me at studio conferences. We understand and respect each other and never have taken each other for granted. Five times he has taken me to newspaper conventions and introduced me as "Miss Smith" and—what a wonderful thing professional loyalty is—the newspaper people accepted me as "Miss Smith" and never in all the years have our names appeared in print together.
>
> The first time I mentioned that I'd like to go hunting and fishing with him, he got a funny look on his face and I knew what he was thinking: "Oh, no, a dame, tagging along." I went with a group. I carried my own gun and my own camera and waded through the streams in the vanguard. And at night when we'd camp, I'd help fix the dinner over an open fire and surprised them with all sorts of snacks packed away in my knapsack and a bottle of brandy.
>
> Other men have been lovers and competitors, but not friends.

Some of this panegyric would appear heavily edited in her autobiography *A Portrait of Joan*. McCabe was a predecessor of Al Steele, her last husband—

a successful businessman with an ego so strong it could not be overwhelmed by a movie star—a quality almost impossible to find in Hollywood.

THE DIVORCE FROM FRANCHOT Tone and the affair with McCabe seem to have made Crawford conscious of an overriding lack in her life—children. If she couldn't sustain a relationship with a man, perhaps children could fill the void. The child who would become known as Christina Crawford was born in June 1939 in Los Angeles and was adopted by Crawford ten days after her birth. The adoption became official in May 1940.

That experience seemed sufficiently encouraging for her to adopt a male child born in June 1941, only to have the birth mother reclaim the child she had named Christopher. She promptly adopted another boy, who had been born in Oklahoma in October 1942. That adoption became final in 1946, with the child also being named Christopher. Those two children would eventually be joined by fraternal twin girls, Cathy and Cindy, who came to live with Joan in the summer of 1947, after their mother died seven days after their birth in Dyersburg, Tennessee. Crawford adopted them from the Tennessee Children's Home, which was closed in 1950 after the director was accused of running a baby-selling operation. Their adoption became official in June 1948.

It was in this period that Crawford bought a 16mm movie camera and began documenting her domestic life. There are about three hours of footage that survive. Some of the footage is in black-and-white, but most of it is in color and involves Charles McCabe.

The home movies feature long panning shots of New York in 1940, apparently taken from the roof of the Hearst Building, and much footage from Christmas 1940—Christina with her nurse, Christina with a new doll, Christina opening gifts. The child is blond and curly-haired, outfitted in a pretty yellow dress. The swimming pool at North Bristol has a fence around it so the child can't fall in.

In one shot McCabe and Crawford are sitting on the grass and Christina walks up and kisses his cheek. In another shot, Christina kisses a portrait photo of McCabe—the same photo he would give to his own children.

In all the shots of Christina, she seems quite happy.

McCabe smokes cigars, Crawford smokes cigarettes, and they travel in a woody station wagon to a hunt club in Millbrook, New York, eighty miles outside of New York City. At one point, McCabe and a group of hunters are standing around a life-sized standee of Wendell Willkie holding out his hand, which provokes the men to engage in a quick flurry of monkey-see-monkey-do handshakes. This would place the Millbrook trip in the fall of 1940, when Willkie was running for president on the Republican ticket against Franklin Roosevelt, and Crawford was on leave from MGM.

Clearly, McCabe trusted Crawford's discretion—the visual evidence could have blown his life sky-high. McCabe is not wearing a wedding ring in any of the shots, and it's clear she's directing him to take specific positions for the camera.

Away from McCabe, there are a few shots of the first Christopher. She gives him milk and burps him.

There's a short sequence of Crawford's birthday on March 23, 1941, full of kids and nannies, followed by "Christina's Birthday, June 11, 1941," complete with mini-airplane rides, horseback rides, clowns, trained pigs, dozens of guests, and a huge birthday cake. Interestingly, there is one Black child among the invitees.

Margaret Sullavan is one of the attendees, along with one of her children, as is Sylvia Lamarr, Joan's stand-in at MGM. In all of these home movies, Crawford's body language is more relaxed, her smile quicker, than in any footage of her before a 35mm movie camera in the same period. The Kodachrome shows off her reddish hair, as well as her freckles, which she didn't bother to disguise except when she went before the MGM cameras.

The home movies peter out around 1941, probably just about the time the affair with Charles McCabe ended, only to be briefly picked up again in 1950, when Crawford was on location in Palm Springs for *The Damned Don't Cry*. Most of that footage involves Steve Cochran dancing and frolicking with girls, although Don DeFore shows up in some random shots at a nightclub.

DESPITE THE MODEST FINANCIAL success of *A Woman's Face*, MGM was obviously beginning to lose interest in the woman who had been one of their franchise players. Case in point: *When Ladies Meet*—another remake, this time of a movie from eight years earlier. The original had starred Ann Harding, Robert Montgomery, and Myrna Loy and was no great shakes. The remake cast Crawford opposite Robert Tayor and the rising Greer Garson and made the original look like a masterpiece. It continued the erratic trajectory of the last several years of Crawford's career at MGM, where a good picture would reliably be followed by an atrocious picture that functioned as a brick wall for the momentum established by the good picture.

Crawford had managed to endure a decade and a half of competing with Norma Shearer and her attendant advantages, but now she had to cope with competition in the person of a redhead from England. Greer Garson was already in her thirties when she came to MGM, but the ace cameramen Joe Ruttenberg managed to disguise that fact. More importantly, she had that ineffable quality of class whose lack had been one of Crawford's primary attributes. As Norma Shearer's career sputtered to a stop, Garson replaced her as MGM's ideal of genteel womanhood.

With the exception of *A Woman's Face*, Crawford's career at MGM after *The Women* is a sad, spavined anticlimax. *Reunion in France* and *Above Suspicion* are innocuous, marginal programmers, but *When Ladies Meet* is a full-fledged embarrassment.

Crawford plays a successful novelist who's in the midst of an affair with her promiscuous publisher, played by Herbert Marshall, who happens to be married to Greer Garson. (The echoes of Charles McCabe must have been deafening.) Waiting in the wings in a ridiculous, insulting part is an overly chipper Robert Taylor, who hangs around just long enough to catch Crawford after Marshall goes back to his wife. This is mostly played as high drama with tremulous line readings and supposed comedy relief from Spring Byington.

The two leading ladies share one interesting scene, where Garson is playing the piano and Crawford comes over, begins to sing, then sits down and is joined by Garson in the song.

There are several ways to play a melodramatic scene like this, and director Robert Z. Leonard opts for unspoken female bonding, which doesn't make much psychological sense and takes the edge off. It also makes Robert Taylor even more expendable than usual. What's clear is that Garson is the focus of both the scene and the movie—she gets the key light and more close-ups.

The gap between moral conflict as portrayed in early 1930s MGM and moral conflict as portrayed in early 1940s MGM is stunning. The former is played for erotic attraction amidst authentic social tension; the latter is plush women's magazine fiction, with the moribund Marshall positioned as an irresistible alternative for two ostensibly smart women. Even Adrian's contributions—it's the last Crawford MGM picture for which he designed costumes—are mostly unattractive.

When Ladies Meet made a profit of more than $800,000.

The picture points up how crucial internal credibility was for Crawford as an actress. She couldn't fake it with technique, had to feel some emotional or psychological connection to the story or her character. That accounts for her rapid rise in a period devoted to stories in sync with her own backstory, and her gradual deflation at a studio with a growing investment in middle-class domestic fantasy.

William Haines remembered her during this period. "[She] never discussed it. She'd drop in at the house to talk but not about that. Just to know someone was there who believed. . . . I'd seen her overcome many things—win a friend from an enemy. She's fearless when she wants something. A bad picture she talks about too much, a good one she never mentions. She's unique. A capacity for lots of things—for work, for friends, for hate and for love."

CHAPTER TEN

WITH HER FINELY TUNED antennae for studio politics, Crawford would have known that *When Ladies Meet* was an X-ray of two careers—one ascending, one descending. She could feel—no, see—the studio beginning a search for the next iteration of Joan Crawford, or, failing that, the next big thing who could replace Joan Crawford.

And there was another problem. Crawford was now high-priced talent. In 1936 she had earned $302,307, in 1937 $351,538, in 1940 $318,365, and in 1941 $266,538. Money like that demanded equivalent returns at the box office, and it wasn't invariably the case.

Crawford's discontent was growing, not because of any one thing, but because of everything—failed marriages, her dislike of most of the pictures she was making. The children were probably an attempt at filling the vacancy she felt in other areas of her life. She would occasionally complain about the lack of quality pictures at the studio, but that wasn't really true. *Mrs. Miniver*, *Random Harvest*, and *Waterloo Bridge* were all examples of quality MGM pictures for a new era. The problem was that none of them starred Joan Crawford.

In the late spring of 1940, a play by a young writer named Tennessee Williams was submitted to Crawford by the Theatre Guild. Williams grumbled that a "film star" without stage credits was the Guild's first choice for *Battle of Angels*—an early draft of *Orpheus Descending*, which in time became the film *The Fugitive Kind*. "They want everything to be subordinated to her part,"

Wiliams wrote, "and of course this is not altogether satisfactory to me and just between ourselves, Miss Crawford, if she takes the part, will have just as much of the play as I think belongs to her."

Two months later, Crawford rejected the play as "low and common," a remark that deeply offended Williams. "Certainly the play is mainly a study of sexual passion," he wrote Lawrence Langner, the head of the Theatre Guild, "but serious rather than titillating, so I don't believe any responsible critic would find any validity in such a charge." Williams seems to have been relieved, and turned his attentions to Miriam Hopkins, whom he thought ideal. His regard for Crawford would increase in later years.

THE MGM METHOD WAS for every publicist to have personal responsibility for three to four stars. Crawford had drawn a young man named Walter Seltzer, who would eventually become a producer of quality pictures (*One-Eyed Jacks, Will Penny*). Seltzer called her the "last of the movie queens. Never in the thousands of times in our association, was she ever less than perfectly dressed, in full makeup. She was never casual, not even if it was for an audience of only 20 fans. She had an image of herself and she lived up to it."

At the same time, Seltzer thought she had a sense of humor about herself. She always had mood music playing in the house, but she would laugh at the performative fakery of it. Crawford told Seltzer that she had to have certain situations in every film: a waitress who married a stockbroker, an heiress who married a chauffeur. That way she would have a mixture of high and low, as well as scenes calling for beautiful clothes.

Seltzer noticed how she would study her stills for hours, looking for flaws. "She hated imperfections in her image." And there was her preoccupation with cleanliness. Seltzer would often find her polishing the furniture at North Bristol whenever he arrived there, and the place was invariably immaculate.

When she wanted to buy Seltzer a present, she would tell him she wanted to buy a present for some other man and ask for Seltzer's advice. She would then take him to a jeweler's in Beverly Hills, ask him to pick out some jewelry, then do some *hondling* over price. After the deal was done, she would hand the jewelry to Seltzer and tell him, "You damn fool, you could have had a watch."

She stood by him when he got into trouble. A studio tour was being given by a guide who happened to be a friend of Seltzer's. The guide told his group that MGM's stages three and four could be connected and form "the biggest sound stage in the world." Seltzer happened to be passing by and said, "You're full of shit; they have a bigger stage at Warner's." A week later he was fired from his $45-a-week job.

Crawford was furious. She was going to go to Mayer to plead Seltzer's case, but Seltzer told her not to, that it might upset a job he was setting up at Warner's.

"What can I do for you?" Crawford asked.

Seltzer told her that she could hire him as a freelance publicist. "Absolutely," she said. "And I'll pay you what MGM did."

Seltzer worked ancillary publicity for Crawford along with his Warner's gig until he enlisted in the Marines in 1943. Crawford couldn't resist sticking it to MGM—she changed her phone number and wouldn't give it to the studio. If they wanted to get in touch with her, they had to call Seltzer first.

CLARK GABLE HAD MARRIED Carole Lombard in 1939, which put an end to his occasional affair with Crawford. In January 1942, Lombard and her mother were returning to Hollywood from a War Bond tour when their plane took off from Las Vegas and promptly slammed into a mountain. Everybody on the plane died instantly. No one has ever been able to figure out the how of the accident—the pilot was experienced, and everyone who flew in that area knew the mountain was there.

Clark Gable came to Crawford when he found out that his wife was dead. Like everyone else in Hollywood, Crawford had adored Lombard for her humor, her zest, and the clarity of her character. Crawford told friends that she and Gable didn't make love, that she just held him while he cried.

Crawford volunteered to take over a picture Lombard had been scheduled to start shooting at Columbia, and donated her salary to charity—$50,000 to the Red Cross, $25,000 to Franklin Roosevelt's Paralysis Fund, $25,000 to the Motion Picture Relief Fund, and $12,500 to Navy Relief. It was a light romantic comedy called *They All Kissed the Bride* opposite Melvyn Douglas.

While she was shooting the picture, the Columbia contract actor Glenn Ford caught her eye, and the two embarked on a brief affair. "We enjoyed each other's company very much for a while," Ford said. "I wouldn't call it a love affair. She was too powerful a presence for that. I don't think she wanted that. She was very much sufficient unto herself."

The cameraman was the great Joe Walker, the ace responsible for the luminous photography in Frank Capra's pictures. Walker remembered going out to a party at Mocambo with his wife on a weeknight. He passed by a table where Crawford and her party were having a good time. "Joe," she yelled. "What the hell are you doing here?"

"I might ask the same of you—what are *you* doing here at this hour? You have close-ups tomorrow."

"Yeah, but goddamnit, you're photographing me—you gotta have your rest!"

As it turned out, Walker did a good job, as did Crawford. *They All Kissed the Bride* doesn't sound like much—a hard-driving female executive is clobbered by the ideal combination of love and lust when she meets a reporter writing a negative book about her company—but it's a pleasant watch, assuming you can stomach the humiliation Crawford's character has to endure in order to get in touch with her inner wife. This was regarded as essential for comedies involving professional women in that period—see *Woman of the Year*.

Crawford was working at an unfamiliar studio, opposite a crackerjack cast of farceurs (Melvyn Douglas, Billie Burke, Roland Young) and with material that wasn't really in her wheelhouse. But she acquits herself very well, with energy, good timing, and an admirable sense of fun, especially considering the circumstances.

WALTER SELTZER SAID THAT Crawford developed a crush on Cary Grant and unsuccessfully pursued him—the only time Seltzer saw her go after a man.

When Seltzer broke the news that Grant had married the dime store heiress Barbara Hutton, she said, "What has Woolworth's got that I haven't?"

Losing out on Cary Grant might have impelled her to marry for the third time, to Phillip Terry, a good-looking actor of no distinction whatever—by all odds the most incomprehensible of her marriages.

Terry was born Frederick Kormann in 1907 to an oil-rigging family and was hired in 1937 by MGM on one of their speculative $75-a-week contracts. He grew to be more than six feet tall, husky, good-looking in a suit or, presumably, out of a suit. Crawford liked him because he was "gentle, understanding, loved poetry and reading aloud." If that sounds vague, so was the marriage. "I've never really known why I married Phillip," she would say in retrospect.

They were introduced by a publicist named Harry Mines, who had met Terry at Paramount. Terry knew Mines and Crawford were friends and indicated he'd like to meet her, so Mines arranged it.

One night Crawford called Mines and asked him to come over to the house. He arrived to find Crawford and Terry sitting on the sofa facing the one where Mines was to sit. Their physical proximity instantly communicated that they were in a relationship.

"I want you to be the first to know that Phil and I are going to marry," Crawford told Mines. He convinced her to give the story to Louella Parsons.

"His very presence was . . . anodyne, comfortable and comforting," remembered Crawford, which sounds suspiciously like a recipe for boredom. "The men who'd attracted me before were passionate, volatile. The man in New York [Charles McCabe] was a dynamo. But I couldn't have him, and here was his antithesis, an easy-going, unpretentious man who seemed to adore me, who was calm and absolutely uncomplicated." Walter Seltzer said Terry's main distinction was that he could knit as fast as Crawford, and "she could knit half of a sweater while watching a movie."

They were married on July 21, 1942, at the home of the prestigious Hollywood lawyer Neil McCarthy. One of MGM's biggest stars had married a bit player, and, with the marginal exception of playing Ray Milland's concerned brother in *The Lost Weekend*, Terry stayed a bit player. What he had going for him was a slight resemblance to a clean-shaven Clark Gable.

In comparison to her first two marriages, the marriage to Terry was dynamically unbalanced. Crawford would come to believe that she "mistook peace of mind for love, and at the time believed in it with all my heart."

What actually seems to have motivated the marriage was less than love, and probably not even lust—Phil Terry was good with Crawford's children, and willing to devote as much of his plentiful spare time to them as was necessary.

WHEN WORLD WAR II came to Hollywood, most stars who didn't enlist still contributed. Crawford did all she could, directly and indirectly. She had stayed friendly with Laurence Olivier after her divorce from Douglas Fairbanks Jr., and the merry-go-round made a full circle when Olivier divorced Jill Esmond to make room for Vivien Leigh. Esmond and her five-year-old son Tarquin Olivier moved to New York and were living with Jessica Tandy in her small apartment, but there was no work. Crawford came to the rescue when she sent a letter to Esmond saying, "Come have a holiday with me." Esmond and Tarquin moved to California in a house next door to Crawford that she rented for her guests.

"Her adopted daughter," wrote Esmond on July 2, 1941, "is charming and Joan is very sweet with her. Joan had just got her adopted son, about seven weeks old. I gave him his bottle and it was lovely to hold a very tiny baby again. I wonder if she will get fed up with them. . . . Apart from the children Joan seemed just the same. We discussed the latest films and talked of Greta Garbo, and after dinner saw a very poor film in her private theater. Just the same dull routine as eight years ago. She is still a bore and has no humor."

So much for refugee gratitude. Tarquin Olivier's own recollection of the house was "of a goody two-shoes atmosphere, all pretend and prissy, like the plastic covers on their chintz cushions."

While Crawford was experimenting with domesticity, John Garfield and Bette Davis came up with the idea for the Hollywood Canteen, which was located at 1415 Cahuenga Boulevard just south of Sunset. The art director Al Ybarra wangled $2,500 of materials from studios, and their employees did the carpentry and installations. The Canteen opened on October 3,

1942, with Spencer Tracy pulling a shift washing dishes and signing autographs. The Canteen was open from 7 p.m. to midnight six days a week and was free for all servicemen who might want to be waited on by Hollywood stars. Mary (Mrs. John) Ford ran the kitchen for the duration of the war, while Kay Kyser and his band reliably held down the music stand on Saturday nights.

Alcohol was not served, but sandwiches, coffee, soft drinks, and cigarettes were all free. The Canteen was racially integrated, although Mary Ford notified the Los Angeles Police whenever she observed interracial dancing. As it happened, interracial dancing was not illegal, so the police forwarded her complaints to her husband in London, who was preparing to fly to Morocco to photograph an Allied invasion. John Ford told the LAPD that his wife "was inclined to become agitated and excited about racial matters" and they "should take Mrs. Ford out of the Canteen" if they so desired.

As Bette Davis remembered, "A soldier might ask Hedy Lamarr to pour another cup of coffee while Marlene Dietrich served sandwiches and Basil Rathbone carried a tray of used dishes back to the kitchen." Five to six thousand men came every night.

Everybody pitched in to aid the war effort. In July 1942, Tyrone Power and his wife Annabella opened their house on Saltair to the public as a benefit for the Free French Relief Committee. Booths were set up in the garden where stars auctioned off personal belongings. Hundreds of people arrived to gawk at the movie stars, not to mention trample the garden.

Fred MacMurray sold off his old hunting equipment, while Crawford's contribution was a selection of lingerie that went for sums Power and his wife thought outrageous.

Otherwise, life went on. One day on Rodeo Drive Crawford ran into Jack Oakie, who asked her why she wasn't working. She told him that she was focused on her children. They chatted for a while and she told him that she had enjoyed taking nude sunbaths on her lawn until the Goodyear blimp started flying over the house at suspiciously low elevations.

"What did you do?" asked Oakie.

"I put a towel over my head so they wouldn't know who I was."

ENTERTAINING WENT ON AS before. Dinners were formal, even if there were only six people there. The evening began at four, and after dinner Crawford would run films, where she would occasionally talk back to the movie. There would be a butler, two maids, and nameplates for the guests, who at this point often included Norman and Sally Foster, Richard Cromwell, Mary Martin and Richard Halliday, Sidney Guilaroff, and Mae Murray, now a dazed relic of the silent days at MGM.

Crawford always made room for a few newbies as well. Once, Cedric Hardwicke and Roland Young were dinner guests when the butler asked if there was anything else he could get them.

"I'll take a mink coat," said Hardwicke. Young countered by saying he preferred a silver fox. The butler consulted Crawford, after which he fetched the appropriate furs. Both men put them on and evidently looked quite fetching.

Crawford retained her nodding interest in Christian Science and would occasionally bring out Mary Baker Eddy's *Science and Health*, even though she thought the philosophy behind the book made its adherents too emotionally cold—Ginger Rogers, for instance. Later, she would say the same thing about Doris Day.

REUNION IN FRANCE WAS directed by Jules Dassin, a thirty-year-old being groomed in the MGM system he had grown to despise. He didn't like the studio and he particularly didn't like Louis B. Mayer, saying that "Mayer's arm around your shoulder meant his hand was closer to your throat."

When Dassin was told that Crawford would be his star, he inquired about the script. "The *script*?" Mayer shouted. "Did you hear me say 'Joan Crawford?'"

As it happened, the script was indeed the problem, working Dassin up into a fine rage that script conferences did little to ameliorate. As far as the production team was concerned, Crawford's wardrobe was more important than the script.

After one argument with producer Bernie Hyman, Dassin was led to a window overlooking the parking lot. "Which is your car?" Hyman asked. Dassin pointed to a car that had a roof, four wheels, and not much else. Hyman pointed to a gorgeous Cadillac and said, "That's my car, and I say the script is wonderful."

The shoot didn't improve Dassin's mood. He yelled "Cut!" whenever Crawford did something he didn't like, and he yelled "Cut!" a lot, which led Crawford to walk off the set, which in turn led Mayer to tell Dassin he was fired. That night, Crawford invited Dassin to dinner at her house.

"Hey, Julie—may I call you 'Julie'?—do you think I'm a bad actress?"

Dassin replied that he thought she was a good actress who made the mistake of sometimes "acting the lady—or what you conceive the lady to be."

"Really? Is that what I do?"

She suggested they start all over again, but asked him not to yell "Cut!" around her.

"If I don't think a scene is right, what do I do?"

"Just run a finger over your eyebrow."

"What if you're not in a position to see it? What if your back is turned?"

"Brother, when I'm in front of that camera, whatever goes on anywhere on that set, *I see*."

Dassin was back on the picture. For the rest of the shoot, he didn't say "Cut!" just ran a finger over his eyebrow, and "wherever she was, she knew it, and the scene would start again."

John Wayne was borrowed from Republic to be Crawford's leading man and wisely concentrated on keeping out of the potential line of fire. His primary memory of the film was watching Crawford enter the stage in the morning followed by her secretary, her wardrobe mistress, and her makeup man. Bringing up the rear was Phil Terry holding her dog.

On the last day of production, Dassin was on a camera boom for a tracking shot on a railroad set. As the actors began to move, so did the camera, and Dassin was amazed to see Crawford gently swing her hip and nudge costar Philip Dorn out of the shot.

Dassin was enraged, jumped off the boom, and confronted Crawford. "I was raised in Harlem," he would remember, "and the street fighter spirit came out in me and I heard myself saying, 'I'm going to punch you in the jaw.'"

Crawford ripped off her hat, threw her purse to the ground, and confronted Dassin. "Go ahead," she said.

Thus challenged, Dassin did the only thing he could do. It was 10:30 a.m., he yelled "Lunch!" and walked off the set.

Joe Mankiewicz had taken over production duties from Bernie Hyman and held an emergency meeting. He told Dassin to finish the picture by giving instructions to the cameraman, who would in turn relay them to Crawford. That was the way the film limped to its conclusion.

After the last shot was in the can, Crawford strode up to Dassin and said, "Hold out your hand." She dropped a beautiful pair of cuff links into them and said, "I enjoyed working with you."

"You *bitch*," replied Dassin. "That is really a nasty thing to do."

Crawford and Dassin eventually became social friends, although she always regarded the picture with disdain. *Reunion in France* was Dassin's last MGM picture. He relocated to Universal, where he made *The Naked City* and *Brute Force*, after which he was blacklisted and went to Europe, then again reconstituted his career with *Rififi* and *Never on Sunday*.

Crawford's last picture under contract at MGM was *Above Suspicion*, opposite Fred MacMurray. They play newlyweds who elude Nazis chasing them through a soundstage Europe. In his last picture before dying of a heart attack while golfing, Conrad Veidt plays a good German, while Basil Rathbone plays a bad German.

Above Suspicion is not a terrible picture so much as a deeply ordinary, inauthentic one. It's more stylish than most movies directed by Richard Thorpe, but the script is played blithely, as if everyone is under the spell of Hitchcock's *The 39 Steps*. As a result, the stakes seem low. Not surprisingly, it mimics a scene in Hitchcock's *The Man Who Knew Too Much* where an assassination is carried out during a concert.

While Crawford was finishing up eighteen years at MGM with indifferent programmers, Greer Garson was making *Mrs. Miniver, Random Harvest*, and *Madame Curie*. The message was clear.

Crawford's correspondence with George Cukor shows that she was fully aware that *Above Suspicion* was junk ("I just finished another Metro stinker. . . . Golly it lasted almost four months"). It also indicates that she had not yet made the decision to leave the studio. She asked Cukor to take a look at an Anita Loos script called "Women in Uniform" that she thought would work well for both of them. "Ask Anita to send you a script, will you?"

By spring she was moving toward a decision. In April 1943, Crawford asked for and was granted six months off from the studio. It didn't take that long for her to make up her mind. In May, she called Louis B. Mayer and told him she wanted out. Back in New York, Nick Schenck wanted to hold her to her contract, which had some time to run. After all, *Reunion in France* and *Above Suspicion* had both made money. Mayer told his boss that it was wrong to try to squeeze the last few shekels out of an actress who had been extremely loyal, not to mention hardworking, and had made the company millions of dollars. Schenck relented. On July 29, 1943, MGM officially canceled Crawford's contract and paid her $100,000 in settlement.

On her last day at MGM, Joan Crawford drove to the studio alone. She cleared out her dressing room by dumping all her belongings into valises, then washed the small kitchen and vacuumed the carpets. Nobody was going to be able to say she left any mess behind.

She loaded everything into her car, then drove through the rear gate. She never looked back.

As Norma Shearer could attest, Crawford was capable of holding a grudge, but her feelings about MGM were more complicated than many imagined. Near the end of her life, she would say, "L. B. Mayer was my father, my father confessor; the *best* friend I ever had." But she still felt she had been ill-used. "Mr. Mayer cried when I told him I was going to leave and said, 'Why, Joan, we practically raised you here; you're one of the family.'

"That was the trouble; I was the sister who did the work and brought home the money. They thought I'd always be around for that." In life, as well as on-screen, she felt cast in the thankless part of the loyal, put-upon child.

A few weeks before MGM issued her the severance check, a small box appeared on the lower-left corner of the front page of the *Film Daily*: "Crawford to Warners Under Long Termer. . . . Warners has signed Joan Crawford, long under contract to Metro, to an exclusive long-term contract. Her first film for the company will be 'Night Shift.'"

CHAPTER ELEVEN

I F MGM WAS A velvet-lined coffin, at least it was constructed of polished mahogany. By comparison, Warner Bros. was a plain pine box.

"It was the whole philosophy of the studio to never give anyone credit, or a percentage of stocks," said the producer Henry Blanke, who came to America in the silent days as Ernst Lubitsch's assistant and spent the rest of his career at Warners. "It was a good philosophy, I must say. The reason they became a big studio was not the invention of sound, but because of this philosophy.

"Jack [Warner] was tough and we were tough as a studio. And we knew it. That was 'our' philosophy. If the other studios were tough, we'd be tougher, more realistic. The only theory we followed was that the characters had to talk like real people. That's the way we got away with it."

As the screenwriter Catherine Turney put it, "You never knew any stars at MGM, they were shielded, [but] everybody knew everybody else at Warner Brothers. It was just one great big unhappy family."

Harry Warner ran the business, and Jack Warner ran production through successive brilliant lieutenants: Darryl Zanuck and Hal Wallis. Harry and Jack never got along, so tended to stay out of each other's way as much as possible. Harry was an observant Jew who believed that movies should serve the social good. Jack was observant about movies and women, unobservant about everything else, and believed in Jack Warner.

"[Jack] won't stand up in a pinch," said Brian Foy, who ran the Warner B movie operation for decades. "He'll shake your hand on Friday and tell you you're set for two years, then go to New York, call on Monday and fire you. I know him well and I like him, don't get me wrong, but he has no guts."

Actually, Jack Warner had plenty of guts, as the cumulative product of the studio attested. What he lacked was loyalty. Jack resented actors—resented paying them a lot of money, resented their fame. Louis B. Mayer liked and appreciated women and placed powerful women throughout his studio—Margaret Booth was head of editorial, Anita Loos was a mainstay of the writers' department. Most importantly, Mayer listened to women—Ida Koverman, Mayer's head secretary, was widely regarded as someone who could make or break careers at MGM.

But Warners had only one woman department head, Jean Burt Reilly, and Jack Warner ignored her. Generally speaking, actresses were miserable at Warners, because Jack was scared of them and compensated by bringing the hammer down at the slightest sign of independent thought. Bette Davis and Jack had epic battles, and in 1943 Olivia de Havilland sued the studio over its habit of putting her on suspension and adding the time spent haggling to the back end of her contract. Amazingly, de Havilland won in court, and the decision began the slow-motion dismemberment of the studio system's standard seven-year contract.

Writers weren't any happier at Warners than actors. "They didn't trust us," said Stephen Longstreet. "They needed us. They needed us to sew the dialogue into the action, because basically that was what movies were—action. We had no real power. No writer ever stopped a scene to tell the director it was being done wrong. The studio always put three or four writers on the same project. You didn't know that. You'd be off doing your version and they'd be off doing theirs.

"Credit stealing was going on all over the place. It was easy to steal a credit from a writer—particularly if you were a smart producer. You would have the writer do all the work and then you would add a few lines . . . and convince the head office that you wrote most of the script. It was before the time of a strong writers' union—we had no real arbitration. We were there to mend story lines, to fix construction. We were not there to write great scripts."

Joan Crawford would assert that she was without work for three years after leaving MGM, but that was a gross exaggeration. It was actually about a year that undoubtedly felt like three years. During that year, she turned down several scripts, many of which had Bette Davis's fingerprints on them. Jack Warner sent Crawford one script featuring a young ingenue, but she sent it back, saying, "I'm too old. Give it to Joan Leslie." She also turned down *Never Say Goodbye*, a script by Edmund Goulding that was later done with Errol Flynn and Eleanor Parker.

While Crawford bided her time, she put in Monday nights at the Hollywood Canteen, working behind the snack bar serving coffee and donuts, then dancing with the servicemen passing through Los Angeles. One sailor danced with her and told her she looked just like Joan Crawford.

"I *am* Joan Crawford," she replied.

"Yeah? Whatever happened to ya?"

That thought had already occurred to Crawford—for the first time in her adult life, she was functionally unemployed. Crawford's cook went to work in a defense factory, while Christina's nurse enlisted in the WAVES. Domestic help slowly vanished, so Crawford and her new husband had to do most of the work. Crawford planted a Victory Garden in the front yard that provided tomatoes, beans, carrots, radishes, and corn. Since help couldn't be found, Crawford closed down part of the house.

Phil Terry would take the children on outings to the Farmer's Market while Crawford cooked, did laundry, tried to exhaust herself, and failed. As she remembered, "Outsiders writing of Phillip and me described these years as the most serene of my life. They were the most difficult. . . . I tried to like it, tried to fill it with meaning [but] . . . frankly I was bored because the actress is half of this woman and the actress had no outlet."

Crawford kept rejecting scripts until Jack Warner shipped off a memo to her saying that actors at Warner Bros. had to earn their salaries. Right after that, Crawford appeared in Warner's office asking to see him. If there was anything that rattled Jack Warner, it was an angry woman. As he disappeared through the back door he told his secretary to inform Crawford he wasn't in.

Crawford left a message for her boss: she agreed with him that actors shouldn't be paid for not working; she therefore wanted to be taken off salary until they agreed on a film project. As of January 1, 1944, Crawford was off salary.

Ten months later, a reporter wrote, "There is a general feeling that Miss Crawford is through as a motion picture actress. In a town where disaster has an almost obscene attraction for the populace, this tidbit is repeated with unction by individuals who have every reason to regard Miss Crawford with admiration and even gratitude."

While all this was going on, Lew Wasserman, Crawford's agent at MCA, kept telling her she was not washed up, that renewed success was only a matter of time. "Lew Wasserman kept my faith bright and shining," Crawford would say.

There was nothing to do but wait for something to happen.

———◆———

THE GENESIS OF *MILDRED Pierce* came in a remark that MGM writer-producer James Kevin McGuinness made to James M. Cain. "There's one [story] that's never failed yet," said McGuinness, "and that's the story of a woman who uses men to gain her ends." Cain said that a light immediately went on. "I thought, well, it's never failed yet, that sounds like a pretty good story to me."

Cain made the title character of his 1941 novel a woman who wasn't a femme fatale, but rather an ambitious housewife with the willingness to use men out of devotion to her daughter.

The problem for a movie adaptation was that, while the story didn't have the sadomasochistic sex that animated Cain's *Double Indemnity* and *The Postman Always Rings Twice*, it was still very dicey material. In September 1941, Val Lewton, who was David O. Selznick's story editor before he became a producer at RKO, wrote Geoffrey Shurlock at the Breen office asking his opinion of Cain's novel.

Shurlock responded with a small but meaningful roster of changes that would be necessary before a film of the novel could even be considered:

The affair between Mildred and Monte Beragon had to go.

Mildred and Monte couldn't marry, otherwise his affair with Mildred's daughter would reek of illicit sex.

The quarrel between Mildred and her husband couldn't be over his affair, but over something else—money, perhaps.

Selznick decided to pass, as did everybody else, but early in 1944 Warner Bros.

bought the novel. They submitted a preliminary treatment, and Joseph Breen responded by telling Warner that although changes could be made to bring it within the bounds of the Production Code, "the story contains so many sordid and repellent elements that we feel that the finished picture would not only be highly questionable . . . but would, likewise, meet with a great deal of difficulty in its release—not only through Censor Boards, but from other public groups as well."

Warners submitted a temporary script for the picture in the middle of August, but before the matter was settled it seemed that half the writers in Burbank took a spin on *Mildred Pierce*. In most cases, the attempts only made things worse.

The roster of writers who worked on the script included Thames Williamson, Catherine Turney, Margaret Buell Wilder, Albert Maltz, Margaret Gruen, and William Faulkner. Faulkner's script had particularly inappropriate diversions. He titled his script "House on the Sand" and spent a great deal of time delineating the financial arrangements behind Mildred's restaurant, apparently because he was offended by James M. Cain's indifference toward money. As one critic noted, in this version, "Mildred's world seems more akin to the Snopes' of Faulkner's novels than it does to either the world of Cain or screenwriter [Ranald] MacDougall."

The producer on the project was Jerry Wald, who wanted to move the story out of the 1930s and the Depression, wanted to give it a sense of upward mobility. Wald pushed the writers to give Mildred's lover Monte a surface elegance barely concealing his moral corruption.

After Faulkner left the project, Catherine Turney worked on a more faithful adaptation that hewed closely to Cain's novel. "I thought James Cain was very sympathetic to the woman's problem," Turney told the historian Joanne Yeck. "But [director Michael] Curtiz didn't understand the story. He couldn't believe anyone cared about a Glendale housewife who baked pies."

Everything changed when Jerry Wald saw Billy Wilder's *Double Indemnity* and, as Turney put it, "decided that he was never going to do another picture that wasn't in flashback form! Michael Curtiz [also] wanted to add a flashback and a murder. I argued with them, but they were determined." Against her better judgment, Turney added the murder, after which Bette Davis asked her to write *A Stolen Life*. Ranald MacDougall completed the script.

Turney worked on pictures for all three of the major female stars at Warner's—Davis, Crawford, and Stanwyck. She liked both Davis and Crawford, Stanwyck not so much. "I don't think she liked women very much. She was polite, but I never felt any warmth there."

In retrospect, Jerry Wald's decision to surround Mildred with a murder mystery was a masterstroke, upping the stakes and giving the story a larger dimension than the basically domestic Cain original. It also served a tactical function: Monte is shot in the beginning, and while the audience is led to think the killer is Mildred, the murderer is actually her morally bankrupt daughter Veda. Monte's death and Veda's eventual capture simultaneously punish both of them for their affair, negating the Breen office's primary objection to that plot point, while giving *Mildred Pierce* the bleak *noir* overtones that help make the picture memorable.

By making Veda a murderer as well as the agent of her mother's destruction, Wald completely changed the parameters of the story, thereby greatly irritating James M. Cain. "Jesus Christ! What kind of fantastic superimposition was that; it had no bearing whatsoever on the theme! It made no sense to me, so I was never really able to praise [the movie of] *Mildred Pierce*."

Cain would eventually express some of his dissatisfaction to Crawford, although in gentler terms, and she replied, "All I can say is, they tried it without the murder, and the thing seemed flat. The murder pulled it together somehow."

As far as the star was concerned, it seems to have come down to either Stanwyck or Crawford. Privately, Crawford would give credit to Lew Wasserman's persistence in convincing Jack Warner to cast her. But Jerry Wald liked the idea of Crawford as well— a favorite saying of his was that "talent was never over, just misplaced." Wald and Crawford would make a batch of pictures together, some of them first-rate.

Martin Jurow would become a successful producer (*Breakfast at Tiffany's*), but at the time he was working as Jack Warner's assistant. According to Jurow, he was looking out the window of Jack's office when he saw Crawford arriving on the lot to test for the part of Mildred. Her posture was that of a weary working woman, shoulders slumped, eyes fixed on the sidewalk.

"Do you think I should go outside and welcome Joan Crawford?" Jurow asked his boss. "Maybe even escort her to the wardrobe department?"

"That has-been?" snapped Warner. "Why waste my time? We're only using her because Stanwyck's too busy! I've got better things to do than say hello to that dame."

That certainly sounds like Warner, who thought actors were overpaid prima donnas who took attention away from where it should rightfully go: the prima donna named Jack Warner.

Jurow went outside to greet Crawford anyway and told her how thrilled everybody was that she was at Warner's. "As I talked, a striking transformation took place. Her posture turned regal. Her eyes glowed. Her smile combined simple gratitude with queenly *noblesse oblige*. Yes, she was indeed thrilled to be at Warner Bros. Yes, she couldn't wait to do the test. And she hoped to do justice to a part as rich and rewarding as Mildred Pierce. Oh, and thank you so much for the personal greeting.

"In a matter of mere moments, Joan Crawford Unemployed Actress became Joan Crawford Movie Star. . . . Even Joan Crawford needed to feel sought-after."

What all this meant was that Crawford's days in the wilderness were over. "The worst time in my life was the period after I left MGM and before I made *Mildred Pierce*," she would say.

MELODRAMA WAS MICHAEL CURTIZ'S meal of choice, often served with a subtle expressionism. His most recent hits had been *Yankee Doodle Dandy* and *Casablanca*, so Crawford and company were getting a director at the height of his powers. Curtiz's dynamic visual flair would carry the film on his back, although there were times when Crawford had her doubts.

By November 1944, the picture was moving toward production, except for the fact that critical details such as the cameraman still needed to be settled. Jerry Wald sent out a memo on November 6 pointing out that Ernest Haller, Bert Glennon, Sol Polito, and Carl Guthrie had all made photographic tests of Crawford, and all had been failures.

"On Tuesday we are making additional tests with Pev Marley," wrote Wald to studio manager T. C. Wright. "This note is not written to you in criticism but rather to ask your advice. We do know that somewhere along the line these cameramen are missing. Both Curtiz and I looked at the film she made at Metro and there is no doubt that men like Bob Planck and Ray June managed to capture on the screen what we are trying to get for Miss Crawford. . . .

"As you know, both Curtiz and I feel that Jimmie [James Wong] Howe would be the logical man for this picture but from my past conversation with you regarding his availability, you hold very little hope that we'll have him in time for our picture."

Crawford correctly regarded James Wong Howe as the best, most versatile cameraman in Hollywood. Whatever the deficiencies of his test, Ernest Haller ended up shooting *Mildred Pierce* and did a fine job.

Another problem was the part of Mildred's viperous daughter, whom she nevertheless adores. A half dozen actresses tested for the part. Ranald MacDougall remembered that "Joan never forgot where she came from and how lucky she was, she felt, to have her stardom. She was the definitive Movie Star, but she never forgot that once she [had] needed help. . . . For *Mildred Pierce* she came into the studio herself to do a test with Ann Blyth, to help her get the role of Mildred's daughter. It was practically unheard of for a star of her caliber to do any kind of test, much less with an unknown trying for a supporting part. But she knew that the actress who played her daughter would affect her own performance and she also knew it would help Ann Blyth. They remained friends for life.

"Crawford was a loyal friend, and, believe me, crews loved her. She never made trouble for anyone, but I think what I remember most is how she showed up to make that test with Ann."

The film was scheduled to begin shooting December 6, but MacDougall was still writing, so the start date was pushed back to the week of December 16. Shooting continued until the week of March 17, 1945, about thirty days over schedule.

Clearly, everybody concerned was trying to make the picture as good as possible, although Michael Curtiz's manner and method were basically identical with that of a Marine Corps drill instructor. When the costumer Milo Anderson brought Crawford on the set to show off a dress, Curtiz was on a camera boom ten feet above the set and exploded: "You fucking little pansy son of a bitch, I told you no [shoulder] pads!"

A couple of days into the shoot, Jerry Wald called Henry Rogers, the founder of Rogers & Cowan publicity, to suggest that he start an Oscar campaign for Crawford.

"But you've only been shooting for two days!" Rogers protested.

"So? How about it?"

Rogers dutifully called Hedda Hopper and told her Crawford was excelling in the part.

"You're full of shit," Hopper replied.

"Do it, Hedda," Rogers said. "What have you got to lose?"

Hopper mumbled something about "That crazy Jack Warner" and printed an item: "Insiders say Joan Crawford is giving such a great performance in *Mildred Pierce* that an Oscar is predicted."

Jerry Wald called Rogers: "Really great work—keep it up!"

"What about Joan?"

"Don't tell her. Just go ahead and do it." Soon, items started appearing in other columns. Far out in the Pacific, a wave began to form.

About six weeks later, Jerry Wald called Rogers at midnight. "I think it's going to work. I just came from a party at Hal Wallis' and he said, 'I think Joan Crawford has a good chance for an Oscar. I don't know where I heard it. I think I read it somewhere.'"

When *Mildred Pierce* opened in the fall of 1945, the reviews were unanimous. "*Mildred Pierce* Smashing Joan Crawford Triumph," headlined *The Hollywood Reporter*, while *Variety* called it "a "potent vehicle earmarked for important boxoffice in all situations and justifies Miss Crawford's two-year wait for the proper story."

Even *The New York Times*, whose movie critic Bosley Crowther always regarded Crawford with disdain, indicated grudging approval: "Joan Crawford is playing a most troubled lady and giving a sincere and generally effective characterization of same. . . . It is a tribute to Miss Crawford's art that Mildred comes through as well as she does."

James Agee was considerably more perceptive as well as enthusiastic, and called the film a "nasty, gratifying version of the James Cain novel about . . . the power of the native passion for money and all that money can buy. Attempt [is] made to sell Mildred as noble when she is merely idiotic or at best pathetic, but constant, virulent, lambent attention to money and its effects, and more authentic suggestions of sex than one hopes to see in American films. Excellent work by Joan Crawford. . . . As movies go, it is one of the few anywhere near honest ones."

The film was passed with very minor changes by censors in Kansas, and with one or two cuts in Ohio. Only Ireland banned the picture outright because "The sanctity of marriage is treated as a joke and moral consideration of any kind is ignored. Seductive situation, dubious dialogue, murder and accommodating husband are minor features of this film."

It was obvious that Crawford was going to get an Oscar nomination at the very least, and she was carried away by the thrill of possibly winning. But the more she thought about it, the more terrified she got. Her old fear of appearing before a live audience kicked in. A few days before the ceremony, she was panicked. "Henry, I don't think I can do it," she told Henry Rogers.

"Do what?"

"Go to the Academy Awards."

"But you've got to."

"I am so frightened. I cannot stand the probability of losing and having people feeling sorry for me. And if I win, there's the agony of walking on the stage."

Rogers called Jerry Wald. "You gotta talk to her. She's got to go."

"I'll try."

On the day of the ceremony, Crawford called Rogers. "Henry, I've got the flu." She claimed a temperature of 104, which would have put her in delirium. Try as he might, Rogers could not convince her to go to the ceremony.

Unfazed, Henry Rogers simply made arrangements for a photographer to be at Crawford's house in case she won, with Mike Curtiz delivering the Oscar afterward, which was exactly what happened. Crawford later claimed that the excitement and the flannel robe she was wearing caused her to overheat, so that her fever conveniently broke.

Right after the ceremony, Crawford wrote Hopper: "Hedda dear, Over a year ago you wrote in your column that I'd win the award—You were so helpful and encouraging. May I say I'm deeply grateful. Joan."

The Academy Award meant a great deal to Crawford. Actually, it meant everything: Status. Excellence. *Acceptance.* A shiny symbol of how wrong MGM had been. "If I had the money, I'd build a house around Oscar," she told a friend. "A shrine at the foot of the stairs," with a light shining on the golden statue. As for the financials, *Mildred Pierce* returned rentals of nearly $6 million on a cost of $1.4 million—a massive hit.

The film that emerged from this welter of hands concerns itself with America's eternal Holy Trinity: money, sex, and class. It's a grim, bleak, incrementally monumental film that doesn't flinch. Mildred, like the woman playing her, is doomed to be victimized—by circumstance, by time, by her own bad judgment, and, ultimately, by her child.

Few Hollywood films have dared to be as unsparing about the costs of being a woman. As David Denby wrote, it's a "bone-wearying job with fringe benefits but no central satisfactions . . . except . . . the neurotic satisfaction of constantly sacrificing oneself for . . . an unworthy daughter." Mildred learns the hard way that a woman can work harder than any man and still lose everything.

Mildred Pierce is the definitive portrait of masochistic female need and resulting maladjustment, beginning with Mildred's relentless focus on a man incapable of loving anybody but himself and rising until the traumatic scene where she is slapped by her own daughter and takes a brutally clumsy fall on a staircase—one of Crawford's finest acting moments. Crawford had long excelled at projecting pain and resentment, but *Mildred Pierce* adds scalding humiliation to the mixture.

The picture's only real flaw is that Mildred's character is rounded, but all the other characters are flat—defined by a single characteristic. Jack Carson's Wally is on the make; Zachary Scott's Monte is a louche country club degenerate; Ann Blyth's monstrous Veda is a murderously spoiled brat.

As with *Casablanca, Mildred Pierce* has retained its hold on audiences, not because of latent romantic idealism—it has none—but for its blunt confrontation with a sordid but recognizable reality: maternal guilt, illicit sex, the costs of prioritizing business over home, and unexpected, shattering death. In the end, Mildred returns to her first husband mainly because there's nobody else left. It's strictly a matter of convenience.

Lucille LeSueur and Billie Cassin had failed to get any traction, but Joan Crawford had finally triumphed. Indeed, Mildred would give Crawford the matrix for the rest of her career. Her characters would never possess the increasingly wizened Yankee integrity of Katharine Hepburn, or the neurotic need to dominate that propelled Bette Davis. In the next phase of her career, Crawford would portray women with a full roster of insecurities perpetually driven toward survival, motivated by inner need and a vital sexual current.

In other words, she returned to playing women much like Joan Crawford.

LATE IN 1945, DOUGLAS Fairbanks Jr. returned to Hollywood from naval service in the war. Fairbanks had served on minesweepers on the Murmansk run, in the Sicilian campaign, and in the English Channel. He earned the Silver Star, the Croix de Guerre, and the Distinguished Service Cross. Men had their heads blown off standing next to him, but Fairbanks never suffered so much as a scratch. After Fairbanks was awarded one of his medals, his friend David Niven wired him, "Well done, dear chum. Suggest that is enough. This can be overdone."

His first party back in Hollywood was thrown by Sonja Henie. Fairbanks and his wife Mary Lee had just arrived when he spotted his ex-wife across the room. The moment was fraught—Mary Lee and Crawford had never met.

Crawford let out a yelp and shouted, "Darling!" She ran across the room and hugged him. "Darling! I suppose you haven't heard—you don't know—I'm no longer with MGM. I'm with Warner Brothers now!"

As Fairbanks remembered the moment, "It was good to be home. Little had changed."

CHAPTER TWELVE

JUST AS WARNER BROS. was enjoying one of its greatest triumphs, it was besieged by a labor catastrophe. In October 1945, the studio was hit by a particularly nasty labor strike over the use of scab labor, among other grievances.

Harry and Jack fought back street-style. Strikebreakers were given large steel bolts from the machine shop and heaved them at the pickets from the roofs of the soundstages. A hidden camera was placed by the automobile gate and photographed employees who were picketing. Crawford showed up at the gate in her limo but didn't cross the picket line.

The Burbank police threw in with the studio and broke through the picket lines. It took eight months for the strike to be settled, with the result being a 25 percent pay increase for the rank and file. The true price was considerably more expensive: Jack Warner's undying enmity.

EVE ARDEN HAD A small part in *Dancing Lady*, so she and Crawford had met before making *Mildred Pierce*, which doesn't quite account for their seamless simpatico. Arden's trademark was a topspin of sardonic humor applied to nearly every line, and it's a mark of Crawford's confidence in her playing of Mildred that she wasn't threatened.

After *Mildred Pierce*, which brought Arden an Oscar nomination, she made a movie with Phillip Terry. Although Arden had just divorced her husband, she became interested in adoption. She asked Terry if he knew anything about the process, and he said he did, but it would make more sense to have Crawford call her.

The next morning Arden's phone rang at 7 a.m. "This is Joan Crawford. I have a baby for you!"

That particular adoption didn't pan out, but Crawford was instrumental in Arden's adoption of three children, and the two remained friendly for years. After Arden adopted her three children, she married the actor Brooks West, and promptly got pregnant and gave birth at the age of forty-seven.

Arden and her family had a ranch in Thousand Oaks that encompassed nearly forty acres, complete with horses, cows, and chickens. One Sunday Arden called Crawford and asked if she was busy that day.

"Not at all," said Crawford.

Arden said that her daughter Liza and she wanted to drop off some presents. When they arrived, they found Crawford in a fancy dress, Christina in organdy and lace, and Christopher in an Eton collar. The twins were also dressed up.

After a while, Christopher asked if he could go out and play. "Not when we have company," his mother said.

It was a formality observed by many people who witnessed the family in action. Shirley Temple remembered Crawford coming to her house for a visit. Temple noticed that Crawford was "impeccably groomed and acutely self-conscious about every fold in her skirt. Her elbow-length black gloves were constantly being adjusted so as to be absolutely even, and her . . . suit of jet black elegantly framed the large golden cross suspended at her bosom. Altogether she was a beautiful and incandescent person, picture postcard perfect."

A few weeks later, Crawford again visited Temple at home and brought Christopher and Christina along with Phil Terry. "Each child performed like a programmed wind-up toy," remembered Temple. At one point, for no reason Christopher drew back a fist and slugged Crawford hard on the thigh. She slapped him on the cheek, and the child let out a wail that startled everyone.

"He struck me," Crawford told Terry. "He struck me!"

The household tour came to an abrupt end. As recompense for the unpleasantness, a few days later Crawford sent over a cocker spaniel puppy, which seemed sleepy. In the morning the dog was dead from distemper.

It was as if Crawford had never seen the way an actual, semi-normal family interacts. In fact, she hadn't. The LeSueurs had all gone their separate ways and spent as little time with each other as possible, whether through intent or necessity. Nevertheless, Crawford attempted to program proper behavior irrespective of personality or psychological indisposition.

The screenwriter Catherine Turney was treated to an impromptu piano concert by Christina at Crawford's house. The composition was "The Happy Farmer," and when Christina hit some wrong notes, Crawford smacked the top of the child's wrist. "Then, of course, the poor kid never did get it right," said Turney. "I often wonder why she adopted [those] four kids, because basically I don't think she was a very motherly type."

CRAWFORD AND PHIL TERRY had a daily schedule distributed to the household help:

8 a.m. Breakfast.

9:15. Facial.

And so forth through the day, culminating at 5:15: Cocktails, usually daiquiris, which they would drink with entwined arms while saying "I love you, my dear." Somewhere in there were notations for playing with the children, as well as "Siesta," which meant lovemaking.

Catherine Turney thought that Phil Terry had been cast in the part of a queen's consort. "That was one thing about Joan, she was very romantic, and always lived in a kind of romantic dream world. I remember she told me she and Phil Terry had met on a dance floor and every time they [went dancing after that] he would dance in the same spot or something like that, and it was all so romantic. And each time she had a romance, it was always a big thing in her life. Which, in a way, was kind of endearing. It, in a way, reflected her insecurity. . . .

"She wanted desperately to be loved for herself. . . . I know I give the impression that she was very hard, but she really wasn't. Actually, she was quite vulnerable."

The scheduling was more ambitious than the marriage, which couldn't be sustained, probably because of the economic and social imbalance between Crawford and Terry. In December 1945, Crawford and Phillip Terry separated. Louella Parsons was . . . *shocked*! "This was one Hollywood marriage I always felt would last," she wrote in a sentence she had written about a dozen other broken Hollywood marriages.

Because Terry was a minor player, the divorce didn't arouse anything like the headlines Crawford's previous divorces had. She filed for divorce in March 1946, shortly after she won her Oscar. Terry agreed to a waiver of his right to contest the divorce, and both agreed to a property settlement. In short, she paid him off.

WITH MARRIAGE NUMBER THREE behind her, Crawford decided to downplay serious romance. Affairs were one thing, but the possibility of another marriage seemed to be off the table, the better to focus on career and children.

She told Louella Parsons that "A real mother doesn't always want her children. An adopted mother always wants them, else she wouldn't adopt them." A single woman adopting children was far more of an anomaly then than now, but even Crawford's friends had some doubts. A friend of Billy Haines's once asked him what Crawford did with her kids when she had to go on location. "Probably puts them in Bekins [Storage]," he sighed.

She could afford it. The IRS reported that Warner Bros. paid Crawford $400,000 in 1946—the highest salary at the studio. Second highest was Dennis Morgan, with $261,000, followed by Michael Curtiz at $258,600. Jack Warner was paid a mere $182,100, a fact that probably amounted to a bone in his throat.

Crawford was once again ascendant, and her opinions about everything were solicited and printed. She was asked to name the ten most important career women, and she responded with, in descending order, Eleanor Roosevelt, Sister Kenny, Marian Anderson, Helen Keller, Emily Post, Dorothy Parker, Elizabeth Arden, Shirley Temple, Hattie Carnegie, and Greta Garbo.

She had been a star since silent movies, an unparalleled run for the period, but she was not nostalgic. She thought current movies were extraordinary.

She singled out *Johnny Belinda* and, a few years later, *Home of the Brave* and *Champion*—intense melodramas that didn't stint on realism. She saw all those pictures with Billy Haines, who told her, "If they're making pictures like that, I think I'll go back into the movies."

She began seeing Greg Bautzer, a lawyer to the stars who managed to bed many of his clients. Bautzer was tall, dark, handsome and knew it. For a time he had kept company with a dazzling young woman named Phyllis Levy, who worked in the publishing business, where she came to be regarded as the Jewish Audrey Hepburn. One night they were at a nightclub when Levy excused herself to go to the bathroom. She had been there approximately thirty seconds when a cigarette girl came in with a flower and a note from Bautzer: "I miss you already."

In short, Bautzer was a master of the sort of premium-quality fawning upon which lucrative careers are erected.

Bautzer played to Crawford's affectations and her ego. He always walked a step or two behind her when she was making an entrance at a premiere or a party or happily transported her dog in his arms. He would confide to friends why he endured all this: "A night with Joan is better than a year with ten others."

Bautzer handled Howard Hughes's legal affairs, which entailed all the billable hours a lawyer would ever need, so money was not a problem. He gave Crawford lavish presents such as a cigarette case covered with rubies and engraved "Forever and Ever." Crawford upped the ante with diamond cuff links from Cartier. She hired him as her lawyer and brought him other clients: John Garfield, Ginger Rogers, and, yes, Franchot Tone.

In her early years, Crawford had been a light drinker, but by the time she started going out with Bautzer she was carrying her own flask of 100 proof vodka to parties, just in case the hostess had only stocked 80 proof. She would order a tonic and ice and supplement that with some vodka from her flask.

According to the maître d' at Romanoff's, the affair with Bautzer was lubricated by equal amounts of Smirnoff's and Beluga caviar, which translated to wild fights and equally wild sessions of making up. After one fight Bautzer tore off his Cartier cuff links and gave them back to her. Crawford flushed the cuff links down the toilet, then remembered how much they cost, which meant she had to lay out $500 for a plumber to retrieve them. Years later,

Bautzer would be talking to a reporter when he pointed out four small facial scars. "She put them there," he said. "She could throw a cocktail glass and hit you in the face—two times out of three."

Hedda Hopper ran an item that the two were considering marriage but concluded with vinegar: "I'll believe that when Greg tells me it's true."

During the times when Crawford and Bautzer weren't speaking, he moved on to Ava Gardner and Merle Oberon. After reconciling, Crawford bought his-and-hers Cadillacs. The relationship sustained until October 1949, when Bautzer made the mistake of going out of his way to greet another, younger actress at a party thrown by Louis B. Mayer.

On the way home, they were passing the UCLA campus in Brentwood when Crawford pulled over to the curb and told Bautzer she thought the right rear tire was going flat. Would he get out and take a look? As he got back to the tire, she gunned the car and drove off down Sunset.

He stood there watching her brake lights disappear. It was 1:30 in the morning. There was no traffic, no public phone anywhere. "That was my discipline," he told the BBC. "That was to serve as my penance for having paid some attention to this very lovely actress whom I had known for quite some time."

Bautzer buttoned his tuxedo and hoofed it three miles to the Bel-Air Hotel. The affair was over, although Crawford still occasionally turned to him for legal advice.

CHAPTER THIRTEEN

Humoresque WAS A PARTIAL remake of a Fannie Hurst story that had been made as a silent film in 1920. Hurst was alarmed by the news of the remake. "'Humoresque' was a Jewish story when first written," she wrote to a functionary at Warners. "I doubt the advisability of trying to turn back the clock and do it in the same mood. In any event I hope Warner and Brothers will grant me the courtesy of an opinion in the matter of filming my story." Her plea for involvement was ignored.

Jerry Wald's first casting impulse was Bette Davis, but that idea met with resistance from Steve Trilling, Jack Warner's right-hand man. On November 17, 1945, Wald sent an early version of the script to Davis, with an accompanying letter full of the expected soft soap: "I think the character of Helen is an exciting one, and I feel that there is no one on the screen who could do as much with it as you can."

Davis didn't share Trilling's enthusiasm. Slightly less than a month later, the picture began shooting with Joan Crawford. It came together more expeditiously than *Mildred Pierce* for the simple reason that much of the script was lifted from a largely unused Clifford Odets script for *Rhapsody in Blue*, a biographical picture about George Gershwin. Jerry Wald simply changed the names of the characters and used the Odets script for the family scenes with the John Garfield character, who is recharacterized as Italian rather than Jewish. The rest of the script was written by Zachary Gold.

Once again, Wald obsessed over every detail, which is more or less the producer's job: "The dress that was designed for Helen's party, with the puffed sleeves, is much too exaggerated in the shoulders and the skirt is too full. . . . It looks too much like the Joan Crawford who was left behind at Metro. We have in our hands a woman who is being recognized for her acting ability, and nothing should be done to distract from that. We know she is a good actress and we shouldn't make the fatal mistake that Metro did by trying to over-dress her."

Although Adrian got screen credit for the costumes, he never had a contract with Warner's, but simply supplied a succession of sleek outfits directly to Crawford that emphasized the predatory nature of the character.

Crawford was playing a bored high-society dame laboring beneath an alcoholic husband and a drinking problem of her own. Wald cast the proletarian John Garfield opposite Crawford—an interesting clash of society and street. When they were introduced, Garfield said, "So you're Joan Crawford, the big movie star. Glad to see you." He then reached out and touched her breast. Crawford exploded, "Why you insolent son of a bitch!" And then she smiled. "I think we're going to get along fine."

"It was wonderful working with Johnnie," Crawford would say twenty years after the fact. "Great, great talent."

Garfield was the bridge between the predominantly personality-based acting of the early twentieth century and the Method, and his path to acting was unusually convoluted. "He had a tragic childhood," said his daughter Julie. "His mother died, and his father was a horrible man—a rabbi on the weekends, a pants presser during the week. His father was very strict and wanted my father to become a rabbi too, but he wasn't interested. They had terrible fights. And then he got involved with gangs."

"He was crazy, in a gang, hanging off the sides of buildings for a quarter. A wild kid. But he fell instantly in love with my mother. She got him a job wrapping packages at Macy's. After that, he got a job selling diaphragms door to door for Margaret Sanger."

Eventually Garfield traded birth control for acting. He found a teacher who fixed his stutter, worked with Jacob Ben-Ami, then got involved with Eva Le Gallienne's company, whereupon acting became his permanent passion. He latched on at the nascent Group Theatre, where he became close with Clifford Odets. Lee Strasberg liked Garfield but never took him entirely seriously because of what Strasberg felt was a lack of intellectual heft. Odets wrote *Golden Boy* for Garfield, but in one of the most bizarre casting decisions of the century, Luther Adler was cast in the title role, while Garfield had to make do with the part of Ziggy. After that came the offer to make movies at Warner Bros.

Garfield's street quality meshed well with what had become Crawford's polished exterior. There was only one problem, according to Julie Garfield: "She complained to the director: 'Why is he always making eye contact with me?' This is a woman who was used to acting for and to the camera, and Daddy wanted to make eye contact. In the end, she ended up making eye contact and it was the best performance she ever gave."

Garfield's wife Robbie told his daughter about the day they shot the big love scene. "That was the day she brought her children to the set. All dressed up with patent leather shoes on the beach. Why bring your kids to the set that day?"

Garfield's marriage, was, said his daughter, "very volatile. Madly in love. One minute they'd fuck, the next they'd fight. She complained about him. He was a movie star, which she didn't like, although I'm sure my mom would have liked to have been a movie star too."

Robbie Garfield was far more of a political creature than her husband. It came naturally—Robbie Garfield's mother's best friend jumped to her death in the Triangle Shirtwaist Factory fire in 1911.

Warner Bros. made Garfield a star, but he didn't particularly appreciate the favor. "He hated what he was doing because he had to do a lot of movies he thought were shit." As a result of his basic dissatisfaction with Warners, and his up-and-down marriage, Garfield generally projected a volatile, pissed-off attitude, which meshed nicely with his gradually accreting image of a doomed proletarian hero.

Humoresque was a basically simple story inside a huge, top-heavy production. Robert Blake, playing Garfield as a child, was cast adrift and intimidated. Blake had a scene on a fire escape, when he's watching the city below and yearning to join the other kids. The large crew, the camera craning up to Blake on the fire escape, the lack of any kind of emotional preparation, left the child adrift.

And then he heard a voice, a loud one.

"Bring that camera down here now! Kill all those fucking arcs. Clear this goddamn set."

It was Garfield, taking over the scene, taking over the direction. He climbed up the stairs to the fire escape set and sat down next to Blake. He took out a pack of Camels and lit one. "I want you to tell me everything that happened when you were a little boy, but don't talk. Tell me, Bobby, what it was like." He climbed back off the set.

The child did the scene, director Jean Negulesco called "Print," and Garfield came back out onto the fire escape. "Wherever you go and whatever you do," he said, "remember there's going to be a camera in front of you and me behind you. Never tell the story to the camera, never tell the story to the audience. Always tell it to me. You attract the camera to you. You do not reach out to the camera to show it anything."

It was the kind of essentially internal behavior that Crawford had never gotten but had to learn the hard way, by watching herself on-screen and finding out what worked and what didn't.

When he wasn't organizing, Jerry Wald acted as cheerleader, sending a memo to Negulesco: "After seeing last night's rushes, I must confess that you really outdid yourself. The weaving pattern of Helen as she drunkenly staggers across the sand, is one of the most interesting and fascinating shots I have ever seen in a picture . . . after *Humoresque*, you will be talked about in the same breath as Curtiz."

There's a dynamic buried in the narrative of *Humoresque* that's simultaneously unsentimental and deeply masochistic: Crawford's character is used to taking lovers without ever being in love. She makes the crucial mistake of falling for Garfield, who is happy to sell out for her connections, but can't quite bring himself to care for her as much as she cares for him. Result: tragedy.

Humoresque is undoubtedly too long and probably too much. It's Crawford's most luxurious film, spectacularly photographed by Ernest Haller with some of the inkiest blacks in movies, and acted with total conviction by everyone. Crawford strides through the film radiating the splendor of a female panther prowling through a diminishing jungle, while simultaneously projecting the self-loathing of the second-stage alcoholic.

Negulesco devises all sorts of gambits for making it look like Garfield is playing the violin. There were actually two professional violinists—one in back of Garfield doing the fingering, another below Garfield whose right hand is doing the bowing. Framed correctly with Garfield's head in the center of the shot, and with Isaac Stern's flamboyant dubbing of the classical score, the illusion is perfect. (Stern was paid $20,000 for the job.) Just when you think you've figured it out, Negulesco throws in a crane shot swooping down on Garfield, isolated from the orchestra. When the camera gets close, the violin comes up, and Garfield begins playing.

One by-product of the production was a close friendship between Garfield and Stern—for a time they lived in the same building. Another was a mink dildo that Crawford gifted her leading man at the end of the shoot. According to Garfield's daughter, it was an expression of wish fulfillment rather than acknowledgment of an affair. "He didn't know what to do with it. He was in a state of shock. A mink dildo?"

Within the studio there was bitching that there was too much classical music in the movie. More importantly, *Humoresque* took forever to make. Production began December 14, 1945, and didn't finish until the second week of April 1946. Crawford didn't start work until January 21. On February 8, she called in sick and stayed sick for eight days. After that, she missed nine more days, while Garfield missed five days. It must have been contagious—Negulesco missed a couple of days as well, and was replaced by Irving Rapper for one of them. In total, the picture ran a whopping forty-four days over schedule.

Humoresque is simultaneously an ornate studio product—the budget amounted to more than $2 million of Jack Warner's grimly grasped dollars, and every cent of it is on the screen—and something of a personal project that's directed with style and conviction. Negulesco even works in one of his own drawings, showing Crawford with her eyes closed. It's prominently displayed on the wall of her character's apartment.

The reviews were not great, but business was. The picture made a profit of about $500,000.

FOR THOSE PEOPLE CRAWFORD liked, nothing was too much. In May 1946, David Niven's wife Primmie died after falling down the basement stairs of their new house and fracturing her skull. She was twenty-eight years old. Her death left Niven surreptitiously depressed for the rest of his life.

Friends rallied around Niven and his two young sons. Clark Gable helped—he had lost Carole Lombard and knew what Niven was going through. Fred Astaire took Niven golfing and Rex Harrison, whom Niven couldn't abide, gave him a boxer puppy. Crawford welcomed Niven's sons into her own house for some weeks until their father took them to Ronald Colman's ranch in Montecito.

For Crawford's next picture, Jack Warner assigned Curtis Bernhardt to direct *Possessed*. Bernhardt had just done *A Stolen Life* with Bette Davis and said, "Compared with Bette Davis, Joan Crawford . . . was as easy to work with as can be." The only difficulty arose when Bernhardt would forget whom he was working with and accidentally called Crawford "Bette." This usually provoked Crawford into throwing her purse at him.

Ranald MacDougall was once again writing, and he and Jerry Wald were invited to a script conference at Crawford's house. "She had two drawing rooms," remembered MacDougall.

> One was on one side of the foyer and was very feminine, with ruffles and organdy flounces and, I don't know, very, very feminine, a lovely room, and the other one was masculine. It had a bar in it. It had leather-paneled walls and was definitely masculine.
>
> And when we came in, we were ushered into . . . the male one. We were men. If we had been women, we would have gone to the other one, I assume. At any rate, we went into that one, and we were sitting around waiting for Joan . . . and I said, "Good God, leather, that's real leather on the walls!" And I turned to Jerry Wald, and I said, "You know, Jerry, that is real leather. It must be like living in a wallet."

Joan knew what being a star was all about.

Supporting Crawford was Raymond Massey, who was fascinated by her. "I discovered the secret of Joan's longevity: she was the best technician I ever met. Could match close-ups and long shots flawlessly. Knew everything about lighting, camera lenses, and dressed for the camera, and not the other actors.

Her face photographed superbly, captured and held the light. . . . Joan talked a lot about one day tackling the theater, but I knew she never would. For one thing, she had an innate fear of people.

"One more thing: During the big party scene she insisted all the crew dress up too, so she'd be in the right mood, and then when we were waltzing, she insisted she lead. After all, she was the star."

Possessed—not to be confused with the 1931 Crawford film with the same title—is a movie that adamantly refuses to make up its mind about what it wants to be. Like its central character, it's profoundly schizophrenic. It begins with a compelling sequence in which a catatonic Crawford trudges through downtown Los Angeles at dawn, after which she is taken to a hospital and we flash back.

The picture starts out as a deep-dish *noir*, feints at a transition into a Gothic, manages to integrate a family in peril, and finally returns definitively to its *noir* roots. It has its moments—the picture is sumptuously mounted and photographed—but the seductive surface is undermined by the narrative whiplashing, which leaves Crawford little choice but to assert dominance in a vain attempt to smooth out the rough edges. Crawford's leading man was divided in two: Raymond Massey as the straightlaced husband opposite Van Heflin, borrowed from MGM to play an indolent alcoholic once too often. The picture did all right—rentals of $3 million against a cost of $2.5 million—but after distribution costs the profit would have been minimal.

Despite the intrinsic problems of *Possessed*, James Agee was impressed. "Miss Crawford, though she is not quite up to her hardest scenes, is generally excellent, performing with the passion and intelligence of an actress who is not content with just one Oscar. . . . A lot of people who have a lot to give are giving all they've got."

Darryl Zanuck borrowed Crawford for a picture at 20th Century-Fox called *Daisy Kenyon*. Crawford's introduction to Zanuck was unforgettable. She was ushered into his office, and he promptly opened a desk drawer so he could proudly display a solid-gold casting of his genitals. Welcome to Fox!

Until it goes off the rails in the third act, with arbitrary character reversals, *Daisy Kenyon* is an intelligent high-end melodrama about a career woman torn between two men: battle-weary veteran Henry Fonda and cheerfully corrupt married lawyer Dana Andrews. To give the movie some visual tension, director Otto Preminger shoots most of it with deep shadows that nicely meld with the characters' neuroses.

Fonda worked in a mood of sullen professionalism. Zanuck disliked Fonda and Fonda loathed Zanuck, mainly because the producer had refused to cast him as Tom Joad in *The Grapes of Wrath* unless Fonda signed a seven-year contract. Zanuck's argument for the contract was simple: "I don't want to put you in a big fuckin' part like this and then have you go over to MGM and play something with Joan Crawford."

Crawford affectionately—and accurately—termed Preminger "a Jewish Nazi." After the first day of shooting, Preminger returned home to find he had been gifted by his star with a new set of garden furniture because "I can't work with any director who owns such old garden furniture."

Preminger's estimation of the experience was that "She did everything I asked [of her] on film"—not exactly a ringing endorsement of the experience. Crawford asked Preminger if he would release her as early as possible on weekdays so she could serve dinner to the twins. It was clear that she was focused on being a good mother.

Crawford's main area of interest on the picture turned out to be Fonda, whom she found extremely attractive. Crawford made some tentative approaches, but they were ignored. Finally she had the wardrobe department make a jockstrap festooned with rhinestones, gold sequins, and red beads, which she presented to him early one morning on the set. Fonda opened the package and turned it over, wondering how to respond. The next scene called for him to help Crawford up a staircase, at which point she murmured, "How about modeling it for me later?" He nearly dropped her.

She had misread the man. Fonda was a throwback to Lon Chaney—acting was his church, and he was not prone to affairs with costars. Nothing happened.

The picture itself went smoothly because both Preminger and Crawford were professionals for whom discipline was paramount. "I think each of them sensed the potential ferocity of the other," said costar Ruth Warrick, who also mentioned that "Joan was very secretive. You could never quite tell what she was thinking, although you felt she had an underlying anger at the world. . . . She demanded deference, and she insisted on protocol because she came from such desperately low circumstances. She was polite to the men in the company, as you would be to a maid, but she didn't acknowledge I was alive; we were like boxers across the room, and I was just as glad because I didn't want to tangle with her."

The only problem derived from Crawford's demand that the set be kept at her usual temperature of 58 degrees, because, it was said, she was going through menopause. When both Fonda and Andrews complained, she gifted them with long underwear. As far as Fonda was concerned, *Daisy Kenyon* was another meaningless Zanuck assignment.

Dana Andrews went through the picture with an air of grim determination, which, come to think of it, describes his basic screen character. He hadn't wanted to make the picture in the first place, but his attorney said he had to or the studio could sue him for $300,000.

With *Daisy Kenyon* in the can, Crawford took a vacation in Hawaii by herself, sailing on the liner *Matsonia* because she remained afraid of flying. Her suitcase carried a couple of scripts. She stayed for only two weeks, because she was wanted back at Warner Bros.

CHAPTER FOURTEEN

◆

ALTHOUGH CRAWFORD WAS ONCE again near the top of the Hollywood heap, the business was changing in ways she didn't like. "I remember when I was in the process of a divorce [from Phil Terry] and I dated a very prominent lawyer [Greg Bautzer] who wanted to go somewhere to eat and dance. . . . [I] wondered what the press would say, [and] he told me, 'Joan, don't you realize the press doesn't give a good goddamn what you do anymore?' And he was right."

She wasn't talking about the public losing interest in Joan Crawford per se, she was talking about the shifting taste that gradually rendered the sunlit values of Louis B. Mayer's MGM passé, about the inevitable passing of the guard that would put the stars of Crawford's era on the endangered species list.

She remained innately competitive, but only with contemporaries she didn't like. With actresses who were friends or whom she respected, she was a continuous booster, even if, like Barbara Stanwyck, they had similar qualities of barely sublimated aggression. And she was also capable of being a rapt fan. George Cukor threw a party at his house for Ethel Barrymore and invited Crawford, who knelt at Barrymore's feet looking, said one observer "like a stage-struck kid. . . . Crawford was as much the enthralled fan as anyone."

At this point, Crawford's team of advisors included Greg Bautzer on legal matters and Bo Roos on financials. Roos was a money manager whose clients included Marlene Dietrich, John Wayne, Fred MacMurray, Rita Hayworth, and Merle Oberon. He was a devout believer in real estate and was open to becoming friends with his occasionally eccentric clients, which didn't always work out. He and Wayne eventually engaged in a lengthy legal fight over what Wayne considered bad financial advice. Roos confided to his daughter that Merle Oberon slept on her back in order to forestall wrinkles, while Crawford was categorized as "one tough cookie, very demanding."

When Roos told Crawford to sell her house in Brentwood and buy an apartment instead, she listened carefully, then ignored him. She kept the house and bought an apartment on the corner of Rodeo Drive and Charleville. One of her tenants would be Harry Rapf and his wife, whose jealousy about Crawford had obviously receded. Mrs. Rapf loved the apartment because she was a professional shopper and the apartment was within walking distance of the premium stores.

After the divorce from Phil Terry, Clark Gable began spending time at Crawford's house. He hadn't yet remarried to Lady Sylvia Ashley Fairbanks, the widow of Fairbanks Sr. It was the rough equivalent of Crawford's marriage to Phil Terry in that it was utterly inexplicable. Crawford was similarly at loose ends. The publicist John Mitchell said that Gable was often at Crawford's house on weekends, and the kids called him "Uncle Clark." If she was aware of a certain repetition regarding the men her mother had referred to as her Uncles decades before in Kansas City, she pretended otherwise. Mitchell said that Crawford never raised her voice to the children—if the kids misbehaved, she simply removed their favorite toys and they would have to be earned back. It was typical of a period in which she seemed to avoid confrontations, perhaps because she had so many problems accruing at the studio.

By the end of 1947, the honeymoon signaled by *Mildred Pierce* and the resulting Oscar was over. On December 15, Jack Warner sent a confidential cable to the New York office of Warner Bros.: FROM PRESENT INDICATIONS APPEARS TO ME WE GOING HAVE LOT TROUBLE WITH JOAN CRAWFORD, TEMPERAMENT AND SUCH THINGS . . . MAY HAVE SUSPEND HER THIS WEEK. SECONDLY, WHAT DO YOU THINK OF DROPPING HER ENTIRELY. WE HAD SEMI FAILURE IN HUMORESQUE AND EXCEPTIONAL FAILURE IN POSSESSED. INSTEAD WORRYING ABOUT HER COULD BE DEVOTING MY

TIME WORTHWHILE PRODUCTIONS AND NEW PERSONAL-
ITIES . . . HOWEVER, THIS ONLY WAY I FEEL TODAY. IF SHE
STRAIGHTENS OUT BY END WEEK MAY NOT FEEL THIS WAY
BUT FACTS MUST BE FACED AS THESE THINGS TAKE ALL YOUR
TIME.

The problems obviously went away, but not completely. From this point on, Crawford's pictures had smaller budgets than *Humoresque* and *Possessed*. Movie attendance was beginning its long decline, and the studios had to adjust accordingly.

If Crawford was aware of the gradual tightening, she gave no sign of it. She still inhabited the Grand Manner as if she had been born to it. When the young Barbara Bel Geddes came to Hollywood in 1947, a friend of Crawford's took her to Chasen's, where Crawford was dining. "Ask her," said Crawford to her friend, "to turn her head this way. I just want to gaze at her. I think she's divine."

BILLY HAINES LIKED TO tell the story of showing up at Crawford's house on North Bristol to be told that the maid and the cook had just quit, and she would sit down with him as soon as she put the kids to bed. After a while, she came into the kitchen, put a chair by the entrance, and told Haines to have a seat. She then proceeded to scrub the floor while they talked. According to Haines, she was wearing an Adrian dress at the time.

This intrinsically incoherent combination of just plain folks and Movie Queen was even present in her relations with the members of the Joan Crawford fan club. For each issue of the club magazine Crawford wrote a letter in tones of primal gush. "Don't you think we have the nicest club newspaper in the whole world?" she wrote in a 1948 issue.

"I am always so excited when I see it in the mail and it's always so full of wonderful surprises for me. . . . Martha Kay's article on the Academy Award presentations was accurate beyond words. I think she has ink in her veins because she is going to make a wonderful reporter. . . .

"Nothing could have made me happier than Loretta's winning the Oscar.

She not only deserved it for *The Farmer's Daughter*, but for *The Bishop's Wife* and many, many more performances she has given throughout the years. Of course, I just jumped up and down when Celeste Holm, Ronald Colman, Edmund Gwenn and Elia Kazan won their Oscars. The goose flesh ran up and down my spine continually the entire evening because I knew the joy the winners would have, and when that sweet Edmund Gwenn made his beautiful speech, that did it—tears flowed, mascara ran, and I was a wreck emotionally."

JERRY WALD REUNITED CRAWFORD and Michael Curtiz for *Flamingo Road*, but this time the mixture didn't quite gel. For one thing, Crawford was at least fifteen years too old for her character: a carny in a burg clearly situated in an unnamed Florida, who falls in with a dissolute crowd of politicians and kingmakers. Crawford's leading men were Zachary Scott and David Brian—cumulatively indicative of the reduced budget. Both of them were playing basically weak characters, and even Crawford is more acted upon than active, which means the melodrama only comes to life when she faces off against the flamboyantly malevolent Sydney Greenstreet.

With power confronting power, those scenes can't help but have juice, but Curtiz's one-size-fits-all style—camera push-ins, foreground objects placed to give a sense of depth to the compositions—feels artificially grafted rather than an integral part of the melodrama.

The actress Iris Adrian was playing the part of a convict in jail with Crawford's character. She laconically tells Crawford that the reason she's in jail is that "my boyfriend stabbed himself with a knife I was holding at the time." Adrian thought Crawford was a "great broad." One day Crawford came up to Adrian and complained that Curtiz had told Jerry Wald he didn't want "that big-eyed dame with the football shoulders" in the picture.

"I've got a contract for five more years," Crawford told Adrian, "so I've got to do this picture, but I wish I could've gotten out of it. It's not easy for me to be cute and darling for such a bastard."

At the end of a long day, Adrian muttered, "Well, home to mother," to which Crawford responded, "Home to *be* mother. And if things don't get better there, I don't know *what* I'm going to do."

Iris Adrian summed up Crawford by saying, "Those kids *and* Mike Curtiz. The poor dame had her hands full."

Flamingo Road proved slightly profitable, but the question of what kind of career Joan Crawford would have in middle age was looming ever larger. A guest appearance in an amusing Hollywood spoof called *It's a Great Feeling* brightened the year but dodged the question. Crawford appears as herself opposite stars Dennis Morgan, Doris Day, and Jack Carson. Carson plays a slight variation on his screen character—a likably boorish ham comedian determined to direct himself in a movie nobody else wants any part of. The premise is set up by a montage of elite Warners directors (Michael Curtiz, King Vidor, Raoul Walsh) rejecting the doomed vanity production.

The film features gag appearances from all the Warners stars, up to and including Errol Flynn for the topper. We pick up Crawford in the wardrobe department looking like a million dollars. She's furiously knitting when she overhears Carson and Dennis Morgan arguing over who gets to date Doris Day next. She flares her eyes, turns around, and says, "You two boys ought to be ashamed of yourselves. Just think of what you're doing to that poor little innocent girl! Two grown men acting like grown men!!!"

When Carson and Morgan protest, she slides into a variation of her vehement speech to Veda in *Mildred Pierce*: "I've never denied you anything. Anything money could buy I've given you. But that wasn't enough, was it? Get out! Get your things out of here before I throw them into the street and you with them!! Get out before I kill you!!!"

She then slaps both of them.

"What was that for?" asks Carson.

"I do that in all my pictures," she says sweetly before exiting the scene.

Self-parody seldom gets more expert than this. Crawford was not renowned for her sense of humor, but her ninety seconds in *It's a Great Feeling* proves she not only had one, but was fully aware of the screen clichés she had created and was able to laugh about them, not to mention herself.

DESPITE HER SOLICITOUSNESS TOWARD Ann Blyth on *Mildred Pierce*, Crawford would develop a reputation as an actress who was easily threatened by attractive younger actresses. What went unreported was an equivalent attentiveness to younger actresses who she felt needed help. In 1949, Crawford called Eleanor Parker, a contractee at Warners who was struggling for traction.

"She called to say she had read a script—she read everything—which I should do," said Parker. "She was too old for it, but it would be great for me. 'Go get it,' she said."

The picture was a Jerry Wald project called *Caged*, and it had some similarities to the Crawford vehicle *Paid* from nearly twenty years before, about the unjust imprisonment of a young woman. Wald was leaning toward Wanda Hendrix for the lead. John Cromwell, who was directing, didn't want Parker. But Jack Warner agreed to let Parker test and she got the part.

Caged brought Parker her first Oscar nomination. "I never expected to win the Oscar, so I wasn't disappointed. When I went home after the awards to change clothes for the party afterward, the phone rang. It was Joan. She was ranting about how wrong it was that I had lost."

VINCENT SHERMAN CAME INTO Crawford's life just as the personal void was merging with professional stasis. The project was called *The Victim*, a transparent rewrite of the story of Virginia Hill, a gangster's moll who became the mistress of Joe Adonis, a New York thug supposedly related to Mob boss Frank Costello. Hill eventually became the mistress of Bugsy Siegel in his last fevered days of overspending in Las Vegas, which got him killed. Steve Cochran was to play the Siegel character, and Sherman was assigned to direct.

Sherman thought that Crawford was still attractive but was far too old to convincingly play a young innocent in the big city, so the writer added a prologue to the script that made Crawford a housewife married to an oil field worker whom she abandons after their child is killed. Crawford liked the changes, and suggested that she and Sherman watch *Humoresque*. When Sherman complimented her on her playing of a sexy scene, she took his hand

and placed it against her breast, then placed her other hand on his knee and began moving it toward his crotch.

Sherman was surprised but not shocked. He had been through a similar situation with Bette Davis, who had also seduced him with the star's *droit du seigneur*. But there was no lock on the screening room door, and Sherman thought it would be bad form to be discovered on the floor with the studio's biggest female star. "I realized that she had been stimulated by her own eroticized image and that I was confronted with a female who went after what she wanted and was masculine in her approach to sex."

Sherman was married to a pleasant woman with a high tolerance for errant husbands. He and Crawford consummated their attraction in Crawford's dressing room. Sherman would direct three consecutive pictures with Crawford, invariably intrigued by her skill and professionalism, not to mention her sensuality.

For the former: "I had never worked with anyone who was so keen, so knowledgeable about filmmaking." As for the latter, Crawford informed Sherman that "The ideal wife is a lady in the living room but a whore in bed."

Crawford invited Sherman and his wife to a dinner party at her house, and Hedda Sherman told her husband, "She's still a stunning woman, and, strangely enough, there's something about her that I like and admire. . . . She's gracious and considerate, and if you can see beneath the Hollywood crap, you can detect a woman who refused to become a loser, who pulled herself up from nothing and made something of her life."

The Virginia Hill project was retitled *The Damned Don't Cry* and plays as a partial return to the woman-in-peril movies of Crawford's early 1930s period. It's a better movie than *Flamingo Road*, if only because Sherman gives it a rapid pace. There is some tasty location footage of Palm Springs circa 1950; it features the comprehensively sleazy Steve Cochran; and it has lush, bitter dialogue: "Self-respect is what you say you've got when you don't have anything else."

Crawford's box office was holding, even though Jack Warner continued to cut budgets. *The Damned Don't Cry* cost $1.2 million, netted a million dollars over that.

Crawford began pressuring Sherman to marry her. He managed to thread the needle—he had no intention of leaving his family, and the affair continued.

The Damned Don't Cry was followed by both Crawford and Sherman being loaned out to Columbia to make *Harriet Craig*, a remake of *Craig's Wife*, which had starred Rosalind Russell fifteen years earlier. The script involved a controlling type A woman with a bad case of House Pride who eventually drives everyone around her into the next state. Sherman thought the story was dated and that modern audiences wouldn't respond to it. Crawford said she could use the money.

Sherman went to Steve Trilling, Jack Warner's assistant, and told him, "Steve, if that's the same script that Crawford asked me to read, I don't want to do that.' (Trilling) said, 'Oh, Gee, Vince, we've already made the deal for you.' I said, 'What happens if I say no?' He said, "You don't want to do that. You would break your contract with us.'"

So a picture that nobody really wanted to make was made anyway. Crawford's wardrobe was designed by Jean Louis, who thought the job was going to be difficult because of Crawford's penchant for broad shoulders and the fact that broad shoulders were out of fashion by 1950.

"She came to see me, and I [thought], 'Well she's still wearing those pads.' No, it was her shoulders. She had square shoulders. . . . She has a very long torso. Short legs. And then you see those big shoulders and I thought, 'My God, those are the Adrian shoulders.' I thought Adrian had made them, but they were hers."

Jean Louis quickly realized that "She had very good figure. Very good. . . . And she had that phobia about ankle-strap shoes. She had to have all the ankle-straps, and they were not in fashion at the time. . . . She told me she couldn't stand regular heels because they wouldn't stay on her feet. She had very small feet, and they'd slip out of the shoes."

Sherman was aware of the synchronicity between the actress and the character: "Her obsessive attitude toward her home; her distrust of men and her desire to control; her power of manipulation; and her concept of the proper way for a man to behave toward his wife. . . . I tried to capture these traits in the film, and although they were a critical comment, she never once objected. So I was never sure she was fully aware of what we were doing."

During the affair with Sherman, Crawford was her usual generous self with gifts: a gold watch, silk pajamas, tailored jackets, Sulka ties, a stereo camera.

Sherman told her she was embarrassing him, and she replied, "It gives me pleasure, so why should you mind?" When they vacationed together at Lake Louise, the gossip columnist Harrison Carroll got wind of the trip and called Sherman's wife. Both Sherman and his wife were upset; a private affair was one thing, public humiliation for his wife quite another.

Back at Warner's, Sherman and Crawford were handed *Goodbye, My Fancy*, a supposed romantic comedy with Robert Young and Frank Lovejoy. Jack Warner had Steve Trilling call Sherman and told him to avoid close-ups of his star because she was "getting too old." Adding to the tension was Crawford's animosity toward Janice Rule, the film's ingenue, and Sherman's continuing refusal to get a divorce.

Goodbye, My Fancy had a been a hit Broadway play with Madeleine Carroll. It concerned a congresswoman going back to her alma mater to receive an honorary degree and finding love. It starts out as a light comedy, complete with Eve Arden as Crawford's assistant, then develops a social conscience halfway through. The larger problem is that Crawford's primary leading man is the charmless Frank Lovejoy, who was born to play tough cops but is instead playing a photographer for *Life* magazine.

With more sensitive casting and appropriately soft-focus photography, it would have been an adequately genteel vehicle for Claudette Colbert or Irene Dunne, but Crawford's public must have found it weirdly uneventful in all the wrong ways—it's a movie where *everybody* is miscast. By this time, Crawford's audience wanted to see her slapping or being slapped, killing or being killed, and *Goodbye, My Fancy* was a feeble romance about characters with little at stake played by actors who were unable to strike sparks off each other.

Goodbye, My Fancy cost $1.2 million and returned the same amount to Warner Bros.—once distribution costs were deducted, a loss of hundreds of thousands of dollars. At this point, Crawford had multiple pictures left on her contract. Following instincts honed over the last thirty years with other female stars who had worn out their welcome (Kay Francis, Bette Davis, Ann Sheridan, Ida Lupino, among many) Jack Warner set about making sure her next picture would be a memorable stinker.

THE AFFAIR WITH VINCENT Sherman ended in squalid fashion. He was leaving her house after an argument and Crawford tripped him. He stumbled, caught himself, turned, and slapped her. Crawford fell down and Sherman went on his way. They saw each other a few times after that, but the ship had not only sailed, but sank. After one final argument, he came home to find his wife eating grapes. Hedda Sherman told her husband that Crawford had called to tell her she was sending Hedda's husband back to her. Sherman's wife thanked her, and that was almost the end.

A few nights later there was a 2 a.m. phone call from Crawford. She murmured, "Goodbye, Vincent" and dropped the phone. Ignoring the fact that Joan Crawford was the least likely suicide in movie history, Sherman drove to her house and found her on her bed dressed in a nightgown, with an open bottle of sleeping pills on the bedside table. Sherman didn't know if she had actually taken any of the pills or was merely playing a scene, but he got her up, poured some coffee in her, and drove back home just before 5 a.m.

Amidst all this melodrama, it fell to the (justifiably) unheralded Felix Feist to direct Crawford's last Warner Bros. movie, the unforgettably awful *This Woman Is Dangerous*. Crawford plays a gun moll who is going blind. She falls in love with the doctor who saves her sight (Dennis Morgan, also playing out his Warner's string), which causes a disruption in her relationships with the thugs (David Brian, Philip Carey) with whom she's consorting.

It was a script that would have been ludicrous in 1932 with Ruth Chatterton and George Brent, but Jack Warner foisted it on Crawford, probably in the hope that she would quit rather than make it. In the early 1950s Hollywood was staggering from the blacklist, not to mention a continuing loss of attendance provoked by television and rotten movies like *This Woman Is Dangerous*. In a cost-cutting move, Jack Warner had closed the story department and was selling off land while openly considering a sale of the studio itself.

What this meant in practice was that the script was being written as it was being shot. "We are still in this picture," Crawford wrote to a friend, "writing it as we go along. The only thing I can say for it is just one complete surprise after another—to us, as actors. I don't know what the hell it's going to be to the audience. After Dennis Morgan and I worked for three days and found that we had to write our own dialogue, he walked out of my dressing room one day and said to the crew around there, 'This would be a pretty damned good picture if she only had time to write it.'"

Crawford rightly considered the film an embarrassment. *This Woman Is Dangerous* wasn't exactly a flop—it just didn't make any money: worldwide rentals of $1.5 million, $200,000 more than the rentals for *Goodbye, My Fancy*, much less than *The Damned Don't Cry*, which earned $2.2 million.

An aging star; mediocre business. The result was a foregone conclusion. On the day after Christmas 1951, Warner Bros. released Crawford from her contract. They agreed to pay her $2,500 a week beginning in April 1952, followed by $1,000 a week beginning in January 1953 until they had paid her $400,000 for the unmade pictures on her contract.

The same thing was happening all over Hollywood to actors who were being thrown onto the open market after years of contract work. Beyond the walls of Warner Bros. lay the uncharted territory of freelancing in a Hollywood racked by professional uncertainty and political upheaval.

Shortly after Crawford walked the plank at Warner's, John Garfield died. Garfield and his politically radical wife had epic battles regarding his decision to testify before the House Committee on Un-American Activities. According to Julie Garfield, "My mother said, 'Don't play their game—they're full of shit. We'll go to Europe and work there. Forget it. Don't stool on your friends.' And he said, 'I can't leave. This is my life. I insist on trying to clear my name.'

"It was a huge fight."

Garfield testified but refused to name names, which meant he remained in professional limbo. "He was so stressed, and he had a heart condition. He pushed it and pushed it and just dropped dead."

John Garfield was thirty-nine years old.

For Crawford, the good times had ended long before the death of one of her favorite leading men, and long before she left Warners. "If I can put my finger on the time of change," she said, "I think that when World War II ended, the fun aspects went out of American movie-making, and that sense of fun never returned."

HOLLYWOOD MAY HAVE BEEN changing, but friends still had to get used to going a long time without seeing each other. Robert Wagner, then in his young-leading-man stage, remembered being in a limo on the way to a premiere when both Barbara Stanwyck and Crawford got into the back seat, pinning him in the middle. He was stunned, because at this point he had never met either of them. He was even more stunned when they completely ignored him and began chattering away, filling each other in on everything that was going on in their lives since they had last met, which seemed to have been months before. "They were obviously very close friends and I had no idea," Wagner said.

This era of professional instability coincided with increasing turbulence at home. The first recorded instance of Christopher running away from home came in March 1951. The cause was his nurse's refusal to put chocolate syrup on his ice cream. He was only a few blocks from the house when the police found him. The *Los Angeles Times* reported that Crawford was planning on taking a hairbrush to his rear end. Six months later he lit out again and after a few days was found at the Santa Monica Pier.

The dysfunction wasn't a complete shock to Crawford's friends. Rosalind Rogers, the wife of the publicist Henry Rogers, remembered Crawford showing her Christopher's bedroom when he was four or five. She was startled to see the boy was tied to the bed at both ends.

When she asked why, Crawford replied, "Because he sucks his thumb."

"But why his legs too?"

"Because he kicks off the covers."

"But doesn't it bother him?"

"No, he's used to it."

Another time Rogers noticed that Crawford was constantly taking the boy's thumb out of his mouth. "He's growing up with buck teeth," Crawford explained.

Rogers shrugged. As Hollywood problems go, it seemed minor. Beverly Hills was full of orthodontists, but Crawford didn't care.

James MacArthur remembered meeting Crawford and Christopher in 1949, when his mother Helen Hayes returned to Hollywood after fifteen years to make Leo McCarey's *My Son John*. "Joan invited mother and me over for

Sunday afternoon and I swam and played with Christina, who was about my age. Christopher was maybe three years younger.

It was a pleasant day. Then I was invited to spend a weekend and sleep overnight. I was in Chris's bedroom and when we got in bed the maid came in and began tying Chris to the bed.

I thought, "My God, this is the Hollywood I've heard about. They tie children of movie stars to their beds. Is the maid going to do it to me next? If so, she's gonna have a fight on her hands."

No, the maid left. I said to Chris, "How can you let them do that to you?" He said, "Don't worry about it." He did a little Houdini-like maneuver and he was out of the ropes in a flash.

The costumer Sheila O'Brien thought there was a basic misalliance between Christopher and his mother. "He did not want to do dishes," said O'Brien, "and I suggested giving him yard work [instead]." Crawford seems to have ignored the suggestion out of a basic lack of emotional suppleness.

Crawford undoubtedly saw all this as inculcating her own strong sense of purpose. If she saw someone with poor posture, she would show them how to put their back up against a wall, or how to carry a book on their head, because that's how she had taught herself to walk—like a movie star.

Her way was the best way. When Rosalind Rogers wanted to throw a party for her husband's fortieth birthday, she had thirty or forty people in mind. By the time Crawford was through micromanaging the event, the guest list had grown to seventy-five or eighty, which was too many for Rogers's house. They ended up having the party at Chasen's, with 180 attendees.

Joe Mankiewicz thought that the basic problem with Crawford's relationship with her oldest children involved her fantasies of proper behavior. "She held the theory that mother was always right. She had read it in screenplays, so that was the way it had to be. Children should grow up with a model and she wished someone had given her that kind of upbringing."

As far as Crawford was concerned, she was only trying to instill a sense of discipline, and if her two eldest children didn't grasp that, she had to mandate it. "I don't believe in progressive education," she told one reporter, "and I can't stand brats."

"I think I was a good mother," Crawford would insist.

I've always thought, too that "father" and "mother" are words that mean disciplinarian. . . . I was strict about some things. The pediatrician told me that if children took naps until they were 12 they'd be the healthiest ever. The kids hated that as they grew older, but it certainly paid off in good health.

They were taught the kind of self-sufficiency I'd had to learn in quite a different way when I was working my way through school. When they were old enough to stand on a stool at the sink they washed out their shoelaces and polished their little white shoes every day before putting them away. They hung up their clothes *if* they were clean—which wasn't very often.

But I didn't stand over them with a whip. If that kind of training is started early enough it becomes second nature. And it leaves you time to get on with more important things.

I was strict when I thought it was necessary, but I balanced it with tenderness, love and plenty of my time.

Between her unsettled private life and her newly unsettled career, it was a difficult time. The actress Nancy Olson recalled a party at Charles Feldman's house, when Crawford dominated the conversation with what Olson called "bitter tales of romance and broken love affairs." She ended her disquisition with a warning to Olson not to trust men.

"She was so strict with the kids," said Rosalind Rogers. "She wasn't mean about it; she felt she was a loving, adoring mother. Once I told her 'They're only kids.' She turned on me. 'Look, I never had a damn thing when I was a kid. I want them to appreciate everything they get.'"

"You're so tough," Rogers told her.

"It's a tough world," she snapped.

THE TRAJECTORY OF CRAWFORD'S career in this period can be charted by naming her recent directors in chronological order: Michael Curtiz, Jean

Negulesco, Curtis Bernhardt, Curtiz again, three for Vincent Sherman, and finally Felix Feist. Two confirmed A-list directors, followed by two competent studio craftsmen, and, bringing up the rear, a dyed-in-the-wool B movie director who could be had cheaply and with good reason.

Nineteen fifty-two was the year of decision regarding television. Every studio was shedding contract talent, and even B movie production was shifting—Monogram was changing its name to Allied Artists because the name Monogram had become synonymous with low-end production, which was now the province of TV. In the future, B movie production would increasingly center on drive-ins that attracted a loyal teenage audience, largely through the efforts of Roger Corman and American International Pictures.

When movie stars like Dick Powell, David Niven, and Loretta Young began fronting successful TV shows, it made the environment even more fraught for those left behind. Crawford had a chemical resistance to TV, for reasons both logical and emotional. Adrian didn't design for television, and James Wong Howe and Ernest Haller didn't photograph television. For actresses of a certain age TV seemed—and often was—slapdash, hence scary. And if you tried it and failed, what was your fallback?

One notable failure was Barbara Stanwyck, whose first TV show was a fast flop. Stanwyck would later have a modest hit with *The Big Valley*, a slavish imitation of *Bonanza*, but not a particularly good show. Stanwyck being Stanwyck, she never let up on her professionalism or intensity.

Crawford edged into TV warily, with an episode of *The Revlon Mirror Theater* in September 1953. "It can harm a player if things aren't exactly right," she said. "They must have the proper story, facilities, and material. I believe in film for television because I think a player, especially an actress, should look the way she looks on the screen—her best at all times."

In 1954, she tried what was known as a backdoor pilot, an episode on *The General Electric Theater* that could be spun off into a series if the response was sufficient. Crawford played a widowed newspaper columnist given to travel where she encounters what would presumably have been a succession of dramatic stories. The show didn't sell.

Crawford tried only one other pilot, a nighttime soap shot in 1965 called *Royal Bay*, opposite Paul Burke, the star of the TV version of *The Naked City*.

Royal Bay also failed to sell, but it got some play as a movie of the week under the title *Della*.

Crawford was still represented by MCA, the talent agency founded by Jules Stein and run by Lew Wasserman and a crew of lieutenants who were mandated to dress in white shirts and black suits. The overall effect was of a group of men who were either assassins, undertakers, or both.

Wasserman would become Hollywood's Pope, the man charged with making deals with the unions. He was universally respected, universally feared, but what set him apart from all the other moguls was that, unlike Sam Goldwyn or Jack Warner, his word was good. A handshake from Wasserman was the equivalent of a heavily lawyered contract with anybody else.

Crawford would work occasionally on TV in the 1960s and '70s on shows both low-end (*Zane Grey Theatre*) and high-end—*Route 66, The Virginian*. The shows were often produced by Universal's TV operation—Wasserman always remained loyal to his old clients. The salaries varied, usually from $5,000 to $10,000 for a week's work. It was top money for the period, but TV would never be Crawford's natural habitat.

Wasserman was rarely quoted directly, but would speak circumspectly and usually off the record. Of Crawford, he would say, "I don't remember having an argument with her, but she certainly was not a patsy. She could be tough and opinionated, but she respected my opinion if my motives were on her behalf. She would listen."

The MCA agent assigned to Crawford on a daily basis was Art Park. Park found that Joan "was great to work with. She worked with you, didn't challenge you, supported you. Joan's biggest problem was having been a star when there was a firmament for stars. She couldn't adjust to changing times. She wanted to play with younger actors, but the younger male stars wanted younger actresses. I told her, 'It's the one thing we have no control over—getting older.'"

In response to Park's honesty, Crawford cried. The same problem was bedeviling Stanwyck and Bette Davis, which was no consolation. Like Norma Desmond, they were all actresses too big for pictures that were getting smaller by the month.

Crawford was now pushing fifty and was coming off a series of flops and near flops. Those can be ridden out when you're thirty, but those same flops are something else entirely when you're middle-aged in a shrinking business.

As Joan Crawford surveyed the landscape, both her professional and romantic futures looked highly uncertain. Because she was Joan Crawford, she did the only thing she knew how to do: forge ahead.

Above: Joan in *Sudden Fear*.

PART THREE

*"I never wanted to be some sort of joke,
and thank God, I haven't been."*

—Joan Crawford

CHAPTER FIFTEEN

CRAWFORD'S FRIENDSHIP WITH KATHERINE Albert had remained strong since meeting at MGM in 1925, so much so that Albert and her husband Dale Eunson had made her godmother to their daughter, whom they named Joan. It seemed like kismet when the young girl was signed to a contract by Sam Goldwyn. She was only fourteen, but she photographed older, so Goldwyn issued press releases saying she was sixteen. Goldwyn was looking for an unknown to play the title role in a picture called *Roseanna McCoy*—about the Hatfield-McCoy feud—and he chose Joan Eunson, who was rechristened Joan Evans.

But Goldwyn had been floundering ever since William Wyler left his employ after *The Best Years of Our Lives*, a problem the producer never quite managed to solve. *Roseanna McCoy* flopped, as did Evans's other Goldwyn pictures, *Edge of Doom* and *Our Very Own*.

"Joan was always wonderful to me," Evans remembered. "Just before World War II, when I was only about six or seven. I stayed with my grandmother in New York for a while. When I was to join my parents in Los Angeles, I made the trip there with Joan on the 20th Century and the Super Chief. You had to change trains in Chicago, then. I'm sure few who were there ever forgot the sight of Joan Crawford descending on Dearborn Street Station with entourage, luggage and tyke in tow. I know I never have."

In time, Joan Evans fell in love with a young man named Kirby Weatherly. He had no show business connections, and her parents didn't approve. They also may have thought their eighteen-year-old daughter was old enough for the movies but too young to be married. In any case, Crawford decided to intervene in a family crisis by holding the July 1952 wedding at her house on North Bristol.

Crawford explained. "They'd have gone off and gotten married anyhow. They were married here at the house and spent their wedding night in Christina's room. I put out a lovely nightgown and pajamas and had champagne on ice and when they were married a year, we had the little anniversary party here in the garden."

Evans and Weatherly stayed married for the rest of their lives, but Crawford's friendship with her godchild's parents was irretrievably broken. "Katherine has never forgiven me," admitted Crawford, "and that's sad, because I've missed her."

The presumption was and is breathtaking, and the episode is fascinating for Crawford's correct estimation of the strength of the bond between young lovers that was far more successful than her judgment regarding her own relationships. For the rest of her life, Crawford referred to Joan and her husband as her son and daughter. Joan Evans managed to reconcile with her parents and kept a photo of Crawford in her office for the rest of her life.

Evans resented what happened to Joan Crawford's reputation. "She always used to be the quintessential movie star, now she's a child-abusing joke." She never saw any evidence of child abuse.

DAVID MILLER, A DIRECTOR who had been at MGM for years, got a call from a producer named Joseph Kaufman. Kaufman announced that he was working on an independent production to star Joan Crawford and "I've had several scripts written, none were satisfactory. We would like you to direct."

Miller had met Crawford when he was working in the short subjects department at MGM, although that didn't explain why he was being asked to undertake a Crawford picture. He read the scripts Kaufman had in hand for the picture but wasn't impressed. Miller then read the novel by Edna Sherry on which the scripts were based and found a paragraph that he thought could be expanded into something cinematic.

Miller called Kaufman and explained. Kaufman was happy to have found someone with an idea. He said he was going to call Miller's agent and make a deal, but Miller told him to call Crawford first. Crawford loved Miller's take, but before Miller agreed to direct the picture he wanted to talk to her. Miller had talked to a couple of directors who had worked with Crawford, and they had both told him it was crucial to level with her at all times.

Kaufman arranged the call.

"Hello, Miss Crawford."

"David, darling! I think your idea is great."

"It's not my idea. It came out of the book."

"Anyway, I like it very much."

"Is it good enough for you not to have script approval?"

A pause.

"Yessss. What happens when you and I can't agree?"

"Then we will have Joe Kaufman arbitrate."

"No, that won't work."

Crawford explained that she needed to be honest with Miller. He agreed, then told her, "I want to be in a position to tell you to go fuck yourself."

She laughed for a long time and asked if the agreement would be contractual.

"Not if I have your agreement," said Miller.

"You have it."

Miller's phrase regarding Crawford was an "honest broad." Kaufman hired Lenore Coffee to write the script using Miller's ideas, and the picture began to move toward production. Crawford wanted Clark Gable as her leading man, but that wasn't going to happen. For one thing, Kaufman couldn't afford Gable. For another, playing a murderer wasn't in Gable's career path and never would be.

David Miller became fascinated by Jack Palance, who had just broken through in Elia Kazan's *Panic in the Streets*. (*Shane*, which made Palance a star, was shot in the summer of 1951, but George Stevens took eighteen months to edit his film, which only came out in August 1953, a year after *Sudden Fear* was released.)

"You must have a reason," Crawford said to Miller after watching the Kazan movie. "You want to use Richard Widmark?"

"No, I don't. I want to use Jack Palance." Crawford's initial reaction was puzzlement—Palance was not handsome/sexy, but dangerous/sexy, not to mention ugly/dangerous. The more she thought about it, the angrier she got.

"She was incensed. She ushered me out of the playroom, then pushed me out of the house."

Miller drove home, got into bed, and then the phone rang. It was Crawford, in tears. "You don't love me. You don't respect me! How can you think of me with such a leading man? I've played with all big stars!"

Miller couldn't help but be moved by this woman, desperately looking for someone she could trust, reaching out in the middle of the night. And if that someone could be convinced of her point of view, so much the better. Miller asked her to run the Kazan film again. That softened her somewhat, and the third viewing softened her some more, but she still didn't understand.

"I want you to level, and I know you will—why this man?"

"It's difficult to tell you."

"You must. *That's what I want!*"

Miller sighed and told her the truth. "In the last few pictures you made, you played not only the female lead, but the male lead as well." He pointed out that Hitchcock worked overtime to make his heroines vulnerable, and an intrinsically menacing actor like Palance could accomplish the same thing.

Against her better judgment, Crawford finally acquiesced. Palance was hired for $12,000 plus his wardrobe, but he proved to be difficult. Palance had made only a few pictures, but he had the confidence of a steely veteran.

Throughout the shoot of *Sudden Fear* in January and February 1952, Palance concentrated on his own performance rather than helping Crawford. When it came time to shoot her close-ups, Palance stood off-camera and didn't give her any perceptible reactions. "I wish you'd tell him when he's not on camera to act as though he was," Crawford told Miller. For his part, Palance said that in the middle of a take, Crawford would break character and say to David Miller, "I don't want a Brando quality in this thing."

Nor did Palance respond to her as a woman, which put Crawford off her feed, as did the presence of Gloria Grahame as the tramp with whom Palance's character is having an affair. "You can't like everyone you work with," Crawford told one reporter. "She's perfect for the part."

Emotional displays aside, Miller thought Crawford gave an expert performance, although he said cameraman Charles Lang Jr. had some difficulties. "She wasn't always easy to photograph at this stage. Her upper face was OK, but the chin was a problem. But she had a knack of being able to go through a scene with her chin up to avoid sag."

Crawford's deal with Joseph Kaufman involved a choice of either a flat $200,000 or 40 percent of the profits. She and Lew Wasserman went to a screening of the finished film and made the right choice—she took the percentage. Because Crawford was a partner in the film's proceeds, she agreed to do a five-week personal appearance tour, which was a success despite her nerves.

Sudden Fear combines two viable genres—woman-in-peril and *noir*—in a very successful melding that's one of the best of Crawford's late starring pictures. Crawford plays Myra Hudson, a successful playwright who falls for Palance's Lester Blaine, an unsuccessful actor. Blaine has a girlfriend, the lusciously duplicitous Gloria Grahame, and they plot to bump off Myra, who discovers said plot courtesy of a recorder accidentally left running.

At that point, the film takes a delicious Hitchcockian turn, as Myra, used to inventing plots, proceeds to devise one that will rid herself of both her antagonists.

The climax is a tense, beautifully shot and edited tour of San Francisco at night, which manages to disguise the fact that it was actually shot around Bunker Hill in Los Angeles. *Sudden Fear* was a good movie as well as a profitable one—cost of $600,000, domestic rentals of $1.65 million. A few years earlier, before the movies began bleeding audience, it would have made considerably more.

Next up was a possibility that flared out. Daniel Taradash was writing the screenplay of James Jones's *From Here to Eternity* for Columbia. As Taradash remembered, "[Burt] Lancaster was almost a given from the word go. Joan Crawford was mentioned for the wife with whom Lancaster has an affair, and [Harry] Cohn kind of liked the idea. [Director Fred] Zinnemann had a long conversation with her, and he said, 'I think she can do it, and she says she'll play it without the frills and the glamour.' She was more or less cast until one day they got a call saying she wanted her own cameraman and makeup. Cohn and Zinnemann shook their heads, and that was the end of Joan Crawford."

It worked out for the picture. Crawford rolling around in the surf with Burt Lancaster would not have had the erotic charge that the pristine Deborah Kerr brought to the scene. But it was a tactical blunder on Crawford's part—*From Here to Eternity* on the heels of *Sudden Fear* would have put her back on top.

———◇◇———

CRAWFORD HAD LONG SINCE realized that she was a business as much as an actress. One writer noted that "There's no good reason why Crawford Preferred shouldn't be listed on the Big Board. . . . Joan sets the example of never neglecting small stockholders. It's a cheerful sight to see her greeting them by name on the street, asking about their children's health and spreading good will for big business. The product involved here is personal glamour."

Despite her reflexive tending of the franchise, despite the success of *Sudden Fear*, there was a growing sense that Crawford was increasingly out of style, if only because the movie business was changing around her. Like Cagney, like Stanwyck, Crawford was a concrete, assertive performer, an artist who had mastered a repertoire of behavior and could shade it on cue.

But what had been the dominant form of acting for a half century was being replaced by a more abstract approach, just as painting and jazz were moving in the same direction. There's a wonderful book by the psychologist James Hillman and the critic Michael Ventura called *We've Had a Hundred Years of Psychotherapy and the World's Getting Worse*. As Ventura writes, "An Olivier or a [Katharine] Hepburn will project their roles at you as precisely as a laser, focusing on a moment's absolute center; [Montgomery] Clift or [Gena] Rowlands will play the same moment at its edge. Olivier or Hepburn will play the same moment when its most itself, where it is *that* moment and no other; Clift or Rowlands will play the moment at the border, where it's begun to change into something else."

The older style concerned itself with narrative told through well-defined characters, while the newer style focused less on specific narrative and more on revealing the paradoxical realities of human nature. The earlier style is centered, the later style less grounded.

There were a few actors who could play in either style—Cary Grant, for instance. Grant is often farcically broad in comedy, simultaneously giving an expert performance and occasionally peeking out from behind the performance in open enjoyment of his own prodigious skill. In his rare serious dramas (*None but the Lonely Heart, Notorious*) he abandons the whirling comic mechanism so we can see a furtive wisp of the bleak disgruntlement he carried with him for most of his life, which makes those dramatic performances seem perennially modern.

Ventura again: "Where Bette Davis and Clark Gable walk into a room as though they're expecting to take it over, Paul Newman and Warren Beatty . . . walk into a room as though they're expecting to have to leave, and very soon too."

One of these styles makes an audience feel secure; the other makes them uncertain, which is why old movies retain a considerable fan base. You pays your money and you makes your choice.

To put it succinctly, a style focused on internal and external commitment morphed into one centered on behavioral and psychological ambiguity. Crawford had the bravado of Olivier or Hepburn, and the same unerring focus on the specific point of a given scene. Crawford knew all about the ambiguities of real life, and, like most of the audience, she wasn't particularly comfortable with them let alone expert at solving them. She was profoundly in sync with the dramatic certainty of movies. The problem Crawford and the rest of her generation of actors would increasingly face as time went on and the later style became codified was finding material—and coworkers—that would simultaneously mesh with their style and the audience's changing taste.

Besides that, there was the problem of younger actresses. One in particular. "It was like a burlesque show," complained Crawford about a recent appearance by Marilyn Monroe at the *Photoplay* magazine awards in 1953. "The audience yelled and shouted and Jerry Lewis got up on the table and whistled. But those of us in the industry just shuddered. . . . Sex plays a tremendously important part in every person's life. People are interested in it, intrigued with it. But they don't like to see it flaunted in their faces.

"Kids don't like her. Sex plays a growingly important part in their lives too, and they don't like to see it exploited. . . . Miss Monroe is making the mistake of believing her publicity. Someone should make her see the light. She should be told that the public likes provocative feminine personalities, but it also likes to know that underneath it all the actresses are ladies."

The transformation from a girl obsessed with a manic Charleston to a theoretically sedate matron who preferred the foxtrot was never more apparent.

FROM ONE OF HER best movies, Crawford segued to one of her worst.

Crawford had been gone from MGM for a decade, but Benny Thau, the longtime head of talent, sent her a script titled *Why Should I Cry?*, an unlikely soap opera about a star of musicals who falls in love with a blind pianist.

It wasn't Louis B. Mayer's MGM anymore. He had been deposed in 1951, and Dore Schary was now running production. The studio had radically cut back from what it had been even a few years earlier, and further economizing was on the horizon. The stock company was thinned out, and budgets and shooting schedules had been reduced accordingly.

Despite all this, Crawford thought it would be fun to go back to the studio she always regarded as home, and asked for Charles Walters, the director of *Lili*, which she had found "delightful." Crawford phoned Walters and asked if she could bring over dinner and some vodka in order to talk about the script. As she read him the script, Walters began to worry. "I found [the script] a little dumb. She was supposed to play a tap dancer, and one of the first shots was supposed to be a close-up of the tap shoes as she's getting into a taxi. I said—to myself—that at her age, Joan Crawford should not be prancing around in tap shoes."

Despite his doubts, Walters was under contract, so he accepted the job. He soon found out the meaning of the phrase "full-court press" as Crawford laid siege to him. At a meeting at her house, he found her in a housecoat but fully made up. Drinks were served, after which she stood up and opened the housecoat to reveal her naked body. It wasn't a sexual move—Crawford would have known that Walters was gay. "It was purely professional," said Walters. "This was our first film together, and what she was saying was, 'Okay, you'd better see what you've got to work with.' She simply wanted to show me the equipment." If Walters admired the equipment, so much the better.

The picture began shooting on April 27, and a large banner proclaiming "Welcome Back, Joan!" was hung over MGM's main entrance on Washington Boulevard in Culver City. Retitled *Torch Song*, the musical had a stringent budget of $1 million. Crawford was nervous, understandably so. She had asked Billy Haines to come and watch her dance rehearsals, and he responded in character: "Only God or a good-looking man could get your legs up that high."

Charles Walters had begun his career at MGM as a dancer, was gradually upgraded to choreographer, and finally became a director. He characterized Crawford with three words: "Ambition, drive, professionalism." He clearly admired and respected her but didn't seem entirely sure if he liked her. "She was a namedropper, and the name she loved to drop the most was Joan Crawford. She intoned it—'Joan . . . Crawford.'"

Walters and Crawford rehearsed the opening number for two weeks before the start of shooting because "I knew she would worry about it through the film." Walters proposed shooting it on the first day of production to get it out of the way, and Crawford agreed.

When she arrived on the set, everyone was there—Dore Schary, Fred Astaire, Ann Blyth. The men on the crew were all wearing carnations in their lapels. There was a basket of Italian delicacies signed "from an admirer"—Clark Gable. Then Crawford brought out her presents: Chuck Walters got a gray cashmere sweater and a dozen lamb chops.

At 8:45 a.m., she was theoretically ready to shoot, but she was in her dressing room. "She called for me," said Walters. "I went in her room and found her sitting on a stool before a mirror. 'I am absolutely petrified,' she said. 'I can't face it. You're going to hate me, but I gotta have a drink.'

"All right, Joan, I think that's warranted."

"You gotta have one with me."

Promptly at 9:45, Walters and Crawford emerged from her dressing room. They were both slightly the worse for wear, but she was sober enough to do the number.

The script of *Torch Song* was a throwback to Crawford movies of twenty years earlier—a dancer loses love, then finds it. The difference was that Crawford was now firmly middle-aged, which mandated a middle-aged actor. The studio's choice was Michael Wilding, who was deep in the bottle over problems in his marriage to Elizabeth Taylor. Wilding had to have his lines pasted on the piano, which led to Crawford upbraiding him. "How dare you come in not knowing the words. This is an insult to your fellow workers. And your breath stinks!"

Needless to say, Crawford and Wilding were never simpatico, but the dialogue scenes were finished by May 23, after which they moved on to the big musical number, which was danced to a song called "Two-Faced Woman." It had been recorded for Vincente Minnelli's *The Band Wagon* but got cut and was being used as a cost-saving measure. Crawford and the rest of the dancers were covered in dark pancake that made everybody look biracial, irrevocably sending the number into the stratosphere of High Camp. *Torch Song* finished shooting on June 2.

Other than the first day, Crawford didn't drink and was unfailingly generous to the entire crew. She gave Walters a rubber tree on which were hanging presents—a stopwatch; vitamin pills. Every Friday she threw a cocktail party for the entire crew and added silk shirts to Walters's stash of gifts.

Walters was generally able to pierce the façade that shrouded divas, but he could never quite manage it with Crawford. "She was always 'On.' I had worked with Garland. I figure it would be better if I knew them better than they knew themselves. I knew Garland better than she knew herself. But Joan's façade never dropped, drunk or sober. She gave me a gold cigarette case and lighter, monogrammed. To show her businesslike nature, she also gave me the bill of sale. 'I know you will need this so you can insure it.'

"Nobody ever knew the woman. She had manufactured an image and it became her."

Walters remembered being invited for a quiet lunch at Crawford's house one Sunday. She had hired John Morris, an accomplished artist, to reframe some of her paintings. Morris had set up shop in the garage and would move the frames out to the yard when they had to dry. "She knew exactly when the Gray Line tour bus would come by. At the right time, she was [outside] painting frames when the bus went by."

Similarly, she was still sending advance copies of her schedule to her New York fan club so they could meet up with her. Walters asked her if she didn't want some privacy.

"They put me where I am," she replied. "If they aren't to be where I am, they goddamn well better know about it. If it wasn't for them, I'd still be in Kansas."

Despite his mingled feelings about her—maybe because of his mingled feelings about her—they stayed friends for the rest of her life. One time they were on a train when Crawford mixed Walters a scotch and soda out of her private liquor case. He got to the bottom of the glass and discovered a stunning set of sapphire and gold cuff links and studs. It was his birthday, and she had prepared by getting him a present. This time there was no accompanying bill.

BY NOW, MOST ARTICLES about Crawford led off with an awestruck acknowledgment of how long she'd been a star, a refrain that clearly got on her nerves. In an article about actresses over forty, and, in some cases, over fifty, i.e., bravely confronting imminent death, a roster that included Marlene Dietrich, Gloria Swanson, Claudette Colbert, Irene Dunne, Barbara Stanwyck, and Crawford, Hedda Hopper pointed out that Crawford was the only one who got touchy when her age was mentioned.

Billy Haines remained Crawford's best friend, and he always saw her clearly, undying affection or not. "I've only known two movie stars," he said.

> Swanson and Crawford. Real old-fashioned classic stars. (Garbo was an import who never settled.)
>
> [Crawford] recognizes herself strongly, knows her weaknesses. Probably that's why she doesn't like criticism—she knows it already, has a thorough inventory of herself. She has a scent for publicity like an animal for a wounded deer. Never misuses it. She's fearless in what she attempts to do, has no shame whatsoever. If she's to sing, she'll sing even if it's not good singing. She has faith in herself.
>
> She has set the pattern for her own life. Nothing halfway. She can be either the worst bitch or the best friend in the world, and in 28 years I've never been bored. She runs the gamut from the *Police Gazette* to *Vogue*.
>
> She is my best friend. We've had some rough times and we each always think the other is at fault. One time she had her secretary call to say she

wanted her curtains cleaned and they had to be back in two days. I politely told the secretary what to tell Joan to do with her curtains, and she did. Joan had the whole room redone just to show me, and we didn't speak for months.

When she's tired, she becomes a little girl again, Billie Cassin—a Southern accent, soft, clinging. When other old friends are around, she's likely to become Lucille LeSueur. Let one foreign face come into the room and she's the grand lady, Joan Crawford. When she calls me playing Billie, I always say, "Who is this?" It infuriates her.

Give her criticism and you get what I call her two cold fried eggs look, and she changes the subject. But she lets you know later on in some little way that she's heeded the advice. . . . She has an instinct for human relationships in her career. Personally, not always.

Haines remembered one incident in particular. It was twenty-five years before, and the party was at his house. Clara Bow was there, a lot of other people. They were dancing to Cliff Edwards records and presumably feeling no pain. A friend of Haines's made a pass at Crawford. She handled it well and politely refused, but the man wouldn't leave her alone.

Haines interceded and told the man he'd have to leave. He refused. Haines picked him up and threw him out the front door. Things went further south, and the two men got into a fistfight in the street. The next day the friend called and told Haines he'd had some teeth knocked out. Haines told him to go to the dentist and he'd pay for it. He tried to collect half of the expense from Crawford, who, reasonably enough, refused to pay for dental issues resulting from the lout's boorish behavior. Haines was furious and they once again entered a period of Not Speaking.

Haines summed her up by saying, "She thrives on challenge. She doesn't trade on her femininity."

Haines said he thought winning the Academy Award had given her a "recognition of self," and the years that had preceded it had likewise given her an underlying sense of imminent professional catastrophe. "I've touched the top rung [but] she'd been too young to understand my problems. It's like walking on nothing. The career of no return.

"She's unique. A capacity for lots of things. For friends, for hate, and for love."

SHE WAS NOW APPROACHING grande dame territory, and had grown used to designating suitable men as a temporary consort. A typical event was meeting someone at a party or some other social event and inviting them to her house for a nightcap, as with Robert Wagner, by now a rising young star.

"She suggested I follow her back to her house in Brentwood," remembered Wagner. "After I got there, she asked me if I would like a swim. She told me there were some trunks down by the pool and I could help myself. I went down to the pool, took my clothes off, put on a pair of trunks and got in the pool.

"After a few minutes, Joan came out of the house with absolutely nothing on, did a very graceful dive off the board, swam the length of the pool underwater, and came up right between my legs."

"Hi there!" she said in her brightest, most vivacious voice. It was a lovely, creative invitation and Wagner responded accordingly. "She was a dynamic lover, both domineering—which you might expect—and yielding—which you might not."

IN SEPTEMBER 1953, CRAWFORD sat for a long interview with Hedda Hopper. The transcript reveals their conversation as respectful but never intimate. There's conversation about *Johnny Guitar*, her first real Western since the days of Tim McCoy, and her physical condition. Her waist was 25 inches, her weight 127.

"What do you think has kept you a star all these years?" asked Hopper.

Crawford took a beat to think about it, then replied, "Honesty. And devotion to my work. I've been really devoted to it." She admitted to being ambivalent about television, even though she'd done one or two shows and was thinking about a series. The plan was to make a numbing thirty-nine episodes in the first year. It never happened, perhaps because it would have meant abandoning her first love—movies—perhaps because the hurry-up-and-get-it-done aesthetic of television would always give her pause.

"There's one day of rehearsal and three days shooting time. On pictures I get up at quarter to five; on television I get up at quarter to four. I must be ready to shoot by 8:00. And one night I worked until 8:30; the next night until 10:00. The next until 12:30. Then I fell on my face."

Willard Sheldon, who had been an assistant director at MGM in the silent days and who liked Crawford, was working at Universal when Crawford did one of her first TV shows and found it an interesting experience.

"She was a woman with a lot of quirks," Sheldon said. One of the quirks involved Kleenex. When her face needed to be cleaned between takes, the Kleenex could touch Crawford's face only once, then had to be thrown away. "She went through boxes and boxes of Kleenex," said Sheldon.

She also needed to feel more centered than TV usually allowed. She had been used to nicely appointed dressing rooms at MGM and Warner's, but Universal never bothered with lavish dressing rooms for guest stars on TV production. For Joan Crawford, they made an exception. She wanted to sleep in her dressing room while making the TV show, so a decently sized dressing room was constructed out of plywood on the soundstage where the show would be made. Sheldon was there to greet her when she arrived for the shoot. When Crawford saw him she let out a yell and came straight over to him, keeping all the executives waiting while she talked with another alumnus of MGM.

When it came time to show her the dressing room, she refused to go in, saying, "There might be someone in there." The director and producer both offered to go in and check the place out, but she refused. When Sheldon said he'd check it out for her, she said, "All right, Willard. I trust you. If you say everything's OK, I'll go in."

It was a fully appointed dressing room with everything she might need. There was a bed, a kitchenette, a table with a couple of bottles of liquor. Sheldon poured himself a quick drink, then came out to tell Crawford it was all clear. "And she said, 'OK' and in she went!"

She addressed the issue of how she'd changed over the years: "At [a] luncheon at MGM the other day, I saw Freddie March. We did *Susan and God* together, but at that stage . . . I had no sense of humor. I was too serious about my career. You have to have a balance of humor. A bad picture is not the [worst] thing in the world. Well, during the lunch Freddie said to me, 'Gee, you're fun.' Then he had a puzzled look and I could read his mind. He was thinking, 'You weren't this way on *Susan and God.*'"

And they talked about young actors and actresses, some of whom she heartily approved of. "I think everybody in the industry should open their arms to [Audrey Hepburn] and say, 'Come in and help us. . . . This girl was born in a camera. . . . She has a kind of magic. I think this child will know intuitively what to do. . . . Audrey Hepburn is like Katie Hepburn in *A Bill of Divorcement*. . . .

"Leslie Caron is in a class with Audrey Hepburn. People say she's not pretty. Who cares? She has talent. Pier Angeli is another—if she doesn't rely on her beauty. . . . Jean Simmons is our greatest young talent outside of Hepburn. And Burt Lancaster told me he'd never met a genius until he met Montgomery Clift."

JILL WINKLER, THE WIDOW of Otto Winkler, an MGM publicist who had died in the same airplane crash that killed Carole Lombard, wrote Crawford with a proposal for a TV pilot that Crawford found interesting but lacking in dramatic potential. Hedda Hopper had acted as go-between, and Crawford wrote Hopper to inform her of her reactions:

> It's now 11:30 at night . . . and I can't call you naturally at this hour. But I did want to talk to you about it. I think Jill's idea . . . is very interesting. And the suggested prospectus of future scripts is fine, too. The only thing I feel—and I must be honest with you, Hedda—I feel that Jill will not be able to get any star to play this part. It's actually plain narration. The star part is inactive. It brings in a lot of interesting characters—like soap operas . . . [and] I think it's a brilliant idea for an unknown or for someone who's done a couple of pictures—but certainly not for a star (and this is merely my opinion). I think that is why Irene Dunne's show is off the air.

Crawford was now between men as well as between pictures. She took to putting Cliquot, her French poodle, into the car and heading out for long excursions toward unplanned destinations. At night, she'd call Hedda Hopper and leave messages about her nonadventures: "Crawford has been having a great time staying at motels all the time," Hopper wrote in her notes.

> Gets up in the morning, goes to nearest lunch counter, then on her way. Doesn't know who gets more attention, she or Cliquot, but is quite sure dog has slight edge. Raving about courtesy of truck drivers who get in the middle of the road if they think car in back is dangerous to pass, but immediately pull over and wave you through if the road is clear ahead. When she gets back wants to do an article about truck drivers.
>
> Staying at Lake Louise for a few more days, then coming down the coast, will take her a week to drive down. Greatest experience of her life, has been wanting to do it for years. Calls home and talks to kids every night. Strong reaction of people in little towns where she stops. They aren't sure whether it is or isn't. In one coffee shop she heard two guys making a bet as to whether it was her or not—she bent over to the guy who bet against it and told him to save his money.

There's something poignant about Crawford piling the dog and some suitcases into the car and hitting the road, seeing sights she had never taken the time to see without the impetus of a movie location.

―――――◆◇――――

IT WAS A MARK of Crawford's shaky career that she jumped into a picture at Republic Pictures. Republic resided on the upper range of Poverty Row, which meant that ordinarily Crawford would have avoided it like leprosy, but the studio was engaged in one of its periodic lunges at classing up the joint—they had produced Orson Welles's *Macbeth* in 1948 and John Ford's *The Quiet Man* in 1952.

Crawford was probably connected to *Johnny Guitar*—the novel had been dedicated to her—because she had bought the movie rights before publication. The novel was written by Roy Chanslor, who had a bent for plots centering on brash women. (Chanslor also wrote *The Ballad of Cat Ballou*, later made into a successful comedy with Lee Marvin and Jane Fonda, and worked uncredited on Fritz Lang's *Rancho Notorious*.)

As screenwriter Philip Yordan told the story, *Johnny Guitar* was on location in Arizona when things fell apart. Yordan got a call late one night from Lew Wasserman—Yordan's agent as well as Crawford's. "Phil, I'm in deep trouble. I've got Joan Crawford and [director] Nick Ray and a bunch of our people in Arizona and they've been shooting for a week. And Joan won't go before the camera because she says the script stinks. . . . If she leaves, Republic will go out of business. They can't take a loss on two million dollars worth of commitment. They'll save only a couple hundred thousand by not shooting. They'll sue me, MCA will sue Joan—but she doesn't care. We can't let that happen. I want you to go there and satisfy her to go before the camera. There's a car on the way to pick you up. I chartered a plane for you and you're leaving right now."

What seems to have happened was that the first-draft script had been written by Ben Maddow, the coauthor of scripts for *The Asphalt Jungle* and *Intruder in the Dust*. But by the time *Johnny Guitar* was ready to shoot, Maddow had been blacklisted, and Yordan was fronting for him, along with several other blacklisted writers. Wasserman called Yordan because he expected him to make the script shootable, if not good.

Yordan flew to Sedona and talked to Nick Ray. "I need this picture," Ray told him. "It can't be abandoned, so do something with her. I can't talk to her anymore. She feels I betrayed her. . . . She needs the money too, but she just doesn't want to go ahead."

Finally, Yordan talked to Crawford, who told him, "It's just a crock."

"Well, listen Joan, you know the situation. If you go, the company goes down."

"Well, I gotta protect my career. I'm not on the way up. And this picture could finish me."

"I agree with you."

"Can you re-write it?"

"Yeah, though with the shooting and all, I don't have much time. But tell me, what bothers you?"

"It's nonsense. I have no part. I just stand around and walk around with boots on and have a few stupid scenes."

"Well, what's your idea?"

"There's Sterling Hayden in the picture, and he's not much, and some other actor and he's not much and Ward Bond, one of the actors who John Ford is always using in those pictures with [John] Wayne and he's not much. So I want to play the man. I want to shoot it out in the end with Mercedes McCambridge, and instead of me playing with myself in a corner, let Sterling play with himself in the corner and I'll do the shoot-out."

"I said, 'Ah, uh, um . . . if I do that, will you do the picture?'"

"She says, 'Yeah.'"

"I said OK."

Yordan talked to Nick Ray and said, "Nick, look, you need the money. I can use the money. MCA is good to us . . . so why don't you get up in the morning and when you shave in the morning, say, 'I'll never work with Joan Crawford again,' and then in eight weeks it'll be over!"

According to Yordan, Ray thought about it and then said, "Never is a long time."

Yordan began rewriting the dialogue of Vienna, Crawford's character, to make it edgier, more commanding:

Johnny: How many men have you forgotten?

Vienna: As many women as you've remembered.

In retrospective stories about moviemaking, someone is always playing the part of the cavalry and riding to the rescue. In Phil Yordan's stories, the rescuer was always Phil Yordan. Nick Ray's version was different and marginally more believable, if only because he wasn't the one riding to the rescue. Rather, he was the one in need of rescuing.

He and Crawford had been brought together by Lew Wasserman and Wasserman's lieutenant Jennings Lang. The plan was to make two pictures, one titled *Lisbon* for Paramount and *Johnny Guitar* at Republic. Ray worked with Andrew Solt and John Lee Mahin on the script for *Lisbon*, which was about a wealthy woman who works as a double agent. Ray and the writers wrestled with the project for months and couldn't make it work. Finally Crawford told him, "Oh, hell, Nick, give it balls. Write it for Gable and I'll play it."

"*That* was the central character of Joan—she would take any challenge," said Ray. *Lisbon* ended up being sold to Republic as a vehicle for Ray Milland. *Johnny Guitar* was the other project and as Ray said, "I set out to break all the rules. First of all, I started out with two women, not men."

According to Ray, he was the one who hired Phil Yordan, who had the reputation of being "a road company Ben Hecht." Hecht would hire young or blacklisted writers for bargain rates and use them to ghost scripts for which he took the credit and most of the money. (Whether Ray knew that Yordan farmed the script out to Ben Maddow is unknown.)

Ray realized that Crawford had reached a stage of life where she could be jealous of younger actresses. The younger actress on *Johnny Guitar* was Mercedes McCambridge, who was every bit as fierce as the star. Crawford and McCambridge loathed each other on sight and spent the production trying to upstage each other. The relationship was complicated by the fact that both actresses were drinking.

Since Crawford was the star, McCambridge was mostly left to stew. In Crawford's memoir she couldn't bring herself to mention McCambridge's name, but referred to her as an "excellent actress but a rabble-rouser. . . . Her delight was to create friction."

McCambridge would say that the relationship got off on the wrong foot when Crawford told her she had wanted Claire Trevor to play her part. "At one point," said McCambridge, "I went to her dressing room and said that we should make up. She asked me to leave." Ray decided to use the antagonism between the two women as fuel for their scenes together. "I wasn't about to encourage sweetness and light."

Crawford's core problem with the script was that she believed her character's behavior needed to be justified. She gave Ray an outline of five new scenes she believed were necessary. While she was talking Ray was calculating what the scenes would add to the picture's cost. He came up with a rough figure of $600,000. Yordan eventually delivered those five scenes, of which Ray used "parts of three scenes." The added cost was a more modest $220,000, "which Republic could afford."

After about six weeks of shooting, Herbert Yates, the head of Republic, returned from Europe and looked at the *Johnny Guitar* footage. He told Ray, "I love it, but the film's in color and I don't see any flowers."

The pressure kept building after the picture relocated to Hollywood. One night Ray called Humphrey Bogart, who was "always a refuge for me."

"I'm at LaRue's with Joan Crawford," Ray told Bogart. "Can I bring her over and we'll play gin rummy?"

"Wait a minute, I'll ask Betty."

Lauren Bacall came back with, "Oh, Christ, bring the bitch over."

Ray went back to the table and told Crawford they were going to Bogart's house.

She snorted. "Not with a written invitation."

Ray said that he and Crawford eventually paired off, but not until the picture was finished. Scheduled for thirty-four days of shooting, it took forty-four. The entire experience left Ray with edgy recollections of catastrophe narrowly averted, and of being trapped between two angry women—a place no man wants to be.

The end result of all this flagrant hostility seasoned with confusion was a very strange picture shot in Republic's Trucolor process, whose bold primary colors can burn the retina if you're too close to the screen. The brand name Trucolor was a blatant lie—it had burnished skin tones and house-on-fire reds, but greens tilted strongly toward brown.

Because it was being written as it was being shot, the picture is dramatically unwieldy, but Nicholas Ray gives it his uneasy neurotic charge—characters who vacillate between ferocity and tenderness for no specific dramatic reason. He also manages to be the first director to get Sterling Hayden to stop bellowing his lines—no small accomplishment. As compensation, he lets Mercedes McCambridge do all the yelling. She seems to be playing a furious lesbian, possibly in preparation for *Giant* two years down the road, where she played a different part in exactly the same manner.

To everybody's surprise, *Johnny Guitar* was a commercial hit, probably the last one Republic had before they went out of business in 1957. It earned $2.5 million in domestic rentals. Ray said because of *Johnny Guitar*, "Warner Brothers thought I had a magic formula, and gave me *Rebel Without a Cause*."

Over time, *Johnny Guitar* became one of the florid one-offs beloved by people whose favorite movies mandate sunglasses. "[Crawford] is beyond consideration of beauty,'" François Truffaut rhapsodized. "She has become unreal, a fantasy of herself. Whiteness has invaded her eyes, muscles have taken over her face, a will of iron behind a face of steel. She is a phenomenon. She is becoming more manly as she grows older. Her clipped, tense acting, pushed almost to paroxysm by Ray, is itself a strange and fascinating spectacle."

It comes down to the difference between people who watch a movie for the story and people who watch a movie for the psychiatric charge. If you belong to the latter group, *Johnny Guitar* is at all times startling and at times extraordinary; if you belong to the former group, it's an out-of-control vehicle in constant danger of heading over the cliff.

Neither the film's commercial success nor auteurist rhapsodies impressed Crawford. To the end of her life, she thought the picture was a blunder from start to finish.

THERE WAS A CHANGING of the guard in Hollywood in the early 1950s. Marilyn Monroe and Burt Lancaster were bigger news than Clark Gable and Joan Crawford, and occasional negative stories about Crawford began to appear, often quoting Sterling Hayden, Mercedes McCambridge, and a smattering of anonymous sources. Crawford's mantle of dignity could make her sound pompous, as she assumed a role as the Queen of Hollywood, pontificating about the movie business and How To Be A Star. As always, she was a combination of show biz bravado and blunt honesty: "If I'm out of work a year, I'm in debt."

In the spring of 1954, Crawford was in New York and had dinner with Franchot Tone several times, which led the newspapers to print dubious reports that they were thinking of remarrying. Crawford said, "Not so fast. I don't think you can ever go back," she said. "Once it's finished, it's finished." She told the gossip columnist Earl Wilson that if she'd had more of a sense of humor the marriage might have lasted. "I adore him."

REPUBLIC WAS THE FIRST and last Poverty Row studio where Crawford worked. For one thing, she blamed Republic for making Cliquot sick. It seemed that the dog nibbled on a carpet at Republic and became ill, which had never happened to her dogs at MGM or Warners. "Cliquot was always happy when I was at the glamorous studios," Crawford explained to a reporter on what was obviously a slow news day. "But when I went to Republic, he got into trouble. Cliquot is miserable when I'm not working. When we go to a studio, he is very happy."

Not content with sharing the details of her dog's digestive tract, Crawford kept going. At upscale studios, "people fed him very much and he gained too much weight. Cliquot usually eats white meat of chicken, ground sirloin, ice cream and ginger ale. He wears custom-made jackets from Hammacher-Schlemmer. They are red with black velvet collars with 'CC' on them. They have heart-shaped pockets with Kleenex in them in case he has to blow his nose. Cliquot and I wear matching costumes. He wears his red jacket when I wear red slacks and sweater. When I wear green, he wears green. And he has a rhinestone collar for evening."

This is the sort of pap that had filled fan magazines since 1915, but by the mid-1950s, the environment was changing and readership was declining. In order to compete, the magazines began catering to a younger audience. Stories about Gary Cooper and Claudette Colbert were replaced with stories about Debbie Reynolds and Eddie Fisher. The content was still pure vanilla, but Crawford complaining about her poodle's stomach issues would have sounded like something emanating from Buckingham Palace.

Billy Haines understood what was going on with his old friend because he saw a lot of it. His clientele skewed older, toward his own generation of stars and producers. His attitude was that he was still part of show business because "many of my friends are my clients. I feel part of them. I'm still an actor who's hanging some curtains. . . . The present run of stars don't have the knowledge and interest in homes that the older ones had. They're a beatnik group of actors with no interest in it at all."

Part of the problem was the look that Crawford had settled on in middle age. Eyebrows so thick they resembled caterpillars, a flamboyant slash of lipstick, and a heavier makeup than she had used years earlier. It all had the effect of making her face less mobile. The result was something akin to a Kabuki mask that inevitably stiffened the face of one of the most expressive actresses of her generation.

Accompanying this was a shift in her body language. The young woman who had sailed into a room with abandon in the early 1930s was gone, and her body language now resembled the physically immobile actors she had rendered archaic. Crawford could still give arresting performances, including two that were among the best of her career (*Sudden Fear* and *Autumn Leaves*), but the growing sense of emotional and physical constriction implied dramatic claustrophobia.

Vulnerability was glimpsed only occasionally. On a promotional tour to Detroit, Crawford did a radio interview with a man named Sonny Steele. He decided to ask a question that went far beyond the usual promotional patty-cake: "Does a star of your caliber ever get lonesome?"

The question is followed by two long seconds of silence, after which Crawford murmurs, "Sure."

"You don't want to talk about it?"

"Well . . ."

Sensing danger, he shifts gears and retreats to safer ground. But the fact remained that at this stage of her life, loneliness was one of the most crucial issues confronting Joan Crawford off-screen as well as on.

Increasingly, Crawford's public pronouncements were couched in the tones of a sniffy Mother Superior. When a magazine published an article slagging aging movie stars such as Gary Cooper, Katharine Hepburn, and Bette Davis, she sprang to their, as well as her own, defense. She didn't believe that the majority of moviegoers were teenagers, as the offending article had asserted. "I'd hate to think what would happen to the picture business if Gregory Peck, Cary Grant, Gary Cooper, Katharine Hepburn, Bette Davis and Jimmy Stewart retired. There's no reason why they should retire."

———◇———

JOAN'S RELATIONSHIP WITH HER brother and mother had not improved and never would. The costumer Sheila O'Brien believed that on some level Joan was jealous of Hal, for reasons that had something to do with their father. Hal had actually known Tom LeSueur before his vanishing act, and Joan seemed envious. "It was a product of her upbringing," said O'Brien. "When I told her tales of my father, she was enormously interested. She got a cute glow listening to me. She was never interested in stories about my mother."

Despite Hal's reputation as a professional layabout, he eventually got sober through Alcoholics Anonymous and earned his five-year chip, none of which cut him any slack in the eyes of his sister. She barred him from her house as a bad influence.

Nineteen fifty-five brought a new secretary into Crawford's employ. Betty Barker had met Crawford when she was a twelve-year-old fan and had filled in as a temp. Barker graduated from high school in 1935, then went to junior college and got a job in Washington during World War II. After the war, she came back to Los Angeles and went to work at RKO, where she eventually became Howard Hughes's secretary and learned all about the prodigious personality malfunctions of the movie industry.

"[Crawford] was so generous," said Barker. "She had a soft heart. Anybody ill, or with marital problems, she would write comforting letters to them. She wrote thousands of letters and Christina complained about that. She was very, very generous. . . . I wasn't a friend of hers because I had to be. I was a friend of hers because she was fun. . . . She was nice; she was kind to me, a wonderful friend."

If the scales were tipped toward the positive side, Barker still saw her friend and employer clearly. She needed to be the star in the room and could be hypercritical: "Why can't she fix her teeth?? Doesn't she have anything better to wear?" Pleasure was difficult for Crawford to access, but on the other hand there was her generosity and her often bawdy sense of humor.

Barker liked Hal, thought he was personable and handsome, but he was one of those men who couldn't get a handle on his own life. She felt the same way about Crawford's mother, who seemed to her to be a "sweet, middle-class woman with few pretensions." But Joan seemed ashamed of her mother, and gave the impression she wished Anna would act like the glamorous mother of a great star.

Where Hal was concerned, there were flares of something that could only be called malice. Barker remembered Crawford inviting him to her house to meet a man she was seeing so he could appreciate what she was up against with her family. Crawford proceeded to serve Hal liquor during dinner. Hal got blind drunk and the boyfriend had to drive him home. The underlying issue as Barker perceived it was that Hal was his mother's favorite and Joan resented it.

OTHER THAN THE VAGUELY lurid title, *Female on the Beach* was and is an unimportant picture, but its production gives a good idea of the radically altered economics of 1950s Hollywood, as well as the extent to which stars now controlled production.

It was produced by Albert Zugsmith, who spent most of his career making exploitation pictures with titles like *Sex Kittens Go to College* and *The Private Lives of Adam and Eve*. He also unaccountably produced two auteurist classics: Orson Welles's *Touch of Evil* and Douglas Sirk's *Written on the Wind*.

Zugsmith initially planned to make *Female on the Beach* with Ann Sheridan in what was to be a partnership with a Spanish producer. The prospective deal was to pay Sheridan a straight 50 percent of the gross. Sheridan's agent asked for $50,000 in advance, but Zugsmith didn't have $50,000. He told his Spanish co-producer that Sheridan was out and asked who should they get to replace her? The producer responded with the names of ten actresses, with Crawford the last one on the list.

It was at this point that Zugsmith was hired by Universal as a staff producer. Zugsmith brought the project with him, and the Spanish co-producer was paid off. Zugsmith thought Crawford was the best idea and sent her the script. Crawford promptly responded that she'd be happy to do the picture for $200,000.

Universal was about to have a great run of success with women's pictures produced by Ross Hunter starring actresses such as Jane Wyman, Barbara Stanwyck, and Lana Turner. Edward Muhl, the production head at Universal, thought Crawford was a fine idea. So did studio president Milton Rackmil, whom Crawford was seeing at the time. With the deal done, Crawford took charge. She grabbed the best bungalow on the lot and chose Jeff Chandler, the biggest male star at Universal before Rock Hudson's ascent, as her costar.

By the time Crawford was through supervising preproduction, Zugsmith estimated that the picture had run through nearly a dozen writers, including an uncredited Ranald MacDougall.

"The story conferences were unending," said Zugsmith. "At her house, mostly at her bungalow. She had a lot of moods and roles she played. Underneath that hard exterior, I sensed a frightened woman. I think she was scared that I wouldn't be able to [present] her in the MGM way."

The difference, of course, was that at MGM Crawford had never been allowed to control her films. But MGM was long ago and far away, and it was clear that *Female on the Beach* was going to be made to her specifications and no one else's. The word from the front office was simple: keep Crawford happy.

The director was Joseph Pevney, who could be classed as a studio workhorse and had worked with Jeff Chandler before. The studio asked Pevney to ask Chandler to do the picture as a personal favor. Chandler's answer was succinct: "Fuck you, Pevney."

Chandler was averse to temperamental female costars and wanted nothing to do with Crawford. Nevertheless, he ended up doing the picture after pressure was applied. "Ed Muhl tried to keep out of it," Zugsmith remembered. "Joe Pevney went along. She picked the cameraman. She called the shots."

Pevney said that Crawford was down-to-earth and sensible, but he thought the picture was on the junky side, and he asked Crawford why she was doing it. Her reply indicated she thought the script was a lot better than he did. She did ask Pevney not to do any close-ups after 4:30 in the afternoon, which was generally when she would take her first drink of the day, a signal that she wasn't going to be on the set much longer.

"She was playing it the way she always played it, the way she was taught to play it," said Zugsmith. "Jan Sterling should have been in the ending, but she sensed that I was favoring Jan. She did everything to cut down Jan's part."

Bob Rains was the head of publicity at Universal and had known Crawford since 1946, when he dated one of her girlfriends. "You couldn't come on strong with her," Rains said. "That was Jeff Chandler's mistake. She could be a lady or a truckdriver."

Even with all the writers, the picture was budgeted at a modest $900,000 including studio overhead, which guaranteed a profit. Zugsmith never had a quarrel with Crawford, and he was surprised when she sent a note to Milton Rackmil: "You've got a jewel in that Zugsmith. I want to help him."

"That was her technique," Zugsmith said. First the slap, then the caress, or vice versa. After production closed, she tried to supervise the edit, but Zugsmith managed to keep her out of the cutting room.

Female on the Beach is not quite as bad as its title would indicate, but it doesn't miss by much. The plot involves a well-off widow who takes over a beach house after the previous inhabitant dies in what appears to be an accident. She gets a love/hate thing going with the neighborhood's resident stud, the somewhat overage Chandler, who was also the boy toy of the previous owner and who may or may not have hastened her death.

Because of the modest budget, there's a definite feeling of second-tier status throughout the picture. The director is not Douglas Sirk, Universal's best director of neurotic love stories, but Joseph Pevney; the leading man is not Rock Hudson, but Jeff Chandler; the film is not in Technicolor, but black-and-white. Crawford seems to have sensed that she was making what amounted to a B movie and responds with an indicative, surface performance.

Zugsmith regarded the film as a difficult experience, but when his production of *Written on the Wind* was nominated for three Academy Awards, Crawford sent him a glowing note of congratulations. Nevertheless, Zugsmith said that he was not anxious to repeat the experience. Neither was the audience.

——◊——

FROM UNIVERSAL, CRAWFORD WENT over to Columbia to make *Queen Bee* for Jerry Wald, which was simultaneously a variant on *Harriet Craig* and an updated, vulgarized version of Lillian Hellman's *The Little Foxes*. Regina in *The Little Foxes* uses money and emotional frigidity to control her degenerate Southern family, while Eva Phillips uses sex and alternating waves of smothering love and fear to control her degenerate Southern family. Wald's production has more texture than it needs, but the acting is generally mediocre and the supporting cast (Barry Sullivan, John Ireland) feels threadbare.

Sullivan had known Crawford at MGM and liked her because of her honesty. He had been handling the microphone for the opening of MGM's interminable biblical spectacle *Quo Vadis* at the Fox Wilshire when Crawford left the theater after the film was over.

"What did you think of the picture?" he inquired eagerly.

"My ass hurts," she replied.

Just as *Queen Bee* was on the verge of wrapping up, a group that included Sullivan, Ranald MacDougall, John Ireland, and Betsy Palmer went out for drinks. Joining the group was Frank Galen, a writer for George Burns and Gracie Allen. The group was fairly well lit when Galen began explaining that the average male member was only five inches, while the average female cavity was seven inches. "That means," he announced, "that there are 27,000 miles of unused snatch in America."

That got John Ireland's attention. "Are those statistics correct?" he asked, which provoked a general collapse.

Two days later, they were shooting the final scene of *Queen Bee* when the cameraman asked Crawford to turn over on a bed because he wanted to measure her.

That gave MacDougall the giggles, which in turn led Crawford to ask what was so funny. Sullivan told her the story, and Crawford laughed so uproariously that work became impossible and they had to add a day to the shooting schedule.

Queen Bee failed to gather much notice from critics or audiences and was generally regarded as a flop.

CONTRASTING WITH THE MOVIES she was making, 1955 brought a pleasant surprise.

The first rumble of Crawford's last marriage came in the first week in May: "Joan Crawford Romance Reported." The man in question was someone different. Not an actor, not even particularly handsome. Alfred Nu Steele was the chairman of the board of Pepsi-Cola, a newly divorced father of two who looked like a white-haired barrel on legs. Steele and Crawford had been introduced three years earlier.

Just three days after the news of their relationship broke, Steele and Crawford were married on May 10, 1955, in Las Vegas in what was clearly an improvisation. The location was the penthouse of the Flamingo Hotel, the time was 2:10 a.m. They had planned to be married in ten days and were having dinner at Romanoff's when Steele suggested, "Let's fly tonight." Despite her fear of flying, Crawford agreed and they boarded Steele's private plane. After borrowing a wedding ring from a friend, the deed was done.

Joan called her children from Las Vegas to give them the news. "I've married Uncle Al. He's your daddy now," she told them. "We really liked him," said Cindy Crawford, "but we weren't that crazy about the marriage at the time because he sort of took her away from us. [We] couldn't crawl into her bed and chat any more."

Crawford had to return to Hollywood for the last few days of work on *Queen Bee*, after which they honeymooned in Capri. Al Steele's capsule version of the relationship was that "I married a lady and found out she was a movie actress." Most of the time he referred to her as "My Bride."

It was the right move at the right time. Crawford had begun to think of herself as a potentially retired actress burdened with a full roster of family troubles, and with good reason.

While Steele and Crawford were on their honeymoon, Christopher Crawford went AWOL twice from Mt. Lowe Military Academy. The first time, the police found him and a friend who had also absconded and returned them to the school. A few weeks later, he went over the wall again with vague plans to end up in Van Nuys. That made four AWOLs for the boy. Clearly, he didn't want to be in military school.

In essence, Crawford seems to have been repeating the failed example of her own mother, who had forced her daughter to live in environments that provoked a sullen rebellion. The fact that her mother had no choice and Crawford did seemed irrelevant. An argument could be made that all this gave Crawford the determination that got her out of Oklahoma and Kansas. There would be no similar upward evolution for Christopher.

A man with a can-do personality and a knack for people, a man like Al Steele undoubtedly struck a harried single mother as a wonderful idea.

CHAPTER SIXTEEN

FOR THE FOUR YEARS of her marriage to Al Steele, Crawford made only two films. The rest of the time she put herself at her husband's disposal as a helpmate and a beacon attracting attention to his product. "This is a team effort," she said, "and I am proud to be on this team."

Al Steele was born in 1901 in Nashville, attended Northwestern, worked in the advertising department of the *Chicago Tribune*, then took over the Standard Oil office in Indiana. A few more jobs in high-end corporations and he became chairman of the board of Pepsi in 1950.

Steele was not remotely comparable to Doug Fairbanks Jr., Franchot Tone, or Phil Terry—he wasn't in show business, wasn't dashing, wasn't particularly handsome. But he was kind and loving, and he was neither submissive nor an actor—there were none of the pressures resulting from the competition of careers. Most importantly, he wasn't threatened or intimidated by his new wife. Crawford would come to regard him as the mature love of her life, surpassing even Clark Gable.

Steele was a practical man with a gift for people. "I enjoy people," he explained. "I like people. Some people are bored by people. People depress them. They have mental intolerance. They think they are so much better than their fellow men. When trying to project their personality, they may irritate others. It would be better if they relaxed and tried to understand the world and the people around them.

"Most brashness is a coverup for inferiority feelings. If I could create mass emotional security the way I create mass customers I'd be a great guy."

For the first time, Joan Crawford had found a practical husband. Steele helped her get over her terrible fear of flying. "He would hold my hand on takeoffs and landings and he would say to me, 'In about four minutes [the pilot is] gonna say, 'Fasten your seat belts. . . . He'll also say there'll be turbulence.' Before two minutes were up, [I would hear] 'This is the captain speaking.' Sometimes they couldn't even serve lunch. But he talked to me and said 'We're going through thunderheads . . . and it'll be quite bumpy.'"

Steele was sharp, he was loving, and he gave her ballast that her other husbands hadn't. "We stimulated each other, out of mutual love and pride," said Crawford. Over the next four years, they traveled to dozens of cities in America, as well as Beirut, the Belgian Congo, Uganda, Kenya, Zanzibar, and Mexico, opening Pepsi plants and spreading the company gospel.

Henry Rogers's wife Rosalind said that the marriage marked a psychological as well as a career shift for Crawford. "She didn't have to apologize for not acting while she was with Steele. She could work on her own time, whenever she chose. There was no great pressure to maintain a career."

"I was more in love with Alfred than any other man in my life," said Crawford. "He wasn't as handsome as Doug or Clark or Franchot or Phillip, but he had a virility, a sense of assurance, that made him the center of attraction in any room. Women were crazy about him and men liked him. He made everyone feel at ease. I fell madly in love with him the night we met and the all-too-few years with him were the happiest years of my life."

With her acting career clearly losing momentum in her fourth decade of stardom, Crawford funneled most of her emotional energy into being the ultimate corporate wife—her final transformation. She worked hard to promote Steele's product. Pepsi became a fixture on the sets of the films she made, and she did hundreds of publicity events for the company. In return, Steele tended her children and her with kindness and devotion. "My mother invariably referred to Steele as her father," says Crawford's grandson Casey. "She adored him, and he adored her."

"He was her best kind of husband," said Cesar Romero. "A solid man. He didn't kowtow as the others did."

Steele made it easier for Crawford to make the difficult decision to leave Hollywood. It was partly a matter of retooling, partly an adroit career shift from movie star to corporate wife. Orry-Kelly, one of the few designers who could give Adrian a run for his money, said that there was something else involved: "Crawford had spent more than her last nickel."

It was an exaggeration, but there was no question that Crawford's lifestyle and overhead had left her with less money than her income would indicate. "Joan Crawford spent a fortune on clothes," Orry-Kelly asserted. "She had a personal dressmaker on her payroll. She bought the finest fabrics, brocades, and embroideries, but somehow—maybe by intention—she dressed for the taste of her multitude of fans, the same fans she continued to inform of her whereabouts, the time she would leave her (house), what theater she would attend, what street she would walk, what nightclub she would be in, even what was cookin' and what have you!"

Billy Haines was invited to a dinner party that Crawford threw to announce that she was leaving Hollywood, and he told Orry-Kelly about the evening. (Orry-Kelly's take on Haines: "[He] was the last word in elegance and good taste, and he would take your last nickel. As Fanny Brice once said, 'He ain't cheap, kid.'")

Crawford had said the dinner was informal, but her definition of informal included fourteen guests, two butlers, and two maids. Among the guests were Jack Webb and his wife and the composer Jule Styne. Crawford proceeded to announce that she was moving to New York to be with her new husband.

All eyes turned to Billy Haines. "I would like to drink a toast to This Old House," he said, raising a glass.

> I have been coming here for years to these little family dinners and I feel that This Old House and her mistress are part of my blood and bones. It was the mother and father of my career, and it makes me sad to see them go. It's like the passing of an era—to me it's the passing of a true and capable friend. I remember when I first started to work on This Old House it was about. . . . four husbands ago. After each husband it was scrubbed, tubbed and recovered, deleted and added to.
>
> I won't admit to myself that you are pulling up all your roots here. I know

you're not, because I have a little cottage where I live for your return, and as the Spanish say, *esta casa es su casa*—this house is your house. There is a guest room there waiting for you—your room—without notice come any time.

But, the day you move in, Cranberry, is the day I move out!

In fact, Crawford hedged her bet—New York became her primary residence, but she didn't sell the house on North Bristol for four more years.

Orry-Kelly thought both Crawford and Haines played their parts totally in character. Crawford summoned her familiar aura of melodrama, and Billy paid tribute to Crawford's bountiful generosity, while at the same time acknowledging that she could be hard to take. Orry-Kelly understood perfectly: "Actors never stop acting, even when their careers are ended. They still 'get on.' They all have implicit faith in themselves."

CRAWFORD'S NEXT FILM WAS a huge leap over *Female on the Beach* and *Queen Bee*. *Autumn Leaves* begins as closely observed soap opera, ascends to domesticated psychological horror, and ends with an ambiguous return to apparent normalcy. It was Crawford's first film with Robert Aldrich, who was never one to shy away from the lurid (*Kiss Me Deadly*, *The Big Knife*, etc.).

Don't be misled by the category of soap opera—*Autumn Leaves* is typical of Aldrich's affinity for violence, whether physical or emotional. Walter Hill wrote of Aldrich that "at the calculated level, Bob espouses left-liberal politics. But at an instinctive level, he . . . [sees] violence as a natural result of the misuse of power. Even more than that, violence as a natural result of the human condition."

Aldrich was a large, bulky man, a former football player who was born into wealth but rejected his family's money as well as their conservative politics. He began as an assistant director for a roster of mavericks: Lewis Milestone, William Wellman, and Charlie Chaplin. His own films add up to volcanically fierce independent moviemaking.

Crawford plays Millicent Wetherby, a typist who lives in a modest garden court apartment off Hollywood Boulevard. She is friends with her landlady and apparently no one else. A flashback tells us that she is alone because she spent years tending her ailing father. After he dies she's marooned in middle age. Millicent is what the shopgirl of 1931's *Possessed* might have evolved into if she was terribly shy and never met Clark Gable.

Millicent falls in love with and marries a younger man (Cliff Robertson), only to gradually realize that he's mentally ill, driven around the bend by his first wife's incestuous affair with his father. (Daddy is overplayed by Lorne Green, the sonorous ham who played Pa Cartwright on *Bonanza*.)

The first draft of the script was written by Jean Rouverol and her husband Hugo Butler, who were blacklisted, living in Mexico and using Jack Jevne as a front. The script derived from a story Rouverol had written for *McCall's* magazine based on a young man who had married into her husband's family. It wasn't a big-money gig—Aldrich originally intended to make the film independently and was paying for the script out of his own pocket. Rouverol recalled they earned $5,500, which went a long way in Mexico in the early 1950s, even after Jack Jevne took 25 percent off the top for the use of his name.

Crawford approached the picture with her usual attention to detail. She and Aldrich had a meeting in New York in June of 1955 where she enumerated her ideas about costumes. Aldrich turned around and sent a memo to Columbia's chief dress designer Jean Louis about her expectations:

1. Wants to see design for swimsuit.
2. Wants to see sketch for what's under robe.
3. Wants to see more fabric.
4. Wants new fabric for blouse with beige skirt.
5. Smaller checks on outfit for beach sequence.
6. Add blouses and new fabric for office work.
7. Would like to see soft cotton fabric for engagement sequence.
8. Would like to double back same outfit for running upstairs in hotel.
9. Design new robe for breakfast and Virginia arrival scene.
10. Wants to see fabric for coat material.
11. Wants to test all clothes.
12. Wants two jackets on sincere suit.

That wasn't all. After requesting and getting cameraman Charles Lang, Crawford had specific requests for her wardrobe mistress, hairdresser, and makeup man, all of which led Aldrich to write another memo: "The degree to which she seemed disturbed and hostile concerning her dressing room arrangements on her last picture here leads me to believe it would be most politic for you to:

Have her dressing room in the make-up building painted.
Have the major pieces of furniture recovered.
Maybe most important of all, have air-conditioning installed.
Onward and upward with the arts.

A further memo specified the colors she preferred (green, coral, and beige). She needed a desk and typewriter, a private phone with, if possible, the same number she had when last at Columbia, a refrigerator, and ample wardrobe space. "She seemed to be super-sensitive concerning the condition of carpets in most Columbia dressing rooms. Take this for what it's worth."

Crawford made a specific request to screen a batch of pictures that were doing good business that she felt "would help her orientate herself with just what is going on in films now," wrote Aldrich. Among the pictures she wanted to see were *The Bridges at Toko-Ri*, *Vera Cruz*, *Bad Day at Black Rock*, *East of Eden*, *Blackboard Jungle*, and *Daddy Long Legs*.

All these requests were made directly to Aldrich as opposed to her agent or an associate producer, which Aldrich found curious. "Perhaps in lieu of directing, the directors on her pictures take care of these little things," he mused.

The picture began inauspiciously with a phone call to MCA agent Art Park one night at 3 a.m. It was Crawford, and she demanded that "I want you to come and see how this man is insulting me."

Park hauled himself out of bed and went to North Bristol. Robert Aldrich was there. Both he and Crawford were drinking and discussing the script at the top of their lungs. Park managed to calm them down, then went back to bed.

The next day Park went to Joan's house. "Joan, we are friends and I work for you, but there's no reason why my work should be imposed on my family. My wife doesn't deserve having her sleep disturbed at 3 a.m."

Crawford was properly embarrassed and promised nothing like that would ever happen again. Instead, Crawford told Aldrich that if her writer didn't attend the first day's shooting, neither would she. Aldrich replied that if her writer showed up, he would ensure that no cameras turned. "Looking back, I really think that's the only way you can properly deal with Miss Crawford. The writer didn't show up but she did."

After this rocky beginning, she and Aldrich came to a place of mutual respect, in spite of Aldrich's impatience with the time Charles Lang took to light a scene. "But he really knew how to do it. Big close-ups of the eyes and bone structure, cutting under the mouth to avoid the sagging chin.

"For the first four or five days she was aloof, referring to me only as 'Mr. Aldrich.' Then one day I watched her in a scene. I suddenly became misty-eyed because of her performance. She came over and embraced me, and from then on she referred to me as 'my director.'"

Aldrich manages to transcend the script's lurches with sincerity, style, and his habitual willingness to go all the way. Crawford plays some beautiful scenes, especially her halting, desperate speech to her husband in the film's conclusion. Millicent is prepared to be alone again, but she's trying to get out of the confrontation as quickly as possible. She can tolerate being lonely—she's been lonely all her life—but she can't bear more humiliation. It's a scene any adult can recognize. There is a (provisional) happy ending, as Nat King Cole's rendition of the Joseph Kosma/Johnny Mercer title song wells up on the soundtrack.

Autumn Leaves eked out a tiny profit—net of $1,032, 853 against a cost of $957,207, and Aldrich won Best Director at the Berlin Film Festival. The film deserved better. Although Aldrich would say that "*Autumn Leaves* did nothing to embellish my reputation," he also confessed that "I liked a lot of things in it that were really corny. I'm not unproud of it."

More importantly, Crawford and Aldrich had reached a place of trust. He would call on her again in a few years.

CHAPTER SEVENTEEN

FOR THE NEXT FOUR years, Crawford downshifted into the role of corporate wife and made only one movie: *The Story of Esther Costello*. Mostly, she worked on the rehabbing of the lavish New York apartment she and Al Steele bought and accompanied him on promotional trips for Pepsi-Cola.

The Pepsi-Cola promotional department assiduously taped the interviews that Crawford and Steele did wherever they happened to be. The tapes ended up on a shelf in Crawford's apartment and were eventually rescued by her grandson Casey. They provide a glimpse into the star's expertise in PR, as well as the personality of Al Steele.

He had a slightly gravelly Midwestern voice and a casual, avuncular deportment. Steele told one interviewer that when he got out of college he possessed nothing but "peanut dust" until he got his first job selling ads at the *Chicago Tribune*. He always tried to personalize banal locations. When they opened a bottling plant in Utica, New York, he told his interviewer, "I've always wanted to open a farm around here. . . . At heart I'm a farmer." He usually does his selling quietly but occasionally lapses into rote boosterism: "[Business] opportunities are greater than at any time in the last century."

As for Crawford, after decades of handling the Hollywood press, she's in her element. "Hi, Chet," she tells an interviewer in Louisville, "it's wonderful to be here. . . . Please call me Joan." When he asks about *Our Dancing Daughters*, she replies, "Oh, let's not go that far back . . ." She portrays herself as a happy wife, and by all accounts, including her own, that's essentially what she was. "I'm much too busy living a full and beautiful life to write a book," she tells an interviewer in Colorado Springs, and she downplays any movie plans.

In the first three years of their marriage, they traveled what Crawford estimated as 850,000 miles on behalf of Pepsi. For Crawford, it was not really that different from the movie business. "I'm just selling a different product," she told one interviewer. "I work at it. It takes planning and organization." A lot of the publicity questions involve the 1950s Housewives Holy Trinity: Glamour/Diet/Clothes. When she's asked domestic questions, they tend to be sidestepped.

"How many children do you have?"

"Four. . . . We fill a room pretty quickly. . . . But sometimes it seems like 16." Her philosophy of childrearing was increasingly fatalistic: "Let them be. You're not going to change them anyway."

She spoke about young actors she liked: Sandra Dee, Diane Varsi, and Anthony Perkins. When she was asked if movies were better than ever, she snapped, "Not generally." Would she consider television? "Under no circumstances."

The trips took her to some far-off destinations, from Omaha, where she did a series of public service ads for the Strategic Air Command, to Mozambique, the Belgian Congo, and South Africa.

In most of these appearances she's in her gracious, temperate Great Lady mode, somewhat in the manner of late-period Greer Garson. Always serene, rarely ruffled.

THE SAME MONTH OF Crawford's last marriage, the FBI got into the Joan Crawford business. The provocation came courtesy of Howard Rushmore, a former communist, later a paid informant for the Bureau, and the prodigiously unprincipled editor of *Confidential* magazine. Rushmore had narrowed his focus to the legend of the Joan Crawford stag film.

Rushmore told the FBI that at some time in the past Joan Crawford had been arrested in Detroit and convicted of prostitution. "Subsequently a motion picture film of Crawford in compromising positions was circulated to be used at smokers. The film was then used for blackmail purposes at the time when she was married to Franchot Tone and the two of them paid approximately a quarter of a million dollars to suppress the circulation of this film. . . . The facts were reported to the Bureau and the Bureau subsequently arrested two individuals. The Post office inspectors were also involved in this case.

"According to Rushmore, the file in the Detroit Police Department is no longer available and the film allegedly was turned over to the FBI at a time when the FBI requested the films during the investigation of the alleged blackmail. . . . Rushmore further related that reports which had reached him were that Joan Crawford over a period of years had worked for the FBI as a confidential informant. Rushmore thought that he should check this story with the Bureau."

A month later, the Bureau's L. B. Nichols reported back to J. Edgar Hoover's associate Clyde Tolson:

> Our records do not support anything like this. There have been recurring rumors of an obscene film. We have never found anybody who had this although the rumors and the information are so persistent that it would lead one to believe that there was such a film in existence. Likewise, Joan Crawford never served in an undercover capacity for the Bureau.
>
> Recently, Howard Rushmore came by the office and I advised him briefly that we had no investigation involving blackmail; that we did not have the film; that we did not have in file, there was no record of her film from the Detroit Police Department and she had never served in an undercover capacity for the Bureau. . . .
>
> Rushmore then told me in the strictest of confidence, with the understanding that the identity of this informant would not be circulated or divulged, that he had been told the story by [name redacted]. . . . We rechecked this matter. I asked the Detroit office to recheck their files under the name of Lucille LeSueur which was the name presumably used by Joan Crawford at the time of the arrest. SAC McIntire informed me that there was absolutely no record in the Detroit office of Lucille LeSueur and there was no . . . indication that the Detroit Office [of the FBI] had any information from the Detroit Police Department.

A further document states that in 1944 and 1945 the Bureau had "conducted considerable investigation" regarding the stag film. One informant "advised that he had talked to over 500 people who had claimed to have seen Joan Crawford obscene film but 'he had never been able to get any of them to produce it for him.'"

Another informant advised that MGM had bought the film, that only a few prints of the film survived, and that these were in possession of top studio executives. "Film is described as being very old and Crawford would not be recognizable."

In 1944, attempts were made to buy a copy of the film, but the informant was told that the movie would be very expensive and that, "due to her age, Crawford did not look like she does today, having a different hairdo, et cetera, and stated that she would not be easily recognizable unless you were aware of her identity prior to the projection of the reel."

Another informant stated that other actresses had once worked as prostitutes: Barbara Stanwyck and Paulette Goddard.

Making a hard-right turn, the document states that informants had advised that Crawford in the 1930s had been "very antifascist and lent her name and prestige to organizations later designated as subversive. During World War II she belonged to organizations such as Russian War Relief. Since World War II she had been one of the anti-Communist leaders in Hollywood."

Despite Nichols's lengthy enumeration of dead end after dead end, the report's conclusion was that "undoubtedly the Joan Crawford film exists but is practically unobtainable."

This mélange of hearsay, rumor, and fantasy was probably stimulated by a stag film performer with dark hair and a vague resemblance to Crawford in the first year or so of her career, when her appearance verged on the generic. An urban legend was born.

In 1958, the alcoholic and unemployable Howard Rushmore shot and killed his wife, then committed suicide.

Crawford's own comment on this rumor was succinct: "Bullshit. By that time I was so far along I wouldn't have had to do anything like that; not only wouldn't I have done it for any money that might have been offered, but what the hell. I would have known better."

In October 1971, Crawford visited the office of J. Edgar Hoover while in

Washington doing a publicity event for Pepsi-Cola. A month later Hoover forwarded to her a copy of the FBI magazine that featured a photo of Crawford and Hoover together. He signed the accompanying letter "Edgar."

———◆———

CRAWFORD'S CAREER WAS STILL afloat, but barely—there are only so many times you can play a middle-aged woman pining for love in commercially marginal movies. Besides that, Crawford now found herself out of sympathy, not just with Hollywood, but with a lot of the people within it, especially younger people who flaunted their wares and by so doing nudged older people a step or two into the shadows.

She could no longer be cast as a vibrant woman looking for love. Rather, she was a middle-aged woman grudgingly accommodating herself to reality, making do with what modest satisfactions were on offer. In other words, she was once again offering herself to her audience as one of them.

The difference was that her performances sometimes lacked the vitality and immediacy that had been the norm in earlier years. Sheila O'Brien thought that the underlying problem was the marriage to Franchot Tone. Because of Tone's influence, Crawford began to approach acting from the point of view of technique. She began to think analytically, intellectually. Process entered into it, and she wasn't primarily that kind of actress, or, for that matter, that kind of person. Her performances stiffened, became less lifelike. "She was more natural in the early MGM films," observed O'Brien.

What kept the later performances interesting was the uncanny mirroring between actress and audience. She still seemed to be enacting something about their shared lives, about the difficulty of confronting diminished personal circumstances in middle age. It was all true, but it wasn't as optimistic as it had been.

———◆———

CRAWFORD'S NEW DESTINATION WITH her new husband was New York, partially because it was Al Steele's headquarters, partially because she was in need of a transition.

Once again Crawford called on Billy Haines. This time she wanted him to design the penthouse at 2 East 70th Street and Fifth Avenue she and Al Steele purchased in March 1956. The building contained eighteen apartments and had been built in 1928. Crawford and Steele purchased two apartments on the thirteenth and fourteenth floors and wanted them converted into one four-thousand-square-foot apartment on the thirteenth floor. They hired the architectural firm Skidmore, Owings & Merrill to do the construction with Haines doing the decorating. Crawford announced she was quitting pictures after *The Story of Esther Costello* in order to be "the best wife in the world."

Beginning in the autumn of 1956 and continuing for the next year, twelve-foot walls were torn down, other walls were erected, and massive reconfiguring was undertaken. By the time it was done, eighteen rooms and six bathrooms had been converted into eight rooms and four bathrooms. On the upper floor, small windows were replaced by a wall of glass overlooking Central Park.

Crawford's bedroom included a heated floor and motorized drapes with the controls built into the headboard of the bed. The view from the living room faced northwest and had a stunning view of Central Park, with the George Washington Bridge in the distance.

When it came to the decorating, Al Steele attempted to take charge, but Haines refused to play nice: "You fucking tycoons. You make a few bucks and you think you can start building things with no taste. Nothing gives you the privilege to do that."

By the time Haines was done, the apartment was a mid-century modern masterpiece, featuring a diamond-shaped dining table, a whirlpool, and a geranium-pink bedroom. The environment emphasized yellows. There was a skylight and a freestanding staircase lined with ferns.

Haines tied the place together with his specialty of white carpets and customized walls covered in treated burlap tinted a pale cream. There were fireplaces in both the drawing room and the bedroom, which also featured a working fountain. Every piece of furniture was custom-made for its specific place in a specific room. Crawford remembered that "There wasn't a dark nook in the whole place, except possibly the broom closet."

The tab for the remodeling was officially reported as $387,000, although it might have gone closer to $500,000. Crawford and Steele had assumed that

Pepsi would cover the costs, and they did, but only after specifying that the money was a loan at 6 percent interest. For those times when she had to go to Los Angeles, Crawford contented herself with renting an apartment in a building owned by Loretta Young.

One friend came to visit shortly after the Fifth Avenue apartment was finished and was treated to the Grand Tour. He was invited for 7:45 a.m. to find the man from the phone company explaining the workings of the answering machine he had just installed. "Joan played it like a movie script, having the telephone man go over it again and again until she got it right."

The morning passed. "Around 11:45 the maid came to interrupt her and remind her of her luncheon appointment! Joan had a well-scrubbed face when she received me at 7:45 a.m. One large hair pin to hold a loosely twisted knot chignon on the nape of her neck. . . . Her face was like a well-hewn sculpture . . . but in a flash under fluorescent lights (which she always used, knowing if she could perfect herself under that kind of light, wherever she would be, she would look far better. It was that hard light test that did the trick) she became Crawford—voila!"

A corporate gadfly questioned Steele and Crawford about the outlay for the apartment at a Pepsi stockholders meeting. He said he had some questions for Miss Crawford, who replied, "Make it brief, boy."

The stockholder began backtracking, saying he thought she would be a welcome addition to the Pepsi board.

"If I were, we'd have long sessions but short speeches."

"May I ask how many shares of Pepsi-Cola you own?"

"It's none of your business. Besides, I owned them before I married Mr. Steele."

At that point, Steele broke in to say that "I let my wife run her business and she lets me run mine."

NEW SURROUNDINGS MANDATED NEW friends and different way of life. Crawford developed an enthusiasm for Nancy Walker, whom she had known only glancingly in Hollywood. "I was one of a group of New York actors who hated

California," remembered Walker, "and (we all) stuck together out of mutual protection—Gene Kelly, Laird Cregar, later Frank Sinatra."

After opening in a show on Broadway, Walker was astonished to get a lovely bouquet from Crawford with a note saying how much she had enjoyed her work. A few weeks later, Walker got an invitation to one of Crawford's cocktail parties. Walker hated cocktail parties but decided to go because Crawford had been so kind to her. The party was at the Sherry-Netherland, and Crawford came down the stairs looking terrific. She opened her arms and said, "You showed! And you've got a show tonight! If you're anything like me, I know you like to get there early."

"If I'm not in the theater by seven o clock, I start shaking," said Walker.

"Then I'm going to get all the time you have while you are here."

Crawford brushed everyone else off and talked only to Walker for a half hour until it was time for her to get ready for her performance.

"Needless to say, I thought she was terrific," said Walker.

IN THE EARLY PART of 1957, Louis B. Mayer was dying, as was his Hollywood. At the same time Joan Crawford was having trouble finding scripts because she was too large for the kind of kitchen-sink movies that were increasingly popular in the 1950s. Movies dealing with outsized, melodramatic emotions—*Rebel Without a Cause, East of Eden*—were generally about teenagers, not fifty-year-old women. Only Ross Hunter at Universal was making movies that could have starred Crawford, and he would be locked in with Lana Turner, who was years younger than Crawford.

In October 1956, Crawford was shooting *The Story of Esther Costello* in London for director David Miller when she wrote a chatty letter to her friend Jane Kesner Ardmore: "I was presented to the Queen last night—nearly died of excitement and fear. Found the Queen very charming, also Princess Margaret. It was one of the most exciting moments I have ever had. Of course, I was not too happy about being presented with that group of people representing the Motion Picture Industry, such as Marilyn-you-know-who, and Anita Ekberg. Incidentally, Marilyn and Anita were howled at because of their tight dresses—they could not walk off the stage. It was most embarrassing."

Dana Andrews was also presented to the Queen that night—he was in England making Jacques Tourneur's *Curse of the Demon*. He had been placed in the receiving line between Ekberg and Brigitte Bardot, which amused Crawford. "Oh, darling, I don't know when I'll ever see you!" said Crawford.

One night at a restaurant, Ekberg was at the next table, in a low-cut dress with long blond hair streaming down. David Miller asked Crawford why she wasn't eating her salad.

"If she'll get her hair out of my salad, I'll eat it."

The Story of Esther Costello emerged as a viable, twisty melodrama about a blind deaf-mute child adopted by an American socialite. The producers were the Woolf brothers, who were coming off *The African Queen* and *Moulin Rouge*. The film was shooting at Shepperton Studios, and Crawford and Al Steele were living at Great Fosters. On weekends they all dined together in London. Miller thought Steele could be alternately tough or tender with Crawford, as the situation demanded. On balance, Miller thought Steele handled her beautifully.

Hedda Hopper seemed surprised. "Joan Crawford's marriage seems to be working out much better than anyone expected," she wrote in a group letter to Janet Gaynor, her husband Adrian, Mary Martin, and her husband Richard Halliday, who had bought a plantation together in Brazil. "She and her husband are cracking out with a party within the next few days. Al bought Joan an apartment in New York . . . so Joan will commute between here and there."

The British film crew respected Crawford's work habits, which remained exemplary. She was always fifteen minutes early and rapped on Miller's dressing room door calling out, "I'm here, David." She never left for the evening without asking, "Is that all you want of me, David?"

It was a happy shoot except for a single traumatic episode that began with Al Steele knocking on Miller's dressing room door.

"May I come in?" he asked.

"Sure."

"There's a problem. Joan is in her dressing room. She's hysterical."

Miller went to Crawford's dressing room to find her eyes swollen, her face red. She was so upset she could barely speak. She was clutching a pack of English currency—her weekly per diem of 500 pounds for a living allowance.

Attached was a note specifying two deductions: one pound 10 shillings for a makeup towel, and 10 shillings for electric light bulbs for her dressing room mirror.

"Who do they think I am?" she asked Miller through her sobs. "A bit player?"

She told him that that she didn't want to hurt him or the picture. He replied that it was a moot point, because she couldn't be photographed as she was. Miller had his assistant call the Woolf brothers, who tried to placate Crawford by telling her the offending person would be fired.

"If you fire him, you'll have to finish this picture without me," she told them. It wasn't about a blundering bureaucrat; it was a matter of respect.

Two hours after icing her face, Crawford was ready to shoot. Eventually, the crew heard about the episode and treated Crawford with even greater respect than they had before.

More than thirty years of stardom, millions of dollars earned, an Academy Award, and thousands of column inches of mostly laudatory print, and none of it had made any real difference. Underneath the carapace of Joan Crawford she was still Lucille LeSueur, a distressed worker with a perpetually endangered sense of self-worth.

The Story of Esther Costello barely nudged rentals of $1 million.

SPENDING MOST OF HER time in New York or on the road meant that correspondence from old friends became increasingly important to Crawford. As always she was attentive to all and sundry. She kept up her usual volume of correspondence with loyal fans. A typical sample:

> My special days just wouldn't be complete without one of your lovely greetings. I cannot tell you how much your sincere friendship has meant to me. Thank you again and again for everything. . . .
>
> I'm sorry to be so delayed in answering but I was away for several months on my first real vacation in fifteen years. What a wonderful time I had and shall never forget it, I know. I spent time in Texas, then on to a ranch in

Mexico, and then on to New York. Here I saw several grand shows, many of my friends and of course did my usual amount of work.

It seemed like the children had grown so much by the time I got back. They were in need of dental and medical care so I was most happy to get back. We spent the week before Easter at the Alisal Ranch. I also took the two children of the Harry James's and what a time those six gave me. I never saw so much energy, but did manage to keep up with them. I need a rest when I got home. . . .

I am rushing today so please forgive me for being in haste. Again thank you from the bottom of my heart for your ever thoughtfulness of me. Until the next time let me wish you the best of everything and a very happy summer.

She replied to a birthday telegram from Ruth Gordon and Garson Kanin in an entirely different tone: "How the hell did you remember the date?" she wondered. "But, Ruth, I thought we were going to take a walk in the Park. My phone number is Murray Hill 8-4500, extension 308. Now that I will be in New York for a while . . . I'll walk any time you like."

Nineteen fifty-eight brought trouble and, presumably, grief. In May, Crawford's son Christopher was arrested and charged with juvenile delinquency for shooting out streetlights in Greenport, New York. In August Crawford's mother died at the age of seventy-three. Anna Bell McConnell LeSueur Cassin's death certificate listed her as "Anna Bell LeSuer aka Anna Bell Crawford" and the cause of death as a stroke. Anna was living with her son Hal at the time of her death.

Crawford and Al Steele flew back from Bermuda for the funeral at Forest Lawn. Little notice was paid to Anna's death, although the newspaper in San Angelo, Texas, recalled that "Miss Johnson was a saleswoman." Ed Blanton, a San Angelo businessman, correctly remembered that Anna was a member of the Salvation Army, "which would play in front of many of the saloons, and Miss Johnson would pass the tambourine within the saloons."

Hedda Hopper ran a brief item stating that Anna was "A fine woman, she never stopped working. Half the coat hangers in my house were made by her. She used to send me delicious preserves and pickles when she made a batch."

Hopper's item kicked off some anonymous letters scoffing at the diagnosis of a fatal stroke: "A more truthful story would be to say that she died of a broken heart. . . . It has been three years since Joan has 'bothered' to even see her Mother. . . . Granted, she has called her by phone, but that is not the same. And a sweeter, dearer person hasn't existed. A very dear old lady. . . . This is the great Joan Crawford!" Another anonymous letter arrived at Hopper's office three days later, presumably from the same person.

That same month the always attentive George Cukor wrote Crawford a fan letter: "The other night I just happened to turn the television on that happened to be running *A Woman's Face*. My God, weren't we good! This would sound very immodest to anyone outside the family. You gave a most thrilling performance, human and sensitive. . . . It's curious how little one remembers. I was constantly being surprised at what I saw, and mighty proud too. I usually cringe when I look at my efforts on TV.

"My grateful thanks, dearest Joan . . ."

BY THE TIME 1959 rolled around, Joan Crawford hadn't made a movie in two years and professed to be perfectly content with that state of affairs. "I can live without movies," she announced. "I didn't think I could before I married Alfred, but I find I can, very easily. If a movie comes along that I'd like to do, and if it doesn't interfere with any of our plans, I'll do it. Otherwise, it's part of the past, another life."

Just because she considered herself semiretired from the movie industry was no reason to cut back on interviews, or on her own brand of honesty. "I wash out my own underwear. You'd think I only have one pair. I got this habit during the years I was dancing in the chorus."

Once again she began to ease into television—game shows such as *What's My Line?* and *Password*, as well as episodic dramas such as *Route 66*, the innovative show about two hunky bachelors tooling around the country in their Corvette and running into dramatic stories every week. The gimmick was that each episode was shot on actual locations. Crawford did an episode shot in Poland Spring, Maine, where she played a well-off woman whose crazy husband escapes from the asylum and tries to kill her. Her physical presence remains striking, but at bottom it's a standard woman-in-peril premise.

The appearance on *Route 66* was no accident. During a late-night tipsy phone call, she had enthused to a friend about George Maharis, the star of the show. "That's one good-looking Greek boy!" she told Raymond Daum. "She really wanted to work with him," said Daum. Unfortunately, by the time Crawford did her *Route 66* episode, Maharis had left the show in search of movie stardom, which proved elusive.

IN 1959, CESAR ROMERO was working as the spokesman for Petrocelli clothes when he ran into Crawford and Steele. They had been on the road for Pepsi for five weeks and had one more week to go, after which they would take a few days in New York before heading off to Jamaica for ten days of vacation.

They had all planned to have breakfast together, but Steele didn't appear at first. When he finally showed up, he mentioned that he hadn't slept well.

"Have you had a checkup?" asked Romero.

"No," Steele said. "My heart's OK."

A week later, on April 19, Romero was in Pittsburgh when he turned on the radio. Al Steele was dead. He and his wife had gone to bed at 12:30 a.m. She woke up at 9:15 a.m. and went into Steele's bedroom. He was on the floor, his face gray, his body already turning cold. She covered him with blankets, called for the maid, called for the doctor. There was nothing to be done.

They had been married one month less than four years. Steele would have turned fifty-eight in a couple of days. An autopsy revealed that he had died of a massive heart attack, and *Variety* reported that "Steele's physical exhaustion called for frequent 'pep-up' pills and/or shots from his medico as this or that speech or pep meeting had to be held."

At the time of Al Steele's death, Christopher Crawford was in jail for stealing a car.

The letters of condolence poured in.

Robert Aldrich: "By now I am sure you have received a multitude of messages that magnificently phrase the shock, the sadness and sorrow that are felt for you at this troubled time. Unfortunately, I have never found words that are potent enough to really be helpful or useful at such times.

"The most anyone is able to say, it seems to me, is that they love you, and feel deeply for you and if there were *anything* they could do, they would want and wish that you ask them to do it . . . *whatever* it might be."

Noel Coward: "Dearest, dearest Joan, my deepest sympathy and love."

Marion Davies: "Dearest Joan, all my love and compassion to you in your great sorrow. My thoughts are with you Joan. May God give you strength to alleviate the pain. If I can help please let me know. . . . All my love and devotion to you."

Douglas Fairbanks Jr.: "Billie dear, Just heard crushing news. Please know how desperately sorry we are and how much affectionate sympathy we send you in this heavy hour. Love Mary Lee and Douglas."

Phillip Terry: "I was so sorry to hear of your recent loss. I had heard of such nice things about Mr. Steele. Please accept my sincere sympathy for your so recent bereavement. If there is anything I can do please do not hesitate to call on me."

Once the shock wore off, Crawford set about restoring order in her usual comprehensive way. All the condolence letters she replied to were stamped "ANSWERED." A typical example, to George Cukor:

Thank you so much for your wonderful wire, and the beautiful flowers. I'm so deeply grateful to you for your loving thoughts. The only consolation I have is that I made this man a very happy fella'. I'm glad he got to know you a little bit.

Thank you for being so wonderful, and thank you too for helping me in my time of need.

Love, Joan.

The only sustained domestic contentment she had ever known had been ripped away. Her friend Bob Rains would say that "Steele gave Joan a sense of security that she never knew before. A sense of being wanted."

As far as can be determined, Al Steele was the last man Joan Crawford loved. She never married again, and it's probable she never even considered it.

Right: Young Lucille LeSueur.

Left: Lucille with her mother, probably in Lawton, Oklahoma.

3.

Left: Chorus girl Lucille LeSueur in the Shubert musical, *The Passing Show*.

4.

Right: Since MGM didn't have a clear idea of what to do with their new contractee, they tried everything. Here, she is dressed as a fetching pirate.

Above: Barely recognizable beneath an unattractive hairstyle and makeup that disguised her eyes, the newly christened Joan Crawford nevertheless made an impact in *Sally, Irene and Mary*.

Below: Crawford's growth as an actress started with working with Lon Chaney in *The Unknown*. Here, she withstands the appraisal of leading man Norman Kerry, Chaney, and director Tod Browning.

7.

Above: The young star, circa 1929.

8.

Left: Crawford in *Our Dancing Daughters*, an archetypal flaming youth movie of the 1920s that propelled her into stardom.

Below: Crawford and first husband Douglas Fairbanks Jr.

9.

Above: Crawford with her mother and brother Hal at MGM.

Below: Holding her own opposite luminaries such as John Barrymore in *Grand Hotel* showed the world that Crawford was far more than an average ingenue.

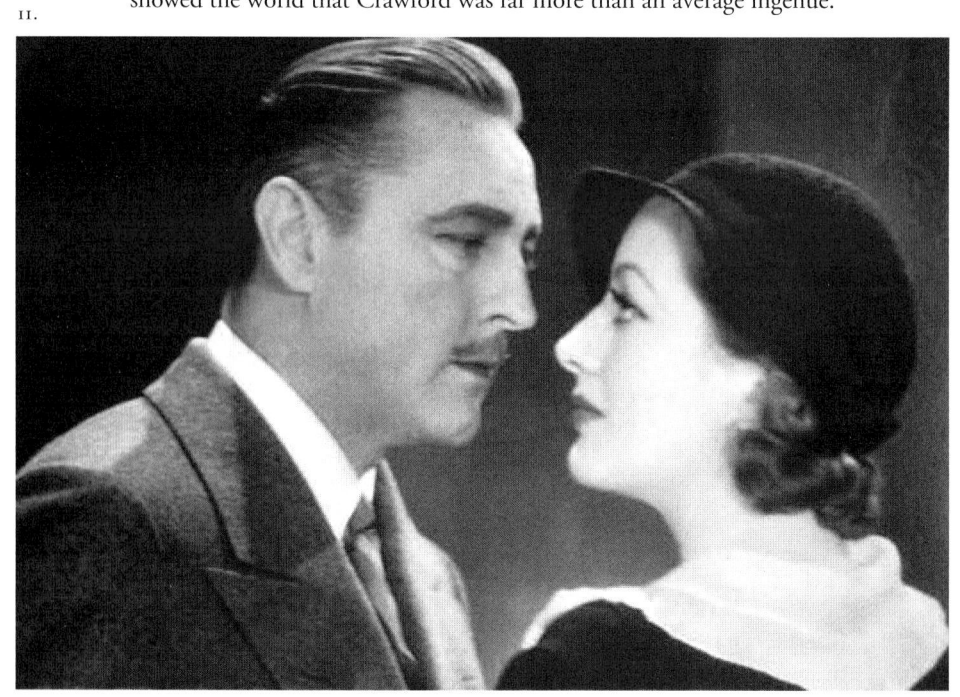

12.

Left: Joan Crawford with second husband, actor Franchot Tone, with whom she made seven films.

13.

Right: Crawford's affair with Spencer Tracy led to a brief enthusiasm for horseback riding and polo.

Above: Designer Adrian and Crawford go over costume designs.
Theirs was a very close and longtime collaboration.

Crawford's two favorite directors were the gentle, fatherly Clarence Brown (*below*) and George Cukor, the latter of whom is carefully situated between his two warring stars and the rest of the cast of *The Women* in the photo above.

Above: Don't let their proximity fool you—Crawford and Norma Shearer disliked each other before, during, and after *The Women*. Crawford models the midriff-baring outfit that appalled Louis B. Mayer.

18.

Above: Even though their affair had been over for years, Crawford and Gable still struck sparks in *Strange Cargo*.

Below: With third husband Phillip Terry in her dressing room during the production of *Above Suspicion*.

19.

Above: Contemplating suicide in *Mildred Pierce*, the film that recharged Crawford's career.

Below: From left, director Michael Curtiz, Crawford, Eve Arden, and dialogue director Herschel Daugherty discuss a scene from *Mildred Pierce*.

22.

23.

Above: With John Garfield in *Humoresque*.

Left: With daughter Christina and son Christopher, arriving via train on one of Crawford's trips east.

Above: Shooting a Pepsi-Cola commercial with the twins and fourth husband Al Steele.

Left: Meeting Queen Elizabeth in October 1956.

Above: Stripped of every vestige of glamour, Crawford gives a naturalistic performance centered on desperation in Robert Aldrich's *What Ever Happened to Baby Jane?*

27.

Above: After Crawford moved back to New York City in 1955, she and Franchot Tone reconnected and saw each other frequently. The year here is probably 1965, when Tone appeared in *In Harm's Way* and *Mickey One*.

28. *Below*: Kim Braden and Crawford in her last motion picture, *Trog*, in 1970.

After his death, her escorts tended to be conspicuously married or gay. To the end of her own life she spoke of Steele as the great love of her life.

It was Al Steele who had gotten Crawford over her fear of flying, holding her hand and assuring her that everything would be fine. He domesticated danger, which counterbalanced some of the reflexive insecurity instilled in her childhood.

Al Steele's death meant she would spend the rest of her life alone—a state that had always frightened her before, but that she now accepted with a sense of grim duty. The only unpleasant residue of the marriage was the debt that was now Crawford's from the expensive remodeling of their apartment.

Joe Mankiewicz understood what Steele had given her—a glimpse of a life beyond movies: "Steele had given her a whole new screenplay after her major film career was over. She was hostess, wife, helpmate. She became a corporate woman equal to her position as a movie star."

Crawford was now cast in one of the few parts that had never interested her—a widow. She was understandably at sea, and more so when she went over the finances. A month after Steele's death she told Louella Parsons that she was effectively broke: "I haven't a sou to my name. . . . It all went for income tax and debts."

She also had two expensive households to run and four children. What that meant was that she finally had to sell the North Bristol house, which was bought by actor and dancer Donald O'Connor. She had to plow through thirty years' worth of possessions, making snap judgments about what was to be thrown out, what was to be given to her children, what could fit into the apartment.

Once again, Jerry Wald came to her rescue. Just five weeks after Steele's death Wald offered her a juicy supporting part in his production of *The Best of Everything*. Wald had been considering actresses as varied as Nina Foch, Patricia Neal, Beatrice Straight, Margaret Leighton, Joan Fontaine, and Dorothy McGuire for the part of an embittered middle-aged editor in the book business who's kept dangling by her married lover. The salary was generous: $75,000 for a part that took only a few weeks to shoot. (The young actresses who were the actual stars of the picture got only between $7,000 and $34,000 apiece.) It was a supporting part, but it was important because it gave Crawford something she desperately needed—work.

Crawford immediately said, "I'll take it."

"Don't you want to read the script?" asked Wald.

"No. I trust you. Thank you for thinking of me."

The Best of Everything is about young career women in publishing surrounded by men who are by turns rapacious or weak. The film occasionally threatens to become good but settles for being highly watchable. Hope Lange is costumed and directed to incarnate Grace Kelly as much as possible, Diane Baker is the Good Girl impregnated by Robert Evans, while the stunning Suzy Parker is an aspiring actress who can't land big jobs because of a lack of talent—typecasting. Jean Negulesco directs everything in a lush, head-on manner until Parker's character starts to lose it, at which point he goes in for Dutch angles indicating imminent disaster. Until Parker's dark night of the soul, *The Best of Everything* flaunts more pastels than *Pillow Talk*.

Crawford plays an office gorgon who has found out the hard way that careers don't love you back and has turned sour as a result. She's quite good, even though she doesn't have anybody to play off of. She always regretted the cutting of a drunk scene where her character waits for the married lover who never shows up. The film was already over two hours, and Jerry Wald was selling Lange, Parker, and Rona Jaffe's provocative best-seller, not a star in her mid-fifties.

Crawford liked Negulesco, who had directed her in *Humoresque*, but he put his foot in it when he told her she had "the most spectacular penthouse in New York City, but the lousiest taste in paintings." Negulesco had long been after her to upgrade her art collection. "He said we should get Modigliani and such, which get more valuable every year," Crawford said. "But Alfred and I bought pictures we liked. And personally, I'll take diamonds."

Negulesco collected Dufy and Dubuffet, among others, and he seems to have taken particular objection to a couple of Margaret Keane paintings on Crawford's walls. The Keane paintings dismayed many of her friends, but Crawford was obstinate: "You don't have to live with them, I do, and they make me happy," she told one friend.

On the set of *The Best of Everything*, "She seemed to be miserable," remembered Diane Baker. "I tried to reach out to her as much as I could and as much as she let me. She was not easy to get to know. There was always a barrier. Her husband had just died, she hadn't made a film in a few years, and, frankly, she seemed panic-stricken. Also, she was appearing on-screen with three women who were much younger than she was, and that could not have been easy for her."

———◇———

A MONTH AFTER STEELE'S death, Pepsi-Cola named Crawford to its board of directors. Her salary was $60,000 a year for a five-year term. It was not a gesture of affection, but rather contractual. Six months before his death, Steele had signed an eight-year contract with Pepsi, which raised his salary from $121,477 a year to $150,000, plus options on 75,000 shares of the company. Steele's death nullified the stock options, but the death benefit held tight—the contract contained a provision that if he were to die before the expiration of the contract, his wife would receive "an amount equal to two years compensation at the rate then in effect," payable over five years.

Crawford's payout was not a pension—she intended to work for it, and work for it she did. Promoting Pepsi would become her primary focus, but the downside was that it kept reminding her that Al Steele was dead. She had always been sensitive to loss, other people's as well as her own, and Steele's death sharpened her antennae for the grief of others.

She and Jane Ardmore attended a dinner party at Cole Porter's apartment at the Waldorf-Astoria. Porter seemed shriveled in his wheelchair and was obviously ill, so much so that he couldn't eat any of the exquisite dinner. Crawford was so upset by Porter's condition that she couldn't eat either.

Ardmore had seen all the latest Broadway shows, and that seemed to rouse Porter. He quizzed her about them with an unusual intensity. It was too much trouble for him to attend in a wheelchair, and talking about the theater was as close as he could get to it.

Over the next few days, Crawford called friends and asked them to call Porter—he was, she explained, withering on the vine. Some did call him, but Billy Haines refused. He and Porter had had some kind of argument, and they weren't speaking. Crawford stood by the phone and began to cry, tears coursing down her face at her old friend's stubborn cruelty to his old friend.

CRAWFORD'S PEPSI SALARY DIDN'T cover her overhead, so she signed on to promote the products of a hat company for an extra $25,000 a year.

When attending Pepsi board meetings, Crawford was tentative at first.

They knew I was learning. They knew I was frightened. If you try to—with your insecurities—prove you've very secure, believe me it shows.

The first time I went to a Board meeting, I said, "What page are you on? What does it mean there? I don't understand it." I didn't. I didn't understand it. But a member of the Board said and underlined what they were talking about: "Turn the page. Double pages. . . ."

I think a man in business, especially a big corporate business, loves to have you remain a female but never use your femininity. Admit your lack of knowledge and brother will they ever help you. Sister and brothers, will they ever help you. . . .

I worked with business managers, actors, directors, story conferences, writers. So I was accustomed and trained in 32 years for that. So when I became a member of the Board of Directors, I was accustomed . . . to nineteen men every morning. I must say I was terrified at the first three Board Meetings because I had been married to the Chairman of the Board, but fortunately he knew my hunger for knowledge, he knew my desire to learn about his business.

It was another part to play, and she would learn to play it very well.

CHAPTER EIGHTEEN

IN THE SUMMER OF 1960, Crawford took a working cruise with her twin daughters Cindy and Cathy. Also on board were Al Hirschfeld, his daughter Nina, and a Wall Street executive named Peter Brochu who was traveling with his son Jim, who was about to turn thirteen. The ship was the SS *Brazil* on a thirty-one-day cruise from New York to Buenos Aires and back, with stops in Trinidad, Rio, and Montevideo.

"My father was incredibly charismatic," remembered Jim Brochu. "He was handsome—he looked like Jimmy Stewart—he was funny, a real catch. My mother was dead, and my father was absolutely certain he never wanted to get married again." Jim Brochu was told that Joan Crawford was on board, which meant nothing to him, but everything to his father. "She's my favorite actress!" said Peter Brochu.

On the second day of the cruise there was a mixer for the teenagers on board, and Jim went to meet the other kids, among whom was a friend of his named Janet Yellen—the future head of the Federal Reserve and Secretary of the Treasury. She lived two blocks from Jim, they did the limbo together, and he had given her his school ring, which, he insists, she never gave back.

At the mixer, Jim met Cindy and Cathy Crawford. "We just hit it off. They said, 'We have games in the cabin if you want to come play.' So we went to the cabin, and there was Mrs. Steele. She was at the dressing table, dyeing her hair. There was a big glass of water in front of her, which in retrospect I don't think was water.

"'Come in, have a Pepsi,'" she said. "It was a working trip for her. She couldn't have been nicer to me. I felt immediately comfortable with her and the twins, and I told her I wanted her to meet my father."

Back in their cabin, Jim told his father that he had met a beautiful lady who was a widow. "I'm not getting married again," Peter Brochu snapped. "No widows!"

That night in the dining room there was applause, and father and son turned to see Joan Crawford and her two girls making an entrance. "My father said, 'That's Joan Crawford!' And she came right over to the table and said, 'Oh, Jimmy, thank you for spending the afternoon with us. Wasn't it fun?'

"And then she turned to my father and said, 'You must be Pete.' And my father didn't know whether to shit or go blind. Then she said, 'Shall we have a dance later and perhaps a drink?' And so they did. And there were several nights when Dad did not come back to our cabin."

Pete Brochu and Crawford saw each other a few times after the cruise was over, but the friendship between Jim Brochu and Crawford, and between Jim and Cindy Crawford, endured.

Pete Brochu never did remarry.

NEW YORK HAD ITS compensations, but Crawford missed her old friends. In the 1940s, she had considered the fan magazine writers Katherine Albert and Ruth Waterbury her closest friends, in spite of the fact that "We [weren't] the type of women to have time for canasta," but the relationship with Katherine Albert was over.

Helen Hayes and Crawford had been close in the 1930s, but Hayes remained devoted to the theater and was working most of the time. "I hear from Helen when she feels like writing," was the way Crawford put it.

Gay friends like Billy Haines and Jerry Asher spent most of their time in California—Asher seemed to take Crawford's move to New York City as a personal affront. Cesar Romero made it a point to see Crawford when at all possible, and she appreciated his loyalty. "Cesar will always break a date to take me out. I'd do the same for him. He gets me with all my problems. One time I got ill. 'Butch, drive up a side street, I'm ill.' I was so embarrassed."

Romero tried to comfort her. "Forget it, Joan, I've been sick many times in my life."

"But not on a side street!"

Crawford and Romero spent many New Year's Eves together at one party or another. "The only problem was that every woman wants to dance with Mr. Romero. One year I sat with soap bubbles and balloons, and finally I just came home."

Otherwise, things were . . . quiet. In 1960, a part in *Return to Peyton Place* was a possibility, but that came to nothing, and in any case it wouldn't have reversed the perceptible sense of slowdown. While her relationship with the twins was and would remain solid, there were continuing problems with Christopher and Christina. The first open declaration of war between mother and daughter came in a 1960 magazine profile headlined "The Revolt of Joan Crawford's Daughter." The article is about 80 percent Christina, 20 percent Crawford.

"It has been 18 years of disappointment," Crawford announced, while the author averred that "when interviewed, mother and daughter often give completely contradictory versions of the same events."

The relationship started well. "Mummy was with me constantly," said Christina. "No matter where she went, even when she traveled across the country, I went along too. . . . And she read poetry to me in that marvelous voice of hers. She read the poems of Edna St. Vincent Millay and the sonnets of Shakespeare. When I learned to read we took turns reciting stanzas. Mother loved poetry and she wanted me to be exposed to it as early as possible."

There were memories of holidays and vacations and visitors to the house. John Garfield made a particularly strong impression on the child. "I thought he was the most marvelous creature in the world and I decided that if I ever married, it would have to be someone like him."

Christina said that things got complicated around the time she was nine or ten, when she began asserting herself and separating her likes and dislikes from those of her mother. The arguments "reached more than average intensity . . .

because the actress held the same rigorously high standards for her children that she had always demanded of herself. There was constant bickering. . . .

"I was told that I was wrong. I would be contradicted so crushingly that I'd turn red as a beet. I was just supposed to do as I was told and keep quiet."

Christina was sent to a convent school. Crawford's marriage to Al Steele in 1955 helped. "I have never felt such warmth, strength and understanding in any person," said Christina. "He was my idea of what a father should be."

Christina thought about studying drama at Northwestern, but chose Carnegie Tech. She quit after a year against the advice of her mother and went to New York, where Crawford got her a job as a receptionist at MCA. She got a part in an off-Broadway play, which was advertised as featuring Joan Crawford's daughter. After the play closed, Christina quit her job at MCA. As one onlooker noted, "Joan Crawford was incapable of giving help to her daughter except on her own terms, and Christina was incapable of accepting help from her mother except on *her* own terms."

As far as Crawford was concerned, Christina's quitting MCA was stupid. It was a job where Christina could make contacts, read scripts, see what was getting made and what wasn't, get her sea legs in the business. "If she couldn't keep the job at MCA, then I didn't feel I could help her any longer," Crawford said. She cut off Christina's allowance. The article ends with the two women metaphorically glaring at each other from opposing corners.

A year later, there was another magazine story in which Christina largely recanted the earlier story. "Because we lived in a goldfish bowl . . . newspaper stories of what went on in our family were so exaggerated that Mother often appeared cruel, which was certainly not the case."

It was right around here that Eve Arden became uneasy about her friend's relationship with her daughter. "She adored Joan and thought she was a great actress," said Arden's son Doug West.

But they had a falling-out. My mother never liked talking about Christina. My mother knew Christina's side, and knew there was some truth to what was claimed.

As I understand it, my mother said something about Christina to Joan just about the time Joan moved to New York, and that was it. She had a sense that Joan was not a forgiving mother, and my mother adored all her kids. We had disagreements, but I don't ever remember being punished by her—she used guilt to keep us in line.

She never really talked about Joan in any detail, because she did not want to say anything negative about people. That's why she didn't write about her six-year affair with Danny Kaye in her memoir—she didn't want to upset [Kaye's wife] Sylvia Fine, so she left it out.

(It gets better. Doug West: "My wife's mother was a dancer on Broadway. When my mother died, we were looking through her memorabilia and there was a playbill from *Let's Face It*, the Cole Porter show she did with Danny Kaye. And not ten feet from my mother was my wife's mother. She was in the chorus, and she was also having an affair with Danny.")

What is striking is the gradually accelerating psychological duel between parent and child. Crawford ordered, Christina resisted; Crawford withdrew, Christina refused to apologize. It was a war of temperament and, ultimately, attrition that could only be settled by the grim reality of actuarial tables.

Things weren't much better with Christopher. His first child was born in 1961 in Florida, where he and his wife moved because her mother lived there. Christopher got work as a cabana boy at the Fontainebleau in Miami Beach, and when Crawford came to Miami he took his daughter and wife to meet his mother. She studied both parents and child then addressed them: "Well, she doesn't look like either of you. She must be a bastard."

CHAPTER NINETEEN

AS MUCH AS BETTE Davis disliked Joan Crawford, she was compelled to admit that she owed her: "I will always thank her for giving me the opportunity to play the part of Baby Jane Hudson," noted Davis.

On October 31, 1961, Robert Aldrich sent Mort Viner, Bette Davis's agent, a copy of the novel *What Ever Happened to Baby Jane?* Viner responded by asking for a meeting with Aldrich around Christmas. On November 18, Aldrich wrote Viner: "I am apprehensive that it would be imprudent to postpone (at least the beginnings) of our conversation until Christmas. What I must determine from you is the conditions and interest of Bette Davis in portraying the role of 'Baby Jane,' her terms, her availability, etc. etc. as both Joe Levine and I (and, I might add, Joan Crawford) are convinced that she is probably the only actress in the world who can do this part justice."

Viner responded by informing Aldrich that his client was tied up with Tennessee Williams's *The Night of the Iguana* on a run-of-the-play contract. Before they could proceed Aldrich needed to make a firm offer. This dance went on until Aldrich wrote Davis on February 12, 1962: "Miss Joan Crawford originally mentioned to me your mutual desire to find a property suitable for joining your considerable and unique talents. At the time she had a vehicle, the name of which escapes me, that I thought perhaps a little less than ideal, but I was, nonetheless, totally intrigued by the possibility of finding the proper property for such an interesting and exciting combination of talents."

He went on to explain that he had found *Baby Jane*, bought the novel, and hired Lukas Heller to write a screenplay. "I would be willing to stake the success of our total relationship (which may only begin by your doing this film) on the flat statement that if this is not the best role in potentially the best picture for Bette Davis that you have seen, read or been offered (Including all your past triumphs) then I reluctantly, but philosophically, withdraw the submission as not being up to the measure of importance and stature that we all think it to be."

While these preliminaries were taking place, Davis was engaged in sabotaging Tennessee Williams's play, which had inexorably segued from "The Night of the Iguana" to "An Evening with Bette Davis." The de-evolution began in rehearsals, when Davis's costar Patrick O'Neal had tried to strangle her shortly after she announced that she was "Sick of this Actor's Studio shit!"

Director Frank Corsaro bailed while the play was still out of town, and an increasingly desperate Williams asked Elia Kazan to take a look at the production and give him some guidance before the New York opening. Kazan wasn't about to board a sinking ship and confined himself to telling Williams, "The play is very well-directed. Davis is gonna do exactly what she's gonna do and there's nothing you can do about it, but don't change the staging."

The cast found Davis "extremely unpleasant." A young actress named Lane Bradbury was playing Charlotte and would sit offstage preparing for her entrance. One night in Chicago, Davis walked by, stopped, and gave her "a very dirty look. Well, the next thing you know, she's talking to the stage manager who then comes over to tell me I couldn't prepare my scenes there anymore, and from that point on, I had to go down four flights of stairs to the basement to do my preparation and then run up just in time to go onstage."

On opening night in New York, Davis's entrance as Maxine was met with a roar from the audience. She broke character, stepped to the apron, and raised her hands over her head in the attitude of a victorious prizefighter. She wasn't playing Maxine, she was playing Bette Davis, which was precisely what her audience wanted.

Tennessee Williams, shaky from amphetamine injections from Dr. Max Jacobson and desperate for a hit, bailed on his own play by asking Davis to stay on at least until the theater party advance was exhausted. Davis left the show in April, months before the end of her contract. She was replaced by Shelley Winters. "It is hard to say which was worse, but at least La Davis drew cash," wrote Williams to Maria St. Just. A definitive version of *The Night of the Iguana* would have to wait for John Huston's excellent film, with Ava Gardner defining Maxine.

Both the novel and the screenplay of *What Ever Happened to Baby Jane?* form a compelling Gothic grotesque that offered strong parts for two actresses who hadn't had one in a long time. Neither Davis nor Crawford was being hotly pursued by other offers, so negotiations didn't take that long, but not before considerable maneuvering about money and billing. Initial offers gave Davis more cash up front but less of a percentage of the profits than Crawford—Davis was to get $60,000 and 5 percent of the profits, while Crawford was to get $40,000 and 10 percent. Billing was to imitate John Ford's *The Man Who Shot Liberty Valance*, where John Wayne got first position on the film itself and James Stewart got first position on all advertising.

But Davis realized that while Crawford's part could conceivably be played by a couple of other actresses, Baby Jane could only be played by someone willing to risk complete embarrassment—an alcoholic sixty-something harridan dressed in a Mary Pickford pinafore and sporting whiteface makeup. By the time the contracts were signed, Davis got top billing and certain consultation rights. The agreement was signed on May 9, 1962, with Crawford signing on for $30,000 and 15 percent of the profits. The contract had initially stated that she and Davis would have equal costar billing, which was crossed out in favor of giving Davis top billing and in the same size as the film's title.

"When it came to the short strokes . . . Davis became difficult, Crawford was ever malleable," wrote Aldrich to an associate.

Contracts finally in hand, Aldrich went shopping for money and couldn't find any. Joseph E. Levine had originally agreed to front the $850,000 budget but dropped out, and every major studio turned the picture down. The problem was the stars, both of whom were regarded as elderly has-beens.

Aldrich remained committed to the picture. He widened his net and finally got the film financed by Eliot Hyman, who owned a company called Seven Arts that had bought the TV rights to Warners' backlog of pictures. Since

Hyman was financing, Jack Warner agreed to distribute the picture on a straight percentage basis.

Aldrich had his stars, but the budget meant he would have to make the picture at top speed; the shooting schedule would be six weeks—a pace the stars hadn't seen since their earliest days in the picture business. What this meant in practice was that there would be no time for time-sucking spats that held up production. This would be a sprint, not a stroll.

What Ever Happened to Baby Jane? began shooting on Friday, July 27, and finished on Tuesday, September 11, 1962. The documentation indicates there were occasional tremors but no actual earthquakes, as with this from a document labeled "Davis Diary": "Call from Director to determine health of Miss Davis . . . met with 'Why is Edna [a] Negro' argument' terminated by hang-up.

"Called Back . . . left name . . . Davis did not return call."

As for the relationship between the two stars, which has occasioned flamboyant fan fiction masquerading as film history and at least one TV series, Aldrich would say that "I think it's proper to say that they really detested each other, but they behaved absolutely perfectly: no upstaging, not an abrasive word in public. . . . They both behaved in a wonderfully professional manner."

Davis's take was grudging: "Joan was a pro. She was always punctual, always knew her lines. . . . She had a deep and gnawing need to be liked, loved, admired, appreciated. She could be touchingly generous. She brought gifts for me to the set and presented them in front of the crew."

But there was a competition, and according to Davis it had begun years earlier, when she had a mad crush on Franchot Tone when they made *Dangerous* together at Warner Bros. in 1935. She couldn't get to first base because it was obvious that he was involved with Crawford back at MGM.

A publicist working on *Baby Jane* planted an item in *Time* magazine about the picture. The editors interpolated a bitchy line about both stars "professing to be 55."

On the soundstage the next day, Davis called out to Linn Unkefer, the publicist: "Linn, come in here!"

"Good morning, Bette."

"Did you have anything to do with this item?"

"Yes."

"*She's five years older than I am if she's a day!*" Davis snapped.

The publicist proceeded to Crawford's dressing room. She also called him in and also had a copy of *Time*. "Well, we're getting off to a good start, aren't we?"

"Bette was very . . . well-educated," said the screenwriter Lenore Coffee, who wrote for both actresses. "Joan was not. Bette came from a good family and was a trained theater actress. Joan had taught herself to speak and she spoke very well. I had great admiration for her."

When she was asked about distinguishing between their personalities, Coffee said succinctly, "I think Joan would be more susceptible. I think Bette could be pretty tough."

In fact, Crawford and Davis embodied many of the same characteristics. Crawford was far more amenable to direction than Davis, who generally treated directors as obstacles God unaccountably placed between her and the audience. She only submitted when confronted with a stronger will—William Wyler, for instance. Both sought to control their professional trajectories as much as possible by seducing their directors, either through charm, dominance, or sex.

And there was another crucial difference. Crawford wanted a happy set, while Davis was stimulated by aggravation and tension. If nothing aggravated her, she'd search for something that would.

Director Vincent Sherman would remember that "In life and offscreen, Bette was simple, forthright, honest and unaffected. The moment she began playing a role she became actorish and theatrical. Joan, on the other hand, was simple, forthright, honest and unaffected when playing a role, but in life she was exactly the opposite: actorish, theatrical and affected.

"Bette dressed poorly and never seemed to care much how she looked, whereas Joan was always well-dressed and highly conscious of how she appeared. Bette never thought of herself as being beautiful or attractive, whereas Joan was sure of her beauty and dedicated her life to taking care of it. Finally, I think sex for Bette was a biological need, while for Joan it was primarily an ego trip."

With his intimate knowledge of both women, Sherman got to the point. "Davis and Crawford . . . disliked each other, but they were really sisters under the skin. Both of their fathers left their mothers when they were very young, so they were afraid of rejection; even expected to be rejected. They distrusted men and, in lay psychology, therefore emasculated them as a sort of defensive preventative measure. They needed to be in control."

Robert Aldrich knew both women quite well and outlined to his associate Eugene Lester how to behave: "I know you would normally think of it but under the terrible pressures you must be operating under you might just forget and, knowing the schizophrenic feline as opposed to the feminine mind of Crawford, I would only suggest that you somehow find the time to 'make her an emotional partner' of everything that has gone on. I don't mean that you should donate your lily-white body but if she feels she has been 'left out' there will be hell to pay. Okay? Okay."

Lester responded by sending a stream of floral bouquets to Crawford, who invariably responded with gracious thank-you notes: "Gene dear, How wonderful it was to see you. Thank you so much for the beautiful red roses. I am so deeply grateful to you. I'm sorry our little visit was so short, but it was good, even briefly, to see that happy face of yours. Bless you and thank you again for your kindnesses."

According to Linn Unkefer, the closest thing to an outburst occurred when Crawford was in her wheelchair on the set while laboring beneath a cold. She asked Aldrich if she could take a break for a few minutes, which led Davis to say loudly, "You'd think by now we'd all be troupers." Crawford stared at Davis, then got up and walked away, while Aldrich took Davis aside and cooled her down. Other than that, there was a minimum of chitchat.

Publicists had to adapt their methods to the individual personalities of the stars. Davis tended toward grumpy, and Unkefer had to cajole her to do interviews. With Crawford, all she had to do was give her a briefing on the reporter so she wouldn't walk into the interview blind.

The only real professional problem arose from the fact that the two stars had different ways of working. Davis went full tilt in both rehearsal and performance, while Crawford walked through rehearsals to get her movements and dramatic beats, but didn't give a full performance until the camera rolled. "I never give until the camera's turned," said Crawford. "You know, how much can you give of yourself? Why give it anyway, for God's sakes, it's not being recorded."

This eventually led to Davis turning to Robert Aldrich and snapping, "*Mr.*

Aldrich!" and stalking into her dressing room. After a while Aldrich emerged to find Crawford had been passing the intervening time by knitting. "Can I be helpful?" she inquired. Davis wanted to know when Crawford was going to "give me some emotion to work against?"

Aldrich had worked with Crawford before and knew how she worked. "Bette," he told her, "when the camera's rolling."

"There was never a feud because it takes two to tango and I refuse to fight," Crawford said more than ten years after the film was shot. "I'm not going to waste my energy on anything or anybody until that camera goes! Nobody can entice me into that; nobody can goad me into it."

While voices were never raised, the underlying tension was real. Davis would claim that Crawford had three sizes of falsies, that Aldrich had to struggle to strip Crawford of glamorous makeup and wardrobe, even though squalor is intrinsic to the characters and the setting.

"I could feel all those evil vibes slipping through the doors," said Anna Lee, who was playing the nosy next-door neighbor. "Bette was quite nice to me because her chunky daughter B.D. was playing my daughter. With Joan there was a polite distance. Cases of Pepsi arrived daily for the crew. . . . It is true that Joan weighed herself down with jockey weights when Bette had to drag her across the floor. . . . It was all quite tense, I can tell you."

What was clear to Aldrich from the beginning was that in spite of all the jostling, the movie was working. "The picture goes in some regards very well," he wrote Eugene Lester toward the end of production.

> It is going to be a fine, perhaps even brilliant film, maybe even a minor classic. Davis' performance is quite beyond belief and in my opinion she is walking away with the picture and has *never* been better in her entire life, which is quite a statement. Nor do I think that I have ever been better.
>
> At present we are four days behind. We may lose one more between now and conclusion, a fact which doesn't seem to disturb anybody yet as there seems to be so much excitement. . . .
>
> Davis has been fabulously cooperative even if explosive and occasionally trying. Crawford, has, sorry to say, been less rewarding. She just can't adjust to making a realistic picture and, try as she may, she stays in constant

conflict with herself between wanting to do what she knows is right but still wanting to remain the old-time movie queen. Consequently, she's in a continuing state of bitchiness and pouts from morning till night. But, it's still one helluva picture.

When the picture was finally completed, Crawford was both exhausted and satisfied. She knew that the movie was good and that she was very fine in it—emotional yet with a reality that, despite Aldrich's fears, ultimately left the movie queen behind.

The final cost was just over $1 million, a sum that was earned in the first week the picture played in New York and Los Angeles. The movie nobody wanted went on to earn more than $9 million in rentals.

Aldrich pitches his film as a claustrophobic black comedy, right up until it becomes a domestic tragedy. Crawford plays a movie star from the early 1930s now confined to a wheelchair in an upstairs bedroom in a decaying semi-Spanish Hollywood mansion controlled by her deranged sister, a former child star. Aldrich uses clips from Davis's films *Parachute Jumper* and *Ex-Lady* and Crawford's *Sadie McKee* as illustrations of their varying career paths.

Davis's Baby Jane exists in a twilight fantasy world much like that of Mae Murray, the silent star whom Crawford had as a dinner guest nearly thirty years before, not to mention Gloria Swanson's Norma Desmond. The performance alternates between childish wheedling when Baby Jane wants something and aggressively cackling theatricality the rest of the time. Davis's performance is extremely funny, then scary, finally sad.

Crawford gives a naturalistic, imaginative performance centered on plaintive desperation, but the character is completely reactive. The movie is structurally dominated by the motivating insanity of Baby Jane, as well as by the extremity of Davis's bravura performance.

The characters are a gallery of grotesques, including Victor Buono as a gay man who hates his mother and is looking to score some money off what's left of the sisters' depleted stash. When Billy Wilder made *Sunset Boulevard*, *Baby Jane*'s thematic predecessor, he made William Holden's Joe Gillis a hack screenwriter who's smart enough to realize he's a hack. Joe gets involved with the crazy Norma Desmond as well as Nancy Olson's nice girl in the script department. In other words, there are a couple of recognizable human beings.

But *What Ever Happened to Baby Jane?* is populated almost exclusively by grotesques and its forward motion is created by Aldrich's basic trait of exploding the conventions of whatever genre he was tackling. *Baby Jane* is a fascinating one-off, often imitated, never duplicated, largely because of the dynamic tension between two equally magnificent but completely different stars. It deserved its success.

THE FIRING SQUADS DIDN'T appear until after the picture was released. The proximate cause was a planned dual appearance of both stars at the Cannes Film Festival. The cost was $32,000, and there was much haggling over whether Aldrich or Warners would pay for it. The thinking was that a deluxe appearance by the two primary movie queens of the 1930s and '40s would increase the foreign grosses for *Baby Jane* by as much as $500,000.

But it all blew up over the Academy Awards, when Crawford announced that she would happily accept the Oscar for any actress who was nominated but unable to show up. Bette Davis was nominated for Best Actress. Crawford was not. Davis took Crawford's offer as blatant upstaging and was furious.

It must have been interesting backstage, because Davis was there to award the Best Screenplay Oscar to Horton Foote for *To Kill a Mockingbird*. Anne Bancroft was working in a play in New York, and when she won Best Actress for *The Miracle Worker*, Crawford accepted for her and read Bancroft's acceptance: "Dear Joan, Here's my little speech: There are three reasons why I deserve this award: [director] Arthur Penn, [screenwriter] Bill Gibson, [producer] Fred Coe. Unquote."

After that, Davis's rage increased by a factor of ten.

"All hell has broken loose in the Davis camp, and Bette is now emotionally disturbed," Warner's lawyer Wolfe Cohen wrote. "Aldrich is trying to placate Davis by assuring that he will cancel out Crawford and take Davis as sole representative to Cannes, but Bette is still in a nervous state."

Aldrich was under the gun because of *Four for Texas*, a comedy Western he was directing for Warners that had a rigid start date because of Frank Sinatra's schedule. Aldrich thought he might have to cancel his own participation in the Cannes trip, and he knew that "Davis will be further distressed when she learns that he will not be riding with her and holding her hand."

But things worked out. Sort of.

Aldrich and Davis appeared at Cannes with *Baby Jane* sans Crawford, who pretended not to mind. She wrote a friend, "About the Bob Aldrich-Bette Davis treatment, well, their bitterness can only hurt them. It couldn't possibly hurt the one whom their bitterness is towards. It can only hurt them because they carry around the bitterness within their hearts, and certainly must reflect in their living and their lives. Hurt? Yes, that I am. Bitter? Never."

NINETEEN SIXTY-TWO WAS A good year for Crawford. Besides the success of *Baby Jane*, her autobiography *A Portrait of Joan* was released in the summer and earned both good reviews and good sales, helped along by an extensive series of personal appearances by its author. Ghosted by Jane Kesner Ardmore, it remains a very readable book and, within the limitations of its period and the personality of its subject, honest.

A hit puts you back in the gossip columns, and by all odds the most absurd item about Crawford in the wake of *Baby Jane* came in a flurry of reports that she was seriously involved with New York governor Nelson Rockefeller. "How can you be engaged to a man who's never asked you for a date?" she asked rhetorically.

The following year brought money from *What Ever Happened to Baby Jane?* and a full social calendar. In the second week of July, Crawford flew to Canada for a reunion with Franchot Tone. The Pepsi corporate plane got her as far as Ottawa, after which she transferred to a tiny Grumman Cub that flew her thirty minutes north to Lac Pemichangan and the Gatineau Fish and Game Club.

John Larcher, the caretaker and guide for Tone's property, was there to meet her and the four suitcases and case of Dom Pérignon she brought with her. Crawford stayed for three nights and she, Tone, and Richard Aherne, an Irish actor who was also visiting with his dog Sally, watched some films—*The Finest*

Hours—a documentary about Winston Churchill in World War II—and *The Pumpkin Eater*, with Anne Bancroft—a special favorite of Crawford's, who thought her "the leading movie star today."

Although Crawford didn't share Tone's passion for fishing, she was willing to help him reduce the supply he brought back from the lake. She thought the water was too cold to go swimming, so she did some sunbathing and at night they sipped their Dom Pérignon and talked. There was no rekindling of the love affair; they had both reached the age where a good friendship was preferable to a bad marriage.

That year she made *The Caretakers*, a stillborn melodrama about the staff and patients at a mental hospital that featured Crawford opposite Robert Stack and Polly Bergen. Crawford thought the script was far better than the movie, largely because of some cuts director Hall Bartlett made in the film that obliterated her character's romantic interest in Robert Stack's character. She wrote Bartlett an angry, almost contemptuous letter of reproval for defacing his own movie.

That same year Hal LeSueur died at the age of fifty-nine. He had been working as a clerk in a motel in Los Angeles before a ruptured appendix put him in the hospital and the resulting sepsis killed him. His sister did not visit him in the hospital, nor did she attend his funeral at Forest Lawn, although she paid for it.

A HIT LIKE *Baby Jane* demands a follow-up, and Robert Aldrich was happy to oblige. He believed that the enmity between Crawford and Davis could be finessed as long as there was money to be made. After making the slovenly Western with Frank Sinatra and Dean Martin, Aldrich approached Crawford about a reunion called *Hush . . . Hush, Sweet Charlotte*. Crawford signed on in December of 1963 for $50,000 plus 25 percent of the profits. A month later, Davis came on board for a flat fee of $200,000. There was a succeeding contract in April of 1964 that added 10 percent of the profits for Davis in addition to her $200,000, with the April contract specifying her agreement to Crawford's presence as costar.

With the contracts ironed out by spring of 1964, Aldrich began providing

Crawford with the usual emoluments—lavish floral arrangements for her birthday or, more likely, for agreeing to work with Davis again.

"Bob Darling, Thank you so much for the beautiful red roses on my birthday. How dear you were to remember! Thank you for the wire and the script. I will read it over the weekend and will see you when you come to New York. Please let me know the exact date. Bless you and my love to you and Hattie. Joan."

A week later, after a conference with Aldrich about the script, followed by yet more flowers for Easter, Crawford replied, "So glad your thinking is so much like mine and that, besides shortening the script, you fully intend to improve it."

Somewhere in here there were more negotiations regarding Davis, her money, and her ideas. Aldrich preserved an undated document labeled "Compromises" in which it was specified that Crawford's 25 percent of the profits was not going to be lessened by giving any of it to Davis. Rather, Davis's 10 percent of the profits was going to be deducted from the shares of Aldrich and 20th Century-Fox. Davis also suggested that Mary Astor would be a better idea for a crucial supporting part than Aldrich's choice of Barbara Stanwyck. Besides the star's preference, Astor needed the money while Stanwyck did not. Astor played the part.

In other compromises, Crawford got two days off to attend a Grocer's Convention in June, presumably for Pepsi-Cola duties, and Monte Westmore, her favorite makeup man, would be hired for a full week's salary for her makeup test. Also amended was the matter of billing—unlike *Baby Jane*, Crawford would get top billing, with Joseph Cotten holding down third position for playing the male lead.

With the contractual jousting completed, the real combat started when the picture began rehearsals on May 18, and then shooting on June 1 with three days of location work in Baton Rouge, Louisiana. Davis and Crawford had only one brief scene together in Baton Rouge, although they worked together on a photo shoot for *Life* magazine. Crawford's old publicist friend Harry Mines was working on the picture and had the job of getting what he called "two tough broads" together.

The photographer had the idea of posing Davis and Crawford on tombstones in a cemetery. Davis thought it was hilarious, while Crawford quietly went along with it. *Life* got their shot, but back from New York came the edict that it be retaken in color instead of black-and-white. Davis was willing, but Crawford said, "Not on your life." The magazine ran the black-and-white version. While the company was in Baton Rouge, Crawford stayed in her dressing room when she didn't have to be on the set, while Davis hung around the camera.

When they started shooting at the studio in Los Angeles, Crawford began to falter. She was perspiring, then standing in front of an air conditioner trying to cool off. When that wasn't enough, she would stand in front of a huge fan. They had completed only a few days of studio work when Crawford was admitted to the hospital on June 15.

That day, Crawford sent a telegram to Aldrich: DEAR BOB, HOW SWEET YOU WERE TO SEND ME THE BEAUTIFUL RED ROSES. AM TERRIBLY SORRY THAT I CANNOT WORK TODAY ESPECIALLY FOR THE JOAN CRAWFORD-BETTE DAVIS DAY DECLARED BY [Los Angeles] MAYOR YORTY. I AM SURE MISS DAVIS IS QUALIFIED TO TAKE CARE OF THE PUBLICITY. THANK GOD THEY PUT ME IN HOSPITAL. IF I HAD NOT ENTERED I MIGHT HAVE HAD PNEUMONIA AND WOULD HAVE HELD UP THE PICTURE. LOVE, JOAN.

On June 18, Dr. E. Gourson examined Crawford in the hospital and reported back to Aldrich, who in turn reported back to Stan Hough, the production supervisor at Fox. "She is, in fact, quite ill," wrote Aldrich. "There is much technical language in his report that has to do with an excessively high white blood [cell] count, a severe post-nasal drip that is causing a throat and lung condition that in all probability caused the original fever, uncomfortableness, etc., etc." Besides all this, Crawford had a serious case of dysentery. "His opinion is that she could be incapacitated for an additional seven to ten days."

A day after that, Crawford wrote to thank Aldrich for another bouquet of flowers and closed with I AM SO DEEPLY GRATEFUL TO YOU AND SO DESOLATE THAT I AM NOT ABLE TO WORK. BLESS YOU, LOVE, JOAN.

On June 26, Crawford was still feeling ill and running a temperature of 101, but was sick of being sick. She left the hospital. The day after that, she had pain in her left lung and a bad cough. On June 28, she was examined at

Cedars of Lebanon hospital by a chest specialist as well as by Dr. Prinzmetal, a well-known internist to the stars. A blood count showed a marked increase of her white cells to 23,300. Chest X-rays showed a clouding at the base of the left lung.

The medical conclusion was that "Miss Crawford has an infection involving the lower lobe of the left lung. . . . When I saw her she appeared in no acute distress except for a frequent cough." Doctors began administering a broad spectrum of antibiotics and estimated that she would be out of commission for the remainder of the week. Once again flowers arrived from Aldrich, once again Crawford responded with a note of thanks: "You aren't half as sorry as I am about this pneumonia, believe me. I just feel dreadful having this happen on any production. God bless, and my love to you."

Production was suspended on Friday, July 3, and didn't resume until July 21. Crawford then worked four days, quitting around noon. Aldrich was clearly growing nervous and decided to get proactive: he hired a private detective. The detective did a stakeout and surveillance on Crawford's apartment at 8313 Fountain Avenue to determine if she left the premises at any time on July 24 or 25.

The surveillance on July 24 was uneventful except for the fact that Loretta Young, who owned the building and also had an apartment there, arrived and parked at 6:20 p.m. On July 25, surveillance began at noon and nothing happened until 5:05 p.m., when a two-tone brown Rolls-Royce left the building. It was driven by a woman "appearing to be the subject. She wore a bandana over her hair and dark sun glasses. There is very little doubt but that this was Miss Crawford, she was alone at that time."

The detective tailed her from Fountain to Linden Drive, where he lost her. As of 11:30 p.m. the Rolls hadn't returned to the Fountain Avenue apartments.

On Tuesday, July 28, Crawford worked five hours and twenty-five minutes. The next day she told Aldrich that she had overtaxed herself, was exhausted, and would leave at lunch. Aldrich consulted with studio head Richard Zanuck and Stan Hough. They decided to suspend shooting that day and give Crawford an additional four and a half days to recoup and recover her strength before Monday.

Aldrich phoned Bette Davis to inform her that she wouldn't be working for the rest of the week. "I am sure there is no need to repeat and/or dramatize her reaction," Aldrich wrote in a memo. Davis told Aldrich that in her opinion Crawford would return for a day or two and then revert to being "too tired." "Whether there is any validity in this I no longer know," Aldrich wrote. Sixty years later, you can hear his exhausted sigh.

If Crawford couldn't return to work on Monday for a full day, "we (Fox and Aldrich) [will] be forced to take some decisive action." Aldrich passed all this on to Crawford. On Friday, July 31, Crawford was again admitted to the hospital.

On August 4, Crawford wrote Aldrich to thank him for a bouquet of yellow roses and closed with, "My heart is just broken that I am not strong enough to give you the hours and certainly not the time and strength that the role demands."

At this point the picture closed down. On August 20, Aldrich wrote Crawford a letter that Fox held back because they believed it amounted to termination, which would be unwise unless Aldrich found a replacement. Aldrich and the studio had been more than patient, but they had to make a decision. There were two options: cancel the picture, with attendant legal and financial complications that could stretch on for years, or find somebody else to play Crawford's part.

Aldrich might have given some thought to hiring Barbara Stanwyck for Crawford's part, but that went out the window when Stanwyck called Crawford and told her under no circumstances would she take over for her friend. Joseph Cotten said that Aldrich's first choice for a replacement was Vivien Leigh, who cabled to his tentative approach, "I could just about stand to be in a southern plantation at 5 a.m. with Miss Crawford. But never with Miss Davis!"

Aldrich claimed that his first choice was Katharine Hepburn, but he wasn't sure if her agents ever showed her the script. In any case, Davis didn't want to work with either Leigh or Hepburn, for reasons that Aldrich would not disclose but said "involved deep-seated personal and historical reasons." The fact that Davis had contractual approval of her costars meant Aldrich's choices were extremely limited. Aldrich also thought about Loretta Young, but she said that "I couldn't do that to my old pal," i.e., Crawford.

Now desperate, Aldrich had little choice but to follow Davis's preference. He got on a plane to Switzerland to convince Olivia de Havilland to take the job for a flat $100,000. "I won't say that Olivia was third choice," Aldrich said, "but Olivia was the first choice that was acceptable [to Davis]." The picture opened up again and went into rehearsals on September 1.

It was at this point that Aldrich replaced the Pepsi machine that had been installed at the start of production with a Coca-Cola machine. Davis, Aldrich, and Joseph Cotten were photographed enjoying their Cokes in a gag photo that was meant for in-house amusement. Unfortunately, the still was leaked to the press.

Aldrich was promptly assaulted with newspaper reports "reflecting Joan's justified anguish that she had not been informed by us but had to read in the papers of her replacement."

Counting rehearsals, Crawford had worked for about thirty-seven days out of a scheduled seventy. The lawyers began haggling—over who owed money to whom, over an insurance settlement, just generally haggling. In the end, insurance paid out $440,000 to cover the costs of shutting the picture down and hiring de Havilland, all of which ballooned the budget from $1.7 million to $2.2 million. Ultimately the picture did well—$4 million in rentals—but nowhere near as well as *Baby Jane*.

Aldrich's final word on the subject was that Crawford was "sick, seriously sick. If she'd been faking, as some reports then suggested, either the insurance company would never have paid the claim or she would never have been insurable again.... There's no such thing as a made-up ailment that they pay you off on."

Aldrich and Crawford never worked together again; she remained angry with him for the rest of her life, although it's hard to see why. In 1973, she told an interviewer that Aldrich loved "evil, horrendous, vile things," to which Aldrich replied, "I'm very fond of Joan. If the shoe fits, put it on."

"She thought we should have waited," said Aldrich. "Her survival mechanism told her so, yet she was a totally tactical, political person. She knew we had to move. The insurance company insisted we replace her or abandon the picture."

As far as what exactly happened, Aldrich believed that Crawford had come to the realization that he had more respect for Davis as an actress than he did Crawford. "Their roles in *Baby Jane* were equal, but in *Charlotte* Bette had the better part.

"None of the doctors could say how long she would be in the hospital because they couldn't diagnose the illness. We worked half days, but her condition got worse."

And then Aldrich got down to cases:

Joan could keep angry for two or three days. But Bette's vindictiveness could last forever. They were pretty even on *Jane*, because the roles were even. That didn't stop them from calling up at night and complaining– "Didn't you see what that cunt did today?"

On *Charlotte* it was a different matter. Bette's role was better. And Joan realized it. In the meantime, Joan had purposely offered to accept the Oscar for . . . [*Baby Jane*] nominees . . . Anne Bancroft, Lee Remick, Katharine Hepburn, Geraldine Page. Crawford held court backstage with a couple of Pepsi coolers filled with booze, served cheese and snacks to the nervous winners and presenters. Bette was furious and she declared war on Crawford. . . .

Bette was too much for Joan. She was critical at all times—"That isn't the way she's going to play it, is it?" to me, within Joan's hearing. She kept up the battle.

Joan's illness could not be explained by the doctors. They gave her every test possible. The physical effects were there; you can't fake a temperature of 104.5 and a blood count. . . . But they couldn't diagnose the ailment. Obviously it was psychosomatic.

In retrospect, Aldrich thought de Havilland made the picture better than Crawford would have. "I think probably the casting damaged the picture commercially, but it helped the picture enormously in believability. Crawford was Crawford and very good, but she'd never have given that kind of role the nuance that de Havilland did. Also, if de Havilland steps out of the cab, we're not sure the butler did it. Anyone else steps out of the cab, you know the butler did it, and the story's over."

The story of *Hush . . . Hush, Sweet Charlotte* leans more on flamboyant Grand Guignol than *Baby Jane* did—at one point Bruce Dern's decapitated head bounces jauntily down a flight of stairs—but at bottom it was another story of female betraying female, and Aldrich again managed an emotionally moving ending that was and is surprising in view of the story that has preceded it.

In retrospect, Aldrich thought the picture's timing was a mistake. "I don't want to be a middle-aged Hitchcock. I think any director gets better by doing a variety of films. I don't think he should do any one kind."

Regarding Aldrich's version of what went down, two things can be true at the same time. Davis's push to destabilize Crawford certainly contributed, but can nerves really induce pneumonia?

The confirmation for an authentic medical issue came from Robert Young and his wife Betty. Just about the time Crawford left the picture, the Youngs were relaxing in Rancho Santa Fe when the phone rang. Their daughter answered. "This is Joan Crawford." Young's daughter replied, "Sure it is." Betty Young came to the phone.

"Let's have dinner," announced Crawford. "I'll bring something from the grocery store." Crawford showed up lugging bags of groceries and proceeded to cook dinner all by herself.

She told the Youngs she was newly sprung from the hospital, where they had been "looking for leukemia," which supports Dr. Prinzmetal's discovery of a high white blood cell count. Despite the burst of bad health, "It was the most relaxed I had ever seen her," said Betty Young, probably because Crawford was out from under a bad situation.

It would have been wildly out of character for Crawford to bail on a movie because of emotional indisposition, especially given the fact that she owned 25 percent of the profits, which were likely to be considerable. From the beginning of her career nearly forty years before she had defined herself as a worker, and prided herself on that fact. Bad scripts, incompetent directors, dreary supporting casts—none of that mattered. Joan Crawford showed up. Absolute professionalism was her mantra, and even people who disliked her admired her devotion to craft.

Years later, Robert Aldrich was asked about his affinity for movies about men who are only truly alive when practicing their gift for violence—*The Dirty Dozen, Emperor of the North, The Longest Yard*, etc. The interview segued to "What was it like working with Crawford and Davis?"

"Same thing," he replied. "Two men."

CHAPTER TWENTY

MUCH OF CRAWFORD'S WORK for Pepsi was promotional in nature, but she would use her leverage as a member of the board of directors when she thought it necessary, which meant she was indirectly responsible for one of the company's most legendary sponsorships.

The last project of the 1964 World's Fair was "It's a Small World," undertaken by Pepsi. The company was working with UNICEF and had been the sponsor of The Golden Horseshoe Revue at Disneyland since the park opened.

Pepsi executives asked Disney to help with "It's a Small World," but Walt and company were already up to their necks in the World's Fair, working on an animatronic Lincoln and the Carousel of Progress. Besides that, Disney executives didn't think a year was enough time to design, manufacture, and install what was supposed to be a signature attraction. But there was one executive who believed that there was always enough time if you wanted to do something badly enough: Walt Disney. "I'll make those decisions," he told his staff. "Tell Pepsi I'll do it."

It was Disney himself who decided that the most effective way to structure the attraction was a boat ride that would salute the children of the world. Likewise, it was Disney himself who thought Mary Blair should design the ride. Blair had a very specific style and had done design work for Disney on films such as *Song of the South*, *Cinderella*, and *Peter Pan*, but had recently been working on children's books out of New York City.

While all of this was going on, the board of Pepsi was basically uninterested. The unspoken question on everybody's lips was, "Why do we need this Mickey Mouse thing?"

Blair had some designs in the style of paper sculptures ready after a few months, with specific colors for specific geographic areas: blues and greens for Africa, pink, orange, and other bright colors for South America, etc. But the board of Pepsi remained indifferent. It was then that Crawford took charge, standing up and declaring, "We are going to do this!"

And so it was that with the addition of the annoying earworm song by the Sherman brothers, Blair's childlike designs portraying innocence through graphic sophistication enchanted audiences in 1964 and have continued to do so ever since.

SHORTLY AFTER CRAWFORD LEFT *Hush . . . Hush, Sweet Charlotte*, William Castle hired her for *Strait-Jacket*, proving she was still employable—probably her main reason for agreeing to make the picture. *Strait-Jacket* was an original screenplay by Robert Bloch, the author of the novel *Psycho*, and it's essentially an awkward stitching of that novel and *Mildred Pierce*.

William Castle had been an efficient but unremarkable director of B pictures at Columbia in the 1940s, directing a mélange of Westerns and series pictures such as *The Whistler*. Castle's problem was how to differentiate himself from all the other B movie directors. In 1947, he was the associate producer on Orson Welles's *Lady from Shanghai*, and the months working with the tempestuously theatrical Welles gradually affected his own filmmaking. "The impact Welles had on dad was profound," said Castle's daughter Terry. "Welles's radio show *The War of the Worlds* gave Dad ideas on how to market. That, and desperation." Castle would come to believe that the quality and content of a movie were less important than the publicity about the movie. Sell the sizzle, not the steak.

Beginning in the late 1950s, Castle hit the mother lode with movies such as *The House on Haunted Hill*, *The Tingler*, and *Mr. Sardonicus*—inexpensive horror pictures sold through massive television ad buys. Castle adopted the publicity-friendly persona of an enthusiastic carny hustler, and his films began making pots of money.

Castle came to Crawford's apartment and was surprised by how small she was compared to how large she seemed on-screen. Crawford agreed to accept $50,000 plus a sliding scale for her percentage of the profits that went from 15 percent to 20 percent, along with approvals of script, cast, and cameraman.

The plot involved a woman who kills her husband with an ax after she discovers him in bed with another woman. After spending twenty years in an asylum, she is released to the ministrations of her brother and daughter. Cue another series of ax murders during which she becomes the prime suspect.

Our Dancing Daughters seemed far away.

"She was always pleasant to me, but she was terrifying," remembered Terry Castle. "And the set was freezing. She said the cold kept her skin taut. I was originally supposed to play her daughter as a little girl, and I was supposed to walk in and see my mother chop off the head of my father and sister. I practiced for weeks. Thank God my mom had the good sense to put a stop to that. I sat on Joan's lap. I remember the clinking of her charms, and I have a memory of ice cubes clinking in glasses.

"If you bent to her whims, she was fine. But she was definitely a star. Definitely Joan Crawford. And Dad treated her as such. He was amused by her and he appreciated her breadth of work. And my mother thought my father was being an idiot, because she didn't like the extra bullshit. Joan came with a lot. The trailer, etc. I think it was indulging."

With *Strait-Jacket*, there was no skeleton strung on a wire emerging over the audience's head at crucial moments, as in *The House on Haunted Hill*, or chairs wired with small electrical charges to provoke audience screams, as on *The Tingler*. On *Strait-Jacket*, the only gimmick was Joan Crawford with an ax and a hideous black wig.

Crawford insisted on rehearsing, which the budget-minded Castle resisted. After the first day of rehearsals, Crawford demanded that Anne Helm, playing her daughter, be replaced. "She's absolutely wrong for the part. I insist we recast." She recommended Diane Baker, who had worked with her in *The Best of Everything*. She also made sure that a carton of Pepsi was prominently displayed on a kitchen counter during a scene.

"I respected her," said Diane Baker. "She was dictatorial at certain moments. A perfectionist. I admired that. . . . But there were moments . . . when . . . I had to stand up for myself. I was young, I hadn't worked with someone of that caliber, that strict, and I had to stand up for myself. There were moments when she ordered me to 'fix your clothes,' or 'your hair isn't right.' She was beginning to be a little too . . . authoritarian."

At the end of the shoot, Crawford gave her director a refrigerator with the Pepsi logo on it. "It was awesome, really cool," said Terry Castle. "That's where the milkman would put our milk."

Crawford had a vested interest in the picture's success, so she went on the road for two weeks on a promotional tour while Castle worked another part of the country lugging the prop ax around to interviews. In New York City, Crawford appeared at three theaters a night on Wednesday and Thursday, five a night on Friday and Saturday. On Saturday, when the route included New Rochelle and White Plains, Crawford was on the road for nine hours.

The tour moved to Philadelphia, then Boston, which was complicated by a blizzard that mandated Crawford take a train instead of a plane. Things got worse when the train's lights went out, followed by the heat. She was undaunted, opening a hamper that contained a roast chicken, some hard-boiled eggs, a salad complete with her own homemade dressing, and some pickles, all washed down with vodka.

The publicity director for the movie at Columbia Pictures was Roger Caras, who would become a close friend of Stanley Kubrick's, as well as the voice of the Westminster Dog Show. His scheduling instructions were specific, exhaustive, and perceptibly condescending toward both the publicity department and exhibitors:

Miss Crawford will be traveling by the Pepsi-Cola executive aircraft. Two people will accompany her: Mr. Bob Kelly, PR representative for Pepsi-Cola in New York; Miss Anna Brinke ("Mamacita") Miss Crawford's maid. She does not speak English.

The following hotel accommodations are to be prepared. The top suite (including three bedrooms) in the hotels indicated. This should be the best suite available. A single room for Mr. Kelly is to be reserved on the same floor.

The three bedroomed suite is for Miss Crawford and Miss Brinke. The single is not to be part of the suite, but is to be nearby. A special Press Conferences room or suite is to be nearby. Press conferences described below are not to be held in the Crawford suite. Press suite to be the size of a normal hotel luncheon room. The two pilots of the Pepsi-Cola plane will have a single room each in the hotel.

The following special arrangements are required at each hotel. . . . There may be no deviations. A uniformed security officer is to be assigned to the door of the hotel suite twenty-four hours a day. You are not to use a city policeman and you are not to use the hotel detective. This security office should be hired from Pinkerton. . . . There is to be a man there twenty-four hours a day, I repeat.

The following items are to be in the suite prior to Joan Crawford's arrival: cracked ice in the buckets; lunch and dinner menus; pen and pencils and pads of paper; professional-size hair-drier; steam iron and board; one carton of Alpine cigarettes; a bowl of peppermint Life Savers; red and yellow roses; a case of Pepsi Cola, ginger ale, soda. There is to be a maid on hand in the suite when Miss Crawford arrives at the hotel. She is to stand by until Miss Crawford dismisses her. The following liquor is to be in the suite when Miss Crawford arrives: two fifths of 100 proof Smirnoff vodka (NOTE: THIS IS NOT 80 PROOF AND IT IS ONLY SMIRNOFF); one-fifth Old Forester bourbon; one fifth Chivas Regal scotch; one fifth Beefeater's gin; two bottles Moet & Chandon champagne (type: Dom Perignon).

Miss Crawford will be met in an air-conditioned, chauffeur driven, newly cleaned Cadillac. Instruct your chauffeurs that they are not to smoke and that they may not at any time drive in excess of forty miles an hour with Miss Crawford in the car. Miss Crawford will be carrying a minimum of fifteen pieces of luggage. . . .

Miss Crawford is a star in every sense of the word, and everyone knows she is a star. As a partner in this film, Miss Crawford will not appreciate your throwing away money on empty gestures. You do not have to make empty gestures to prove to Miss Crawford or anyone else that she is a star of the first magnitude.

If the detailed instructions above have given you the impression that money is no object, then carefully note the following, because exactly the opposite is true: the detailed instructions above are to tell you how far you may go. They are very explicit for the precise purpose that we do not want money over and above that required . . . to be spent. WATCH THE COSTS OF THIS TOUR. NEITHER MISS CRAWFORD NOR THIS OFFICE WILL APPRECIATE YOUR THROWING MONEY AWAY. YOU ARE ACCOUNTABLE FOR EVERY CENT YOU SPEND—WATCH IT— AND SUBSTANTIATE IT!

Strait-Jacket makes *The House on Haunted Hill* look like *Diabolique*. Crawford manages some nice moments of plaintive loss after her character is released from the asylum, but after that it's just a matter of waiting for the next ax murder. The polyglot cast seems to have been recruited by a random walk through a studio commissary in search of cheap talent—Leif Erickson, Rochelle Hudson.

Besides the black wig, Castle outfits Crawford with dangling bracelets that sound like sleigh bells. What makes the film watchable is Castle's lurid humor—the Columbia logo at the end of the picture shows the decapitated head of the lady holding a torch resting at her feet. *Strait-Jacket* had only one other thing to recommend it—it put money in Crawford's pocket.

The financials for *Strait-Jacket* provide a fascinating look into the brave new world of independent filmmaking and profit participations in 1960s Hollywood. Columbia invested just over $600,000 to make the picture, and the picture earned about $2.1 million domestically, initially netting Crawford just over $60,000 on top of her salary. After that, the checks steadily diminished until by 1973 she was getting around $2,000–$3,000 a year, before taxes. By 1975 she had earned more than $74,000 from her percentage.

Back in New York, Crawford invited Diane Baker to a dinner she was hosting at "21" in honor of Mary Martin. Baker was staying with her friends Melvyn Douglas and Helen Gahagan Douglas when she got Crawford's phone call. She told Crawford she'd be delighted to come and wanted to bring her makeup man as her guest.

"Oh, no," Crawford said. "I can't invite *my* makeup man."

"I'm so sorry, I can't come."

Melvyn Douglas was in the living room and heard the conversation. "Who's that you were talking to?" he asked.

"Joan Crawford."

"Come into the living room," Douglas said. He then launched into a tutorial on how to humor a star, telling Baker of his own experiences working with Crawford.

Crawford eventually acquiesced to Baker's choice of a guest. The result was that Baker had "a lovely evening. I had great respect for her as an artist (but) I felt personally sorry for her as a human being. She was very needy."

Specifically, Baker and the makeup man found the company a trifle sedate and wanted to have some fun. After dinner Baker began to make her apologies and made a move to go, but Crawford grabbed her by the wrist. "You can't leave!" Crawford said. "If you leave, everybody else will leave."

In that moment, said Baker, "I saw everything. . . . I realized this is a very vulnerable human being who is sad and lonely."

***STRAIT-JACKET* WAS THE BEGINNING** of Crawford taking work she would have rejected even five years before, work that provided income and kept her in the public eye but at a cost. She was clearly downshifting and taking whatever was on offer—not just making shoddy horror movies, but hosting the premiere of *Lord Jim* for a Los Angeles TV station and accepting awards for still being alive.

More upscale was hosting the *Hollywood Palace* on ABC for the standard $10,000 fee. It was a luxurious vaudeville-style show that ran for seven years on ABC and was hosted by a succession of legendary stars from an earlier era—Crosby, Astaire, Garland, etc.

Producer William Harbach got used to dealing with the host's individualized foibles. The perfectionist Fred Astaire would shoot a dozen takes of a dance with his partner Barrie Chase, but nobody except Astaire could ascertain any difference between them. Bing Crosby would work until three or four in the afternoon, then call out, "When do you need me tomorrow, boys?"—the unfailing signal he was about to leave. Genial with the crew, he was cold and strict with his sons, who were clearly terrified of him.

There was Frank Sinatra, whom Harbach characterized as "generous and exciting, but you had to change your underwear a lot." Milton Berle was simply a bastard. "I saw him slap Martha Raye," said Harbach. "When Berle got scared, he could be incredibly mean. Lethal."

Judy Garland passed the time by telling heartrending stories about her horrible mother. Garland was popping uppers, downers, and everything in between. She had trouble getting through Burt Bacharach's "What the World Needs Now" because the herky-jerky rhythm of the song threw her off. She finally hit the wall after multiple attempts. They didn't finish taping the show until 2:30 a.m., whereupon Garland locked herself in her dressing room and refused to come out. Harbach had to get a locksmith to open the door.

They found vomit everywhere, and obscenities scrawled across the walls in lipstick. "We carried her out of the dressing room at five in the morning," remembered Harbach. And then, just as dawn was breaking, Harbach watched Garland in an empty theater, clinging to the night light, perfectly singing the Bacharach song a cappella, just for the two of them.

As for Crawford, she was, as usual, totally professional even though she kept nipping at her vodka throughout the taping. She never showed the slightest sign of inebriation, but Harbach was still nervous.

A YEAR AFTER *STRAIT-JACKET*, Crawford was back in harness with William Castle for *I Saw What You Did*, this time at Universal. The story involved a couple of teenage girls making prank phone calls. It's all giggles until—what are the odds?—they accidentally call a man who's just murdered his wife. Crawford, in an extended cameo, would play a neighbor who's having an affair with him.

Castle had originally offered the part to Barbara Stanwyck, who would eventually work with him on a picture called *The Night Walker*, the gimmick of which was reuniting Stanwyck with her ex-husband Robert Taylor. But Stanwyck was involved with *The Big Valley* TV series, so Castle turned to Crawford. Her part only involved a few days of shooting, for which she got $50,000 and a percentage.

Castle worked cheap, so speed was of the essence, which tripped up an assistant director, who called out, "Okay, bring 'em on!" referring to Crawford and costar John Ireland. Crawford rose to her considerable emotional height and responded imperiously: "Young man, I don't know who the hell 'em' is on this set, but let me tell you something. This is *Mr.* Ireland and I am *Miss* Crawford. I suggest you learn your craft and manners on some other set, not mine."

Crawford understood that the Castle pictures were far down the food chain from *Mildred Pierce* and *Humoresque*—for that matter, they were far down from *What Ever Happened to Baby Jane?* But she met her duties with the press head-on and refused to play any part off-screen that wasn't worthy of Joan Crawford.

"She casts a spell," wrote John Kobal about his interview with her. "It may be confiding at times, silky, sensitive, tremulous at others, but this is steel talking, fine steel—it may flex, it may bend, but it snaps back, and the point could kill...

"When you listen to her, it's a one-act drama, and you see every inch of her face: the shift of bones beneath the fine, unlined, freckled skin; the muscles showing shifting signals in her forehead, the jaw line, the cheekbones, it's this Rolls-Royce model of a human body, nothing is left to chance. Her laugh... was like a gearshift on a Rolls-Royce. You hardly noticed, but you had been shifted!"

"I owe everyone on that street, including the doorman, when I walk out, to look like Joan Crawford, movie star," she told Kobal. "You see me in a pair of beautiful Italian pink silk slacks. This is my day at home working. I have a beautiful silk blouse on, matching.... So you see me in my working clothes, but I know a lot of people who would go out on the street like this. The only time I would be seen on the street like this is in Jamaica, where it's proper, or Barbados."

IN THE FALL OF 1965, Crawford spent a few days visiting Alfred Lunt and Lynn Fontanne at their house in Genesee Depot, Wisconsin. Lunt had recently told Hedda Hopper that he would write George Cukor except for the fact that he couldn't afford a stamp.

One feature of the Lunt-Fontanne house was a mural painted by Lunt. It showed Adam on one side and Eve on the other. Crawford stared at the mural, but there was something off about it.

"I know, they're odd," Lunt said. "You see, Lynn posed for both of them."

JIM BROCHU CAME BACK into Crawford's life in 1966. They had kept in loose contact since meeting on the South American cruise in 1960, staying in touch with an occasional letter or phone call. There was the time Brochu and his best friend went to the Frick Museum. They were leaving when Brochu looked across the street and pointed out Crawford's apartment house at 2 East 70th Street. "A beautiful apartment," Brochu told his friend. "Everything's white so you have to take your shoes off."

"You know her?" asked his friend.

"Sure."

They went across the street and Brochu told the doorman he'd like to see Mrs. Steele. "Call her up and tell her Jimmy Brochu is here."

The doorman thought it was a dubious request, but he complied and his face immediately changed. "Mrs. Steele says you may go up. But use the service elevator."

The service elevator deposited them directly into Crawford's kitchen, where they encountered Mamacita, Crawford's maid. Despite the Hispanic nickname, Mamacita was a sturdy German lady. Mamacita looked very surprised. It was at that point that Crawford walked into the kitchen.

"What are you doing here?"

"Well, this is the way they told me to come up," said Brochu.

Crawford proceeded to get on the house phone and give the doorman holy hell:

"This is the way you treat my guests?"

The carpets were still all white, so the boys had to take their shoes off. Cindy and Cathy were home from school, and Crawford, in Brochu's words, "couldn't have been more gracious."

"Can I get you something to drink?" she asked.

"Sure, I'll have a Coke," said Jim.

There was no visible reaction. "Sorry, Jim, we don't have Coke. How about a nice Pepsi? Try one with lots of ice."

They sat and talked for an hour.

When Brochu was cast in his high school play, his father invited Crawford to opening night. She didn't show up, but did send a telegram: "Jimmy dear, congratulations on your opening night. Joan Crawford."

A few years later, the show business bug had bitten Brochu. "I was twenty and lost," he remembered. "The actor David Burns was my mentor, my best friend. Dad wanted me to go to Wall Street, and I wanted show business. I wrote to Joan, saying 'Help! What do I do?'"

Crawford wrote back and told Brochu to come see her.

When he arrived, she opened the door. She was wearing a housecoat, with her hair in a pink turban and no makeup. For the first time, Brochu could see her face was covered with freckles.

"Joan?"

"Well, who the hell else do you think it is?"

They went into the kitchen, where they sat down. A pizza commercial came on the TV, and Crawford sighed and said it would be wonderful to have a pizza. Brochu took the hint and suggested they go get a pizza.

"Jimmy," she replied, "I can't leave this apartment. It would take me two hours." Brochu realized that she was a prisoner of her own image, wedged between her and the audience's mutual expectation that she always look like a movie star. She was actually comfortable without the carapace of Joan Crawford and all that she represented, but only with people she knew and trusted, and that clearly did not include her fans. They had to be overwhelmed; they had to be seduced.

But in the womb of her home, she would let friends see her as she was and try to give them good advice. "She was always wonderful and caring to me," said Brochu. In this particular case that meant trying to talk him out of becoming an actor.

"She told me I was too tall, which would make it hard to get cast. And then she said, 'It's *so* hard. Acting is hard work, and few people make it.' The thing that she emphasized was the word discipline. That's what she was—very disciplined."

She was, of course, wasting her breath. Brochu would ultimately ignore both her and his father and become an actor.

In 1967, Crawford was named Woman of the Year by the City of Hope. Jimmy Durante headlined, former California governor Goodwin Knight presided, Claire Trevor offered the toast, and David Wolper put together a film tribute. Trevor called Crawford "A tiger, a dancing daughter, a glamorous star, a full-blown dramatic actress, a top Hollywood hostess, a comedienne, an Academy Award winner, a conscientious mother of four, a business executive."

Crawford got up to accept her award and said, "If you think I'm about to get into politics you're crazy; if you think I'm about to compete with Claire Trevor you're crazy; but if you don't think I'm not angry about Duke and I not being up here together you're crazy."

At which point John Wayne ran to the podium to once again pair up with her as she held a large spray of yellow roses.

That same year, Franchot Tone wrote Crawford a letter of apology from his home in Canada for breaking an appointment.

Darling Joan, I was sick—smog, excitement, convivial excess, etc.—and under sedation and I truly didn't remember after I awoke, until [his son] Pat told me.

I am ashamed. Please forgive. I pray never again to let you for a moment think I do not love and glorify and thank you for all your kindness and thoughtfulness. (Is that a word???)

Hope to reach you by phone.

Love, Franchot

When Crawford wasn't working for William Castle, there was always Pepsi, which came with its own challenges. In 1968, she broke her ankle in Cincinnati when she slipped while wearing high heels. She resolutely insisted that there had been no men in her life since Al Steele's death. "I've had no interest in any man since my husband died," she told one reporter. "Unfortunately, I think a woman, to be a full-fledged woman, should always have a love interest.

"I have gone with a number of men, but . . . I would never push myself at a married man no matter what I felt for him. Their wives are off in the country with their babies, and if I have to go to dinner with a married man, I always see there are four or five others along instead of just one."

She would talk about her children if asked. Christina was now married to Harvey Medlinsky and Christopher was in Vietnam. Crawford had clearly begun to write off both of them. "I used to think environment obliterated heredity," she had commented in her memoir. "I was wrong. Unlike Christina and Christopher, the twins don't resent my life, they're pliant, joyous, they link arms with me and off we march into whatever life may offer."

By 1968, nothing much had changed. When a reporter asked her about Christopher, she replied, "He's in Saigon, that's all I know. He's been running ever since he was five; this is the one place he can't run from. It will make a man of him." In August of 1968, she attended the wedding of her daughter Cathy to a petty officer in the Navy named Jerome LaLonde.

FRANCHOT TONE WAS DIAGNOSED with prostate cancer that had metastasized and moved to his lungs. Tone had part of one lung removed but worked when he could. His son Pat had graduated from the University of North Carolina in 1966 and was pursuing an acting career when he wasn't taking care of his father.

Tone and son would reliably spend about one night a month at Crawford's apartment, having a pleasant dinner that she cooked herself while in her bathrobe. The apartment was the combination of the luxe and bargain basement that confounded so many—Haines's custom furniture coexisting with plastic covers on the couches, the impeccably carpentered pull-out drawers full of clothes and shoes. The emotional atmosphere was loving and friendly. "My father respected her, appreciated her as a person," said Pat Tone. "He had a deep underlying fondness for her, as she did for him."

That said, Pat didn't think his father ever proposed remarriage to Crawford, as some reports had it—the romantic and erotic aspect of their lives was firmly buried, replaced by mutual respect and friendship.

After dinner, Franchot would return to his penthouse at 158 East 52nd Street while Pat and Crawford played gin rummy until she finished the bottle of Dom Pérignon—she played a good, tight game of gin. Occasionally they would talk about Cornel Wilde, Pat's stepfather, and his mother, the actress Jean Wallace. Crawford knew them, but not well.

Pat never asked Crawford about her divorce from his father—they had each been married four times, and the subject might be embarrassing. Joan would occasionally have a party, and Franchot and Pat would be invited. One night Irwin Shaw and Paul Green were there, as was the political novelist Allen Drury. Drury was a closeted gay man but felt comfortable enough to bring his partner to the party. Pat Tone said that Crawford was Republican, but only theoretically. "She wasn't interested in politics. Not even slightly."

A few times Christina was there. Pat Tone described Christina's attitude toward her mother at this point as "Servile. Obedient." Pat met Christopher only once and was unimpressed; the young man was clearly on some kind of drug.

After dinner with Crawford on September 17, 1968, Pat took his father back to his penthouse and tucked him into bed. Franchot was scheduled to go to Lenox Hill Hospital the next morning for more treatments. Pat gave Franchot his usual dose of painkiller, but his father asked for a double dose. After that, Pat gave him oxygen. Franchot gasped, threw his head back, and told his son, "That was almost like an orgasm."

When Pat returned at 6:30 a.m. to take his father to the hospital, he found him dead in bed.

At the funeral, just as the service was scheduled to start, Joan made her entrance, sweeping down the aisle with panache and sitting with the family. Burgess Meredith, Franchot's best friend and Pat Tone's godfather, delivered an elegant eulogy: "[Franchot] could build lean-tos in the winter drifts with an axe; he could literally stalk game in the moonlight; he could outsmart fish and find forgotten trails and shoot a hawk out of the sky."

Meredith noted that as the cancer whittled away at Tone, "his wit would sabre to small pieces any pity that was offered to him." He closed by suggesting a line from *Hamlet* as an appropriate epitaph: "Sir, in my heart there was a kind of fighting/That would not let me sleep."

In the limousine afterward, they all had a drink to the deceased—Joan brought the vodka. She was kind and supportive to both of Tone's sons, but not grief-stricken. "She knew that Dad was on the way out," said Pat. "She was resigned."

Dinner was at the Chalet Suisse, and Crawford couldn't get her head around it. "Do you realize this is the first time in decades I've eaten anywhere but '21'?"

Afterward they went back to Crawford's apartment. Pat Tone noticed that two of the few pictures on display included one of his father and another of Al Steele.

For the rest of her life, Crawford made sure to send Pat Tone greetings on his birthday; for the years he was president of a college in Switzerland, the greetings would arrive by Western Union telegram.

THAT SAME YEAR, CRAWFORD was asked to do an episode of *Here's Lucy*, opposite Lucille Ball. In front of the camera Ball was a high-end professional, but behind the camera she could be tough. The episode had been written for Gloria Swanson, and Crawford's nerves about TV were exacerbated by Ball's demeanor. Crawford was unable to remember her lines due to her terror of live audiences.

At one point, Ball came to Crawford's dressing room to discover her with her face hovering over her open purse. In her mouth were two straws that led to a flask of Smirnoff's.

"[Lucy] was the only person who ever fired Joan Crawford," said costar Gale Gordon. "She was very, very late for rehearsal. Lucy called her up and said, 'Be on time.' The next day, ten o clock came, and then came eleven. Joan hadn't called or shown up. Lucy called her on the phone from her dressing room on the stage and the door was open. So we heard her conversation. She got some lame excuse from Joan that she overslept or something. Lucy said to her, 'Well, *listen*, if you're not here tomorrow morning at ten on the nose, you're *fired*. You *get* that? Fired!'"

Crawford showed up on time the next morning, knew her lines, and worked hard, but Ball still hammered her. Crawford was rehearsing a Charleston number, when Ball stopped her and said, "I don't like the way you're dancing—how *did* you win a Charleston contest in Texas? You *can't* dance!"

Crawford asked to try it again. "OK, we'll do it once more. But if you don't get it this time, it's out—finished." Crawford went to her dressing room and began to cry. Herbert Kenwith, a TV director Crawford knew who had been watching the proceedings, came into the room and told her, "Don't let her bother you. She does this to everyone. It's a test."

"I don't *want* to be tested. I've *been* tested. I don't want to be on this half-hour show to endure this."

Kenwith told her to go back and pretend nothing had happened. "How *can* I? She's embarrassed me in front of all these people." Kenwith got Crawford back onstage, but Ball continued to criticize everything Crawford did, which reminded Kenwith of Jack Benny's line after doing a show with Ball: "Herbert, you ought to call a psychiatrist for her."

When the show was completed without any further problems, Crawford's last word on the subject was, "My God, they tell me *I'm* a bitch—Lucy can outbitch me *any* day of the week." The show ran the last week of February 1968, and there's no trace of any problems in the finished product. Crawford is introduced cleaning her house and is interrupted when Lucy and Vivian Vance's car breaks down. They ask to use her phone and supposedly comic complications ensue. As was her wont, Ball mugs as if she's in a contest with Red Skelton. It was a lot of angst for a $5,000 guest star fee, and Crawford began choosing her TV shows with more care.

The problem for actresses of Crawford's generation was simple: finding work that was rewarding and not demeaning. Myrna Loy had a late-career boost headlining the road company of Neil Simon's *Barefoot in the Park* opposite Richard Benjamin and Joan Van Ark as the newlyweds. Benjamin and Van Ark left the company in Chicago to give Hollywood a try, and Christina Crawford came in to play the bride.

"The idea of Joan's daughter playing the role delighted me," remembered Loy, "until I discovered how recalcitrant this child was. I've never known anybody else like her—ever. Her stubbornness was really unbelievable. She would not do a single thing that anyone told her to do. You'd go out there on the stage and you couldn't find her. One thing an actor needs to know is exactly where people are on the stage; Christina completely disregarded her blocking, throwing the rest of us off."

Crawford was coming to Chicago on a press tour for Pepsi, and Loy asked Christina if her mother would come to the play.

"Of course not!" Christina snapped. "She wouldn't come to the play. If she came she'd have to make a Joan Crawford entrance. She'd wait until the curtain went up before she came in, and they'd have to turn up the house lights as she walked down the aisle. The audience would applaud her, and she'd curtsy, as if she were the star of the show, before sitting down."

Loy replied that Christina's mother was far too professional to do anything like that. In any case, Crawford didn't attend. Richard Benjamin had been hired to stage the London company of the play, and at Loy's request came back to Chicago to see if he could impose some order. As Loy remembered it, "he worked with her, but couldn't do anything with her—absolutely nothing. She was going to do it her way."

Word of all this reached Neil Simon, and he flew in from New York. After seeing the performance, he told Loy, "It won't do."

Loy believed that Christina's problem was twofold—she wasn't just in competition with her mother; she wanted to *be* her mother. Loy thought that Christina envied her mother, grew to hate her, and eventually wanted to destroy her. "I think that's the basis of the book she wrote afterward and everything else. I saw what her mind created, the fantasy world she lived in.

"What would you do with a problem child like that? I wanted to beat the hell out of that girl after only one rehearsal."

There would be more difficulties between mother and daughter, as well as occasional periods of fragile rapprochement. In 1968 Christina landed a part on the CBS soap opera *The Secret Storm*. Producer Gloria Monty had hired her without knowing she was Joan's Crawford's daughter. When she found out, she asked Christina to ask her mother to invite them to dinner. "It was a lovely, gracious evening," remembered Monty. "She told stories of Doug and Franchot."

In October that same year, Christina got sick and had to take a hiatus from *The Secret Storm*. "What can I do?" Crawford asked Monty.

"Get another actress," she replied.

"Gloria, I'll play it."

"Are you sure?"

"I'll take it!"

It was work, as well as a challenge. It could also be interpreted as a shot across her daughter's bow. Monty called Fred Silverman, the head of CBS daytime, who thought it was a great idea. Monty went to Crawford's apartment, where the star told her, "I know this character like this," snapping her fingers. "It's Mildred Pierce!"

"Let's not talk too much," said Monty. "Just read the scene." They rehearsed on a Saturday and planned to tape on a Sunday—expensive, but worth it. "She was scared stiff," said Monty. "And courageous." Monty told Crawford that there would be no set for rehearsals, but Crawford shot back, "I need walls, baby. I need furniture." Monty quickly had the crew cobble together some sets for her. The work went slowly because Crawford was nervous and was buttressing that nervousness with an occasional shot of vodka brought by her chauffeur.

Since there was at least thirty-five years between Christina and her mother, it all made for a head-spinning transition for the audience, but viewers of soaps are used to radical recastings and character reversals. The four days that Crawford appeared on the show stimulated a publicity bonanza but did not result in a permanent truce between mother and daughter.

As with every parent who finds their adult children rough sailing, much time was devoted to pondering just where things went wrong. Crawford came up with a fairly obvious explanation: it was show business. But more than that it was the obvious fact that show business took precedence.

"I really don't think the stars of my time should have had children, whether we bore them ourselves or adopted them." Crawford referred to Brooke Hayward's book *Haywire*, about her mother Margaret Sullavan, and father Leland Hayward.

> I know the problems Maggie and Lee had, especially Maggie. She was a truly great actress and a fine woman, but she was so unstable she could barely cope with her career and she certainly couldn't cope with her children. I know their kids got the dirty end of the stick, but that was Hollywood. Nobody knew how to cope with realities. . . .
>
> Take the time element, to begin with. If you were working—and I worked almost constantly while the children were young—you got up at the crack of dawn five or six days a week, and came home at dusk, if you were lucky.

You didn't see your kids in the morning and at night you were so goddamn tired it was all you could do to smile and kiss them goodnight.

On the weekends you were tired, exhausted, absolutely shot, and you'd have welcomed some quiet hours with the kids, but usually there were the social things you had to do for the studio, for your career, and sometimes, but so rarely, just for and with friends.

So all of a sudden your son or daughter had a birthday, and there was nothing to do but arrange a big party, and you invited the Fonda kids, and the Hayward kids, and the studio brats and your lawyer's kids, and you bought very expensive presents and the kids coming to the party brought very expensive presents. . . .

What it boils down to is the fact that a part of us wanted a real, personal private life—husband, kiddies, fireplace, the works—but the biggest part of us wanted the career, and that the biggest part had to live up to the demands of that career.

THE APARTMENT ON EAST 70th Street was very expensive to run, and Crawford's pension from Pepsi had ended in 1964. In June 1968, she finally made the decision to sell the apartment. In October she moved to the Imperial House on 150 East 69th Street, where she took up residence in apartment 22-G.

The move had the general result of making her morose, if only because it was made for economic reasons. Joan would talk about Madeira linens she had bought in a French convent and how the bed had been brought up the side of the building and through a window.

She and the decorator Carleton Varney moved over as much of Billy Haines's furniture as she had room for, and she told Varney to remember that she didn't want anything elegant, i.e., something that would show off his style. Rather, she "wanted something for me." She did, however, tell Varney to pay special attention to the kitchen, because Billy always said, "If the kitchen is in the right place, everything else will fall into place."

Being tied to another designer's style must have been difficult for Varney, but he adjusted. "I was really a cosmetician more than anything else. I changed the dress of the furniture rather than the pieces themselves."

THE CONSTANT PRESENCE OF vodka was an obvious signifier of a drinking problem. "Joan was a functioning alcoholic," says Jim Brochu. "So was my father. No two ways about it. Most of the time she could control it, and you'd never know she was drinking. When Joan did the Lucy show, Lucy became very angry because she was fucking up and she was a little drunk. Lucy was going to fire her, and Herbert [Kenwith] stepped in and straightened her out and straightened Lucy out.

"A movie studio is a womb, a very safe, secure place. An audience introduces the element of danger, of being embarrassed in front of strangers. One time there was a rumor going around New York that she would head up a theatrical revival of *Sleuth*, with a female cast, and I knew that was impossible. The audience terrified her."

As far as movie work was concerned, working for William Castle meant that other déclassé talents came calling. Next up was Herman Cohen, who had made *I Was a Teenage Werewolf* for American International in the 1950s and had since relocated to England. He had a script titled *Circus of Blood*, and Crawford signed on for the picture, which was released under the title *Berserk!* The script was cowritten by Aben Kandel, who had written the passionately proletarian *City for Conquest* for James Cagney in earlier, better days.

William Castle possessed the sense of humor that would come to be known as camp, but Cohen's preferences ran more toward overt sadism. Cohen realized that he had to keep his star happy, so he put a Rolls-Royce with a chauffeur at her disposal. Crawford arrived with several cases of Smirnoff's and worked a poster for Pepsi into the background of one shot. Cohen remembered that "In spite of her sipping, she was very professional with me and would never take a drink unless I okayed it. She always knew her lines and was always on time. She would come in very early and make breakfast for her 'team,' i.e. her makeup man, hairdresser, etc."

Berserk! had flashes of nasty violence, but it was basically a cheater—sixty minutes of plot buttressed by thirty minutes of random circus acts, with a cast that included Diana Dors—England's answer to Jayne Mansfield—all in lurid Technicolor. It was one of many stories of violence set in circuses that followed in the wake of DeMille's *The Greatest Show on Earth—Ring of Fear, The Big Circus*. Crawford plays it like Harriet Craig at the Circus, but there's really no other way to play it, and she looks amazingly good in leotards. *Berserk!* was extremely profitable—rentals of $1 million domestic and another $2 million foreign.

The success of *Berserk!* meant that in the summer of 1969 Crawford was back in England working for Cohen again in what would prove to be her last movie. *Trog* involved Crawford as an anthropologist who discovers an Ice Age caveman troglodyte, hence the title. The makeup of *Trog* involved a former wrestler wearing an ape-man mask reputedly left over from Kubrick's *2001*. Crawford's salary was $70,000.

To a reporter, she said that "Inactivity is one of the great indignities of life. Through inactivity people lose their self-respect; their integrity. The need to work is always there, bugging me. Anyway, I'd never played a scientist or a doctor, and I love science-fiction, and thought this would be fun to do."

There are two ways to play movies like *Trog*: the arched-eyebrow American school popularized by Vincent Price in which the actor subtly—or not so subtly—signals his awareness of the surrounding absurdity and thus holds himself slightly apart, and the straight-faced English school, in which everyone plays the text as if it were Shakespeare, as in the Hammer horror films.

Surrounded as she was by the English, and by her own innate seriousness about her craft, Crawford plays *Trog* absolutely straight, which results in scenes in which her character treats a murderous caveman with the forbearance of a cultured matron coping with a recalcitrant puppy.

Just when you think the movie can't get any worse, at the two-thirds point Cohen splices in five minutes of mediocre stop-motion footage of prehistoric creatures lifted from a 1956 movie called the *The Animal World* to pad the running time.

A nineteen-year-old actress named Kim Braden was playing Crawford's daughter and remembered that Crawford "treated me like she treated everybody else—charming and far removed. The first time I met her, she said Bette Davis was 'a lovely woman.'"

That was at the Dorchester Hotel, where Braden had gone to get the once-over from the star. "I was young and pretty green, and so I went to the hotel to get her approval. She opened the door and there was this tiny little old lady wearing a mumu who had a slight mohawk down the center of her head. She looked about a hundred and twelve.

"'Oh, Kim,' she said, 'how lovely to see you.' She had that low, beautiful voice.

"I almost said, 'Are you Joan Crawford?' because she was unrecognizable. And she was lovely and we chatted and it was fifteen minutes and it was great and I left."

Braden didn't see her again till the first day of production. The director was Freddie Francis, a legendary British cinematographer whose ambition to be more than a cameraman earned him a slot directing horror pictures. Kim Braden:

The first morning we were all there and I hadn't said anything except to my boyfriend about the tiny little lady in the mumu. Joan had to make a long-distance call to Wally Westmore about her eyelashes. She arranged to airmail her used eyelashes to Wally in America to have them recurled, because Wally knew how she liked them.

When she came out of her trailer, she was the Joan Crawford we all knew. She had that slight mohawk on her head because it helped hold her wig in place, and she had put clips in her scalp to pull her face back. The result was that she looked forty-something. She had the corsets, she had the eyelashes and she looked phenomenal!

Her eyes were everywhere. She didn't want too much money to go out. Never pulled rank, never got angry. If she had pulled rank I'm sure it would have been passive-aggressive: "I don't think that's really working, dear." She liked Freddie, who was a dear man.

She only became Joan Crawford when she dressed like Joan Crawford. When she was in the mumu she was a tiny little old lady.

Everybody on the picture, even the wrestler playing Trog, knew the picture was atrocious, so there was little of the *joie de vivre* of a happy company. "She was very nice on set except one time, and even then she was subtle," said Kim

Braden. "There was a scene with she and Michael Gough about Trog and what to do with him. And she suddenly forgot her lines. For about forty-five minutes she kept not remembering her lines, and when they made cue cards so she could read her lines they were too far away. So they kept having to move the camera and the cue cards closer and closer. And finally when the camera was in a full close-up she miraculously remembered all her lines.

"When Michael turned away after the scene, he muttered, 'That's the way you get a single [close-up].' None of us believed she was having any trouble with the lines whatever. She wanted a close-up at that point, and she went about getting it without demanding it."

Crawford must have taken a liking to Braden, because she kept giving the young actress her old mumus. "They looked like curtains sewn together, but I was polite. She sort of liked me, possibly because I was so ignorant. She did mention to me that I was 'the best of the young English girls I've worked with,' which I took as a slam against [Crawford's costar in *Berserk!*] Judy Geeson.

"I never saw her lose her temper; she was very calm. Drinking? I don't think so. I would have noticed. I never got a sense of who she was. I think she thought she could be whatever she needed to be at any given time. I don't remember her sitting with people and telling stories. She was in her trailer. She was the star and the rest of us were there for her needs."

When they got to the end of shoot, Braden was on the fence about whether to buy Crawford a gift. She asked her agent, who thought it was a good idea.

"I was nineteen, not wealthy, so I went to a shop on Bond Street and bought her a lovely potpourri jar. Michael Gough and I went in at the end to say thank you and here's a little something. I handed her my box and she looked at us, and said 'I have something for you.' And she opened a drawer and handed us pens with 'Pepsi-Cola' printed on the side."

A few years later, Braden worked with Bette Davis and asked her about Crawford. All Davis did was giggle. "Bette was funnier, more outgoing, more mischievous than Joan. I would think that Joan felt superior to Bette as a human being. There was a seriousness to Joan. She was very grand, but not unfriendly, not overwhelming."

William Haines was in England redoing Winfield House, the residence of the American ambassador, and visited Crawford on the set of *Trog*. He was obviously appalled. "Cranberry, why do you persist?" he asked. She explained that work was all that was left. Al Steele was dead, her relationships with Christina and Christopher were deeply problematic, and the twins were living their own lives. What else was there but work?

Trog was released on the bottom of a grindhouse double bill with *Taste the Blood of Dracula*. Crawford put up a good front and did publicity, but she was too much of a realist to take any pride in what she was doing. Both reporters and star moved off the specific and onto the general as quickly as possible.

The end result of this pyramid of need was a dismal movie that played drive-ins—an ignominious ending to a forty-five-year career that neither asked for nor needed any apologies.

"She wanted to work, and it didn't really matter what it was as long as she was on the set and playing a character," said Jim Brochu. "In *Berserk!* and *Trog*, she gives it her all, with material that is beyond stupid. But she makes it work as much as she can and work was one of the most important things in the world to her. Maybe the most important."

The only positive residue of the film was a friendship with Freddie Francis marked by a series of affectionate letters between the actress and the director/cameraman. She wrote him that he had directed *Trog* with "great gentleness, and you allowed the tragic story of the cruelty of society to come through as the heavy. . . . The editing is fast and to the point. Thank you for being so wonderful Freddie."

She sympathized with him when he went through a bad experience on a picture with "an inefficient crew and unit," which she called "Hell." In another letter she asked for a new picture of Francis's family because "the children must have grown very much since I saw them."

In September 1970, as *Trog* was playing across the country, Francis sent her a script for another film. "The script you sent me is actually very good, or at least it has good potential," Crawford replied, "and I know, with your delicate touch, it could really become something. But, I don't trust producers and the exploitation on a picture of this kind.

As a matter of fact, what they have done with "Trog" is pathetic. It is being shown, on a double billing, with "Dracula's Blood"—no promotion at all in any city!

I believe the one mistake in this . . . script is that you show all the murders, instead of leaving something to the imagination. Why can't they get back to a "Rebecca"-style type story and make it really mysterious without the total image of murder, murder, murder?

Think about what I've said and write me. I am returning the script to you under separate cover.

You were a dear to think of me. My love to you, Pam, Suzanna, and Gareth.

But there would be no further collaborations with Francis because there would be no more movies.

For an interview about *Trog*, Crawford offered some pro forma comments about the general lack of discipline she saw in the younger generation, then abruptly stopped. "Who the hell am I to talk?" she grumbled. "I raised four kids with discipline. One was a runaway at four. . . . They're a combination of the naïve and the sophisticated."

At times she was clearly overwhelmed by unhappiness. Patricia Neal remembered that occasionally Crawford "would call me at some unearthly hour, dead drunk, and talk my ear off, and she would snarl, 'All right, goodbye!' and slam the phone down!"

Her predominant mood at this time was loneliness. "I don't know anyone who isn't lonely. I didn't have much chance to be lonely during my marriage [to Steele], but I've been pretty darned lonely since then.

"You just learn to live with it. You don't dwell on it. That's the only way to handle it. You read a good book about other lonely people."

When Judy Garland died, Crawford wanted to talk to her neighbor Anne Anderson about whether she thought Garland was a suicide or an accidental overdose. Crawford was firmly against suicide—it was a coward's way out. She believed in willpower; it was everyone's responsibility to make the most of their life. "She was personally affronted by suicide," said Anderson.

LEW WASSERMAN REMAINED LOYAL, making sure that Crawford got work in Universal TV shows that might appeal to her. Her favorite TV shows included *Marcus Welby*, *The Waltons*, *The Name of the Game*, and *The F.B.I.*

More importantly, in 1969 she starred in the premiere episode of Rod Serling's *Night Gallery* and was accorded more money and perks than other guest stars got.

Robert Wagner was working at Universal when he heard the *whomp-whomp* of an overhead helicopter and watched it land beside a nearby soundstage. When the blades stopped, Joan Crawford got out and proceeded down a red carpet that led to the soundstage where she would be working. Universal didn't hire helicopters for Vera Miles.

The *Night Gallery* episode proved both the most difficult and the most memorable effort of Crawford's final years before a camera. Universal had signed Rod Serling to do a follow-up to *The Twilight Zone* with a similar approach—ironic moral tales centering on "What fools these mortals be . . ."

A twenty-two-year-old named Steven Spielberg had been put under contract by Universal for $250 a week and was assigned to direct one of the trilogy of tales that made up the show's pilot. It was a typically prefabricated television project—the script had been written, the cast, cameraman, and editor assigned before the director. According to Tom Bosley, who was also in the episode, Serling had written the script for Bette Davis and Martin Balsam, but Wasserman nudged the studio into casting Crawford and Barry Sullivan.

Spielberg introduced himself with a phone call and found Crawford ebullient, although worried by Serling's dialogue, which she found excessively metaphorical and hard to memorize. The story involved an imperious rich bitch who has gone blind and pays a man thousands of dollars for his eyes so she can once again see. The surgery is a success but she doesn't know it because the New York City blackout hits just as she takes off the bandages.

"I didn't cast Joan Crawford, I wanted Jo Van Fleet," remembered Spielberg. "They came to me and said, 'We just made a deal with Joan Crawford. We're paying her $50,000 for seven days work on this forty-five-minute episode. You've got a lot of responsibility now. Do a good job.'" (Universal was actually paying Crawford $10,000 a week with a guarantee of two weeks.)

Spielberg went to meet Crawford at her apartment in Los Angeles and found her wearing a blindfold and memorizing the placement of the furniture. She took off the blindfold and was clearly stunned at his youth.

"Are you anybody's son in the Black Tower?" she inquired.

"No, I'm just working my way through Universal," he replied.

"Well, let's have dinner."

They went to a Polynesian place called The Luau, where the maître 'd said, "It's nice to have you back, Miss Crawford."

"Having to take her to dinner that night was the most frightening moment of my life," said Spielberg. She told him not to let anybody in the Black Tower give him a hard time—if anybody did, she'd take care of it. "She'd worked with Cukor. . . . She was my guardian angel."

Beneath the comforting initial meeting, Crawford was worried. She called Lew Wasserman and asked him if he couldn't find another director. "Joan," Wasserman said, "if you're unhappy with him, don't complain. Because if you do, they'll fire you." So Crawford did what had long since become her pattern: she put her head down and kept moving forward.

On the first day of production, Crawford arrived at 7:45 a.m. and addressed every crew member by their first name. Spielberg had never met any of the crew and he was amazed to find they were all wearing blazers, hats, and ties instead of the jeans and open-necked shirts he had expected. "They thought [I] was a joke. . . . I couldn't get anybody to take me seriously for two days because I was so young."

Spielberg had never directed television before, so he wasn't used to being under the gun of the schedule or coping with Universal's mandated high-key, overly bright lighting. In TV, all that really matters is getting the episode done on time. The basic rhythm was ten pages of script a day. The first few days Spielberg would come to the set with twenty-five shots in his head and would get perhaps half that many. By eleven in the morning, he would be wrapping his second shot of the day, so lunch was taken up with restructuring his shot list.

It was a baptism of fire.

"If I lose a shot I don't know what I'm going to do. It's sort of like losing your bishop on your second move, and here's Joan Crawford coming to me and saying, 'I look better on this side. No high-hat shots from the floor.'"

Barry Sullivan dropped by the set on a day he wasn't scheduled to work to see Crawford and meet his director. "Barry Sullivan treated her beautifully," said Spielberg. "He treated her like a regular guy, razzing her, punching her in the arm."

Sullivan was not equally enchanted. "Spielberg looked like a 14-year-old Jewish choir boy," he grumbled, but he was moved by what he called Spielberg's "utter respect for a legend." Contrary to Spielberg's own memories of the crew's veiled hostility, Sullivan said that the crew reserved judgment about their young director, but within thirty minutes he won them over. "He did it his way," Sullivan said.

What ultimately saved Spielberg was Crawford. "She was not Mommie Dearest," he said. "She was kind and understanding . . . *elegant!* And she was selling Pepsi-Cola left and right.

"Joan could have been a problem, but instead she was the only person on the crew who treated me like I'd been working for fifty years. She was just sensational. She understood that I probably shouldn't have been there making that particular show, that I should have been doing something more out of my imagination, but she was very compassionate."

Spielberg was awed by Crawford's star quality. "I loved to see her move. Rather than push the camera into Joan, I let her pull the camera to her. . . . In a two-shot with anyone, you looked at her. She was imperious, at the same time childlike, haughty yet tender.

"She had no great range as an actress, but within her range no one did better. She would hold back in a medium shot, and give it all in the close-up. When I suggested a close-up, you could see the generator going. She was an *objet d'art* . . . a Stutz in the showroom."

Spielberg realized very quickly that Crawford knew more about filmmaking than he did. "She (could) look at a light and say, 'Steven, that's F4, not F11' . . ." If Spielberg liked a take, she sparkled. "You couldn't bullshit her; she could tell what I thought through my voice."

After shooting for a couple of days, Crawford got a sinus infection. Spielberg walked into her dressing room to find her on her stomach studying her script. Surrounding her were two nurses, a doctor, and a secretary. Her underpants were off and she was getting a shot in her ass. She missed the next two days of the shoot. Spielberg spent one of the days shooting Barry Sullivan's close-ups, which had the dual virtues of keeping the show on something approaching the schedule and giving Sullivan more attention from his director, who up to that time had been concentrating on Crawford.

There was only one crisis, a scene that had worried Crawford—when her character regains her sight simultaneously with the New York blackout. Spielberg had promised to take time to help her with anything she found difficult, but he had let issues of the schedule dominate. And then he was told that his star was in her dressing room.

She was crying.

"The roof had fallen in," he remembered. "You have let me down," she told him. "I rarely ask anyone for help. It is now five to six and we haven't talked. I'll be embarrassed to watch this. You won't like me, and I won't like me."

Spielberg hugged her, apologized, and wrapped the company. They sat together for an hour talking about the scene, with Spielberg conjuring everything he knew about script and performance. He held her hand, told her he'd be there throughout the scene and would do as many takes as she felt necessary.

He was moved as well as surprised by her vulnerability, but it taught him something he never forgot: whatever the problems with the production and the shooting schedule, the actor has to take precedence.

The episode got finished, albeit two days over schedule. Spielberg has never made any claims for it, but it's easy to see why he was Universal's fair-haired boy. Crawford's segment is well acted, creatively shot, briskly told—head and shoulders above the other two parts of the pilot's trilogy. Crawford's final moment, when she screams, "*I want the sun!*" is hair-raisingly primal and as good as any scene she ever played. If the material was there, and she felt safe, she could still deliver.

Although the series didn't have the success of *The Twilight Zone*, Crawford was noticeably positive about the experience, as she should have been. It was the first time in years she had a project of which she could be proud. As for Spielberg, he didn't work for a year, partly out of design. That year was spent writing the story of *Sugarland Express* and thinking about what he wanted to do with his career as a director.

He figured it out.

IN 1970, CRAWFORD WAS lured back to Columbia, Missouri, where she attended a weekend celebration at Stephens College—her only experience of higher education, unless you count Louis B. Mayer's MGM. The questions involved everything from Women's Lib ("I have come to the conclusion that all the women that don't want to be women haven't learned how beautiful it is to be a woman") to how to get ahead in the theater: "Do your job and go to acting studio at night and work with, I would think, Lee Strasberg." The blacklisted actress Jean Muir, who was teaching at Stephens, suggested Sandy Meisner as a more effective alternative, but Crawford thought the Actors Studio was better because of a communal spirit that reminded her of the Group Theatre.

"I've been an observer for many years there. I was married to Franchot Tone, who was quite the great actor and being an observer [of] every actor—there was Marilyn Monroe, Patricia Neal, I can't name them all who were all observers—they didn't participate, but the actors all get together, do a one-act play in front of other actors and the public who are interested in Actors Studio, and you get a lovely, lovely all-encompassing audience."

One of the students asked Crawford if she ever got depressed, and she responded, "Everyone has their own fears, their own doubts about themselves, their own insecurities, and only experience and lending [themselves] to life itself and learning from every experience will get you over the fears. . . .

"I get in knee deep sometimes. I find that I get into a rut sometimes when I don't have enough activity and I just start reading good poetry, good books, and most of all look for a good script and go to work."

Of all these things, it was work that had always motivated her and lifted her out of troughs, but work was sparse.

That same year, Billy Haines had hernia surgery, and George Cukor reported back to Crawford. "On Friday I had tea with him—yes, tea—at his luxurious home on Lorna Lane. He was full of beans, jumping about, giving a lot of cheap orders, and thoroughly enjoying himself. That night he had people in for dinner. From then on he's never looked back—he's back to work. The whole thing is a triumph of will. Those old-timers are pretty tough. I hope that kids like me will be as 'with it' when we reach his advanced age. He seemed to have mellowed, too. Mind you, there's no danger of him becoming an old peach or an old dear."

AT CHRISTMAS 1971, DOROTHY Manners visited New York and called Joan, who invited her over for Sunday brunch at her apartment. It was just the two of them, so Crawford didn't have to give a social performance. She cooked the meal herself—Tex-Mex dishes comprised of red and green peppers they both loved, powdered chili and eggs, preceded as well as accompanied by Bloody Marys.

"Only a couple of dames like us who were born in Texas could eat this food for breakfast and not die," Crawford said. She told Manners that she had come to the conclusion that timing was everything. "Someone once said that half the battle of achievement is being there at the right time. I'd say it is 99 per cent of the battle."

It was a dark, rainy day, and they talked all afternoon until the lights came on all over New York City. She told Manners how much she had loved Al Steele. She felt he had achieved in his life the equivalent of what she had achieved in hers—they could meet as equals, which had never been the case with her other husbands.

The conversation inevitably moved to the latest generation of movie stars. Crawford felt sorry for them. "They have no joy, no pleasure in what they're doing. They don't like to give interviews. They almost [seem to] feel guilty."

Summing up, she said, "They think it's dross. Believe me, it was solid gold!"

IN JULY OF 1972, Crawford was back at Universal making an episode of a series called *The Sixth Sense*, which undoubtedly made her appreciate how good the *Night Gallery* episode was. She told reporters that she'd like to do more television. "Three or four a year and perhaps a two-hour TV feature. I've been earning my own living since I was 9. I like to work. I need to work." The problem was that "they usually call me in New York on a Thursday and ask if I can catch a plane Friday and be able to work Monday. I say, What's the script? They say you'll see it when you get here. I say, What about wardrobe? What do I bring? What do I wear?

"It's impossible. So unprofessional."

If *Night Gallery* was an unexpected triumph, *The Sixth Sense* was . . . product.

Robert O'Neill was the associate producer, and he was impressed both by Crawford's memory and her attitude. One of her asks was for the cameraman Enzo Martinelli, who had shot her before and knew what she wanted to look like. "I'm no longer an ingenue," she confided to O'Neill. She was punctual, utterly professional, and expected others to be as well. Depending on the coworkers, she could be motherly with one young actress or gruff with another.

Crawford wanted a specific dressing room, but that was being used by the star of a movie. She was understanding: "She's making a feature; I'm just doing a TV show." O'Neill found her a dressing room situated between Rock Hudson and Dean Martin, and this pleased her. "You're a love. I love being with handsome men!"

The cast of the *Sixth Sense* episode skewed young—Anne Lockhart, Scott Hylands, and David Ladd, the son of Alan Ladd. Ladd had grown up with movie stars, but Joan Crawford was simultaneously special and ordinary.

> The overriding thing I remember was her insistence that the stage be kept at 58 degrees. Why I remember that number, I don't know, but I do. It was part of keeping her on top of her game.
>
> There was not a trace of the grande dame; she was very nice to everybody. She had done TV before, so she knew what to expect. I remember she had her dressing room on the set, which was extravagant for television. So was keeping the set at 58 degrees.
>
> Like a lot of the people from the studio era, she drank, but it didn't show. Not drinking. Sipping. Vodka. I had met her once before when she came over to my parents' house for dinner, and she had brought her own bottle of Blue Label vodka. And that's what she drank. 100 proof.
>
> The Joan of it all didn't seem strange. It was a set like any other set. The temperature was the thing. It was shot in a heat wave, and the crew was bundled up in parkas.
>
> I was braced for temperament, but she had none. She was anything but

a prima donna. Other than her trailer and the temperature, I saw nothing but a very professional woman. By this time I had worked with a lot of fine actors who were old pros, and it was always amazing how professional people brought up in the studio system were, including my father.

The episode was titled "Dear Joan: We're Going to Scare You to Death," which gives a good idea of the proceedings. Crawford plays a woman whose daughter has drowned. Her car breaks down on an isolated road and she seeks refuge at a nearby house, which turns out to be the wrong place to go for help.

The writing is from hunger, the direction no better, but despite the obstacles Crawford is quite good and easily outclasses her surroundings. The episode of *The Sixth Sense* ran in September 1972 and constituted Crawford's hail and farewell to acting. After this little remembered episode of a little remembered show, it was lights out for work in her profession.

BASICALLY AT LOOSE ENDS, Crawford filled some time by collaborating on another memoir called *My Way of Life*. The publisher was Simon & Schuster, and the book was handled by editor-in-chief Michael Korda, who came to her apartment for a conference. She asked him what he'd like to drink.

"Bourbon," he said.

Crawford replied that she was not an afternoon drinker. Was there anything else she could offer? He inquired hopefully about a split of champagne, which she happily supplied.

"After that," said Korda, "she always had caviar on ice and champagne for our editing sessions. *Excellent* caviar.

She was never difficult to edit. She was difficult to tour. She wanted security—she had a whole briefing book! It was very difficult for the publicity department, who thought she had died years before. She had very high expectations as to how she would be treated and was vehement when those expectations weren't paid attention to.

She was a movie star! She was intent on going on the road with the book, and I think that was half the attraction. She felt she was out of the mainstream, and that the book would put her back.

With me she was very approachable, never made any attempt to be grand. She never talked about her career—I grew up in the motion picture business, so it wouldn't have worked with me. She could be very funny. Witty. *Scathing!*

I think one of the reasons we got along is she perceived me as a knowledgeable movie person. Certainly, she and Merle Oberon, my aunt, always spoke well of each other, but that was probably professional courtesy.

Korda's takeaway from the experience was as much about Joan's apartment as about her. He didn't expect a palatial setup, but he was surprised to find it so modest. "It was a five-room apartment," he remembered dismissively.

My Way of Life is partly a memoir, partly a lifestyle guide. There are details on how to throw a party and even some recipes. Crawford particularly vouched for her coleslaw, which involved shaved cabbage, green peppers, finely chopped pimento and pineapple, with a dressing consisting of mayonnaise, dry and prepared mustard, the juice of six lemons, olive oil, cider vinegar, hot peppers, and spices and herbs.

The book's core problem was identity and audience—who was it for? The women who had grown up with Crawford and her movies had presumably managed to form their own social identities by this time, and if they hadn't their mid-sixties were probably too late, while it was simply irrelevant for younger women.

Billy Haines seems to have enjoyed the book:

Dear Cranberry,

I bow to you, oh Empress of Motion, when I think how much I enjoyed your book. Then too I am so deeply moved and flattered that you gave me so much consideration and space. Perhaps with this splendid praise I can pull out of life a few more rewarding years—

Now, Madame, alas it has turned out the pupil has beaten the shit out of the teacher. So be it!

Con Amore . . .

My Way of Life brought her together with Jeanine Basinger, a film professor at Wesleyan University who was about to teach a class about Crawford and introduced herself at a book signing.

"I expected to meet a glamorous movie star, and that's what she was," remembered Basinger. "Beautifully dressed. Impressive. Very warm, friendly, but imperial. She sat straight, way more beautiful than I had imagined. Her eyes were like lasers when she evaluated you. She had the power of stardom."

All that changed when Basinger came to Crawford's apartment for an interview.

> She opened the door. She had on flip-flops and a housedress—a real housedress, a Sears Catalogue housedress. Cotton, with a square neck. Not a stitch of makeup. Freckles. Her hair was totally gray, very long, hung down her back and was tied at the back, neat and together.
>
> She offered coffee, then brought it out herself. She still had the penetrating look, but I was there to talk about her career, and I was not a professional writer. I was teaching a class on her, and she focused on that and was very interested.
>
> She told me all about the films, answered every question. She was intelligent, articulate, totally committed. She asked why I was doing it. She was tremendously interested about it. Called George Cukor for me, then gave me his phone number.
>
> As I got to know her, I realized what she was referring to when she said, "I'll get my Joan Crawford suit on." She had a sense of herself as a role she must play, that she could play, and it was her best role. She knew how to do it. She didn't have the Cary Grant ambivalence. She understood that being Joan Crawford was her job, and she was happy to be Joan Crawford. She was really smart about her career, she remembered everything, and she asked questions.

It was the beginning of a late-life friendship that would extend to shortly before Crawford's death. Near the end of the interview, Basinger told Crawford that she wanted to host an event for Crawford at Wesleyan.

"'Oh, no, I could never do that.' She explained that she was busy with

Pepsi, which was a bit of a fantasy at that point, but I saw that the idea shook her. She was essentially a shy person but had learned to perform as Joan Crawford."

· Shortly after Basinger's visit, Patricia Bosworth did an interview with Crawford in *The New York Times* that treated her as a relic and struck Basinger as tacky and cheap. She wrote a letter to Sy Peck, the editor of the Arts & Leisure section, taking him to task for running it. Peck called her a few days later and offered to run her letter as an article.

The morning Basinger's article ran, her phone rang at 7:30 a.m. It was an unmistakable voice. "Jeanine. This is Joan. You are a very great lady, and I appreciate what you have done for me very much. Now, about my visit to your school . . ."

"That was the definition of her right there. She had decided it was going to happen and it *was* going to happen. And she came. I was terribly nervous, practically hysterical. It was 1972, and Wesleyan was a radical campus." As it turned out, 1,300 people packed the place and 3,000 more were turned away. "And she had a list of the twelve fans she had in the Hartford area and they all came with roses and gifts."

The only problem arose because Wesleyan's dining hall, where the Q&A took place, could only be accessed from above, down a long flight of wide stairs. "Jeanine," said Crawford, "I'll be nervous, I'll be wearing high heels." Crawford stopped to count the steps. "There's got to be another way to enter."

"In my cleverness, I said, 'This is it, you'll be fine.'

"'No. If I make one wobble of my ankle, everyone will say I'm drunk. You can't tell me they'd build a building and not have another entrance.'

"Finally she laser-beamed me with her eyes, and I said, 'Well, there is a garbage elevator.' And she said, 'What do I care about garbage? I'll come up in that elevator as long as none of it sticks on me when I get out of it.'"

Basinger chuckled at the memory. "She had a great sense of humor. You know, the job of a teacher is evaluating basic intelligence and the ability and willingness to learn. Joan was intelligent and super willing to learn. She wanted to *know*. And she had learned to ask every possible question."

AS THE WORK THINNED out, then went away, what was left were friends . . . and fans. Sometimes the latter became the former. Carl Johnes was working at Columbia Pictures in New York when his boss asked him to go over to Joan Crawford's apartment. It seemed she had asked for someone who knew something about books. When Johnes got to Crawford's apartment, he found her floor-to-ceiling bookshelves overloaded and sagging. She knew she wanted to give away some of the books to her children, some to her grandchildren, some to charities, and some to Brandeis University, but she didn't have a clear idea of which ones to keep.

Johnes began plowing through the stacks and quickly categorized volumes signed by Noel Coward, Allen Drury, and James M. Cain as keepers. The Rod McKuen and Jacqueline Susann books struck him as expendable, but she snatched Susann's away from him, saying, "She's one of my dearest friends!"

Johnes was struck by her emotional accessibility and by the fact that "Her sense of humor never abandoned her for long." He was a movie buff and became one of her young friends. She taught him to play backgammon, at which she was extremely competitive and not always patient: "Honey, please look at your board!" she would snap.

"Joan played for blood," was the way Johnes remembered it.

There were weekly backgammon evenings during which they talked about current events. Generally speaking, he found her vulnerable and shy. She was losing touch with cultural trends and was avoiding dinner parties because, "Among other things, I don't like to sit around a dinner table and have to talk about people who are dead."

When he sent her a bouquet, she responded with one of her effusive thank-you letters: "Carl, my darling, Thank you so much for the most beautiful blue iris and yellow and white spider chrysanthemums I have ever seen. I ran out of vases so they are in my large yellow wastebasket in the kitchen—and when you come, you will see for yourself how much beauty I have in my kitchen. Much love, dear friend."

Johnes appreciated the note because he hadn't known what the flowers were, only that they were beautiful.

The twins and their families were around, but Christina and Christopher weren't. When Johnes asked about that, Crawford said, "Tina and I have nothing to say to each other anymore. I hear she's found another man, and

I hope she's happy. Anyway, Tina and Christopher are just waiting for me to die. That's all they want."

"Surely there's something you can do about that?"

"Yes, there is, I can cut them out of my will."

THE COMMON DENOMINATOR THAT Crawford looked for in her friends was the Roman fortitude exemplified by Billy Haines. Louis B. Mayer hadn't wanted an out gay man acting at MGM? Very well. Haines didn't sulk, feel sorry for himself, or drink himself into a daily stupor and an early grave. Instead, he reinvented himself.

As Crawford put it, "I hate—and I do not have as friends and will not have as friends, let me put it that way—whiners. I cannot tolerate self-pity. Oh my God, I can't stand them. I cannot waste my time with them. . . . We [all] have our problems, but I don't inflict mine on my friends."

And then came the loss that could not be endured, let alone rationalized. In 1972, Billy Haines was diagnosed with lung cancer. Prognosis: terminal. Typically, he didn't burden his friend. At Christmas that year he wrote her:

> *Dear Cranberry—*
>
> *Mr. James Shields and friend wish to extend to the Ms. Billy Cassin, Lucille Le Sueur and Joan Crawford their sincere thanks for the Xmas wine but most of all for the long years of deep and holy friendship.*
>
> *Come to think of it the Messrs Shields and Haines can not decide which of the three ladies they love the most. So we will roll all three into a "Tootsie Roll" and eat it.*
>
> *Con Amore . . .*

At the same time, Billy's partner Jimmy Shields began to have memory issues. At a party, Jimmy mentioned that they should have invited Polly Moran, whom they hadn't seen in too long. "The reason we haven't seen her," Billy snapped, "is because she's been *dead* for 20 years."

Joan called Billy several times a week. Some days Billy couldn't speak, so Jimmy would update her.

William Haines died on December 26, 1973.

Shortly after that, a writer named Lyn Tornabene came to visit for an interview for a book she was writing about Clark Gable. Crawford came to the door typically dressed in what Tornabene said was a "a $6.95 dress" and the flip-flops. She gave the writer a tour of the apartment, pointed out some of Billy's furniture, and mentioned that he had just died and that he was "a great man."

Outgoing letters were laid out on towels on the dining room table; an open closet revealed rows of pastel wedgies, purses, and fur coats in a row. Crawford had always had dogs—three dachshunds in the 1930s, other small breeds later on—but apartment living meant she was down to one dog, a Shih Tzu named, appropriately, Princess. Princess had weekly treatments to de-mat her, which included a shampoo and crème rinse. The groomer said "that dog was like one of my own. . . . It's not so good for the coat to do it every week, but that's what Joan Crawford wanted."

Princess was brought in after a bath looking like a "snow-white fur pillow," and was carried from room to room by Mamacita; the dog apparently never touched the floor.

Joan asked Tornabene if she wanted to see how Princess ate. Mamacita held the dog's ears up and Joan fed her with a spoon. After that, it was time for Princess to relieve herself, so she was taken into a bedroom where there was a baby's playpen containing a "piddle pad." Everybody said, "Wee-wee, Princess." Princess complied. Tornabene was impressed, or pretended to be.

During the interview, Crawford sat at a makeup table with her back to Tornabene and talked to her reflection. If she didn't approve of the question, Crawford would change the subject from Clark Gable to Princess. At one point she recited the Desiderata. As she talked and applied her makeup, her face began to take on its familiar shape in the mirror.

In her telling, the relationship with Gable was basically a star-crossed romance without an appropriate ending—*An Affair to Remember* minus the climactic reunion. Throughout the interview, it was clear that Crawford was laying down a challenge. It was also clear that Tornabene was losing.

She finally turned around to face her interviewer. She looked to be about forty-five, as opposed to the seventysomething woman who had opened the door. The crowning touch was a pair of gold lamé wedgies that Mamacita fetched that added several inches in height.

The transformation was complete; the interview was over.

AMONG CRAWFORD'S FRIENDS WERE the producer David Brown and his wife, Helen Gurley Brown. They frequently took a limousine to "21," where Crawford insisted on sitting upstairs, which was preferable to downstairs. She usually ordered liver. Tino, the upstairs captain, provided them with Joan's vodka. She would sit facing the door with her glass on a napkin. When the glass was empty, she would nod, and a waiter would bring her another.

Despite the fact that Crawford was now effectively retired, she remained a star with a star's prerogatives, which could become wearisome to other people. Years earlier there had been a party for Hedda Hopper and Louella Parsons, which entailed a drive of approximately ten blocks. Crawford hired a limousine, complete with champagne and hors d'oeuvres.

In January 1973, Joan was honored at the Players Club. Jim Brochu had ignored her career advice, become an actor, and had been a member of the Players for a year or so. "It was part of a series where they hosted a star and they would show a movie that the star chose. She called and asked me if I would escort her. I said I'd love to.

> There was an electricity in the air. When she turned it on, she was what a star was all about. She provoked excitement in the room. There was a palpable transformation from Joan Crawford to *JOAN CRAWFORD!*
>
> The adoration flooded in and lifted her up. The thing that surprised me was the film they showed. It was a film I had never seen and she said it was her favorite: *A Woman's Face*. An extraordinary performance!
>
> There was an actor named Lester Rawlins she wanted to meet because she watched a soap opera he was in. She would go from *One Life to Live* to *General Hospital* to another one. So she wanted to meet Lester Rawlins, and in the meantime she was holding court.

The sofa we were sitting on was facing the stairs so we could see people coming up the stairs. I was sitting next to her and up the stairs comes Joan Fontaine. Joan, with the biggest smile, said "It's Joan Fontaine!" and then, under her breath, added, "That bitch!"

IN WHAT WAS INCREASINGLY coming to seem like retirement, some of the haughtiness that occasionally flared up in years past was leaching away. "When she looked at you," said David Brown, "there was no one else in the room for her, no furtive glancing over your shoulder to see who else (and more important) might be arriving. Joan Crawford was a friend." Like Cinderella, she was usually home by 10 p.m.

Leonard Spigelgass, her frequent dinner guest on North Bristol, had become a successful Broadway playwright with *A Majority of One*, and he reconnected with her in New York. Once, at "21," she was wearing a big red hat with roses on it, and Spigelgass told her that the hat gave her a pink glow.

"Why the fuck do you think I wear it?"

For any Spigelgass event, Crawford would send him a handwritten note of congratulation specifying the event. Similarly, cards would arrive for birthdays and Christmas. A reply thanking her for her solicitousness would provoke yet another card thanking him for his thanks.

Spigelgass wondered why she was going to such extremes, then realized it was simple. "She was filling her life up."

When it came to conversation, Crawford preferred talking to women rather than men. She never verbalized it, but she seemed to feel that women were inherently more trustworthy.

At a party she rescued the stranded, even if they weren't personally close, even if it wasn't her party. She introduced people, making sure they mixed, giving strangers brief biographies of other strangers so they could talk to each other. Although she could not be said to have tended overmuch to her immediate family, she seemed to take pleasure in tending to strangers and friends.

"She had a lot of fear," said Jeanine Basinger. "When she moved to the smaller apartment she gave me a bunch of stuff. I would hear ice cubes clinking when we talked on the phone, but I never knew her to be drunk. Socially, not at all. She was very careful. And she wanted to be sharp. I would say she didn't have to drink if she didn't want to.

She was a loyal friend, a caring friend, a devoted friend who would do for you if you needed it no matter what. Once she decided you were her friend, she would be there. How many people in your life can you really say, no matter what you needed, this person from outside the family—and God knows whether family will do anything—will come to your rescue? She was that person. A friend, a loyal and caring friend.

She remembered crisis. Not having anything. Having to find a way. Having to find someone she could trust and count on. She made soup!

She was ironic. She saw ludicrousness, she saw phony. And she was self-deprecating. She made little jokes about herself. Not a lot, but she had a sense of humor about herself, which nobody ever believes. And she was kind of sentimental. She loved *The Waltons*, loved things that were reassuring to her about the MGM vision of life.

There were friends from Hollywood who continued to check in. Barbara Stanwyck would call, and Crawford and Myrna Loy would get together whenever Loy wasn't touring with a play. But all of her closest friends (Stanwyck, Loretta Young, Rosalind Russell, Cesar Romero, Virginia Grey, Jane Ardmore) lived in California, which meant she had to find new friends in New York.

Shortly after she moved to the apartment in the Imperial House, she called her neighbor Anne Anderson to come up for a drink. The apartment was still a jumble, but there was a photo album of the children near the couch. Crawford went through it page by page, telling Anderson what each child was doing at that point in their lives. "I was strict," she told Anderson. "I wanted them to be independent. I didn't want to coddle them." She dwelled on how unhappy she had been as a child at Christmas because there had been no presents. More importantly, there had been no sense of joy.

Curtiss Anderson, Anne's husband, was a magazine editor, and Crawford came to trust him sufficiently to do a long interview with him. He endeared himself to her by telling her that as a boy in Minneapolis, he had been fired from his job as a movie usher because he was paying more attention to her movies than the customers. "I saw *Above Suspicion* twenty-eight times," he told her.

"You deserve a medal," she replied. "I couldn't stand it once."

She asked Anderson if there was any way she could get to their floor without taking the regular elevator. She felt that if she got in the regular elevator accompanied by other tenants, she would need to be dressed up and she preferred wearing caftans. He told her to go down to the basement and take the service elevator, which she did precisely once. She found it depressing and resumed dressing up for the regular elevator.

In August 1973 she made the decision to move again, down the hall to 22-H, a slightly smaller apartment, which necessitated paring still more possessions. She offered the Andersons her large TV and asked Anne Anderson to take her choice of Crawford's wardrobe.

"I'm only moving to another apartment in the same building," she wrote George Cukor, "but it might as well be to Switzerland. Dear God, the things we collect."

Part of the motivation for the move seems to have been that the building had gone co-op, and she was able to pick up the new place for the bargain price of less than $100,000. Once again she hired Carleton Varney to follow in the footsteps of Billy Haines, and the new place was ready to move in by November.

The problem was that the new place was yet another diminishment from the baronial showplace Billy had designed for her and Al Steele. 22-H had a reception room that led to a 29 x 15 living room, which in turn led into the dining room that was 18 x 12. The kitchen measured 15.6 x 8. There were also two bedrooms and two baths, along with some walk-in closets, two smaller closets, and a small terrace.

As New York apartments go it was a perfectly livable space, but compared to the house on North Bristol and the New York apartment that came after, it felt like yet another step on a downward trajectory. Perhaps the worst of it was that the smaller space meant that more of Billy Haines's custom furniture had to be jettisoned. The end result was a feeling of deprivation and depression.

The diminishment continued with dental surgery in July of 1974. The lack of work, not to mention the creeping sense of age, gave her more time for introspection, and she came to the conclusion that she was drinking too much. According to Crawford, her drinking began to get out of control after Al Steele died.

"Joan was a prodigious drinker," said Robert Aldrich. "She would take a bottle of vodka in the seven-seat limo from her home to a theatre in Westwood or Hollywood. I could possibly drink half a bottle of Scotch—this was during my drinking days. But Joan would put away the whole bottle during the evening."

The more she thought about it, the more it became obvious she had been a heavy drinker long before Steele's death. People who worked with Crawford during her drinking days said that she didn't get sloppy or rude when she was drinking, just tougher. It undoubtedly got worse after Steele died.

The light finally went on one night when Crawford was talking to her daughter Cathy on the phone. She suddenly realized she couldn't remember why she had called her daughter or what they had just talked about.

So she stopped drinking cold turkey. She never went the AA route, possibly because AA replaces a reliance on alcohol with a reliance on what they euphemistically call a "Higher Power," and Crawford's idea of a Higher Power began and ended with Louis B. Mayer. "She just made up her mind not to drink," was the way her publicist friend Bob Rains put it.

Other than the absence of alcohol, nothing else changed. When Rains and his wife were in New York, they would occasionally go to a movie with Crawford, and she always insisted on buying her own ticket. She'd been paying her own way for her entire life and wasn't about to stop now.

———◆◇◆———

ONE OF HER REMAINING pleasures was cooking. She threw a surprise birthday party for Anne Anderson and spent two days in preparation before she asked Anderson to come over for a cocktail. She had made pot-au-feu and a salad. Anderson remembered that her pork chops were particularly good—two inches thick, seasoned with cinnamon. Similarly, a meat loaf would contain a whole bottle of A-1 sauce.

When Anderson did something for Crawford, it would always be reciprocated—she had to return every favor times two. Strangers made her nervous, but a dinner party was a dinner party. "She was uneasy," remembered Curtiss Anderson, "but she turned the corner, shoulders back, head up."

One guest at a party was thunderstruck by Joan Crawford in the flesh and gasped, "Oh my God, I know who you are!" Joan kissed her hand and said, "I'm so glad you do." After a party, even if it was in someone else's apartment, she would reliably be found in the kitchen, doing the dishes or helping to clean up. Similarly, if Anne sent over chicken tarragon, the plastic containers came back scrubbed clean. She even returned chutney jars.

Selma and Marty Mertz lived across the hall from Crawford, and she grew comfortable with them as well. Gin rummy and backgammon helped fill the hours. Joan taught Anne Anderson how to play backgammon, but she could get impatient with Anderson's inexperience. "Why can't you understand?" she demanded. Crawford had made do with a bottom-shelf backgammon table until one Christmas she bought herself one made of marble.

Jeanine Basinger would visit, and there were frequent phone calls as well. "She liked to go to Lutèce for dinner. She once said, 'You have to look your best when you go out.' Can you imagine walking through a crowd of people who could say things like, 'She doesn't look like she used to, her hair looks terrible.'

"She loved her dogs. She would talk about the twins. She never mentioned her son. Once in a while she would say something about Christina."

The new apartment had splashes of color and, yes, there were plastic covers on the couch. "She would take you in the kitchen, where she'd be cooking. She had a lot of yellow and green, bright, colorful yellow, and chartreusy green. And those Keane paintings, several of them. I hated those things, they haunted me. And some of the Billy Haines furniture, which she loved and kept.

"The apartment had a sort of sterile look. She was very into cleanliness, but there was a lot of color. I felt fine in it, because of the kitchen. If Joan was in the room, with housedress and her freckles, she was a commanding presence. Everything else around her was not as interesting. She laughed and smiled and it was like seeing someone you've only seen in a picture on a distant wall and there she was—suddenly *alive!*"

As for Mamacita, "She hovered. It was a ballet of domesticity. I never saw her be unkind to Mamacita, or have Mamacita show anything other than reverence.

"Joan was pretty down-to-earth in her privacy. That was indicated by the way she dressed and that she was unafraid to show herself to people she trusted inside the walls."

If Crawford was in a good mood, the memories would start pouring forth, sometimes with a startling intimacy.

She talked about Douglas Fairbanks Jr. "We were so in love. And it's never the same after that." I never really believed any of that Bette/Joan feud stuff, because she almost never brought Davis up. They weren't at the same studio in their prime, and by the time Joan was at Warner's Davis was producing her own pictures.

The person Joan complained about was Norma Shearer. Always! She resented her. And despite Franchot Tone, the man she talked about was Gable. She told me the story about Gable coming to her house after Carole Lombard died. They had a powerful bond of mutual understanding of their situation, their fear and lack of preparation for their careers. Yet at the same time they had total dominance and mastery of being movie stars.

Sometimes she was conscious of feeling constrained, I think. "I have to be Joan Crawford. People expect it, and I expect it. It's my job. It's what I do." I think she felt she had worked all her life for it, and it was up to her to honor the success she'd had. She talked about the people who'd supported her. They *mattered* to her!

She understood the bargain, and I don't think she ever questioned it. Joan could face reality. She could face truth. She had to do it all her life, and she chose a fantasy profession to help her not have to do it.

CRAWFORD AND GEORGE CUKOR carried on their correspondence of gratitude for Christmas and birthday presents, and there was time for other old friends as well. She sent a note to Jack Oakie, her boyfriend of nearly fifty years before: "You are the best ex-boy friend this ex-girl friend ever had. You not only have taught me the value of friendship, but have inspired me."

She introduced a series of her movies on New York television in return for the station running a series of spots promoting her favorite charity: Muscular Dystrophy. She insisted on *Mildred Pierce* and agreed through gritted teeth to the showing of *Rain*.

On the day of the recordings, her discomfort with television reared up and she was nervous. She had brought a selection of wigs and jewelry to the station and began to feel more comfortable as the crew treated her like a queen. They had gone to the trouble of hiring her preferred lighting man, and when the lights hit her she relaxed.

"She looked great, she sounded great. She was an odd combination of strength and vulnerability," said Michael Stevens, who was shepherding the shoot. When it was all over, she wrote thank-you notes to every one of the thirty-five people who had been on the crew.

Crawford hit a nerve with a letter to George Cukor about how much she deplored cheap nostalgia. Cukor wrote back saying that her attitude was both "eloquent and realistic. Do you remember the nonsense we had to go through timing a kiss with a stop watch—checking your decolletage within a sixteenth of an inch—and what about when a husband and wife were in a nuptial bed, one of them had to have their feet planted on the floor? As for a non-husband and wife in a non-nuptial bed—heaven forbid!

> But it takes two to tango so one should face up to what in part brought this threat of censorship on. The vulgarity, the stupidity, complete lack of taste, the sacrificing of everything for the fast buck. Another pernicious effect of all this tastelessness is that it alienated the great big, family audience. Unhappily all this filth happened at a time when Nixon and his sanctimonious, holier-than-thou mealy-mouthed hypocrites are running things. . . .
>
> Louis B. Mayer wasn't particularly nice to me. He put up with me, I suppose, because I was under contract to Metro and a friend of his daughters'—and let's face it—he may not have thought I was a good director. But he was a showman, practical and wise. His daughters told me that he was firm in his belief that pictures are family entertainment, and the moment that was abandoned there'd be disaster. Louis (although I never dared to call him that) had very high moral standards—if you didn't inquire too carefully

into his personal carryings-on—Ginny Simms, Ann Miller, Hedy Lamarr and on and on.

I must confess that I'm very often taken aback at what I see on the screen, and I don't mean hard-core porno stuff. I'd hate to take mama to see *Last Tango in Paris* although it had some wonderful things in it. But it extends also to untalented pictures. The other day I saw *Forty Carats* (spare yourself that) and for no reason at all—in this light comedy—people spewed obscenities at each other. As for nudity, there was infinitely more eroticism generated by ladies like you—fully clothed.

With these few words, dearest Joan, I send you all my love....

Crawford contributed a piece to *The New York Times* that spun off the Supreme Court decision enshrining "community standards" as the standard for pornography. The usual suspects said the usual things: William F. Buckley "vigorously" applauded the decision, while filmmakers (Paul Mazursky, Melvin Van Peebles) thought it ludicrous.

In some ways, Crawford was psychologically conservative, in others libertarian, but her knowledge of the practicalities of filmmaking pushed her in the direction of freedom of expression:

I deplore going back—way, way back to the censor boards and regulatory bodies that would piously and unilaterally proclaim what we should read and what we should see. With a single stroke of their repressive pens, the majority opinion . . . of the Supreme Court has told us that community standards would provide the final answer to all of our problems with prurience. What a blow to all of our talented and creative people who will no longer be able to tell a cinematic story with honesty and forthrightness. The local censor will be looking over the shoulder of our director, into the camera of our cinematographers, impugning the integrity of our writers, and inhibiting the work of our actors.

How can movie makers meet the new "community" standards? Will they make "covering" shots for Memphis, or Omaha? Perhaps St. Louis or Binghamton, New York needs a special handling of a unique scene. Are we going to codify our prints hot, cool, or cold, or mild, medium, or the TRUTH?

That's it—that's what we'll be missing ultimately—the truth, and without it we will sink back into the unrealities and banalities of the past. To preserve our true liberties, we must read and see whatever we please. Boredom will pronounce its own death sentence on repetitive pornography.

SHE NEVER STOPPED TRYING to improve herself—for a time she took a literature course from a private tutor. If she was in a good mood, she'd reminisce about movies. Ann Blyth had been a problem on *Mildred Pierce* because she was a kind, sympathetic person who had trouble playing a pathological bitch. Crawford told her, "Ann, no one is going to believe the story—you're too nice." Crawford got down on her knees and grabbed Ann's legs and squeezed until they hurt. "Now can you be tough?" It took the combined efforts of Crawford and Michael Curtiz to bring Blyth up to the necessary level of mean.

On December, 10, 1974, Crawford had been scheduled to come over to the Anderson apartment for dinner when she called and asked them to come to hers. They were shocked to find her with an eye half-shut and half her face swollen and bruised. They thought she had been beaten, but she told them she had been writing notes and blacked out, hitting her face on the edge of the table.

"As you can see, I can't come to dinner." It was typical—she wanted them to know her excuse was valid. She had a doctor come to her apartment, a reflection of the MGM years, when the studio gave their stars customized service. Some people assumed she had been drinking and passed out, but Carl Johnes asserted that in all their times together he had never seen her inebriated.

Anne Anderson thought she was fascinating, a living, breathing *objet d'art*, but occasionally a burden. "She was not an easy friend. We went off on a weekend one time without notifying her. Joan called a friend and she was hysterical until we were finally located. She was very possessive of her friends."

Needless to say, she was lonely. Myrna Loy admired her because of her attentiveness. "She remembered anniversaries and milestones in the lives of her friends. She never forgot names, dates, or obligations."

Loy suggested she give the theater a try. Loy was still doing *Barefoot in the Park* in dinner theaters and still loving it, and Gloria Swanson had done *Butterflies Are Free* in New York and on tour. Gloria had her limitations—she tended to plant herself onstage as if positioning herself for a close-up—but she sold out houses for audiences of women who wanted to see what she looked like. If Loy and Swanson could do it, Joan could too.

But the idea of being out onstage alone, without the adjacent support of a director or crew, still terrified Crawford. "I envy you like mad," she told Loy, "you've latched on to the secret of growing old gracefully—and usefully." Loy understood, as most did not, that Crawford's bravura performances were just that—performances.

Barry Sullivan would always call whenever he came to New York. He took her out to see Cliff Gorman in *Lenny*, Julian Barry's play about Lenny Bruce. They dined at "21" before the show, and Crawford held court until 1 a.m., long after the play was forgotten. Sullivan realized that it was better that way; she probably wouldn't have liked *Lenny* anyway.

She had reached that stage where there was more life behind her than there was in front of her, so it followed that she talked more about the past than the future. She believed that Douglas Fairbanks Jr. "gave me laughter, Franchot was stimulating, Philip gave me comfort." As for Al Steele, he gave her an enveloping sense of security . . . until, through no fault of his own, he didn't.

CHAPTER TWENTY-ONE

PEPSI RETIRED CRAWFORD IN April 1973, when she had supposedly turned sixty-five. Despite the fact that her income was lessened, she continued to make generous donations to her favorite charities as well as Christian Science.

A theatrical press agent named Michael Sean O'Shea approached Crawford regarding Joe Papp's Shakespeare in the Park. Papp was looking for a donation of $25,000 in order to get a grant of $50,000 from the city. Crawford told O'Shea she couldn't swing $25,000 by herself, but she used her celebrity to raise money for Papp, hosting tea parties at $50 a ticket and signing upward of six thousand fundraising letters.

O'Shea became another one of the gay men with whom Crawford had an affinity, and in turn he became her loyal defender. For all of Crawford's efforts on behalf of Papp, O'Shea was always peeved that there was never any mention of her—or, for that matter, O'Shea—in Papp's interviews.

"She didn't send flowers to funeral homes," said O'Shea. "She sent flowers to the homes of the survivors. When I came home after my mother's funeral, she had sent turkey, ham, and Dom Pérignon.

She often wore shirts and leotards—she had great legs. . . . She'd lay on the floor to watch her old movies, chin in hands, intent. She'd call about her own movies [on TV]: "watch the next segment; an actor is going to do something marvelous."

If you knew how to handle her, you could get along. She never saw a psychiatrist in her life—she didn't believe in it. When she got sick, she believed the Bible would help her, and she refused doctors.

For current events, she read *The Wall Street Journal* and *Harper's*. Her other reading matter consisted of lifestyle publications: *Architectural Digest, Women's Wear Daily, Vogue, Town & Country,* and *House & Garden*.

Most current movies left her cold, but she loved the Robert Redford version of *The Great Gatsby* because "everyone looked so lovely." She hated violent movies or TV shows and liked soap operas because they gave her a chance to appraise young actors. If she thought an actor had talent, she'd watch the credits for their name and send them a letter of appreciation. She watched Walter Cronkite every night and *Bonanza* every week. And she still watched *The Waltons*, mostly because of Ellen Corby's Grandma.

She liked Carol Burnett's parody of *Mildred Pierce*, which was called *Mildred Fierce* and phoned Burnett to tell her so, although privately she told friends she thought it too long and too arch. She hated Burnett's parody of *Torch Song*.

Around the apartment, she wore leotards and a shirt, or mumus. Because of Christian Science she rarely went to doctors. Likewise, she had never been involved with or had her children involved in any kind of conventional religious structure. Her grandson Casey thinks that she might have been looking for something to pour herself into that would take the place of acting, and Christian Science certainly fills the devotional bill.

She believed that most people used medicine as an emotional placebo as much as for actual medicinal effects, and that with faith and patience the body could often right itself. She had the negative example of a long list of Hollywood actors who shortened their lives because they relied overmuch on alcohol and/or drugs.

Part of the interest in Christian Science derived from her antipathy to conventional religion as she'd seen it practiced. She bridled at those who used religion as a cudgel and believed Rosalind Russell was an admirable example of a woman whose strong religious beliefs were never imposed on anybody else. There was also a continuing fear of knives, which might have been the reason she never had a facelift.

In short, she was one of millions of gainfully unemployed senior citizens existing within a gradually shrinking environment who had to find contentment in small pleasures.

"Take away the last thing she had, the connection to Pepsi," said Joseph L. Mankiewicz. "That might have destroyed her. She had just run out of proxy identities. When the makeup comes off for the last time, what's left?"

Her last official public appearance was on Sunday, April 8, 1973, at a career tribute with the publicist John Springer at New York City's Town Hall. She and Springer had been friendly for years. When he was in uniform during World War II, he had danced with her at the Hollywood Canteen, and she had treated him as a person, not "just another nameless, faceless kid in uniform, which is how some of the other stars, lesser stars, [treated] you."

After the war Springer became a publicist and had worked on *Sudden Fear*, among others. It was around this time that he was dancing with her again at a party at Chasen's.

"I had hoped I'd see you at the party last week," he said.

"I wanted so much to go, but I had nobody to take me. I sat home alone—like I did New Year's Eve and so many nights."

He thought she was being intentionally ridiculous. "Oh, sure. That will be the day—when Joan Crawford is poor Cinderella, crying into her pillow because she doesn't have anyone to take her to the ball."

She looked at him and said, "Yes. That's the way it is," and he realized she was absolutely serious.

When Springer got married, Crawford sent a large box decorated with gardenias. The box contained several dozen monogrammed glasses of the finest crystal. After the wedding, Springer and his wife had a tour of Crawford's Fifth Avenue apartment, when Crawford pulled out a hat and told June Springer, "June, this hat is you. You must take it!" It was a wide-brimmed hat with a veil, the sort of hat that only a movie star or a fashion model could get away with. June Springer never wore it, but she always kept it.

Springer's first series of conversations with screen legends was planned to include Sylvia Sidney, Myrna Loy, and Jean Arthur. When he told Bette Davis about his plans, she insisted on being included, "as long as Crawford is not on the list." Springer told her that they weren't a sister act, which satisfied Davis. The pathologically shy Jean Arthur begged off, so Springer substituted Ginger Rogers, who later withdrew.

That meant Springer had a vacant spot, and he went for Crawford despite his promise to Davis. "Oh, Johnny, I couldn't face it." Later, she called him: "If you're really in a spot . . ."

"I am."

"I'll do it. For you." As always, she was extremely nervous about appearing in public without a script.

There were seventy minutes of film clips, then an intermission, after which Crawford was to make her entrance. Awaiting her cue, she froze. "I can't go on," she told Springer with panic in her voice.

He pushed her onstage and into the spotlight, and the wave of love hit her. "First I had fear that the audience wouldn't be filled. . . . I walked out on stage, tried to sit down, and I had to keep walking. . . . They threw flowers all around me! . . . then I started to cry."

For more than an hour she took full possession of her subjects with a mixture of humor and candor. As she put it, "My nervousness ceased."

She reiterated her love and respect for Louis B. Mayer, but thought Jack Warner was "a stinker." Bette Davis was "my greatest challenge ever, and I mean that kindly. She likes to scream and yell and I just sit and knit. During 'Baby Jane' I knit a scarf from Hollywood to Malibu."

When it was all over, she told Springer, "It was one of the greatest evenings of my life, and I'll never go through it again."

She posed for Richard Avedon in his "What Becomes a Legend Most" series of ads for Blackglama. Crawford is sheathed in mink, and the image focuses on her face and those luminous eyes gazing up into the light. It's the last great photograph of a woman who had made thousands of them, probably more than any other star.

Peter Rogers, the ad man behind the Blackglama campaign, became friends with her and said she was "a loving, giving friend who liked to have a good laugh, frequently at her own expense." The only thing for which he could not forgive her was thrashing him at backgammon.

But none of this was work. Styles had changed and Joan Crawford had defiantly remained herself. There was talk that the American Film Institute was planning a tribute to her. Crawford called up a friend and complained, "I don't want a tribute, I want a job!"

But there would be no AFI tribute to Crawford, not then, not ever.

MANY OF CRAWFORD'S FRIENDS thought Christian Science was a strange enthusiasm, but what was perceptible about this phase of her life was a new clarity. She was dropping the affectations that had acted as armor between her and the world, just as she had dropped the comforting veil provided by vodka. James Baldwin wrote about "the ability to look at things as they are and survive your losses [and] . . . the zest, joy and capacity for facing and surviving disaster." It was back to basics—friends, solitude, those members of her family and extended family she liked and who liked her.

When it came to society in general, Crawford was a typical member of her generation. The fashions and music of the period left her cold (the miniskirt was "ridiculous"), and as for the women's movement, ""they don't want to be women." Someday, she said, the women in the movement "are going to have to find men and become women."

Occasionally she watched movies. She liked Glenda Jackson ("She has bite, but glamour, too"). Her last extensive interview came in June 1974, with Curtiss Anderson, who had been an editor at *Ladies' Home Journal* but never published the interview. The transcript shows her veering from Mother Courage to stark self-appraisal to Jerry Lewis–level sanctimony.

ON CHILDREN:

"[My] kids are fine, they're happy. I don't see the others because Cindy and Cathy, twin sisters, live so far away. . . . And the others have their own lives. I've never asked my children, 'You know, I raised you, now you owe me something.' That awful jazz. I raised them for their lives and that's the way it should be. Once they have them, leave them alone. If they need you, they'll call you. Usually collect."

ON EXPLOITATION:

"What's the difference between exploitation and publicity? I was sold to the public. I was a star when I was 19. If that's called exploitation, then I was exploited."

ON DOMESTICITY:

"You'd think I'd hate cooking after cooking my way through school for 30 children. . . . I learned by trial and error really, but I love it, it's great therapy for me.

"Housewife, homemaker, actress, and business woman: well, you have to love what you're doing or you don't do it well. And I think you can teach yourself to love it. I love challenges, and for example one day, damn it, I am going to make a souffle. I have never been able to be successful with that. It falls! You would think three elephants tromped through my kitchen every time I make one. Fortunately, I've never tried it with guests."

ON ACTING:

"We trained ourselves, there was no acting school. If you wanted to learn you left your own set when you weren't in front of the cameras and went over to other people's sets. Now, being exposed to Jean Hersholt, three Barrymores . . . if you can't learn from them, you'd better just stop. And get another job.

"I learned concentration from Lon Chaney. Total. You get your character, which I learned from him, and nothing should disturb that thought and that character."

ON THE MOVIE BUSINESS:

"People say it's tough now. It's *always* been a tough business. They don't train them. They get success too soon. They don't know how to handle the success when it comes too soon. They haven't served their years of apprenticeship, because I feel that acting is a tremendous craft, a beautiful craft. . . .

"Did you see Cybill Shepherd on the Academy Awards? She couldn't even read a cue card. My God, I read the review of *Daisy Miller* and I tell you I don't know how they get away with it. There isn't one [female star] on the screen today that has what we called audience identification. I can't identify with anyone on the screen today, or the characters they play.

"There are no Hepburns—Katharine or Audrey. There are no Garbos. And they're not training anyone."

ON FANS:

"I've never called them fans. I've called them friends. Before I could afford a secretary I used to write [letters] by hand. And I answered every one of them. I'm not going to have somebody write me and tell me they adored me in *Dancing Daughters* or *Modern Maidens* or any picture—and they're not going to get an answer from me? Why, I couldn't sleep nights. I really couldn't. I wouldn't know what to do with myself if I left them alone."

ON INDOMITABILITY AND VULNERABILITY:

"Thank God they think I'm vulnerable, which I am. I think that's what makes us strong, being so vulnerable, being able to be hurt. The only problem is . . . most women . . . become . . . bitter rather than indomitable, and the bitterness will always show. It starts in the eyes and ends with the mouth. . . .

"I guess if I had been born a man I would have been a Major General. Regimenting, regimenting, regimenting. Organized, organized, organized. Get it done, get it done, get it done. Do it at the right time. Get it over with. I even make notes at night on first things first to do the next day. And I mark it one, two, three, four, five, so when I get up I know [what] to do first."

ON HER COMPETITION:

"All the Jean Arthur comedies were just sensational as far as I was concerned. The Cary Grant–Irene Dunne pictures. *It Happened One Night*, Gable and Colbert. They had a knack for those lovely comedies. . . . The business balanced the heavy with the light. The epics with the comedies. That's timing."

ON BETTE DAVIS:

"She painted with a broader brush than I did. She very often telegraphed so you knew the ending. I [could see it] because that's my business. I'm not sure the public did, not that it harmed her performance. It sometimes didn't give me enough suspense storywise. But having seen all of her pictures, I felt that Blanche, my character [in *Baby Jane*], should underplay, underplay, underplay.

"I know it must have been very distracting to Bette. You see I've never rehearsed a violent or hysterical scene. I go through the motions, not emotions, and read my lines where they've marked me to walk and get it down perfect, so I don't have to look at my marks. I can *smell* them. . . .

"The scene where I have to go round and round and round after I look at the dead bird. I did the lid taking off, but I said to Mr. Aldrich, 'Please do not have the bird in there until you're ready to take it. I'll never get it as good as I'll get when I actually look at that dead bird the first time.'

"He knows how I work. [He told me] 'I'm going to have a camera in the ceiling . . .' I didn't know I was going to react, but the damndest noise, sound came out of me. It was much better than if it had been rehearsed. . . .

ON NORMA SHEARER:

"I had great rapport with all the notable stars in [*The Women*], a kidding relationship. Except with Miss Shearer. She didn't like me because I was playing Crystal who hated her supposedly, but she goaded me. She had my dresses changed constantly hoping that would throw me."

ON WATCHING DAILIES:

"I religiously looked at my dailies every night. And I studied myself. You see I was very lucky—all of us were—who grew up and had the golden years. But I wanted to know how I was coming out shooting out of continuity so much. And I would study and at end of the dailies I ask to talk to the director. Could we start reel two and run that close-up again? Cause we haven't shot three scenes before that. I don't think I was high enough. If I'm too high I can always cure it because when I do the preceding scenes I can always build and build and build and build. But if I'm not high enough [when] I shoot a very emotional scene . . .

ON WATCHING HERSELF ON-SCREEN:

"Once in a while I'll look at a picture I made. I'll look at everyone else—Bette Davis, Olivia de Havilland, Garbo—I'd be transfixed there. Once in a while I'll look at *Flamingo Road*. I wasn't happy with it at the time, I thought I could have done much better. And I've looked at that a couple times when it's on to see where I failed. Technically. The ones I know I did the best I could I don't bother to look at."

ON MOVIE MOGULS:

"(Harry) Cohn could make anyone a star, and he did that with Kim Novak. It takes far more to make a star than Harry Cohn, whom to me was not the brightest man in the world. It takes more than a makeup department, a hairdresser and a good script. It takes a little thing that's called talent. And a little thing that's called humanity. And a little thing that's called magic. And no one can give you that if you don't have it. You cannot pick it up like a hot dog. It has to be latent in you. You have to know that it's there and develop it and develop it and develop it. That is only up to you. We have to search and find it. No Harry Cohn can implant that in you."

WHAT FILLED UP SOME of Crawford's time were her grandchildren.

Once or twice a month her daughter Cathy would drive her grandchildren Casey and Carla to New York from their home in Allentown, Pennsylvania. They would arrive at their grandmother's apartment by midmorning, and Crawford would babysit the kids for the rest of the day and night while her daughter and son-in-law went out on the town.

"She was lovely," says her grandson Casey LaLonde. "She doted on us. She'd greet us in a housecoat and slippers, but with her face and hair perfectly made up. I always associate the smell of Estée Lauder's 'Youth Dew' with her. That was her scent. We loved to slide around on her parquet floors. Looking back, she was very indulgent. We were kids and could be rowdy, but she never told us to keep it down or anything like that. I think she enjoyed having us because it brought some youth back to her life.

"The only concession we had to make was that she didn't want to be called 'Grandma.' We always called her 'JoJo.'"

Casey noticed the plastic slipcovers on the furniture and loved climbing up onto the ledges by the sealed windows to look down on Manhattan. "I didn't know from Joan Crawford, but even as a kid I knew she was special. She had a cool apartment, full of neat things and knick-knacks from all over the world. The furniture was beautiful—William Haines chairs!—and then there were my mother's stories about traveling with her."

She would make lunch for her grandchildren. First she would roast a chicken, then pull the meat off the bones, add mayonnaise, salt, a little onion and serve chicken salad—not on sandwiches, just the salad itself. For dinner, she would gather the kids and head off to Chinatown, which Casey and Carla found wildly exotic. She never took them to the movies. The last picture she was offered was *Airport '77*, but she wasn't interested. "I'll never let them dump me in water and make me look like a hag," she snorted to a friend. Olivia de Havilland signed on for the film.

A workaholic turning her back on the profession that had defined her is not a normal circumstance, but her grandson says it was really very simple. "She couldn't stand the way she looked. She would have people over to the apartment and entertain, but she didn't want to go out and be photographed. In her mind she no longer looked like Joan Crawford. It wasn't 1929 or 1939 anymore, and she couldn't get past it. It's not that she looked awful, she just looked her age. She hadn't had any plastic surgery—she looked like a seventy-year-old woman, and to her that was unacceptable."

On her birthday, the apartment overflowed with flowers from friends and admirers, and that could bring out her humor. A friend walked in and was overcome by the smell of the flowers. "It looks like Campbell's Funeral Home," he said.

"I know," she replied. "I'm afraid to lie down."

Other than occasionally groping for a name, age had not particularly affected her. She had trouble remembering Angie Dickinson's name and would substitute "Burt Bacharach," and that was gradually replaced by singing a few bars of "Raindrops Keep Falling on My Head," which became a running gag.

Otherwise, like many people who had been semiretired by changing times, her world spun at a noticeably slower rate. She kept up a correspondence with Pearl Bailey. They generally addressed each other as "Sister Pearl" and "Sister Joan." "Your sentiments, your thoughts—they say so much," she wrote Bailey. "Would that we could always be talking to 'ourselves' as you have."

AT THE END OF 1974, Crawford made the decision to begin pulling back from the perpetual spinning wheel of her correspondence. She sent out a Christmas letter with this notice: "With the economy and the world situation as they are, next Christmas and thereafter, the time and energy I spend greeting each of you will be devoted instead to the charities which are so important to the less fortunate people, especially, children of the world. This, I believe, is in keeping with the truer meaning of Christmas. My heart is filled with thoughts of friendship and love for you now and always."

In February 1975, she wrote a costumer friend that "I know exactly what you mean by the new crop of directors, etc. out there. They not only don't know their A.B.C.'s, I'd say from working with some of them, they don't know their 'A' from a hot rock. I'll take the Wassermans and the Cukors any day. . . . You are not the only one looking for a job. You should read the so-called scripts submitted to me—Trash—Junk—I cannot finish reading half of them.

"This too will pass."

To another friend that same year, she wrote that her hair was now salt-and-pepper, but "silver I'm not. I wish I were—I'd love it." She turned down an interview from that same friend for *Modern Maturity* magazine because "I've been modern all my life and mature most of my life," and "it's the living of it, not the talking about it that's important."

In February 1975, Leonard Spigelgass asked her to present an award on behalf of Mayor Ed Koch. She replied that she was glad to hear from him, but she had been dieting all her life, had stopped, and had no interest in ever appearing in public again. It wasn't true—she never gained as much as five pounds over her movie weight, but it sufficed as an excuse.

The proximate cause for her withdrawal was a September 1974 event John Springer had for the publication of his book *They Had Faces Then*. He had convinced Rosalind Russell to attend and asked Crawford to attend as well. Crawford didn't particularly want to come, but she was close to Russell and liked Springer. According to Springer, she showed up and did her professional Joan Crawford appearance, then asked Springer, "Have I lived up to everything expected of me?"

Springer assured her that she had, and she left.

The next day the newspapers printed photographs of Russell and Crawford that were cruelly chosen to emphasize their age—Russell had terrible arthritis and was on heavy doses of steroids that puffed her up.

"If that's the way I look," Crawford told Springer, "I won't be seen anymore." The problem was simple: she had been a name-above-the-title star for more than forty-five years, and, through attrition, the nature of the business, and some of her own decisions, she no longer was. A component problem was that she had taken herself out of the movie swim by moving to New York. Age completed a picture she didn't want to see in the papers, not then, not ever.

In September 1976, she wrote to the actress Virginia Grey, with whom she had worked in *The Women*. She commiserated with her over leaving her home of decades for a garden apartment. Crawford could relate. "A year and a half ago, I gave up an eleven room apartment and moved into a [five] room one. With no help, now, I do everything myself—in addition to mail, paper work, filing. It has taken me a year to find a place for only the essentials. And I cannot tell you how happy I am. Content beyond belief! My lawyer's wife said, when she moved recently, 'Joan, dear, I'll never love anything again that can't love me back.' And you know she is right.

"Make a beautiful life for yourself in your new garden apartment, dear friend."

Isolation began to take a greater hold as she began to retreat behind the door of her apartment. She remained affable on the phone, but she began turning down dinner invitations from friends in her building, justifying her decision by saying, "I've spent my whole life being told what to do. I now have time to learn who I am."

With her friend Bob Rains, she was invariably solicitous and kind. Even though she had stopped sending Christmas presents and cards, she continued to send Rains boxes of apples for the holidays. When he had to go out of town for a while, she personally checked out a kennel where he boarded his dog.

The last time Jane Kesner Ardmore saw her was Thanksgiving 1976. Joan had prepared a fine meal for them at her apartment, and Ardmore remembered it as "an exquisite evening," but there was something missing. In one sense, she was the same Joan, but there was a perceptible sense of slowing down, as if she had downshifted from third gear to second. "And that had been one of the attractive things about her—her sense of purpose," said Ardmore.

The last time Myrna Loy saw Crawford, they went out to lunch at "21." As usual, Crawford hired a limousine. She was on her game, funny and effervescent. Loy complained about the age spots on her arms, and Crawford invited her back to her apartment to pick up some lotion her doctor had prescribed that banished the spots. "You know what's just as good?" she told Loy. "Horse pee!"

Crawford's friends were divided between those who saw her stagnating, and those who saw her settling into a life that, after a lifetime of striving, gave her what she needed—no more, but not much less either. One fan was invited to her apartment several times and spoke to her often. "She was mentally and physically energetic, vital as ever, and always without makeup, still incredibly beautiful. Her withdrawal from New York social life was self-imposed.

"'I have done it all and now I am living exactly the way I please.' She was a warm, thoughtful and generous friend who went out of her way to be helpful."

There were no more problems with Christina or Christopher because they hadn't spoken in years. It had long been obvious that most of Joan's family relationships were compromised, and some of her friends thought part of the problem was Crawford's tendency toward being hypercritical. Things had to be perfect. She would complain about a friend who didn't have good teeth or dressed badly.

There were things about Crawford that her secretary Betty Barker never understood, just learned to accept. Her attitude toward money, for instance. Crawford had no sense of her own finances—when she was in England she spent pounds as if they were dollars and didn't seem to grasp the difference. If she had grasped the difference she probably wouldn't have cared. Crawford didn't travel for pleasure, particularly, only for work, but she liked to hear stories of other people's experiences in other countries.

Running counter to all this were her more positive qualities—the generosity, the ribald sense of humor, the positive force field of her personality. Both Jane Kesner Ardmore and Betty Barker asserted that Crawford and Christina simply irritated each other. Barker said that Crawford bought Christina a Thunderbird when she was living in New York, but Christina got so many parking tickets for parking on the wrong side of the street during street cleanings that Crawford took the car back and sold it.

"Then Joan would take her back into the fold and something would happen," said Barker. "Christina would do something and Joan wouldn't like it, and they would be apart again." Ardmore said that Christina and Joan hadn't seen each other since 1972, and both of them seemed content to leave it that way.

LATE IN 1976, CRAWFORD began to lose weight. Betty Barker hadn't seen her for two years, but they talked nearly every day. "She let me know that her back hurt," said Barker. "She wasn't feeling so well. She wasn't drinking and she lost a lot of weight."

Barker believed that Crawford's interest in Christian Science was more of a flirtation than what she actually needed: a full-fledged commitment to something . . . or somebody. "She was disappointed in life. She let go of life. She deteriorated. Her physical body deteriorated. She had terrible backaches [and] she wasn't a hypochondriac." Barker would come to believe that on some level, "She was ready to die."

Jane Ardmore concurred. "Work was crucial to her. Love was crucial. Without either a demanding job or a beloved man, life had no meaning for Joan. She literally let go of living."

On those increasingly rare occasions when Crawford would see Curtiss Anderson and his wife, she would wrap her caftan tightly around herself and ask, "See how much weight I've lost?"

Crawford resisted all offers of help, but she was willing to bend to the extent of accepting help for her housebound dog Princess. Her neighbors the Mertzes would run Princess up and down the hallway to give the dog some exercise.

The pain in Crawford's back grew steadily worse, so she had a hospital bed installed in her bedroom but refused to see a doctor. The only medicine in the apartment was aspirin.

For Christmas 1976, she sent out some cards that contained a photograph taken by John Engstead a few months earlier—a soft-focus close-up of Crawford holding Princess. Crawford looks beautiful, the eyes still burning with light, but this time mixed with something softer, something like acquiescence. Accompanying the photograph was a note:

My hair is quite gray—but doesn't look it in b & w.
   Isn't Princess beautiful?
She is such a good friend.

Love, Joan.

She sent the same photograph to Vincent Sherman: "Vincent dear, This was taken the last week in September, 1976. The Shi Tzu is Princess Lotus Blossom Crawford—who is such a good friend. Isn't she beautiful?

"You can throw the photograph away—I won't mind."

One of the few serious letters she wrote was to Betty Barker, who was now a grieving widow. Crawford's handwriting and thoughts are still decisive:

My Very Dear Bettina,

Thank you for your Christmas card. How good of you to remember me at this special time of the year.

I know my dearest friend this Christmas without Norman will be very different for you—I know because I've been there.

It's been eighteen years since I've been there—it isn't easy—but God gives you the strength to live through it—and to learn to live with it—

The only thing that saved me—was and is to remember how fortunate we were to share so many glorious experiences and join together. Try it my darling—try to dwell only on the joys.

Constant love,

Joan

Jeanine Basinger got a note like the one Crawford sent Vincent Sherman and intuited its meaning. She promptly called Crawford and asked to see her. "It's interesting who's called," Crawford told her. "[But] I need to be private." Basinger told her that she understood, that it was fine she needed to do that. Crawford relented and told her she come could come for a short visit—no more than a half hour.

"She was leaning back on the couch," remembered Basinger. "Not lounging, resting against the couch. She asked about my husband and daughter and our mutual friends David Hayes and his wife. I did not see Mamacita—she had gone back to Germany. That's when I knew [Joan] was dying.

And then she said, "Now, Jeanine, after I'm gone, Christina is writing a book about me. I don't want you to feel upset. It's going to be upsetting, but I don't want you to be upset." In my midwestern way, I said, "How bad can it be?" And she sat up like a bolt and said, "How bad? You'll see how bad. It will be terrible." And then she fell back against the couch.

She looked beautiful. It was just before Christmas. I don't know how many people she let visit, but I did go.

I liked her very much. I still have a recipe she gave me for Jerusalem artichokes.

After that, Joan Crawford went to ground. She would talk on the phone, but sightings grew rare. Betty Barker said that Crawford steadfastly refused to see a doctor, even when her Christian Science practitioner recommended it. The practitioner hired readers with medical knowledge and kept Barker informed of the situation.

In April 1977, Crawford wrote a chatty letter to Harry Mines, referring to the rave reviews of Brooke Hayward's memoir *Haywire*, about the perils of being raised by Margaret Sullavan and Leland Hayward. "I just wonder what Margaret and Leland would have to say about raising those three children. That could be an enlightening book too, you know."

She was interested in Vincent Price's one-man show about Oscar Wilde, and she seems to have approved of his new wife Coral Browne. "They really know how to enjoy their life together," she noted. Her approval did not extend to Olivia de Havilland: "Her years in Europe have left her with a grandiose opinion of herself, I'm afraid."

She wrote to the teenager she had known as Gretchen and grudgingly taken on jaunts to the Cocoanut Grove more than fifty years before. Gretchen had long since changed her name to Loretta Young, but was happy to hear from her old friend, although there was a perceptible sense of her own losses in the letter:

> Joan Dear—Thanks for your sweet note—I loved it. You forget we were all beautiful then. The whole world was more beautiful then—and in all honesty I don't think we appreciated it. But then that's about par for youth. In a way it's

> too bad. It takes so long to mature—to understand the true values in life—
> I often wonder if I'm not really one of the very few slow ones.
>
> Still I plow ahead, hoping and praying each day to get a little closer to Him, a little farther from my own selfish self. . . . Forgive me for going on so—these are just some very personal thoughts which seemed to spill out to you—I only meant to let you know how much I appreciate your thinking enough of me to drop your note. God bless you Joan dear, I pray for your happiness or peace of mind or whatever you call it in your private heart, you know what I mean.
>
> Love, Gretch

The last time her grandchildren came to visit was in March 1977. Casey LaLonde remembered that she was "rail-thin." As they usually did, Casey and his sister began sliding around on the parquet floors. Their mother began to shush them, but Crawford told her to leave them alone. They were just being children.

In late April, Irving Mansfield called and asked how she was doing. "I'm slowly coming around," Crawford replied. "Slowly." Michael Korda called to thank her for a blurb she had given him for a book. She had Korda read it back to her, and she told him she "had spent hours writing it." He asked about getting together and she replied, "I don't think I want to see anybody yet." Carl Johnes spoke to her for the last time at the end of April. Her voice was weak and wavering, nearly unrecognizable.

To offers of help, she was kind but firm. As her neighbor Selma Mertz said, "She wouldn't let anyone help."

In the first week of May, she gave away Princess to a friend, a clear signal that she knew the end was near. By that time, she was down to about eighty pounds. Cooking was now impossible, so her favorite restaurants would send over food. Joan would call David Hartman, the host of *Good Morning America*, because she knew he kept odd hours and could drop off takeout without much trouble.

When Crawford and Myrna Loy talked on the phone, Crawford was cheerful, without a trace of self-pity. She never mentioned cancer to Loy or anybody else. As a result, Loy never quite realized her friend was dying.

In the first week of May the Mertzes checked on her, and it was obvious that Joan had dragged herself to the door to assure them that she was okay, which she clearly was not. When they got back to their apartment, Selma told her husband, "Marty, this woman is dying."

On May 9, the Mertzes again checked on her. "How are you, Joan? Is there anything I can do? Can I send out for food?"

"No," she replied. "Everything is fine."

Crawford knew better. She asked Margaret Campbell, her Christian Science practitioner, "Am I dying?"

"God is life," replied Campbell. "A sunbeam can't die. Your spirit has to go on, but not in this fleshly body."

Crawford took this in, then said, "That's the first time I could see that." A little later, she said, "I'm so at peace with the world that I'm even thinking good thoughts about Bette Davis."

May 10, 1977, was a Tuesday. That morning she insisted on getting out of bed to make breakfast for her housekeeper and Bernice Oshatz, a charter member of her fan club who had become a good friend. She went back to bed to watch some soap operas and called out to the women to inquire about their breakfast and make sure they were eating. Then she went silent.

At 10 a.m., the housekeeper went in to check on her and found Joan Crawford dead in bed. Although family and friends believed that she was suffering from pancreatic cancer, the death certificate would list her cause of death as "acute coronary occlusion."

Joan Crawford died precisely the way she had lived—on her terms.

CHAPTER TWENTY-TWO

ENEMIES, PERCEIVED OR ACTUAL, always served as a stimulant for Bette Davis, and now she was exultant. At a party that night, Davis walked up to Burt Reynolds and said, "Well, the cunt died today!" Reynolds had been talking to the film critic and professor Arthur Knight, whose eyes lit up. Davis noted his reaction and tried to recoup: "But she was *always* on time."

Three days after Joan Crawford's death, a private Christian Science service was held at the Campbell funeral home. The urn holding Crawford's ashes was surrounded by a bank of flowers. A Christian Science practitioner read selections from the Bible and Mary Baker Eddy. The ceremony lasted only fifteen minutes and was attended by all four of her adopted children, Myrna Loy, Anita Loos, Geraldine Brooks, and Franchot Tone's son Jeffrey. As per the instructions in her will, Joan Crawford's ashes were placed with those of Al Steele in a crypt at the Ferncliff Cemetery in Hartsdale, New York, about twenty-five miles from Manhattan.

Four days later, a memorial was held at All Souls Unitarian Church. Pearl Bailey sang "He'll Understand," and eulogies were spoken by Anita Loos, Geraldine Brooks, and Cliff Robertson. Her three daughters attended; her son Christopher did not.

People wrote to the trade papers with admiring Crawford stories. The literary agent H. N. Swanson contributed a remembrance about how Crawford believed he had saved her career with *Mildred Pierce*. For years afterward she would call or drop Swanson a note asking if he had anything suitable from James M. Cain, James T. Farrell, or Arthur Hailey. "She was really her own story department," wrote Swanson.

A month after Crawford's death, there was another memorial at the Academy of Motion Picture Arts and Sciences in Los Angeles. Anthony Slide, who was on the committee, recalled that "Walter Mirisch, who was the president of the Academy at the time, didn't want to do it, but Cukor insisted. Walter finally said that if Cukor paid for the theater, he could do it. Cukor put a committee together and ran the meetings himself. It was clear that he saw Crawford as a symbol of her era. Nobody we asked to speak turned us down."

Cukor had always been terribly moved by Crawford's earnestness, her willingness to go past her comfort zone, as well as by the devotion she showed to her friends—all qualities shared by Cukor.

On June 24, 1977, people stood in line at the Academy theater for hours waiting to get in. "Christopher Isherwood was there, wanted to get in early, and couldn't," said Slide. The speakers included John Wayne, Robert Young, Steven Spielberg, Myrna Loy, George Cukor, Leonard Spigelgass, and Fay Kanin, as well as publicist Emily Torchia, film archivists Robert Cushman and Ron Haver, and publicist turned producer Walter Seltzer. Spielberg told the audience that "She always treated me like I knew I was doing, which I didn't. And I loved her for that."

Myrna Loy flew in from New York, and Howard Strickling drove in from San Diego. The silent film star Carmel Myers paid tribute to an eager young girl from Texas as "living on nothing but coffee for two weeks so she would be slim enough for the camera."

Cukor recalled Crawford's personality and gifts with the sympathy and the deft insight into character that marked his work:

> She was the perfect image of the movie star, and, as such, largely the creation of her own indomitable will. She had, of course, very remarkable material to work with: a quick native intelligence, tremendous animal vitality, a lovely figure and, above all, her face, that extraordinary sculptural construction of lines and planes, finely chiseled like the mask of some classical divinity

from fifth-century Greece. It caught the light superbly, so that you could photograph her from any angle, and the face moved beautifully. . . .

The nearer the camera, the more tender and yielding she became—her eyes glistening, her lips avid in ecstatic acceptance. The camera saw, I suspect, a side of her that no flesh and blood lover ever saw. . . .

I thought Joan Crawford could never die. And as long as celluloid holds together, as long as Hollywood means anything to anyone, she never will.

When it was all over, an exultant Cukor sent out thank-you letters to the members of the Committee. "We did it!" he wrote. "We did it!"

JOAN CRAWFORD'S ESTATE AMOUNTED to just under $1.4 million, including cash, stocks, her percentages of *What Ever Happened to Baby Jane?*, *Berserk!*, and a few other pictures. (She had evidently sold off her piece of *Sudden Fear* years earlier, as it was not included in the estate inventory.) The value of her percentage of *Baby Jane* was estimated as $30,733.92—a massive understatement. Her Academy Award for *Mildred Pierce* was estimated as having "no value."

Her stock holdings included 2,246 shares of Exxon, 250 shares of General Cinema, 2,400 shares of PepsiCo, 800 shares of Standard Brands, and an apartment whose worth was estimated at $76,500. Her life insurance policy was only worth $7,000.

She left bequests of $77,500 apiece to her daughters Cathy and Cindy, while her secretary, makeup man, and wardrobe woman received amounts that ranged from $5,000 to $35,000. The rest of the estate was spread out among a long list of her favorite charities such as the USO and the American Cancer Society. A few months after her death, her apartment sold for $85,000.

The estate inventory included 35 travel books, 20 art books, 18 volumes of George Bernard Shaw, 17 volumes of Shakespeare, 12 volumes of Oscar Wilde, and 150 other miscellaneous books. She had leather-bound scripts of *Mildred Pierce*, *The Damned Don't Cry*, *Daisy Kenyon*, *Sudden Fear*, and *Humoresque*. Among the pieces of jewelry was an engraved bracelet that read, "Joan Darling,

You are all that Woman was Meant to Be." She had kept dozens of pieces of Al Steele's jewelry—watches, rings, tie clasps.

Crawford's will directed that her profit percentages be paid directly to the Motion Picture Home, a longtime favorite charity of hers. Her daughter Cathy inherited all her personal property.

Why didn't she leave the twins more than five-figure bequests? "She expected them to be self-sufficient," said her grandson Casey Lalonde. "She didn't want her children to rely on her for their lifestyle. She had come from nothing and saw no reason why they couldn't be responsible for their own lives."

Her will ended with a curt closing sentence: "It is my intention to make no provision herein for my son Christopher or my daughter Christina for reasons which are well known to them."

In November of 1977, Christina and Christopher sued to invalidate Crawford's will, claiming that their mother "was not competent to make her will in that at that time she was not of sound mind and memory and/or under the undue and unlawful influence of one Jerome LaLonde and wife. . . .

> That on October 28, 1976 [the date of the will], deceased was suffering from an acute and advanced cancerous condition. . . . That on October 28, 1976, deceased was experiencing intense physical pain due to said cancerous conditions. . . .
>
> That deceased was a Christian Scientist and was not under a physician's care in respect of her cancerous condition. . . .
>
> That on or about December, 1974, decedent experienced a serious fall occasioned by drinking which inflicted severe injury to her head. . . . The Last Will and Testament of the deceased was the direct result of a mind and will distorted by her intense pain and/or clouded by alcohol.

The petition went on to claim that Cathy LaLonde and her husband "took deliberate advantage of decedent's seclusion and weakened and distorted mental and physical condition to insinuate themselves into the decedent's favor. . . . That contestants and deceased were always bound by the closest ties of filial and parental affection." Christina and Christopher demanded "parity," i.e., a payout of $77,000 apiece, while Christina also wanted a bust of Crawford from 1941 that had "For Christina" inscribed into the base.

The complaint asked for a jury trial and that the will not be admitted to probate. This meant that legally Crawford would be deemed to have died intestate, meaning the estate would have been divided equally between all four children.

There were all sorts of problems with the suit, among them the fact that Crawford had been sober for several years prior to making her will. James McNally, the guardian ad litem, wrote that "in my opinion, the contestants would not be successful [but] it may well be however, that . . . the theory of monomania could be made out for the consideration of the jury."

He was referring to a supposed *idée fixe* on Crawford's part that Christina had been intent on seducing Al Steele, which was supported by a deposition by Steele's valet: "I was well aware that Joan Crawford was passionately jealous of Christina and extremely resentful of any attention paid Christina by Alfred Steele. . . . Her perception of Christina's and Alfred Steele's relationship was totally distorted."

In a deposition, Christina testified that she hadn't seen her mother since 1972 and hadn't spoken to her for "approximately four years, maybe five years." Christopher, who was working as a telephone lineman, had recently fallen from his hydraulic lift and didn't testify.

Early in 1978, Crawford's belongings began to be auctioned off—two hundred pairs of shoes, a mink fedora, a Balenciaga dress with matching hat that brought $500. Other dresses went for $274 to $500 for lots of six. A carton of sheets and pillowcases went for $275. The leather-bound script from *Mildred Pierce* went for $625, Clifford Odets's script for *Humoresque* brought $600.

There was a gold charm bracelet, a pair of gold earrings engraved but unsigned. One earring was inscribed, "Let me whisper again." The other: "I love you." Also on offer were oil paintings, scrapbooks, steamer trunks, and 250 pairs of false eyelashes.

Andy Warhol showed up and bought six dresses as wardrobe for "transvestites" in an upcoming film. Cumulatively, the auction brought in $42,850, while another auction at Christie's brought in more than $150,000.

In May of 1978, Christina and Christopher offered to settle for $77,500, the amount to be split between them, but they wanted the settlement to be free from estate taxes. They finally settled for $55,000 tax-free, which cost the estate about $80,000.

That same month, a year after Crawford's death, a boxed ad appeared in the back pages of *Variety*. There was a picture of Crawford, a headline reading "In Remembrance" with the date of her death. It was signed by some of her neighbors in the apartment building, friends, and Princess, her Shih Tzu.

It was at this point that news broke about the impending publication of Christina Crawford's memoir *Mommie Dearest*. The agent Bob Bookman at CAA sold the paperback rights for $750,000, with another $300,000 for the film rights.

"The movie deal was with Frank Yablans at Paramount," remembered Bookman.

Christina was testy. Not outrageously so, but testy. I got a call from Christina about her insecurity regarding Yablans. "Would you feel better if your husband was a producer?" I asked her.

"Oh, that would make such a difference!"

So her husband became a producer on the picture, which meant Faye Dunaway's husband also had to be made a producer. Neither of the husbands had ever had anything to do with movies, which shows how much a producer credit means in Hollywood.

I believed the book, but I had no reason to think otherwise, and it was in my professional interest to believe it. The odd thing was that all of Christina's bitterness was in the book, but it didn't go away.

Mommie Dearest was published in October 1978. It basically characterized Crawford as Cruella de Vil, a vindictive whirlwind of rage and grievance fueled by alcohol. Christina related stories of being locked in a closet with the lights off; of night raids with her mother assaulting her while screaming, "No wire hangers!"; beatings with a bottle of Bon Ami cleanser; rage fits resulting in her mother cutting down every rosebush in the middle of the night, then moving on to an orange tree.

Christina even accused her mother of being a lesbian with a story about her making a pass at one of Christina's nurses. All of this infuriated Betty Barker, especially the lesbian accusation. "I know that full story," said Barker. "I was a fan of Joan's then, and the nurse was a friend of mine. Joan fired her because she was letting Christopher smoke in the basement of the house on Bristol Ave. (The gas water heater, etc. were all nearby.) He was only twelve years old at the time [and] the nurse smoked like a fiend.

"Then the fired nurse saw Christina in New York later, she felt she had to give a reason for not still working for Joan, and she came up with that ridiculous lie. What's more—the fired nurse continued to send birthday cards and Christmas cards to Joan for years afterward. Joan never answered them. Joan was not a lesbian, for God's sake."

The book's comprehensive catalogue of abusive hysteria convinced the credulous and damaged Crawford's reputation for more than a generation. Even people who thought Joan had been too demanding of the children believed that "Christina's book is too much the other way," as screenwriter Catherine Turney put it.

The plethora of specific detail was superficially convincing, even when common sense dictated otherwise. Arthur Bell of *The Village Voice* presciently prophesied that while readers would undoubtedly salivate over the horror show, there would be little resulting sympathy for Christina.

Mommie Dearest was the first book in a mini-genre that can be categorized as "What My Vicious Celebrity Relative Did to Me." Other contributions focused on Bing Crosby (general misanthropy and corporal punishment of his sons), Olivia de Havilland (insufficient affection toward her sister Joan Fontaine), and, yes, Bette Davis (rampant narcissism and even more rampant alcoholism).

All of these books sold well and eventually went away without particularly distorting ongoing public appreciation for their subjects. But *Mommie Dearest* created an entirely new narrative for Joan Crawford and made her a camp joke. If Crawford wasn't already dead, *Mommie Dearest* would have killed her.

Corroborating Christina's narrative was her brother Christopher. "I hated the bitch," he told a reporter from *Newsday* in what seems to have been his only interview. "She was a fantastic actress, but she was not a mother. She was not a family. I honestly to this day do not believe that she ever cared for me."

Christopher was still working as a lineman for an electrical company on Long Island and making $200 a week. He said his mother had basically washed her hands of him by 1961. He had attended ten schools before he was thirteen, and there had been numerous involvements with the police. Three months before her death she had refused to take a phone call from him.

At the time of the *Newsday* interview, Christopher was married to his second wife, while his seventeen-year-old daughter had just given birth to his first grandchild. He needed dental work and had small scars on his face and large ones on his back from jumping onto a barbed-wire fence to escape an exploding mortar in Vietnam. He referred to Crawford as "J.C."—what a psychiatrist would call a distancing mechanism.

He thought Christina's book "very factual. . . . The book wasn't written for greed or for revenge. She's doing it for reasons that probably a lot of people won't understand. I think she needed to write that book, to let her conscience be at peace. It's a love story, a very, very sad love story. Tina cared about that bitch. She still cares."

The people who knew Crawford in her Hollywood days were, with very few exceptions, livid at what they regarded as a brutalist fiction.

Douglas Fairbanks Jr. thought the book was "about someone I never knew, only someone with the same name. But I don't recognize this person as anybody I ever knew!"

Franchot Tone's son Pat was deeply offended by the book's obnoxious Poor Little Rich Girl tone that attempted to have it both ways—enumerating all the considerable privileges Christina's adoptive parentage gave her, while focusing on what she characterized as neglect born of alcoholism and/or egocentricity as well as incidents of physical abuse Pat believed to be pure invention. "Those of us who were raised by actors and actresses had to learn to make allowances for the fact that they lived by and through emotions," said Tone. "As for the abuse, I didn't believe Christina for a second."

The writer and actress Illeana Douglas, the granddaughter of Melvyn Douglas, remembers a conversation between her grandfather—who had made four films with Crawford—and Myrna Loy at Douglas's apartment at 50 Riverside Drive in New York.

"Myrna was close friends with Joan, and my grandfather and Myrna were close friends as well. I would see her often.

> The book had just been published and Myrna was saying that nothing in the book was true, that it was all made up, and she couldn't understand it. She asked my grandfather if he had ever seen anything like that.
>
> "No," he said. He only mentioned Crawford bringing the kids to the set dressed up like little dolls, with perfect manners.
>
> They continued to have a conversation about why would somebody that had, in their perception, such a nice childhood, write such a terrible book about their mother. They were both adamant that they had never observed any kind of negative behavior on Joan's part toward her children in any shape or form. Myrna was deeply distressed. My grandfather always referred to Crawford as "Joanie"—always very affectionate toward her.

And so there evolved two diametrically competing narratives. The first was that the book amounted to an act of matricide—a revenge narrative and, beneath that, a classic example of failure punishing success. The other was that it was reportage, more in sorrow than in anger.

Countering all this were steadfast denials from Cathy and Cindy Crawford that anything remotely like what Christina described ever happened. It had always been clear that there was a demarcation between the children. Christina and Christopher were difficult at best, rebellious at worst, while Cathy and Cindy were basically well-behaved.

Both Cathy and Cindy insisted to their own dying days that they received nothing but love from their mother. Cathy said, "Our childhood, our feelings and memories of our mother are in complete contrast to those described in Christina's [book]. Her twisted lies should not be given credence." Cathy's characterization of Crawford's mothering was "firm" but never abusive. Otherwise, Cathy would never have allowed her mother to babysit her own children.

"My mother always made it clear that when they were home, Joan was

200% there for her kids," says Casey Lalonde. "She did not delegate to nannies or au pairs. Yet the book insists she was beating children, while the other two kids in the house never saw or heard it."

"I think the book reflects Christina's jealousy and bitterness towards mother," said Cathy. "When you raise a child and live with them you know the child, and mother knew Christina. And I think she tried to keep Cindy and I away from that. . . . I think Christina wanted to be Joan Crawford."

"I almost always knew that Tina hated mother," said Cindy. "She always used her. What she wanted was to have everything, to be everything Mother had and was."

According to Cindy, the worst punishment she ever received was breakfasting on the previous night's dinner that she had refused to eat. Cathy said that the worst punishment she ever got was a spanking with a hairbrush after she and her sister used their beds as trampolines. Other punishments were mundane—standing in the corner.

"One last thing: I never saw my mother drunk in my life. Never saw her out of control. She didn't drink. She sipped."

For most of Crawford's friends, the book seemed to be yet another example of a relationship that had always been compromised. "[Christina and Joan] had their ups and downs all the time," said Betty Barker, Crawford's secretary. Barker agreed with Myrna Loy's opinion that Christina was in psychological competition with Crawford—her determination to undertake an acting career an example of that. "She wanted to be better than Joan," said Barker.

Barker also said that some of Christina's stories were logistically impossible; that Crawford wouldn't come home from the studio till 7 or 8 p.m. and would be in a state of complete exhaustion. She would have one drink, a quick meal, then go to bed with her script. She didn't have either the inclination or the strength to chop down trees and rosebushes in the middle of the night.

Jim Brochu knew Barker and considered her a "dear, dear friend" who embodied the entire history of Hollywood. "She was particularly incensed about the wire hanger story," said Brochu. "'It never happened,' she said. *'It never happened!'*"

Jane Kesner Ardmore also came to Crawford's defense, calling her "one of the most sensitive, insecure human beings I've ever known. . . . She painted on that slash of red mouth, those black and brazen brows the way a male actor dons a beard and swirls a cape—for courage. Under the makeup—and she never wore it in her home—was a far more beautiful, very tender, woman's face."

In 1990, Cindy and her son took a trip to Los Angeles and looked up Jim Brochu. "Joan had been dead for thirteen years at this point," he remembered. "We met for lunch at Universal, and she told me that they had taken the tour on a tram, and she pointed out her mother's dressing room. 'The people on the tram looked at me like I was crazy,' she said. She was still very upset about Christina. 'Why would she lie like that?'"

Cindy told Brochu that Crawford would swim with the twins in the pool, and sometimes the twins would sleep outside in sleeping bags placed by one end of the pool—not in the hopes that they might drown, but in the Brentwood version of camping out.

"I'll miss her all my life, and so will . . . [my] children. I loved being with her, talking with her, as an adolescent, as an adult. She was so wise and realistic, such a good friend."

Cathy said that "Mommie was very affectionate. My twin sister and I used to crawl into bed with her in the morning and she would like that, and we did, too. I always liked riding with her on our holiday trips to Carmel. I would snuggle up to her while she drove up there. We always had wonderful times during our visits to Carmel. Mommie didn't have to go to work, and it was so beautiful there."

Cindy believed that "What mother wanted me to learn was what life is really about. She handed us nothing on a platter like other movie star mothers. We didn't get Grand Prixs to run around in. She said if you want to light up a cigarette, light it in front of me, not behind my back. We used to light mother's and father's cigarettes and choke afterwards. She offered us $1000 if we wouldn't smoke until we were 21. We both forfeited the money.

"She wanted us to be realistic; she wanted us to be prepared for life."

.500 is a great average for baseball, not so good for children. Dorothy Manners said that the primary reason Crawford was not a total success as a mother was simply that it didn't come naturally. "She saw children as a necessary adjunct to her life and career. All her friends had children, so . . ."

William Haines put it another way: "Cranberry is about as domestic as a hitching post."

THE FILM VERSION OF *Mommie Dearest* ran through an assortment of screenwriters good (Abraham Polonsky, Robert Getchell), indifferent (James Kirkwood), and lousy (too many to name, among them the producer, Frank Yablans). Anne Bancroft had been pegged to star until shortly before production began, when she was replaced by Faye Dunaway. Franco Zeffirelli backed out of directing and was replaced by Frank Perry. The result was a necrotic catastrophe so over-the-top it functioned as its own Carol Burnett parody. The film's sole positive attribute was that it seriously damaged the careers of everyone connected with it.

IN MAY OF 1979, on the second anniversary of Crawford's death, another full-page ad appeared in *Variety*. It carried the names of dozens of family, friends, and fans: Betty Barker, Jeanine Basinger, Robert Bloch, Jim Brochu, George Cukor, Sydney Guilaroff, Edith Head, Van Johnson, Crawford's daughters Cathy and Cindy, Adela Rogers St. Johns, Myrna Loy, Robert Nathan, Mrs. Jack Oakie, Cesar Romero, Howard Strickling, Barry Sullivan, Pascal Franchot Tone, Joan Evans, Robert Young, and dozens of others. In the center of the page was a picture of Joan late in life. Underneath was her signature and beneath that was this: "Your Friends Love You and Miss You. May 10, 1977."

The ad ran for ten years, always on the anniversary of her death.

After the haggling over the estate ended, disbursements finally began in the summer of 1979. At that point, the law firm representing the estate submitted a bill for $125,000, slightly less than 10 percent of the estate's value. The state of New York objected: "If the legal fee is fixed as requested, proponent's law firm will realize more from this estate than charitable residuary beneficiaries." The legal fees were eventually set at $90,000.

THIS EXTRAORDINARY WOMAN, THIS extraordinary life.

One writer enumerated Joan Crawford's more prominent characteristics: "She was regal, vulgar, cold, warm, highly sexed, puritanical, egotistical, modest, commanding, insecure, tender, tough, principled, amoral, kind, cruel, generous and selfish."

In other words, she embodied all the contradictory facets of the human condition.

Jim Brochu said that the image that defined her was only a small component of her actual personality. "Her image was glamour, but she was very down-to-earth. I can still see her caring for a houseguest while wearing a babushka and making bouillabaisse. She wanted to nurture because she had never felt nurtured herself."

The film historian Anthony Slide remarked about her willingness to tend strangers with the same level of care she gave to close friends. "She has been underappreciated in terms of the kind of human being she was. She was extremely generous and helped a lot of people.

"*Mommie Dearest*? Basically disgusting and probably counterfactual. The equivalent of Damien Chazelle's film *Babylon*."

In her career, Joan Crawford first anticipated, then dramatized every new social trend that affected women—the eroticized good-time girls of the 1920s; the downtrodden but striving shopgirls with the water at their chins in the dismal 1930s; the neurotic, fatalistic dames of the 1940s who earned money and position but at a higher cost than anticipated; and finally, the simultaneously independent and discontented career women of the 1950s.

She didn't hover above the audience as did, for instance, Garbo or Dietrich, but as one critic noted "marched through life at the head of an invisible host, demanding fealty from her fans, who saw in her broad-shouldered, smoldering . . . allure a transcendental version of their everyday experience."

She invited the audience to share in her tragedies, to revel in her successes. In some respects, she was like many—most?—people: she understood friendship more than she understood love. In other ways, she was one of a kind—she had a profound, instinctive knowledge of what it takes to succeed in the world, and for a long time she was willing to pay the price.

"What is the strength of any artist?" Jim Brochu asked. "Passion! Always passion! Joan *loved* what she did. She *loved* being an actress. And like so many actors, she wanted to hide herself in other people, hide her weaknesses, hide her horrific childhood."

But she never disguised her shabby beginnings or her romantic flailings, and the audience responded to her emotional honesty. She didn't hide from her audience; she was one of them writ large, avid for life and love, or, if she couldn't get love, for passion.

It was George Cukor who understood her particular gift, her specific power: "Whether you liked her or did not like her on the screen, you could not deny her existence nor deny her quality."

It's all there in her movies. It's even there in her stills, which function as extensions of her performances. As Mick LaSalle wrote, "A picture of Crawford was and is an effort at intimate engagement. She's connecting with somebody. *You*, to be specific. And, in that moment of connection, time disappears. Look at that face—modern, arch, knowing, passionate, ready to eat the world. . . . That's *today* looking right at you."

"She had qualities that are admirable, and don't grow on trees," said Jeanine Basinger. "The kind of loyalty and concern and attention she paid to people. Birthdays, her generosity with gifts. And she was *interested*—she wasn't just talking about movies or her career. She always wanted to know what I was reading. And she was a very good actress. That's an aspect that is not written about. She totally fulfilled the concept of gorgeous movie star and then she went far beyond that."

On the personal level, there was, according to Betty Barker, her "good sense—she was loyal to her friends, and she had far more great qualities than bad ones."

And there's something else, something fundamental. Her intrinsic electric current, her emotional size, meant she was incapable of being dull. From the beginning of her career to its end, she projects a restless energy. George Cukor put it best: "Her real talent is the way she moves. All she has to do is walk across the room, from one side to the other, and you notice that something very special is happening. The way she carries herself, the way her arms move, the position of her head . . . She attracts attention simply by moving and she arrests you. She wouldn't have to open her mouth—just walk—and she would be superb."

The cumulative message she projected was that life is often grim, satisfaction elusive, and happiness so expensive many people can't afford it. Despite that knowledge, she tended people the same way she tended her stardom, probably the way she hoped someone would tend her, but only Al Steele filled the bill. "In private life she was a lovable, sentimental creature," said George Cukor. "A loyal and generous friend, very thoughtful; dear Joan Crawford, she forgot nothing—names, dates, obligations."

Although she didn't have Stanwyck's protean versatility, she gave some performances Stanwyck probably envied. What she did have was a restless sensuality, an equally vivid vulnerability, and a rage to succeed. The result was that Joan Crawford, as Jeanine Basinger wrote, "personified the dreams and disappointments of the American woman for over four decades."

"People are always asking me if there's anything I regret, or would change," Crawford said. "The answer is no! If I hadn't had the pain, I wouldn't be me."

She once said that her mother was proud of her when she went to college for that single semester because she "thought she had the smartest child in the world. I didn't dare tell her [the truth]. Laundry and scrubbing probably were better for me than algebra."

Maybe, maybe not, but she needed to think that it was, needed to think that experience was the best teacher.

We live in a different show business world than the one Joan Crawford inhabited. Stars are different now, as are their careers, their friendships, and their relationship to the audience, but Illeana Douglas believes that Joan Crawford and Elizabeth Taylor were and still are the ultimate female movie stars.

> They fulfilled the idea of what a star is, and at the same time they let the fans know that Crawford and Taylor were roles. They were playing the part, and they made it look effortless. We were endlessly fascinated by the different aspects of their personalities, but we also knew they had sacrificed everything to be what we wanted them to be. They created, curated, and maintained an image almost as if it was an altar.

And they made pivotal choices in their acting career that cemented their legacy. Crawford's choices were so perceptive. Her ability to use clothes as a character choice, to define who the character was? Unmatched.

Crawford's decisions about when to make a turn—to make *Grand Hotel*, to make *The Women*, to make *Mildred Pierce*, to make *Johnny Guitar*. Taylor's decision to make *Who's Afraid of Virginia Woolf?* They knew the right time to do movies that changed their image and bolstered it at the same time. They knew the right time to poke fun at their image.

And Crawford's stunt when she won the Oscar and invited the cameraman into her bedroom! You have to admire someone who could pull that off. That is someone so in command of their legacy, of what you need to do to maintain yourself as a brand.

And they both had across-the-board audience appeal. Straight men admired them, gay men admired them. Women admired them and wanted to look like them. And they had massive sex appeal—their on-screen roles normalized the enjoyment and allure of sex, of love, of affairs, of love gone wrong. They made it clear that they liked sex, that they had human desires that needed to be fulfilled.

There is, of course, another similarity between Crawford and Taylor—both ended their careers ignominiously, Crawford with low-rent horror pictures, Taylor with shabby TV movies and *The Flintstones*. It doesn't matter. Nobody watches *Trog*, nor should they, but *Grand Hotel* and *Mildred Pierce* are always playing somewhere.

And there's something else. They were special actresses, but also special women. Both Crawford and Taylor sustained lifelong relationships, not just with their fans, but with friends. It's not that way anymore.

"What I have found with modern actresses I have gotten to know is they take you in and you'll be their best friend," says Illeana Douglas.

But if you get too close, you're shut down. Nobody can shut you down like a star actress. Suddenly you're best friends, and you're in the inner circle. Then something doesn't go right and suddenly you're out. The expectation from huge stars is that you're part of their machine twenty-four hours a day.

You're there to give them ideas and keep their secrets. But at a certain point, they get afraid. It's all transactional.

In the past, stars accepted that being a movie star was a role, and when you weren't on-camera you could be yourself because you had more protection.

Joan Crawford got a lot of grief for selling Pepsi-Cola, but look around—every single star actress today has a side hustle. Every. Single. Star. Actress.

Geraldine Brooks told of Crawford taking her aside when they made *Possessed* in 1947. Brooks was only twenty-two years old, and Crawford wanted to teach her the self-protective necessities that went into being a movie actress. She explained the magic of the key light, the primary illuminating source for the crucial close-ups.

"Look, honey," Crawford told her. "That's your light. Don't ever forget it. Don't look at it, but always know where it is. It's yours!"

Lucille LeSueur and Billie Cassin struggled to find their light because they were beset by waves of insecurity, by an overwhelming sense of all the things they weren't. By the time Joan Crawford began to understand her power and leverage her need, she had mastered the part she played for the rest of her life, a part that enabled her to move through the screen and into the emotional lives of her audience.

As both actress and woman, she forged ahead, determined to outrun squalor and damage, to transcend the fear that coexisted with the other primary qualities she brought to the movies, and to her life: courage . . . sexual energy . . . vitality . . . defiance.

Joan Crawford learned to love the light, and the light loved her back.

ACKNOWLEDGMENTS

THIS BOOK BEGAN MORE than ten years ago on the Turner Classic Movies Cruise. Casey LaLonde and I were both guests, and I was fascinated by his presentation of his grandmother's home movies. Here was a Joan Crawford I had never seen before—freckled, playful, unposed to the point of dishevelment, surrounded by children, dogs, friends, and one anonymous (at the time) lover.

That screening impelled me to begin collecting string for this book. Casey gave me access to all of his memories and files regarding his grandmother, asked for no permissions or approval of the manuscript. I thank him for his trust and hope that I have given him a picture of a woman in full that he knew only as a doting grandmother.

I've been a Simon & Schuster author for more than thirty years—the second-longest relationship of my life. Bob Bender agreed with me that Joan Crawford's life was worth closer examination than had previously been made of it, and edited the book with his accustomed finesse. Bob edited and published eight of my books, the longest editor/writer relationship I have ever had and the happiest. After Bob's retirement, Mindy Marqués saw the book through to publication in what I trust is the beginning of a beautiful friendship.

The unflappable Johanna Li made all of our lives consistently smoother than they otherwise would be. Fred Chase did his usual impeccable copy edit and saved me from bursts of irrational enthusiasm, among other failings. And a special shout-out to Jackie Seow, who designed the stunning dust jacket, and to my agent Luke Janklow, who carries on the traditions of his father Mort—a great agent and a great man.

The book would have been impossible without the help of my astonishingly skilled researcher, Will Coates, who, among other triumphs, found a husband of Crawford's mother who no one, probably including Crawford, knew existed. Will is irreplaceable as both researcher and valued friend.

While Will set about finding the archival Joan Crawford, I set about finding people who had known her, as well as plundering my files for people I interviewed about Crawford who were no longer aboveground. This mosaic of documentation and memory, as well as my own long-gestating ideas about stardom in the early and middle twentieth century, made the book possible.

Will and I express our gratitude to: at USC, Bree Russell, curator of the Warner Bros. Archive, and Sandra Garcia-Myers for access to the Robert Aldrich papers.

At the Margaret Herrick Library of the Academy of Motion Picture Arts and Sciences: Louise Hilton, Clare Denk, Caroline Jorgenson.

The entire staff at UCLA Special Collections.

At the Shubert Archive: Mark E. Swartz for bringing to light previously unpublished photographs of Lucille LeSueur as a chorus girl, not to mention playbills.

My friend Michael Blake supplied some rare photographs of Crawford in her early days at MGM that captured her vibrancy as well as her connection with Lon Chaney. Leonard Maltin, whom I've known for nearly sixty (!) years, helped out as well, while Alan Rode rode shotgun with sage advice and constant support.

Special thanks to Suzanna Francis Charlton, the daughter of Freddie Francis, for sharing Joan Crawford's letters to her father.

I owe a considerable debt to Karen Swenson, author of a fine biography of Greta Garbo, who called me out of the blue and offered me the interviews she gathered for a Crawford biography she began but never finished thirty years ago. Karen's generosity was and is overwhelming.

So is the patience of Lynn Kalber Eyman, by my side for nearly forty years of movies, travel, and laughter, not always in that order. Her steadfast love makes everything else possible.

For their time and insights regarding Joan Crawford both in the past and the present, my gratitude to: Jeanine Basinger, Michael Blake, Bob Bookman, Kim Braden, Jim Brochu, Clarence Brown, Terry Castle, Illeana Douglas, Douglas Fairbanks Jr., Julie Garfield, Robert Gottlieb, William Harbach, Michael Korda, David Ladd, John Lee Mahin, Tom Mankiewicz, Maurice Rapf, Burt Reynolds, Joseph Ruttenberg, Anthony Slide, David Stenn, Pascal (Pat) Tone, Robert Wagner, Doug West.

—Scott Eyman

*Los Angeles, Venice, Santorini, Istanbul,
Lone Pine, New York City, West Palm Beach*

BIBLIOGRAPHY

Agee, James. *Agee on Film*. New York: Modern Library, 2000.
Allen, Woody. *Apropos of Nothing*. New York: Arcade Publishing, 2020.
Bakewell, William. *Hollywood Be Thy Name*. Metuchen: Scarecrow Press, 1991.
Balducci, Anthony. *Lloyd Hamilton: Poor Boy Comedian of Silent Cinema*. Jefferson: McFarland, 2009.
Basinger, Jeanine. *Silent Stars*. New York: Knopf, 1999.
———. *The Star Machine*. New York: Knopf, 2007.
Basinger, Jeanine, and Sam Wasson. *Hollywood: The Oral History*. New York: Harper, 2022.
Bawden, James, and Ron Miller. *Conversations with Classic Film Stars*. Lexington: University of Kentucky Press, 2016.
———. *You Ain't Heard Nothin' Yet*. Lexington: University of Kentucky Press, 2017.
Behlmer, Rudy, ed. *Memo from David O. Selznick*. New York: Viking, 1972.
Behlmer, Rudy. *Inside Warner Bros*. New York: Viking, 1985.
Black, Shirley Temple. *Child Star*. New York: McGraw-Hill, 1988.
Blake, Michael. *Lon Chaney: The Man Behind the Thousand Faces*. Vestal: Vestal Press, 1990.
———. *A Thousand Faces*. Vestal: Vestal Press, 1995.
Blake, Robert. *Tales of a Rascal*. Los Angeles: Black Rainbow, 2011.
Blauvelt, Christian. *Hollywood Victory: The Movies, Stars and Stories of World War II*. Philadelphia: Running Press, 2021.
Bogdanovich, Peter. *Who the Devil Made It*. New York: Knopf, 1997.
———. *Who the Hell's in It*. New York: Knopf, 2004.
Brown, David. *Let Me Entertain You*. New York: Morrow, 1990.

Buscombe, Edward, et al. *BFI Dossier Number 1: MGM*. London: British Film Institute, 1980.
Chandler, Charlotte. *Not The Girl Next Door*. New York: Simon & Schuster, 2008.
Coleman, Terry. *Olivier*. New York: Henry Holt, 2005.
Cowie, Peter. *Joan Crawford: The Enduring Star*. New York: Rizzoli, 2009.
Crawford, Joan. *My Way of Life*. New York: Simon & Schuster, 1971.
Crawford, Joan, with Jane Kesner Ardmore. *A Portrait of Joan*. New York: Doubleday, 1962.
Crowther, Bosley. *The Lion's Share*. New York: Dutton, 1957.
Davis, Bette, with Mickey Herskowitz. *This 'N That*. New York: Putnam's, 1987.
Davis, Ronald L. *The Glamour Factory*. Dallas: Southern Methodist University Press, 1993.
Drew, William M. *At the Center of the Frame: Leading Ladies of the Twenties and Thirties*. Lanham: Vestal Press. 1999.
Drinkwater, John. *The Life and Adventures of Carl Laemmle*. New York: Putnam, 1931.
Ellenberger, Allan. *Ramon Novarro*. Jefferson: McFarland, 2009.
Eyman, Scott. *Cary Grant: A Brilliant Disguise*. New York: Simon & Schuster, 2020.
———. *Lion of Hollywood: The Life and Legend of Louis B. Mayer*. New York: Simon & Schuster, 2005.
Fairbanks, Douglas, Jr. *A Hell of a War*. New York: St. Martin's, 1993.
———. *The Salad Days*. New York: Doubleday, 1988.
Fantle, David, and Tom Johnson. *Hollywood Heyday: 75 Candid Interviews with Golden Age Legends*. Jefferson: McFarland, 2018.
Finch, Christopher, and Linda Rosenkrantz. *Gone Hollywood: The Movie Colony in the Golden Age*. Garden City: Doubleday, 1979.
Fonda, Henry, as told to Howard Teichmann. *Fonda: My Life*. New York: New American Library, 1981.
Fontaine, Joan. *No Bed of Roses*. New York: William Morrow, 1978.
Ford, Peter. *Glenn Ford: A Life*. Madison: University of Wisconsin Press, 2011.
Garrett, Murray. *Hollywood Candid: A Photographer Remembers*. New York: Abrams, 2000.
Gillespie, A. Arnold. *The Wizard of MGM*. Duncan: Bear Manor, 2011.
Gottlieb, Robert. *Garbo*. New York: Farrar, Straus & Giroux, 2021.
Grissom, James. *Follies of God: Tennessee Williams and the Women of the Fog*. New York: Knopf, 2015.
Guilaroff, Sydney, with Cathy Griffin. *Crowning Glory: Reflections of Hollywood's Favorite Confidant*. New York: General Publishing Group, 1996.

Guiles, Fred Lawrence. *Tyrone Power: The Last Idol*. Garden City: Doubleday, 1979.
Gutner, Howard. *Gowns by Adrian: The MGM Years, 1928–1941*. New York: Abrams, 2001.
Hay, Peter. *MGM: When the Lion Roared*. Atlanta: Turner Publishing, 1991.
Heimann, Jim. *Out with the Stars: Hollywood Nightlife in the Golden Era*. New York: Abbeville Press, 1985.
Hillman, James, and Michael Ventura. *We've Had a Hundred Years of Psychotherapy—And The World's Getting Worse*. New York: HarperOne, 1993.
Hirsch, Foster. *Hollywood and the Movies of the Fifties*. New York: Knopf, 2023.
———. *Otto Preminger: The Man Who Would Be King*. New York: Knopf, 2007.
Horwitz, James. *They Went Thataway*. New York: Dutton, 1976.
Johnes, Carl. *Crawford—The Last Years*. New York: Dell, 1979.
Jurow, Martin, with Philip Wuntch. *Marty Jurow Seein' Stars*. Dallas: Southern Methodist University Press, 2001.
Kazan, Elia. *A Life*. New York: Knopf, 1988
Kennedy, Matthew. *Edmund Goulding's Dark Victory: Hollywood's Genius Bad Boy*. Madison: University of Wisconsin Press, 2004.
Kobal, John. *People Will Talk*. New York: Knopf, 1985.
Kotsilibas-Davis, James, and Myrna Loy. *Myrna Loy: Being and Becoming*. New York: Donald I. Fine, 1988.
Lahr, John. *Tennessee Williams: Mad Pilgrimage of the Flesh*. New York: Norton, 2014.
Lambert, Gavin. *Norma Shearer*. New York: Knopf, 1990.
Lang, Rocky, and Barbara Hall. *Letters From Hollywood: Inside the Private World of Classic Hollywood Moviemaking*. New York: Abrams, 2019.
Lasalle, Mick. *Complicated Women: Sex and Power in Pre-Code Hollywood*. New York: St. Martin's, 2000.
Livingston, Nancy Olson. *A Front Row Seat*. Lexington, KY: University Press of Kentucky, 2022.
Lockwood, Charles. *Dream Palaces: Hollywood at Home*. New York: Viking, 1991.
Lord, Graham. *Niv*. New York: St. Martin's, 2003.
Lucas, David R. *New History of the 99th Indiana Infantry*. Rockford, IL: Horner, 1900.
Maltin, Leonard. *The Great American Broadcast*. New York: Dutton, 1997.
———. *Leonard Maltin's Movie Crazy*. Milwaukee: Dark Horse Comics, 2008.
Mann, William. *Wisecracker: The Life and Times of William Haines*. New York: Viking, 1998.
Marx, Samuel. *Mayer and Thalberg: The Make-Believe Saints*. New York: Random House, 1975.

McCarthy, Todd. *Howard Hawks: The Grey Fox of Hollywood*. New York: Grove Press, 1997.
McClelland, Doug. *Forties Film Talk*. Jefferson: McFarland, 1992.
McGilligan, Patrick. *Backstory*. Berkeley: University of California Press, 1986.
———. *Film Crazy: Interviews with Hollywood Legends*. New York: St. Martin's, 2000.
Miller, Eugene L., Jr., and Edwin T. Arnold. *Robert Aldrich Interviews*. Jackson: University Press of Mississippi, 2004.
Morley, Sheridan. *Tales from the Hollywood Raj*. New York: Viking, 1984.
Newquist, Roy. *Conversations with Crawford*. Secaucus: Citadel Press, 1980.
Oakie, Jack. *Jack Oakie's Double Takes*. San Francisco: Strawberry Hill Press, 1980.
Oldham, Gabriella and Mabel Langdon. *Harry Langdon*. Lexington: University Press of Kentucky, 2017.
Olivier, Tarquin. *My Father Laurence Olivier*. London: Headline, 1993.
Orry-Kelly. *Women I've Undressed*. London: Allen & Unwin, 2016.
Paris, Barry. *Louise Brooks*. New York: Knopf, 1989.
Phillips, Brent. *Charles Walters: The Director Who Made Hollywood Dance*. Lexington: University Press of Kentucky, 2014.
Pratt, George. *Spellbound in Darkness*. Greenwich: New York Graphic Society, 1973.
Price, Victoria. *Vincent Price*. New York: St. Martin's, 1999.
Ralston, Esther. *Some Day We'll Laugh*. Metuchen: Scarecrow Press, 1985.
Rapf, Maurice. *Back Lot*. Lanham: Scarecrow Press, 1999.
Reynolds, Burt, and Jon Winokur. *But Enough About Me*. New York: Putnam, 2015.
Ross, Lillian, and Helen Ross. *The Player*. New York: Simon & Schuster, 1962.
Rouverol, Jean. *Refugees from Hollywood: A Journal of the Blacklist Years*. Albuquerque: University of New Mexico Press, 2000.
Sanders, Coyne Steven, and Tom Gilbert. *Desilu: The Story of Lucille Ball and Desi Arnaz*. New York: It Books, 2001.
Saville, Victor, with Roy Moseley. *Evergreen: Victor Saville in His Own Words*. Carbondale: Southern Illinois University Press, 2000.
Schulberg, Budd. *Moving Pictures*. New York: Stein & Day, 1981.
Server, Lee. *Screenwriters: Words Become Pictures*. Pittstown: Main Street Press, 1987.
Shearer, Stephen Michael. *Patricia Neal: An Unquiet Life*. Lexington: University of Kentucky Press, 2006.
Sherman, Vincent. *Studio Affairs*. Lexington: University Press of Kentucky, 1996.
Sikov, Ed. *On Sunset Boulevard: The Life and Times of Billy Wilder*. Jackson: University Press of Mississippi, 2017.
Silke, James. *Here's Looking at You, Kid: 50 Years of Fighting, Working and Dreaming at Warner Bros*. Boston: Little, Brown, 1976.
Silver, Alain, and James Ursini. *Whatever Happened to Robert Aldrich?* New York: Limelight, 1995.

Skal, David, with Jessica Rains. *Claude Rains: An Actor's Voice*. Lexington: University of Kentucky Press, 2008.
Slide, Anthony. *Inside the Hollywood Fan Magazines: A History of Star Makers, Fabricators and Gossip Mongers*. Jackson: University Press of Mississippi, 2010.
Spoto, Donald. *Laurence Olivier: A Biography*. New York: HarperCollins, 1992.
Springer, John Parris. *Hollywood Fictions: The Dream Factory in American Popular Literature*. Norman: University of Oklahoma Press, 2000.
Stanley, Leonard. *Adrian: A Lifetime of Movie Glamour, Art and High Fashion*. New York: Rizzoli, 2019.
Stern, Sydney Ladensohn. *The Brothers Mankiewicz*. Jackson: University Press of Mississippi, 2019.
Stevens, George, Jr., ed. *Conversations at the American Film Institute with the Great Moviemakers*. New York: Knopf, 2012.
Sylvester, Christopher, ed. *The Grove Book of Hollywood*. New York: Grove Press, 1998.
Thomas, Bob. *Clown Prince of Hollywood: The Antic Life and Times of Jack L. Warner*. New York: McGraw-Hill, 1990.
Thomson, David. *Showman: The Life of David O. Selznick*. New York: Knopf, 1992.
Vieira, Mark A. *Hollywood Dreams Made Real: Irving Thalberg and the Rise of MGM*. New York: Abrams, 2008.
———. *Hurrell's Hollywood Portraits*. New York: Abrams, 1997.
———. *Irving Thalberg: Boy Wonder to Producer Prince*. Berkeley: University of California Press, 2010.
Wagner, Walter. *You Must Remember This*. New York: Putnam, 1975.
Walker, Alexander. *Joan Crawford: The Ultimate Star*. New York: Harper & Row, 1983.
———. *Stardom*. New York: Stein & Day, 1970.
Wellman, William A. *A Short Time for Insanity*. New York: Hawthorn, 1974.
Williams, Tennessee. *Selected Letters of Tennessee Williams*, Vol. 1., ed. Albert Devlin and Nancy Tischler. New York: New Directions, 2000.
Wilson, Victoria. *Steel-True: A Life of Barbara Stanwyck, 1907–1940*. New York: Simon & Schuster, 2013.
Young, Gwenda. *Clarence Brown: Hollywood's Forgotten Master*. Lexington: University of Kentucky Press, 2018.

ABBREVIATIONS USED IN SOURCE NOTES

AMPAS: Academy of Motion Picture Arts and Sciences
My Way of Life: Joan Crawford, *My Way of Life* (New York: Simon & Schuster, 1971)
NEWS: Newspapers.com
PCA: Production Code Administration

Portrait of Joan: Joan Crawford, with Jane Kesner Ardmore, *A Portrait of Joan* Garden City: Doubleday, 1962
UCLA: University of California at Los Angeles
USC: University of Southern California

SOURCE NOTES

PROLOGUE

4 *"In New York, I had met a marvelously mature man"*: Portrait of Joan, pp. 133–34.
5 *"a sparse rag"*: Allen, p. 60.

PART ONE

7 *"I think most of our fears"*: UCLA, Bob Thomas papers, Curtiss Anderson interview with Joan Crawford, box 32, folder 14.
7 *"I was born working"*: My Way of Life, p. 6.

CHAPTER ONE

9 *"Joan Crawford was born in San Antonio:* "Who's Who at Metro-Goldwyn Mayer, 1939," in author's collection.
10 *by the late 1920s, only about 80 percent of Texas births:* Texas Birth Certificates, Familysearch Historical Records website.
10 *Her paternal ancestor was David LeSueur:* familysearch.org/ark:/61903/1:1:NV1B-D45, accessed 7-27-2023.
10 *In 1861 James LeSueur was mustered into the Confederacy:* familysearch.org/ark:/61903/1:1:FSN6-N3B, accessed 8-24-2021.
11 *William Johnson, who fought for the Union in the 99th Indiana Infantry:* Lucas, p. 223.
11 *"I've never admired perfect beauty"*: UCLA, Bob Thomas papers, Curtiss Anderson interview with Joan Crawford, box 32, folder 14.

12	*"when they were on the streets battling against Satan":* NEWS: *Daily Texarkanian,* 1-25-1898.
12	*"Captain Johnson is a man of great pride":* NEWS: *Southern Standard,* Arkadelphia, Arkansas, 1-28-1898.
12	*"after a long illness":* NEWS: *Arkansas Democrat,* 11-4-1902.
12	*The cause of death was listed as "congestion":* Findagrave entry for Daisy McConnell.
12	*Slightly more than three weeks later she married LeSueur:* NEWS: *San Angelo Press,* 11-26-1902.
13	*In 1938 he died broke in Abilene:* NEWS: *San Angelo Standard Times,* 12-15-1996.
13	*Anna and her brood were living at 204 Second Street:* NEWS: San Angelo City Directory, 1908, p. 213.
13	*Cassin was managing the Opera House:* NEWS: *Lawton Daily News-Republican,* 10-7-1908.
13	*"and was highly esteemed and popular":* NEWS: *Lawton Daily News-Republican,* 7-14-1909.
13	*in 1907 he had served on the committee:* NEWS: *Lawton Daily News-Republican,* 12-7-1907.
13	*"Lawton is entitled to just as good amusement":* NEWS: *Lawton Daily News-Republican,* 6-26-1909.
14	*"He is especially qualified for this position":* NEWS: *Temple Tribune,* 3-17-1910.
14	*"She was just the little girl":* NEWS: Bill Crawford, *Lawton Constitution,* 5-11-1977.
14	*"taught me at a very early age":* AMPAS, Joan Crawford biographical file, "How I Broke Into the Movies," *L.A. Daily News,* 4-6-1953.
14	*"It seemed to me that I was always blamed":* Portrait of Joan, p. 37.
15	*"I inhaled the smell of greasepaint":* Portrait of Joan, p. 37.
15	*"When I was a kid I used to run out":* My Way of Life, p. 162.
15	*"In all the Big Pasture town of Lawton":* NEWS: *Oklahoma City News,* 10-5-1934.
15	*One time she organized an "Indian parade":* NEWS: *Oklahoma City News,* 10-5-1934.
15	*"I remember when Garvene Gooch":* NEWS: "Why Joan Crawford Left Lawton," *Lawton Constitution,* 5-22-1977.
16	*In 1916, a legal notice appeared:* NEWS: *Lawton News,* 8-31-1916.
16	*a notice about a Halloween party:* NEWS: *Lawton Constitution,* 11-1-1916.
16	*Anna got a job at a department store:* NEWS: *Oklahoma City News,* 10-5-1934.
16	*"The minute I started serving at table":* Portrait of Joan, p. 44.

NOTES - 399

16 *The 1918 Kansas City Directory:* Kansas City Directory, 1918, p. 831.
17 *"I did not have time to enter a classroom":* UCLA, Bob Thomas papers, Stephens College seminar transcript, p. 10.
17 *"Hollywood is like life":* Portrait of Joan, p. 54.
17 *Anna's father died in Phoenix:* NEWS: *Arizona Republic,* 5-27-1921.
18 *Walter had become the secretary at Stephens:* NEWS: *Kansas City Star,* 1-27-1929.
19 *"Boys, boys and more boys":* NEWS: *Kansas City Star,* 1-27-1929.
19 *"college was only comprehensible":* Portrait of Joan, p. 46.
19 *Never quit a job until it's finished:* My Way of Life, p. 7.
19 *"took a few courses and did receive grades":* UCLA, Bob Thomas papers, Merwin to Thomas, 8-12-1977.
19 *attended a steak roast:* NEWS: *Columbia Missourian,* 4-3-1923.
19 *"I didn't understand a damn thing":* UCLA, Bob Thomas papers, Stephens College seminar transcript, p. 11.
20 *"She was popular with University of Missouri boys":* UCLA, Bob Thomas papers, Merwin to Thomas, 8-12-1977.
20 *"a girl with real pretty eyes":* Stephens Life, 5-1970.
20 *"You're not a quitter":* UCLA, Bob Thomas papers, "Stephens—Interim Prior to Stardom for Actress," Stephens Life, 5-1979.
20 *"She was extraordinary":* AMPAS, Joan Crawford biographical file, Adela Rogers St. Johns, "Love Laughter and Tears," *L.A. Examiner,* 2-25-1951.

CHAPTER TWO

22 *"I [had to] reshape myself":* My Way of Life, p. 143.
22 *"I didn't even make the first line of the chorus":* UCLA, Bob Thomas papers, Stephens College seminar transcript, p. 14.
23 *"A happy, snappy syncopated revue":* NEWS: *Kansas City Star,* 1-25-1924.
23 *"some new faces":* NEWS: *Kansas City Times,* 1-26-1924.
23 *"I went to his office":* NEWS: *Allentown Morning Call,* 3-31-1929, p. 22.
24 *"Down the rainbow pathway of the stage":* NEWS: *Daily Oklahoman,* 3-19-1924.
24 *His death certificate:* Tennessee death certificate for "J Cassin," who died 10-25-1922.
25 *Oakie told her he was nineteen:* UCLA, Bob Thomas papers, Jack Oakie interview, box 32, folder 16.
25 *"Our beds stood in a row like the dwarfs":* Portrait of Joan, p. 51.
26 *Lucille had been making $35 a week:* UCLA, Bob Thomas papers, Jack Oakie interview, box 32, folder 16.

27 *LUCILLE LESUEUR YOU HAVE BEEN PLACED UNDER CONTRACT*: *Portrait of Joan*, p. 7.
27 *The first memo in her MGM employment file*: Walker, *Joan Crawford: The Ultimate Star*, p. 10.
27 *"Structure and vitality"*: *Portrait of Joan*, p. 53.
28 *"I'd been on my own since I was nine"*: *Portrait of Joan*, p. 8.
28 *"I ain't seen ya looking like that since"*: Oakie, pp. 152–53.

CHAPTER THREE

29 *"Sharon belonged to Hollywood"*: Springer, pp. 118–24.
30 *In 1911, the population of Hollywood*: Drinkwater, p. 170.
31 *"Irving was (basically) an invalid"*: Sam Marx to SE. All quotes from Sam Marx derive from this interview.
32 *In May 1925, the* Los Angeles Daily News: NEWS: *L.A. Daily News*, 5-8-1925.
32 *The same two kids appeared*: NEWS: *L.A. Daily News*, 5-10-1925.
32 *Two days after that*: NEWS: *L.A. Daily News*, 5-12-1925.
33 *"Essential to change name"*: Walker, *Joan Crawford: The Ultimate Star*, p. 12.
33 *"Joan Arden, along with Sally O'Neill, Estelle Clark"*: NEWS: *L.A. Times*, 7-9-1925.
33 *The studio even managed*: NEWS: *L.A. Daily News*, 7-12-1925.
33 *"There was a . . . showgirl"*: Slide, p. 35.
33 *Lucille LeSueur had been informally replaced*: NEWS: *Lawton News*, 5-26-1916, p. 1.
33 *Indeed, she had been Lucille Cassin*: NEWS: *Shelby County Herald*, 12-5-1923, p. 1.
34 *"She was formally rechristened"*: NEWS: *L.A. Daily News*, 8-20-1925.
34 *The* Los Angeles Times *ran a photo*: NEWS: *L.A. Times*, 9-5-1925.
34 *"Of all the girls at MGM in that period"*: AMPAS, Jane Kesner Ardmore papers, folder 100, "Joan Crawford Memories," by Pete Smith.
34 *"Gillum was especially proficient"*: AMPAS, Jane Kesner Ardmore papers, folder 100, "Joan Crawford Memories," by Pete Smith.
35 *"You weren't like the others"*: Walker, *Joan Crawford: The Ultimate Star*, p. 16.
35 *"Don't stick your head out the porthole"*: Sam Marx to SE.
35 *"She was a bit plump"*: Rapf, p. 9.
35–36 *"I can't tell you if my father had an affair"*: Maurice Rapf to SE.
36 *"Viola Dana and Joan"*: Academy, Jane Kesner Ardmore papers, folder 100, "Joan Crawford."
36 *"Look at that Shearer person"*: Morley, p. 111.
37 *"ravenous for attention"*: Lambert, p. 106.

37 "*the most beautiful eyes*": Vieira, p. 109.
37 "*Spit it out*" AMPAS, Joan Crawford biographical file, Joan Crawford, "My Past, Present and Future," *Look* magazine, 9-26-1939.
38 *She also shows up in an equally unbilled:* My thanks to Jay Weissberg of the Pordenone Silent Film Festival and especially David Pierce for pointing me toward this heretofore uncredited part.
39 "*She was bovine*": AMPAS, Jane Kesner Ardmore papers, folder 100, Joan Crawford, William Haines interview.
39 "*She dieted viciously*": AMPAS, Jane Kesner Ardmore papers, folder 100, Joan Crawford, William Haines interview.
39 "*Is the movie star there?*": AMPAS, Hedda Hopper papers, Hopper/Crawford interview, 9-8-1953, folder 988, Joan Crawford.
40 "*The Oasis was on Hollywood Boulevard*": Anthony Slide, "The Regulars," *Films in Review*, April 1978.
40 "*I couldn't keep up with her*": AMPAS, Jane Kesner Ardmore papers, folder 100, Joan Crawford, William Haines interview.
41 "*Joan had great body tension*": Heimann, pp. 37–38.
41 "*My skirts were a little too short*": *My Way of Life*, p. 123.
41 "*[Joan] had as much love of life*": UCLA, Bob Thomas papers, Adela Rogers St. Johns interview, box 32, folder 17.
42 "*a gum-chewing dame*": Cowie, p. 13.
42 "*I lived in a little room a few blocks from the studio*": AMPAS, Joan Crawford biographical file, Gladys Hall, "The Mirror of Her Selves," *Dance* magazine, 9-1930.
43 "*Pretend that the news you hear*": *Portrait of Joan*, p. 23.
43 "*I think it was on this scene*": AMPAS, Jane Kesner Ardmore papers, folder 100, Joan Crawford.
44 "*She was beautiful, all right*": Paris, p. 135.
44 "*Eddie Goulding started teaching me how to act*": Kennedy, p. 54.
45 *In a 1929 interview:* Oldham and Langdon, p. 109.
45 "*I wasn't so sure I wanted to be in the movies*": *Portrait of Joan*, p. 29.
45 "*Take off your shoes*": AMPAS, Joan Crawford biographical file, Crawford and Jane Kesner Ardmore, "The Story I've Never Told," *Women's Home Companion*, 1-1955.
46 "*I wouldn't pay a dime to cross the street*": Horwitz, p. 271.
46 "*Joan, your career is coming along nicely*": Thomas, p. 66.
46 "*She was a great gal on the set*": UCLA, Bob Thomas papers, Tim McCoy interview, box 32, folder 16.
47 "*Here was the most tense, exciting individual*": *Portrait of Joan*, pp. 30–31.
48 "*Browning took a lifelike character*": Michael Blake, *A Thousand Faces*, p. 192.

48   "*Chaney's films, at their individual best*": Michael Dempsey, "Lon Chaney: A Thousand and One Faces," *Film Comment*, May–June 1995.
48   "*Crawford is a tremendous plus in the movie*": Basinger, *Silent Stars*, p. 362.
48   "*He admired her seriousness*": Michael Blake to SE.

CHAPTER FOUR

50   *The house cost $28,000 fully furnished*: Walker, *Joan Crawford: The Ultimate Star*, p. 34.
50   "*The cadets were putting on a dress parade*": AMPAS: Joan Crawford biographical file, George Frazier, "Handsome Joan from San Antone," *Redbook*, 3-12-1949.
51   "*a hyper-sexy, provocative redhead*": Bakewell, pp. 18–19.
52   "*Father didn't know why I was going to work*": Fairbanks to SE.
53   "*fell in love at once*": AMPAS, Jane Kesner Ardmore papers, folder 100, Joan Crawford.
53   "*enormous pains to give minor but helpful criticisms*": Fairbanks Jr., *The Salad Days*, p. 121.
53   "*The total effect was magnetic*": Fairbanks Jr., *The Salad Days*, p. 123.
54   "*Don't you blame Joan now!*": Fairbanks Jr., *The Salad Days*, p. 134.
55   "*I can't remember anyone ever being late*": Basinger, *The Star Machine*, p. 132.
56   "*Billie, Doug feels terrible*": Ellenberger, p. 83.
56   "*I remember every one of my important roles*": Lillian Ross and Helen Ross, p. 64.
56   "*I really knew I was a star*": Basinger, *The Star Machine*, p. 55.
56   "*He knew how to build and protect his properties*": Walker, *Stardom*, p. 284.
56   "*the quintessence of what the term 'flapper' signifies*": Pratt, p. 456.
57   "*Diana's personality is described*": AMPAS, PCA files, *Our Dancing Daughters* file, "The Dancing Girl."
58   "*I think from this time on my life was never again carefree*": AMPAS, Joan Crawford biographical file, Lawrence Quirk, "Joan Crawford," *Films in Review*, 12-1956

CHAPTER FIVE

78   "*We've got ourselves a new star*": Marx, p. 157.
79   "*Please do whatever you think*": Guilaroff, p. 49.

CHAPTER SIX

85 *"Poor Larry was very disillusioned"*: Olivier, p. 42.
86 *"Doug was always a good husband"*: Swope to SE.
86 *"With Douglas I played the part"*: AMPAS, Jane Kesner Ardmore papers, folder 100, Joan Crawford.
86 *"When a man asked her to bed"*: UCLA, Bob Thomas papers, Adela Rogers St. Johns interview, box 32, folder 16.
86 *"Joan was a pal to male stars"*: UCLA, Bob Thomas papers, Howard Strickling interview, box 32, folder 17.
87 *"Actresses are not good lays"*: UCLA, Bob Thomas papers, Howard Strickling interview, box 32, folder 17.
87 *"Because I can send a girl"*: UCLA, Bob Thomas papers, Howard Strickling interview, box 32, folder 17.
87 *"I suppose there were some career conflicts"*: Wagner, p. 100.
88 *"She woke up in the morning"*: UCLA, Bob Thomas papers, Howard Strickling interview, box 32, folder 17.
89 *"She didn't know what her part was about"*: AMPAS, Jane Kesner Ardmore papers, folder 100, "Joan Crawford Memories" by Pete Smith.
90 *"You are a female Johnny Weissmuller"*: *My Way of Life*, p. 125.
90 *"Joan was athletic"*: AMPAS, Jane Kesner Ardmore papers, folder 100, Joan Crawford.
90 *"Adrian reserved many"*: Gutner, p. 103.
91 *"Adrian always played down"*: Eyman, *Lion*, p. 214.
92 *"If she was dedicated to an idea"*: UCLA, Bob Thomas papers, Sheila O'Brien interview, box 32, folder 16.
92 *He would sometimes assume a Chinese accent*: Gutner, p. 41.
92 *"I found that meeting with a star"*: Stanley, p. 60.
92 *"I felt the fitting [should] be private"*: Stanley, p. 68.
93 *"Every film star I ever met"*: Grissom, p. 279. I have rearranged some of the sentences in this quote.
93 *"the most decorative subject"*: Cowie, p. 59.
94 *"arrogant, egotistical bastard"*: Vieira, *Hurrell's Hollywood Portraits*, pp. 30, 68.
94 *"Crawford was a natural at posing"*: Vieira, *Hurrell's Hollywood Portraits*, p. 143.
94 *"She'd put Bing Crosby records on"*: Kobal, p. 260.
95 *"George Hurrell used to give me just one key light"*: Vieira, *Hurrell's Hollywood Portraits*, p. 196.
95 *"He shot [Marilyn] Monroe"*: Stenn to SE.

95 "*Don't let them interview you*": UCLA, Bob Thomas papers, Howard Strickling interview, box 32, folder 17.
96 "*Joan was the queen*": Slide, p. 81.
96 *Crawford went out of her way to become friends:* Robert Wagner to SE.
96 "*Joan Crawford was a real star*": Basinger and Wasson, p. 421.
96 "*It was uncanny*": Newquist, p. 37.
97 "*She was very good in script conferences*": Basinger and Wasson, p. 412.
98 "*I want everything an actor knows*": Young, p. 47.
99 *Crawford's films were average in cost:* Mark Glancy, "MGM Film Grosses, 1924–48, The Eddie Mannix Ledger," *Historical Journal of Film, Radio and Television*, vol. 12, no. 2, 1992, p. 134.
99 "*Clarence Brown was very firm*": Young, p. 135.

CHAPTER SEVEN

102 "*I felt a certain something in this play*": Vieira, *Irving Thalberg*, p. 176.
102 "*The thing that is most important is this*": Kennedy, p. 113.
103 "*I think Kringelein's speech can be cut*": Vieira, *Irving Thalberg*, p. 177.
104 "*And my knees turned to water*": UCLA, Bob Thomas papers, Curtiss Anderson interview with Joan Crawford, box 32, folder 14.
104 "*If I fall flat on my can*": Kennedy, p. 117.
104 "*Six years before*": *Portrait of Joan*, p. 94.
104 "*There are two ways to watch*": LaSalle, pp. 120–21.
105 "*Garbo invents her own genre*": Gottlieb, p. 165.
105 "*Crawford had trouble coming into*": LaSalle, p. 121.
106 "*married to the most wonderful man*": Mahin to SE.
106 "*her role models were clearly*": Basinger, *The Star Machine*, p. 365.
106 "*Mr. Hearst looks after Marion*": UCLA, Bob Thomas papers, Howard Strickling interview, box 32, folder 17.
107 "*They were never unpleasant*": UCLA, Bob Thomas papers, Kay Mulvey interview, box 32, folder 16.
107 "*her reaction was not one of sadness*": UCLA, Bob Thomas papers, Maxine Thomas interview, box 32, folder 17.
107 "*Marsh was an extremely capable cameraman*": Finch and Rosenkrantz, pp. 30–31.
108 "*I, Joan Crawford, believe in the dollar*": Lockwood, p. 228.
108 "*I want to do some really fine things*": *Variety*, 7-12-1932.

CHAPTER EIGHT

109 *"I [only] became conscious"*: Gutner, p. 119.
110 *United Artists paid MGM*: Walker, *Joan Crawford: The Ultimate Star*, p. 90.
111 *"weakened the structure considerably"*: UCLA, Bob Thomas papers, Lewis Milestone interview, box 32, folder 16.
112 *"She hated it"*: Ronald Davis, p. 115.
113 *"familiar strangers"*: Fairbanks Jr., *The Salad Days*, p. 199.
113 *"I told him the truth"*: AMPAS, Jane Kesner Ardmore papers, folder 100, Joan Crawford.
113 *"Don't bother to call her"*: Fairbanks Jr., *The Salad Days*, p. 203.
114 *"You can't take my picture with Miss Crawford"*: AMPAS, Joan Crawford biographical file, *L.A. Times*, 11-11-1933.
114 *"Are they kidding, Howard?"*: McCarthy, p. 179.
115 *"I was in love with Clark"*: AMPAS, Jane Kesner Ardmore papers, folder 100, Joan Crawford.
116 *"He's taken no part in the experimental work"*: Kazan, p. 75.
118 *"Look, Mr. Selznick"*: Thomson, p. 158.
118 *"I can walk down the hall"*: Fantle and Johnson, p. 165.
118 *Astaire had just married his wife Phyllis*: UCLA, Bob Thomas papers, Fred Astaire interview, box 32, folder 14.
118 *"I've never known him to be rude"*: *Portrait of Joan*, p. 98.
119 *"Baby, she may be a big"*: Kobal, p. 605.
119 *When Eleanor Powell came to MGM*: Kobal, p. 232.
120 *"Why Norma and Joan were at odds"*: Vieira, *Hollywood Dreams Made Real*, p. 148.
120 *"I don't know who was more frightened"*: Vieira, *Hollywood Dreams Made Real*, p. 186.
120 *"Why do her lips have to be glistening wet?"*: Walker, *Joan Crawford: The Ultimate Star*, p. 102.
121 *"All he did was stand in my kitchen"*: NEWS: Jerry Parker, "Joan Crawford Outlasted Everyone," Times-Post Service, *Longview Daily News*, 6-16-1973.
122 HE APPRECIATED OUR FEARS: AMPAS, PCA files, Trotti to Joy, 10-21-1931.
122 *"this theme is usable when handled in good taste"*: AMPAS, PCA files, *Possessed*, "Resume," 10-21-1931.
123 *"the grave danger lies"*: AMPAS, PCA files, Trotti (?) to Joy, 10-22-1931.
123 *"the chief reason the Code was amended"*: AMPAS, PCA files, Joy to Breen, 12-15-1931.

123 "*The adaptation and treatment*": AMPAS, PCA files, *Forsaking All Others*, Breen to Mayer, 9-25-1934.

123 "*We are gravely concerned about it*": AMPAS, PCA files, *Forsaking All Others*, Breen to Mayer, 11-27-1934.

124 "*I just want to say that*": AMPAS, PCA files, *Forsaking All Others*, Van Dyke to Breen, 12-4-1934.

124 *Robert Young remembered doing a radio show:* Maltin, *The Great American Broadcast*, p. 23.

124 "*With a camera . . . it's different*": Walker, *Joan Crawford: The Ultimate Star*, p. 100.

124 *All this meant that the Theatre Guild's offer:* AMPAS, Joan Crawford biographical file, *L.A. Examiner*, 2-7-35.

125 "*What cold?*": UCLA, Bob Thomas papers, J. Watson Webb interview, box 32, folder 17.

126 "*She was a star without trying*": Price, p. 70.

126 *Melvyn Douglas and his wife Helen Gahagan Douglas:* UCLA, Bob Thomas papers, Leonard Spigelgass interview, box 32, folder 17.

127 *Joan's only problem with Barbara's new relationship:* Wilson, p. 433.

127 *Romero would become a close friend:* UCLA, Bob Thomas papers, Cesar Romero interview, box 32, folder 17.

127 "*There was something predatory about her*": Kazan, p. 77.

127 "*There wasn't the slightest doubt in my mind*": *My Way of Life*, p.16.

128 *he taught her how to play chess and bridge:* Pat Tone to SE.

128 "*The limo would pick us up at 7 a.m.*": Pat Tone to SE.

128 "*Anyone who had a sick cat*": AMPAS, Joan Crawford biographical file, *L.A. Times Sunday Magazine*, 5-21-1939.

128 *MGM publicist Maxine Thomas:* UCLA, Bob Thomas papers, Maxine Thomas interview, box 32, folder 17.

129 *Asher was gay, extremely shy:* Robert Wagner to SE.

129 "*I used to walk up 14 flights*": AMPAS, Jane Kesner Ardmore papers, folder 100, Joan Crawford.

129–30 "*He took me over the coals*": Walker, *Joan Crawford: The Ultimate Star*, p. 109.

131 "*She woke up like a movie star*": Cowie, p. 154.

131 "*I was madly in love with him*": Stern, pp. 133–34.

131 "*Joan was the essential movie star*": UCLA, Bob Thomas papers, Joseph L. Mankiewicz interview, box 32, folder 16.

133 "*If she came through the door in sables and emeralds*": UCLA, Bob Thomas papers, Joseph L. Mankiewicz interview, box 32, folder 16.

133 "*This should have been mine*": Tom Mankiewicz to SE.

134 "*You're too modern*": Walker, *Joan Crawford: The Ultimate Star*, p. 110.

134   *"Franchot hated his part, loathed it"*: *Portrait of Joan*, p. 114.
134   *"I'd watch in amazement"*: These comments combine two interviews: Young, p. 197, and Bawden and Miller, *Conversations with Classic Film Stars*, p. 84.
135   *"He was intelligent*: UCLA, Bob Thomas papers, Joseph L. Mankiewicz interview, box 32, folder 16.
135   *"When she walked in a room"*: UCLA, Bob Thomas papers, Milton Weiss interview, box 32, folder 17.
138   *"But she was not confident in herself as a person"*: UCLA, Bob Thomas papers, Robert Young interview, box 32, folder 17.
139   *"Christian Science fit her philosophy"*: UCLA, Bob Thomas papers, Dorothy Manners interview, box 32, folder 16.
140   *"Well, she'll be footloose and Franchot-free!"*: Hay, p. 179.
140   *"[Crawford] made herself over completely"*: AMPAS, Joan Crawford biographical file, "Joan Crawford Sues for 'Brief and Easy Divorce,'" *L.A. Examiner*, 2-11-1939.

PART TWO

143   *"I've been told"*: BBC Shepperton Studios interview with Joan Crawford archived at the George Eastman House.

CHAPTER NINE

145   *"intelligence and acting"*: Kobal, p. 245.
147   *"You're growing up, aren't you?"*: Sylvester, p. 234.
148   *"On The Shining Hour"*: UCLA, Bob Thomas papers, Joseph L. Mankiewicz interview, box 32, folder 16.
149   *MGM held Selznick's feet to the fire:* Thomson, p. 268.
149   *"some such combination"*: Behlmer, Memo, p. 143.
149   *Selznick claimed they told him:* Behlmer, Memo, p. 141.
149   *"That didn't work either"*: UCLA, Bob Thomas papers, James Stewart interview, box 32, folder 17.
149   *"She herself was so disciplined"*: UCLA, Bob Thomas papers, Lew Ayres interview, box 32, folder 14.
150   *"If made into a picture"*: AMPAS, PCA files, *The Women*, Breen to Riskin, 1-8-1937, and Breen to Hammell, 3-8-1937. I have quoted the letter to Hammel.
150   *By February 1938:* AMPAS, PCA files, *The Women*, Joseph Breen Memorandum for the Files, 2-7-1938.

150 *"The role is that of an outright bitch"*: Walker, *Joan Crawford: The Ultimate Star*, p. 127.
151 *"George said to go for the broadest comedy"*: Bawden and Miller, *Conversations with Classic Film Stars*, p. 249.
151 *"Notwithstanding the provision"*: Lambert, p. 276.
151 *"I now agree that both"*: Lambert. p. 277.
151 *"because of the wholesale characterization"*: AMPAS, PCA files, *The Women*, Breen to Mayer, 4-21-1939.
152 *Breen now became an uncredited screenwriter*: AMPAS, PCA Files, *The Women*, Breen to Mayer, 4-25-1939.
152 *On Shearer's first day*: Lambert, p. 278.
152 *"Shearer wasn't satisfied"*: Joe Ruttenberg to SE.
152 *She did so while knitting*: UCLA, Bob Thomas papers, Charles Walters interview, box 32, folder 17.
153 *"Mr. Cukor, I think Miss Crawford"*: Crowther, p. 272.
153 *She refused*: Lambert, p. 278.
154 *"Must stay home today"*: Gutner, p. 178.
154 *"the picture looks magnificent"*: AMPAS, PCA files, Stromberg to Breen, 6-6-1939.
155 *"Nobody"*: Kobal, p. 376.
155 *"And Crawford sort of enjoyed"*: Kobal, p. 376.
156 *"We're waiting"*: Kobal, p. 377.
156 *WE SAW THE WOMEN THIS AFTERNOON*: AMPAS, PCA files, *The Women*, Breen to Schenck, 7-19-1939.
156 *DEAR JOE KNOW YOU WILL BE PLEASED*: AMPAS, PCA files, *The Women*, Stromberg to Breen, undated.
157 *"Who would have thought"*: Gutner, p. 103.
157 *"I am sorry you are going"*: Stanley, p. 142.
158 *"unable to rehearse"*: Walker, p. 137.
158 *"Know of no promises regarding billing"*: Walker, p. 129.
160 *"This one has got to be good"*: Saville, p. 143.
160 *"and a little gold dust on her skin"*: Saville, p. 143.
162 *"He lives his newspaper the way"*: AMPAS, Jane Kesner Admore papers, folder 100, Joan Crawford.
163 *"Those two children would eventually be joined"*: NEWS: "Quest Led Joan Crawford Twins, Others to Tenn.," *Memphis Commercial Appeal*, 9-11-1995, p. A-1.
166 *"[She] never discussed it"*: AMPAS, Jane Kesner Ardmore papers, folder 100, Joan Crawford.

CHAPTER TEN

167 *In 1936 she had earned $302,307:* Finch and Rosenkrantz, p. 325.
167 *"They want everything to be subordinated":* Williams, p. 255.
168 *"last of the movie queens":* UCLA, Bob Thomas papers, Walter Seltzer interview, box 32, folder 17.
170 *"We enjoyed each other's company very much":* Ford, p. 41.
170 *"Joe," she yelled:* McClelland, p. 242.
171 *"I've never really known":* Portrait of Joan, p. 135; also AMPAS, Jane Kesner Ardmore papers, folder 100, Joan Crawford.
171 *"Terry knew Mines and Crawford":* UCLA, Bob Thomas papers, Harry Mines interview, box 32, folder 16.
171 *"His very presence was":* Portrait of Joan, p. 135.
172 *"mistook peace of mind for love":* Portrait of Joan, p. 135.
172 *"Come have a holiday with me":* Eyman, Cary Grant, p. 196.
172 *"Her adopted daughter":* Olivier, p. 95.
173 *"was inclined to become agitated":* Blauvelt, p. 104.
173 *"A soldier might ask Hedy Lamarr":* Bette Davis, p. 125.
173 *Fred MacMurray sold off his old hunting equipment:* Guiles, p. 145.
173 *"I put a towel over my head":* UCLA, Bob Thomas papers, Jack Oakie interview, box 32, folder 16.
174 *"I'll take a mink coat":* UCLA, Bob Thomas papers, John Mitchell interview, box 32, folder 16.
175 *"Which is your car?":* Walker, *Joan Crawford: The Ultimate Star*, p. 139.
175 *His primary memory:* UCLA, Bob Thomas papers, John Wayne interview, box 32, folder 17.
175 *On the last day of production:* Walker, p. 141.
176 *"I just finished another Metro stinker":* AMPAS, George Cukor papers, folder 734, Crawford to Cukor, undated but early 1943.
177 *On July 29, 1943:* Walker, p. 142.
177 *"L. B. Mayer was my father:* Kobal, p. 279.
177 *"That was the trouble":* AMPAS, Joan Crawford biographical file, Kyle Crichton, "Lady in Waiting," 10-28-1944.

CHAPTER ELEVEN

178 *"It was the whole philosophy of the studio":* Silke, p. 119.
178 *"You never knew any stars at MGM":* Turney to Swenson, 5-7-1997, courtesy of Karen Swenson.

178	*"[Jack] won't stand up in a pinch":* Silke, p. 119.
179	*"They didn't trust us":* Silke, p. 72.
179	*Joan Crawford would assert that she was without work: Portrait of Joan*, p. 138.
180	*"I am Joan Crawford":* Fontaine, p. 128.
180	*Domestic help slowly vanished: Portrait of Joan*, pp. 136–37.
180	*"Outsiders writing of Phillip and me": Portrait of Joan*, pp. 137–38.
180	*As of January 1, 1944:* AMPAS, Joan Crawford biographical file, "A Dancing Daughter Grows Up," *N.Y. Times*, 10-7-1945.
181	*Ten months later:* AMPAS, Joan Crawford biographical file, "Lady in Waiting." *Collier's*, 10-28-1944.
181	*Shurlock responded with a small but meaningful roster:* AMPAS, PCA files, *Mildred Pierce*, Shurlock memo, 9-19-1941.
182	*"the story contains so many sordid:* AMPAS, PCA files, *Mildred Pierce*, Breen to Warner, 2-2-1944.
182	*"I thought James Cain was very sympathetic":* Joanne Yeck, "An Interview with Catherine Turney," *Magill's Cinema Annual 1987*, pp. 34–43.
183	*"I don't think she liked women very much":* Server, p. 237.
183	*"Jesus Christ!":* McGilligan, *Backstory*, p. 129.
183	*Privately, Crawford would give credit:* UCLA, Bob Thomas papers, Walter Seltzer interview, box 32, folder 17.
183	*"Do you think I should go outside":* Jurow, p. 1.
184	*"As I talked, a striking transformation":* Jurow, p. 2.
184	*"The worst time in my life":* NEWS: Bob Thomas, *Spokane Chronicle*, 1-22-1955, p. 5.
184	*"On Tuesday we are making additional tests":* Behlmer, *Inside Warner Bros.*, p. 254.
185	*"Joan never forgot":* Basinger and Wasson, p. 426.
185	*"You fucking little pansy":* UCLA, Bob Thomas papers, John Mitchell interview, box 32, folder 16.
186	*"But you've only been shooting":* UCLA, Bob Thomas papers, Henry Rogers interview, box 32, folder 17.
186	*"nasty, gratifying version of the James Cain novel":* Agee, p. 165.
187	*"The sanctity of marriage":* AMPAS, PCA files, *Mildred Pierce*, memo, 9-2-1946
187	*"Henry, I don't think I can do it":* UCLA, Bob Thomas papers, Henry Rogers interview, box 32, folder 17.
189	*"Well done, dear chum":* Fairbanks to SE.
189	*"Darling! I suppose you haven't heard":* Fairbanks Jr., *A Hell of a War*, p. 266.

CHAPTER TWELVE

190 *"My face is my future":* Silke, p. 299.
191 *"Not when we have company":* UCLA, Bob Thomas papers, Eve Arden interview, box 32, folder 14.
191 *Christopher drew back a fist and slugged Crawford:* Black, p. 212.
192 *"Then, of course, the poor kid":* Catherine Turney to Swenson, 5-7-1997, courtesy of Karen Swenson.
192 *"That was one thing about Joan":* Catherine Turney to Swenson, 5-7-1997, courtesy of Karen Swenson.
193 *Terry agreed to a waiver of his right:* AMPAS, Joan Crawford biographical file, "Joan Asks Third Divorce," *L.A. Herald Express*, 4-25-1946.
193 *"Probably puts them in Bekins":* Mann, p. 280.
194 *"If they're making pictures like that":* AMPAS, Joan Crawford biographical file, Louella Parsons, "Joan Crawford," 6-12-1949.
194 *For a time he had kept company:* Robert Gottlieb to SE.
194 *She would order a tonic and ice:* UCLA, Bob Thomas papers, Henry Rogers interview, box 32, folder 17.
195 *"I'll believe that when Greg tells me it's true":* NEWS: Hedda Hopper column, *N.Y. Daily News*, 3-16-1947.

CHAPTER THIRTEEN

196 *"'Humoresque' was a Jewish story":* USC, Warner Bros. archive, *Humoresque* story file, 2 of 2, Hurst to "Wilke," 10-13-1941.
196 *Jerry Wald's first casting impulse was Bette Davis:* USC, Warner Bros. archive, *Humoresque*, story and correspondence, 11-1-1945/12-6-1945, Wald to Trilling, 9-25-1945.
196 *"I think the character of Helen":* USC, Warner Bros. archive, *Humoresque*, memos and correspondence, Wald to Davis, 11-17-1945.
197 *"The dress that was designed for Helen's party":* Behlmer, *Inside Warner Bros.*, p. 268.
197 *Although Adrian got screen credit:* USC, Warner Bros. archive, *Humoresque*, Obringer to Trilling, 2-28-1946.
197 *"So you're Joan Crawford, the big movie star":* Julie Garfield to SE.
197 *"It was wonderful working with Johnnie":* Kobal, p. 278.
197 *"He had a tragic childhood":* Julie Garfield to SE. All quotes from Garfield derive from this interview.

198 *"Bring that camera down here now!"*: Robert Blake, pp. 216–17.
199 *"After seeing last night's rushes"*: USC, Warner Bros. archive, *Humoresque* 3-1-1946–4-30-1946, memo dated 4-11-1946.
200 *In total, the picture ran a whopping forty-four days over schedule*: USC, Warner Bros. archive, *Humoresque* Production Daily Progress reports, 1488, box 2 of 2.
201 *Friends rallied around Niven*: Lord, p. 140.
201 *"Compared with Bette Davis"*: McClelland, p. 248.
201 *"She had two drawing rooms"*: Basinger and Wasson, p. 422.
201 *"I discovered the secret of Joan's longevity"*: Bawden and Miller, *You Ain't Heard Nothin' Yet*, p. 375.
202 *"Miss Crawford, though she is not"*: Agee, p. 361.
203 *"She did everything I asked [of her] on film"*: UCLA, Bob Thomas papers, Otto Preminger interview, box 32, folder 16.
203 *Finally she had the wardrobe department*: Fonda, p. 176.
203 *"I think each of them sensed the"*: Hirsch, *Otto Preminger*, p. 148.
204 *She stayed for only two weeks*: NEWS: *Honolulu Star-Bulletin*, 9-24-1947, p. 1.

CHAPTER FOURTEEN

205 *George Cukor threw a party*: Garrett, p. 49.
206 *He was a devout believer in real estate*: Olsen, p. 234.
207 *Billy Haines liked to tell the story*: AMPAS, Joan Crawford biographical file, George Frazier, "Handsome Joan from San Antone," *Redbook*, 3-12-1949.
207 *"Don't you think we have"*: AMPAS, Joan Crawford biographical file, George Frazier, "Handsome Joan from San Antone," *Redbook*, 3-12-1949.
208 *"great broad"*: McClelland, p. 2.
210 *"She called to say she had read a script"*: UCLA, Bob Thomas papers, Eleanor Parker interview, box 32, folder 16.
211 *"I realized that she had been stimulated"*: Sherman, p. 201.
211 *"I had never worked with anyone"*: Sherman, p. 204.
211 *"The ideal wife"*: Sherman, p. 203.
212 *"Steve, if that's the same script"*: Silke, p. 293.
212 *"She came to see me"*: Kobal, p. 447.
212 *"Her obsessive attitude toward her home"*: Sherman, p. 209.
213 *"getting too old"*: Sherman, p. 212.
215 *They agreed to pay her*: USC, Warner Bros. archive, release contract between Warner Bros. and Joan Crawford, 12-26-1951.
215 *"If I can put my finger on the time of change"*: Cowie, p. 169.

216 *"They were obviously very close friends"*: Wagner to SE.
216 *Six months later:* AMPAS, Joan Crawford biographical file, "Joan Crawford's Son Takes Another Jaunt," *L.A. Times*, 9-15-1951.
216 *"Because he sucks his thumb"*: UCLA, Bob Thomas papers, Rosalind Rogers interview, box 32, folder 17.
216 *"Joan invited mother and me"*: UCLA, Bob Thomas papers, James MacArthur interview, box 32, folder 16.
217 *"He did not want to do dishes"*: UCLA, Bob Thomas papers, Sheila O'Brien interview, box 32, folder 16.
217 *"I don't believe in progressive education"*: AMPAS, Joan Crawford biographical file, "Joan Crawford, Unhappy Success," *Look*, 10-29-46.
218 *"I think I was a good mother"*: *My Way of Life*, p. 80.
218 *"bitter tales of romance and broken love affairs"*: Olson, p. 48.
218 *"She was so strict with the kids"*: UCLA, Bob Thomas papers, Rosalind Rogers interview, box 32, folder 17.
220 *"I don't remember having an argument with her"*: UCLA, Bob Thomas papers, Lew Wasserman interview, box 32, folder 17.
220 *"was great to work with"*: UCLA, Bob Thomas papers, Art Park interview, box 32, folder 16.

PART THREE

CHAPTER FIFTEEN

227 *"Hello, Miss Crawford"*: UCLA, Bob Thomas papers, David Miller interview, box 32, folder 16. All quotes from David Miller derive from this interview.
228 *"I don't want a Brando quality in this thing"*: AMPAS, Joan Crawford biographical file, Rory Heard, "When Joan Crawford Is Crossed," *L.A. Mirror*, 5-20-1954.
228 *"You can't like everyone you work with"*: AMPAS, Joan Crawford biographical file, "Joan Admits She'd Re-Wed, but Adds 'If,'" *Hollywood Citizen News*, 4-1-1952.
229 *"[Burt] Lancaster was almost a given"*: McGilligan, *Backstory 2*, p. 318.
230 *"There's no good reason why"*: AMPAS, Joan Crawford biographical file, "Jon Whitcomb's Page," *Cosmopolitan*, 1-1953.
230 *"An Olivier or a [Katharine] Hepburn"*: Hillman and Ventura, p. 110.
231 *"It was like a burlesque show"*: AMPAS, Joan Crawford biographical file,

Bob Thomas, "Joan Crawford Gives Marilyn Monroe Tip," *Hollywood Citizen-News*, 3-2-1953.

232 *"I found [the script] a little dumb"*: Phillips, p. 163.
232 *"It was purely professional"*: Phillips, p. 164.
233 *"Only God or a good-looking man"*: Phillips, p. 165.
233 *When she arrived on the set*: AMPAS, Joan Crawford biographical file, Sidney Skolsky column, *Hollywood Citizen News*, 5-6-1953.
234 *"She knew exactly when the Gray Line tour"*: UCLA, Bob Thomas papers, Charles Walters interview, box 32, folder 17.
235 *One time they were on a train*: Phillips, p. 169.
235 *"In an article about actresses over forty"*: AMPAS, Joan Crawford biographical file, "How They Stay Glamorous After 40," *Look*, 1-3-1951.
235 *"I've only known two movie stars"*: AMPAS, Jane Kesner Ardmore papers, folder 100, Joan Crawford, William Haines interview.
237 *"She suggested I follow her back to her house"*: Wagner to SE.
238 *"She was a woman with a lot of quirks"*: Sheldon to Karen Swenson, 7-9-1997, courtesy of Karen Swenson.
239 *"It's now 11:30 at night"*: AMPAS, Hedda Hopper papers, folder 988, Joan Crawford.
240 *"Crawford has been having a great time staying at motels all the time"*: Walker, *Joan Crawford: The Ultimate Star*, pp. 155–56.
241 *"Phil, I'm in deep trouble"*: McGilligan, *Backstory 2*, p. 352.
243 *"excellent actress but a rabble-rouser"*: *Portrait of Joan*, p. 164.
243 *"At one point"*: AMPAS, Joan Crawford biographical file, Bob Thomas, "Joan, Mercedes End Feudin' and Fussin'," *L.A. Mirror*, 11-19-1953.
243 *"I love it, but the film's in color"*: UCLA, Bob Thomas papers, Nick Ray interview, box 32, folder 17.
244 *"I'm at LaRue's with Joan Crawford"*: UCLA, Bob Thomas papers, Nick Ray interview, box 32, folder 17.
245 *"If I'm out of work a year"*: AMPAS, Joan Crawford biographical file, Earl Wilson, "Years Fly by but Joan Is Still Tops," *L.A. Daily News*, 4-3-1954.
245 *"Not so fast"*: AMPAS, Joan Crawford biographical file, "Joan Crawford Would Marry Again, Except—," *Hollywood Citizen-News*, 3-12-1954.
246 *"Cliquot was always happy"*: Goodman, pp. 323–23.
246 *"many of my friends are my clients"*: Goodman, p. 372.
247 *"I'd hate to think what would happen to"*: AMPAS, Joan Crawford biographical file, Dave Kaufman, "'Aging' Crack Riles Crawford," *Variety*, 7-3-1957.

247 *"It was a product of her upbringing"*: UCLA, Bob Thomas papers, Sheila O'Brien interview, box 32, folder 16.
248 *"[Crawford] was so generous"*: AMPAS, Jane Kesner Ardmore papers, folder 100, Joan Crawford.
249 *The underlying issue as Barker perceived it:* Barker to Swenson, 1-4-1998, courtesy of Karen Swenson.
250 *"The story conferences were unending"*: UCLA, Bob Thomas papers, Zugsmith interview, box 32, folder 17.
250 *Chandler's answer was succinct:* UCLA, Bob Thomas papers, Joe Pevney interview, box 32, folder 16.
250 *She did ask Pevney not to do any close-ups:* UCLA, Bob Thomas papers, Joe Pevney interview, box 32, folder 16.
252 *"Are those statistics correct?"*: UCLA, Bob Thomas papers, Barry Sullivan interview, box 32, folder 17.
252 *"Joan Crawford Romance Reported"*: AMPAS, Joan Crawford biographical file, Louella Parsons, "Joan Crawford Romance Reported," *L.A. Examiner*, 5-7-1955.
253 *"We really liked him"*: AMPAS, Jane Kesner Ardmore papers, folder 100, Joan Crawford.
253 *"I married a lady and found out"*: George Eastman House, Joan Crawford audio files.
253 *Most of the time he referred to her as "My Bride"*: George Eastman House, Joan Crawford audio files, "Al Steele in Tulsa."
253 *The first time the police found him:* AMPAS, Joan Crawford biographical file, "Joan Crawford Son Leaves School Again," *L.A. Times*, 7-29-1955.
253 *That made four AWOL's:* NEWS: *Washington Evening Star*, 7-29-1955, p. 60.

CHAPTER SIXTEEN

254 *"This is a team effort"*: George Eastman House, Joan Crawford audio files.
254 *"I enjoy people"*: AMPAS, Hedda Hopper papers, Al Steele interview with Dora Albert, 4-20-1959, folder 988, Joan Crawford.
255 *"He would hold my hand"*: UCLA, Bob Thomas papers, Curtiss Anderson interview with Joan Crawford, box 32, folder 14.
255 *"She didn't have to apologize"*: UCLA, Bob Thomas papers, Rosalind Rogers interview, box 32, folder 17.
255 *"My mother invariably referred to Steele"*: LaLonde to SE.

416 - NOTES

255 *"He was her best kind of husband":* UCLA, Bob Thomas papers, Cesar Romero interview, box 32, folder 17.
256 *"Crawford had spent more":* Orry-Kelly, p. 326.
256 *"[He] was the last word in elegance":* Orry-Kelly, p. 327.
257 *"at the calculated level":* Walter Hill, "Anarchic Instincts," *Film Comment,* 11-2013.
258 *Rouverol recalled they earned:* Rouverol, p. 85.
258 *"1. Wants to see design for swimsuit":* USC, Robert Aldrich papers, #2684, box 38.
259 *"The degree to which she seemed disturbed":* USC, Robert Aldrich papers, #2684, box 38, Aldrich to Richard Pearl, 7-23-1955.
259 *Among the pictures she wanted to see:* USC, Robert Aldrich papers, #2684, box 38, Aldrich to Goetz, 8-11-1955.
259 *"Perhaps in lieu of directing":* USC, Robert Aldrich papers, #2684, box 38, Aldrich to Goetz, 8-4-1955.
259 *"Joan, we are friends":* UCLA, Bob Thomas papers, Art Park interview, box 32, folder 16.
260 *"For the first four or five days":* UCLA, Bob Thomas papers, Robert Aldrich interview, box 32, folder 14.
260 Autumn Leaves *eked out a tiny profit:* USC, Robert Aldrich papers, #2684, box 38.

CHAPTER SEVENTEEN

261 *"I've always wanted to open a farm around here":* George Eastman House, Joan Crawford audio files. All quotes from Steele and Crawford in this section derive from these audio files.
262 *"Subsequently a motion picture film":* Crawford FBI file, 5-11-1955, courtesy of Casey LaLonde.
264 *"Film is described as being very old":* Crawford FBI file, 5-17-1955.
264 *"Bullshit":* Newquist, p. 139.
265 *A month later Hoover forwarded:* Crawford FBI file, 11-11-1971.
265 *"She was more natural":* UCLA, Bob Thomas papers, Sheila O'Brien interview, box 32, folder 16.
266 *"You fucking tycoons":* Mann, p. 332.
266 *There were fireplaces in both the drawing room:* AMPAS, Joan Crawford biographical file, unsourced clipping, circa 1957, "California in Central Park."
266 *The tab for the remodeling:* Mann, p. 333.

NOTES - 417

267 *"Joan played it like a movie script"*: Ben Garber letter to Betty Barker, 11-15-97, courtesy of Karen Swenson.

267 *"Make it brief, boy"*: AMPAS, Joan Crawford biographical file, "Living It Up with Pepsi," *Time*, 5-19-1958.

267 *"I was one of a group of New York actors"*: UCLA, Bob Thomas papers, Nancy Walker interview, box 32, folder 17.

268 *"I was presented to the Queen last night"*: Lang and Hall, p. 229.

269 *"Joan Crawford's marriage seems to be working out"*: AMPAS, Hedda Hopper papers, folder 1417, Janet Gaynor file.

269 *"I'm here, David"*: UCLA, Bob Thomas papers, David Miller interview, box 32, folder 16.

270 *"My special days just wouldn't be complete"*: Concluding Chapter of Crawford website, Crawford to Spaelti, 5-17-54.

271 *"How the hell did you remember the date?"*: Concluding Chapter of Crawford website, Crawford to Gordon and Kanin, 4-3-56.

271 *"Miss Johnson was a saleswoman"*: NEWS: *San Angelo Evening Standard*, 8-18-1958.

271 *"A fine woman"*: NEWS: Hedda Hopper column, *N.Y. Daily News*, 8-20-58.

272 *"A more truthful story"*: AMPAS, Hedda Hopper papers, anonymous to Hopper, 8-15-1958 and 8-18-1958, folder 988, Joan Crawford.

272 *"The other night I just happened to turn the television on"*: AMPAS, George Cukor papers, folder 734, Cukor to Crawford, 8-5-1958.

272 *"I can live without movies"*: NEWS: Margaret McManus, "Joan Crawford in TV Role, Epitome of Movie Queen," *Waco Tribune Herald*, 1-4-1959.

273 *"That's one good-looking Greek boy!"*: Daum to Karen Swenson, 9-97, courtesy of Karen Swenson.

273 He was on the floor: *Portrait of Joan*, p. 195.

273 *"Steele's physical exhaustion called for"*: AMPAS, Joan Crawford biographical file, *Variety* obituary for Alfred Steele, 4-22-1959.

273 At the time of Al Steele's death: NEWS: Jerry Parker, "Joan Crawford Left Sordid Mess Behind," *Anniston Star*, 9-28-1978, p. B-1.

273 *"By now I am sure"*: All the messages of condolence are reproduced on the Concluding Chapter of Crawford website.

274 *"Steele gave Joan a sense of security"*: UCLA, Bob Thomas papers, Bob Rains interview, box 32, folder 17.

275 *"I haven't a sou to my name"*: AMPAS, Joan Crawford biographical file, Louella Parsons, "Joan Crawford Admits She's Broke," *L.A. Examiner*, 5-1959.

418 - NOTES

276 *"Don't you want to read the script?": My Way of Life*, p. 51.
276 *"the most spectacular penthouse": My Way of Life*, p. 51.
276 *"He said we should get Modigliani":* NEWS: Sheilah Graham, "Joan Crawford Carries On," *Washington Sunday Star*, 6-14-1959.
276 *"You don't have to live with them":* Johnes, p. 123.
276 *"She seemed to be miserable":* Hirsch, p. 409.
277 *Six months before his death:* NEWS, J. A. Livingston, "Joan Crawford Gets $60,000 a Year from Husband's Firm," *Boston Globe*, 4-26-1959.
277 *She and Jane Ardmore attended a dinner party:* AMPAS, Jane Kesner Ardmore papers, folder 100, Joan Crawford.
278 *Crawford's Pepsi salary didn't cover her overhead:* UCLA, Bob Thomas papers, Peter Rogers interview, box 32, folder 17.
278 *"They knew I was learning":* UCLA, Bob Thomas papers, Joan Crawford seminar at Stephens College, 1970.

CHAPTER EIGHTEEN

279 *"My father was incredibly charismatic":* Jim Brochu to SE. All quotes from Brochu derive from this interview.
280 *"I hear from Helen when she feels like writing":* AMPAS, Jane Kesner Ardmore papers, folder 100, Joan Crawford.
281 *"Cesar will always break a date":* AMPAS, Jane Kesner Ardmore papers, folder 100, Joan Crawford.
281 *"It has been 18 years of disappointment":* AMPAS, Joan Crawford bio file, Morton J. Golding, "The Revolt of Joan Crawford's Daughter," *Redbook*, 10-1960.
282 *"Because we lived in a goldfish bowl":* AMPAS, Crawford bio file, Christina Crawford as told to Peter J. Oppenheimer, "My Mother's Discipline Helped Me After All!" *Family Weekly*, 9-10-1961.
282 *"She adored Joan":* Doug West to SE. All quotes from West derive from this interview.
283 *"Well, she doesn't look like either of you":* Janit Crawford McClure to Karen Swenson, 1-14-98, courtesy of Karen Swenson.

CHAPTER NINETEEN

284 *"I will always thank her":* Bette Davis, p. 134.
285 *"extremely unpleasant":* John O'Dowd, "A Real-Life Steel Magnolia," *Classic Images*, 1-2020, p. 58.

NOTES - 419

286 *"It is hard to say which was worse"*: Lahr, pp. 428–38.
286 *"When it came to the short strokes"*: USC, Robert Aldrich papers, box 45, Aldrich to Lester, 5-14-1962.
286 *Since Hyman was financing, Jack Warner agreed:* Thomas, p. 234.
287 *"Call from Director to determine health"*: USC, Robert Aldrich papers, box 44, "Davis Diary," July 3, 1962.
287 *"I think it's proper to say"*: Miller and Arnold, p. 49.
287 *"Joan was a pro"*: Bette Davis, p. 134.
287 *"Linn, come in here!"*: UCLA, Bob Thomas papers, Linn Unkefer interview, box 32, folder 17.
288 *"Bette was very . . . well-educated"*: McGilligan, *Backstory*, pp. 147–48.
288 *"In life and offscreen"*: Sherman, p. 218.
288 *"Davis and Crawford . . . disliked each other"*: Todd McCarthy, "Many Expected Successes of an Unexpected Life," *Variety*, 9-22-1995.
289 *"I know you would normally think of it"*: USC, Robert Aldrich papers, box 45, Aldrich to Lester, 3-2-1962.
289 *"Gene dear, How wonderful"*: USC, Robert Aldrich papers, box 45, Crawford to Lester, 6-14-1962.
289 *"I never give until the camera's turned"*: UCLA, Bob Thomas papers, Curtiss Anderson interview with Joan Crawford, box 32, folder 14.
290 *"There was never a feud"*: UCLA, Bob Thomas papers, Curtiss Anderson interview with Joan Crawford, box 32, folder 14.
290 *"I could feel all those evil vibes"*: Bawden & Miller, *Conversations with Classic Film Stars*, p. 218.
290 *"The picture goes in some regards very well"*: USC, Robert Aldrich papers, box 45, correspondence 1962, Aldrich to Eugene Lester, 8-20-1962.
291 *the final cost was just over $1 million:* USC, Warner Bros. archive, *What Ever Happened to Baby Jane?*, folder 631, news item, 11-14-1962.
292 *"Dear Joan, Here's my little speech"*: George Eastman House, Joan Crawford audio files.
292 *"All hell has broken loose"*: USC, Robert Aldrich papers, Cohen to Abeles, 4-11-1963.
293 *"About the Bob Aldrich-Bette Davis treatment"*: Crawford to Quirk, 5-31-1963, Concluding Chapter of Crawford website.
293 *"How can you be engaged"*: NEWS: "Joan Crawford Denies Rockefeller Nuptial Plans," *Lawton Constitution and Morning Press*, 3-24-1963.
293 *Crawford stayed for three nights:* NEWS: *Ottawa Citizen*, 7-9-1965, p. 26.
294 *He had been working as a clerk:* AMPAS, Joan Crawford biographical file, "Joan Crawford Brother Dies in Obscurity," undated clipping.

295   *"Bob Darling, Thank you so much"*: USC, Robert Aldrich papers, box 52, correspondence 1964, Crawford to Aldrich 3-25-1964.

295   *"So glad your thinking"*: USC, Robert Aldrich papers, box 52, correspondence 1964, Crawford to Aldrich, 4-1-1964.

296   *Davis thought it was hilarious:* UCLA, Bob Thomas papers, Harry Mines interview, box 32, folder 16.

296   *She was perspiring:* UCLA, Bob Thomas papers, Chuck Moses interview, box 32, folder 16.

296   *DEAR BOB, HOW SWEET YOU WERE:* USC, Robert Aldrich papers, Box 52, Correspondence 1964, Crawford to Aldrich 6-15-1964.

296   *"She is, in fact, quite ill":* USC, Robert Aldrich papers, correspondence 1964, box 52, Aldrich to Hough, 6-18-1964.

296   *I AM SO DEEPLY GRATEFUL:* USC, Robert Aldrich papers, 1964 correspondence, box 53.

297   *"You aren't half as sorry":* USC, Robert Aldrich papers, Correspondence 1964, Crawford to Aldrich, 6-30-1964.

297   *The surveillance on July 24 was uneventful:* USC, Robert Aldrich papers, Correspondence 1964, Hambleton to Aldrich, 7-27-1964.

297   *"I am sure there is no need to repeat":* USC, Robert Aldrich papers, box 54, correspondence, Aldrich to Richard Zanuck, 7-30-1964.

298   *"My heart is just broken":* USC, Aldrich collection, correspondence 1964, box 52, Crawford to Aldrich, 8-4-1964.

298   *"I could just about stand":* Bawden and Miller, *Conversations with Classic Film Stars*, p. 67.

298   *"I won't say that Olivia was third choice":* Arnold and Miller, p. 50.

299   *Aldrich was promptly assaulted with newspaper reports:* USC, Robert Aldrich papers, box 54, Aldrich to Rosen, 8-28-1964.

299   *"sick, seriously sick":* Miller and Arnold, p. 50.

299   *"I'm very fond of Joan":* Miller and Arnold, p. 84.

299   *"She thought we should have waited":* UCLA, Bob Thomas papers, Robert Aldrich interview, box 32, folder 14.

300   *"Joan could keep angry for two or three days":* UCLA, Bob Thomas papers, box 32, folder 14, Robert Aldrich interview.

301   *"I don't want to be a middle-aged Hitchcock":* Bogdanovich, *Who the Devil Made Its?*, p. 785.

301   *"Let's have dinner":* UCLA, Bob Thomas papers, Robert and Betty Young interview, box 32, folder 17.

301   *"Same thing":* Reynolds, p. 63.

CHAPTER TWENTY

303 *"We are going to do this!"*: Paul F. Anderson, "It's a Small World," *Persistence of Vision*, 1995.

303 *"The impact Welles had"*: Terry Castle to SE. All quotes from Castle derive from this interview.

305 *She was undaunted*: AMPAS, Joan Crawford biographical file, Richard Oulahan, "A Well-Planned Crawford," *Life*, 2-21-64.

305 *"Miss Crawford will be traveling"*: Walker, *Joan Crawford: The Ultimate Star*, pp. 168–69.

307 *Columbia invested just over $600,000*: Financial statements reproduced in Concluding Chapter of Crawford website.

307 *Back in New York, Crawford invited*: Baker relates this story to Foster Hirsch in an interview on YouTube.

308 *"When do you need me tomorrow, boys?"*: William Harbach to SE. All quotes from Harbach derive from this interview.

310 *"She casts a spell"*: Kobal, pp. 279, 284.

310 *"I owe everyone"*: Kobal, p. 282.

310 *Lunt had recently told Hedda Hopper*: AMPAS, George Cukor papers, folder 734, Crawford to Cukor, 11-19-1965.

311 *"I know, they're odd"*: *My Way of Life*, p. 68.

311 *"You know her?"*: Jim Brochu to SE. All quotes from Brochu derive from this interview.

313 *"Darling Joan"*: Tone to Crawford, 8-10-67, posted on starsandletters.blogspot.com, authenticated by Pascal Tone.

314 *"I used to think environment obliterated heredity"*: *Portrait of Joan*, p. 154.

314 *"He's in Saigon"*: AMPAS, Joan Crawford biographical file, Judy Michaelson, "The Bubbles Still Rise to the Top," *New York Post*, 2-24-1968.

315 *"[Franchot] could build lean-tos"*: Burgess Meredith eulogy for Franchot Tone, courtesy of Pat Tone.

316 *"[Lucy] was the only person who ever fired Joan Crawford"*: Sanders and Gilbert, pp. 311–12.

317 *"The idea of Joan's daughter"*: Loy, pp. 324–26.

318 *"It was a lovely, gracious evening"*: UCLA, Bob Thomas papers, Gloria Monty interview, box 32, folder 16.

319 *"I really don't think the stars"*: Newquist, p. 145.

320 *"wanted something for me"*: AMPAS, Joan Crawford biographical file, *Architectural Digest*, March/April 1976.

322 *"treated me like she treated everybody else"*: Braden to SE. All quotes from Braden derive from this interview.

325 *"Cranberry, why do you persist?"*: Mann, p. 373.
325 *"great gentleness"*: Crawford to Francis, 8-11-1970, courtesy of Suzanna Francis Charlton.
325 *"an inefficient crew and unit"*: Crawford to Francis, 1-25-1971, courtesy of Suzanna Francis Charlton.
325 *"the children must have grown very much"*: Crawford to Francis, 12-30-1972, courtesy of Suzanna Francis Charlton.
325 *"The script you sent me"*: Crawford to Francis, 9-24-1970, courtesy of Suzanna Francis Charlton.
326 *"Who the hell am I to talk?"*: NEWS, Kevin Thomas, "Joan Crawford One of Few to Retain Film Status," *Calgary Herald*, 1-3-1970, p. 28.
326 *"would call me at some unearthly hour"*: Shearer, p. 407.
326 *"I don't know anyone who isn't lonely"*: AMPAS, Joan Crawford biographical file, Roderick Mann, "Crawford: 'Listen,' She Says, 'I Like to Work,'" *N.Y. Times*, 8-24-1969.
327 *"I didn't cast Joan Crawford"*: Stevens Jr., p. 598.
328 *"Having to take her to dinner that night"*: Stevens Jr., p. 598.
328 *"If I lose a shot"*: Stevens Jr., p. 602.
329 *"Spielberg looked like a 14-year-old"*: UCLA, Bob Thomas papers, Barry Sullivan, box 32, folder 17.
329 *"She was not Mommie Dearest"*: Spielberg to Ben Mankiewicz, YouTube.
329 *"Joan could have been a problem"*: Stevens Jr., p. 601.
329 *"I loved to see her move"*: UCLA, Bob Thomas papers, Steven Spielberg interview, box 32, folder 17.
329 *Surrounding her were two nurses*: UCLA, Bob Thomas papers, Steven Spielberg interview, box 32, folder 17.
330 *"The roof had fallen in"*: UCLA, Bob Thomas papers, Steven Spielberg interview, box 32, folder 17.
331 *"I've been an observer for many years there"*: UCLA, Bob Thomas papers, Joan Crawford Stephens College seminar, 1970, p. 9.
331 *"Everyone has their own fears"*: UCLA, Bob Thomas papers, Joan Crawford Stephens College seminar, p. 13.
331 *"On Friday I had tea with him"*: AMPAS, George Cukor papers, folder 734, Cukor to Crawford, 7-16-1970.
332 *"Only a couple of dames like us"*: UCLA, Bob Thomas papers, Dorothy Manners interview, box 32, folder 16.
332 *"Three or four a year"*: AMPAS, Joan Crawford bio file, "Joan Crawford Making TV Film," *L.A. Times*, 7-20-1972.
333 *"She's making a feature"*: UCLA, Bob Thomas papers, Robert O'Neill interview, box 32, folder 16.

333 *"The overriding thing I remember"*: Ladd to SE. All quotes from Ladd derive from this interview.

334 *"She was never difficult to edit"*: Korda to SE. All quotes from Korda derive from this interview.

336 *"I expected to meet a glamorous movie star"*: Basinger to SE. All quotes from Basinger derive from this interview.

338 *"Her sense of humor never abandoned her"*: Johnes, p. 19.

338 *"Honey, please look at your board!"*: Johnes, p. 45.

338 *"Joan played for blood"*: Johnes, p. 47.

338 *"Among other things"*: Johnes, p. 128.

338 *"Carl, my darling, Thank you"*: Johnes, p. 66.

338 *"Tina and I have nothing to say"*: Johnes, p 162.

339 *"I hate—and I do not have as friends"*: UCLA, Bob Thomas papers, Curtiss Anderson interview with Joan Crawford, box 32, folder 14.

340 *"The reason we haven't seen her"*: Mann, p. 376.

340 *"a great man"*: UCLA, Bob Thomas papers, Lyn Tornabene interview, box 32, folder 17.

341 She usually ordered liver: UCLA, Bob Thomas papers, Irving Mansfield interview, box 32, folder 16.

341 Crawford hired a limousine: UCLA, Bob Thomas papers, Jacques Mapes interview, box 32, folder 16.

342 *"When she looked at you"*: Brown, p. 44.

342 She introduced people: UCLA, Bob Thomas papers, Curtiss Anderson interview with Joan Crawford, box 32, folder 14.

343 But all her closest friends: Betty Barker letter to Fred Guiles, 3-21-1995, courtesy of Karen Swenson.

343 *"I was strict"*: UCLA, Bob Thomas papers, Anne Anderson interview, box 32, folder 14.

344 *"You deserve a medal"*: UCLA, Bob Thomas papers, Curtiss Anderson interview with Joan Crawford, box 32, folder 14.

345 22-H had a reception room: The Concluding Chapter of Crawford website features pictures of the apartment taken in 1975 for *Architectural Digest*.

345 *"Joan was a prodigious drinker"*: UCLA, Bob Thomas papers, Robert Aldrich interview, box 32, folder 14.

345 *"She just made up her mind not to drink"*: UCLA, Bob Thomas papers, Bob Rains interview, box 32, folder 17.

346 After a party: UCLA, Bob Thomas papers, Curtiss Anderson interview with Joan Crawford, box 32, folder 14.

347 *"You are the best ex-boy friend"*: UCLA, Bob Thomas papers, Jack Oakie interview, box 32, folder 16.

424 - NOTES

348 *"She looked great"*: UCLA, Bob Thomas papers, Michael Stevens interview, box 32, folder 17.
348 *"eloquent and realistic"*: AMPAS, George Cukor papers, folder 734, Cukor to Crawford, 8-24-1973.
349 *"I deplore going back"*: NEWS, *N.Y. Times*, 8-5-1973.
350 *but Carl Johnes asserted:* Johnes, p. 93.
350 *"She was not an easy friend"*: UCLA, Bob Thomas papers, Anne Anderson interview, box 32, folder 14.
351 *"I envy you like mad"*: Kotsilibas-Davis, p. 326.
351 *"gave me laughter"*: AMPAS, Jane Kesner Ardmore papers, folder 100, Joan Crawford.

CHAPTER TWENTY-ONE

352 *"She didn't send flowers"*: UCLA, Bob Thomas papers, Michael Sean O'Shea interview, box 32, folder 16.
354 *"Take away the last thing she had"*: UCLA, Bob Thomas papers, Joseph L. Mankiewicz interview, box 32, folder 16.
354 *"I had hoped I'd see you at the party"*: AMPAS, Joan Crawford biographical file, "The Classic Crawford: A Montage of Memories," *After Dark*, 3-1978.
355 *"First I had fear"*: George Eastman House, Joan Crawford audio files.
355 *"It was one of the greatest evenings of my life"*: UCLA, Bob Thomas papers, John Springer interview, box 32, folder 16.
355 *"a loving, giving friend"*: AMPAS, Joan Crawford biographical file, Herman Rosenthal, "Legends," *L.A. Times*, 9-23-1979.
356 *"they don't want to be women"*: UCLA, Bob Thomas papers, "Joan Crawford in S.A.," *San Antonio Express*, 9-11-1970.
356 *"[My] kids are fine, they're happy"*: UCLA, Bob Thomas papers, Curtiss Anderson interview with Joan Crawford, box 32, folder 14.
360 *"She was lovely"*: Casey LaLonde to SE. All quotes from LaLonde derive from this interview.
361 *"With the economy and the world situation"*: UCLA, Bob Thomas papers, Crawford to "Johnny," Christmas 1974.
361 *"I know exactly what you mean"*: Crawford to Michael Woulfe, 2-11-1975, reproduced on Concluding Chapter of Crawford website.
362 *She replied that she was glad to hear from him:* UCLA, Bob Thomas papers, Leonard Spigelgass interview, box 32, folder 17.
362 *"If that's the way I look"*: UCLA, Bob Thomas papers, John Springer interview, box 32, folder 17.

363   *"an exquisite evening"*: Ardmore to Karen Swenson, 7-15-1997, courtesy of Swenson.

363   *Loy complained about the age spots:* Loy, p. 327.

364   *"She was mentally and physically energetic"*: Ronald Bowers, *Films in Review*, Aug/Sept. 1977, pp. 443–44.

364   *"Then Joan would take her back into the fold"*: AMPAS, Jane Kesner Ardmore papers, folder 101, interview with Betty Barker.

365   *"She was disappointed in life"*: AMPAS, Jane Kesner Ardmore papers, folder 101, interview with Betty Barker,

365   *"Work was crucial to her"*: AMPAS, Joan Crawford biographical file, Jane Kesner Ardmore, "The Truth About Our Mother, Joan Crawford," *Sunday Woman*, 10-22-1978.

365   *Her neighbors the Mertzes would run Princess:* UCLA, Bob Thomas papers, Selma and Marty Mertz interview, box 32, folder 16.

365   *"My hair is quite gray"*: UCLA, Bob Thomas papers, Harry Mines interview, box 32, folder 16.

366   *"My Very Dear Bettina"*: UCLA, Bob Thomas papers, Betty Barker interview, box 32, folder 14.

367   *The practitioner hired readers:* Barker to Karen Swenson, 1-4-1998, courtesy of Swenson.

367   *"I just wonder what Margaret and Leland"*: Crawford to Mines, 4-20-1977, Concluding Chapter of Crawford website.

368   *"She wouldn't let anyone help"*: UCLA, Bob Thomas papers, Selma and Marty Mertz interview, box 32, folder 16.

368   *She never mentioned cancer:* Loy, p. 328.

369   *"God is life"*: UCLA, Bob Thomas papers, box 32, folder 14, Margaret Campbell interview.

CHAPTER TWENTY-TWO

370   *"Well, the cunt died today!"*: Burt Reynolds to SE.

371   *"She was really her own story department"*: AMPAS, Joan Crawford biographical file, Letter to the Editor, *Hollywood Reporter*, 6-7-1977.

371   *"Cukor put a committee together"*: Anthony Slide to SE. All quotes from Slide derive from this interview.

371   *"She always treated me"*: AMPAS, Joan Crawford biographical file, Kevin Thomas, "Academy Pays Tribute to Joan Crawford," *L.A. Times*, 6-22-1977.

371   *"She was the perfect image"*: AMPAS, Joan Crawford biographical

file, Kevin McDonald, "Crawford Gathering Salutes Her Kindness, Generosity," *Hollywood Reporter*, 6-27-1977.

372 *Her Academy Award:* Joan Crawford probate file, p. 1666.

372 *Her stock holdings:* Joan Crawford probate file, p. 1327.

372 *"She expected them to be self-sufficient":* Casey LaLonde to SE.

374 *"I was well aware":* Joan Crawford probate file, Jimmy Murphy deposition, 9-21-1978.

374 *"approximately four years":* Joan Crawford probate file, examination of Christina Crawford, 2-10-1978, pp. 134, 136.

374 *Cumulatively, the auction brought in $42,850:* AMPAS, Joan Crawford biographical file, "Joan Is Gone, but Her Fans Still Remember," *L.A. Herald Examiner*, 2-2-1978.

375 *They finally settled:* Joan Crawford probate file, p. 1295.

375 *"The movie deal was with Frank Yablans":* Bob Bookman to SE. All quotes from Bookman derive from this interview.

376 *"I know that full story":* Betty Barker letter to Fred Guiles, 3-21-95, courtesy of Karen Swenson.

376 *"Christina's book is too much the other way":* Turney letter to Swenson, 5-7-97, courtesy of Karen Swenson.

376 *Arthur Bell of* The Village Voice: AMPAS, Joan Crawford biographical file, Arthur Bell, "Bell Tells," *Village Voice*, 10-16-1978.

376 *"I hated the bitch":* NEWS: Jerry Parker, "Joan Crawford's Bitter Legacy," *Newsday*, 10-8-1978.

377 *"about someone I never knew":* Fairbanks to SE.

377 *"Those of us who were raised by actors":* Pat Tone to SE.

378 *"Myrna was close friends with Joan":* Illeana Douglas to SE.

378 *"Our childhood, our feelings":* AMPAS, Joan Crawford biographical file, Jerry Parker, "Joan Crawford's Bitter Legacy," *Newsday*, 10-8-1978.

379 *"One last thing":* AMPAS, Joan Crawford biographical file, Jane Kesner Ardmore, "The Truth About Our Mother, Joan Crawford," *Sunday Woman*, 10-22-1978.

379 *"[Christina and Joan] had their ups and downs all the time":* AMPAS, Jane Kesner Ardmore papers, Betty Barker interview, folder 101, Joan Crawford.

380 *"What mother wanted me to learn":* AMPAS Jane Kesner Ardmore papers, folder 101, Joan Crawford.

380 *"She saw children as a necessary adjunct":* UCLA, Bob Thomas papers, Dorothy Manners interview, box 32, folder 16.

381 *"Cranberry is about as domestic":* AMPAS, Jane Kesner Ardmore papers, folder 100, Joan Crawford.

381 *"If the legal fee is fixed as requested":* Joan Crawford probate file, p. 1238.

381 *The legal fees:* Joan Crawford probate file, p. 1469.
382 *"She was regal":* Newquist, p. 16.
382 *"She has been underappreciated":* Slide to SE.
382 *"marched through life":* Cowie, p. 1.
383 *"Whether you liked her":* NEWS: George Cukor, "She Was Consistently Joan Crawford, Star," *N.Y. Times*, 5-22-1977.
383 *"A picture of Crawford was and is an effort":* Cowie, p. xiv.
383 *"good sense—she was loyal to her friends":* Barker letter to Fred Guiles, 3-21-1995, courtesy of Karen Swenson.
383 *"Her real talent is the way she moves":* Program for "The Films of George Cukor," a retrospective at the University of Connecticut, 1973, p. 13.
384 *"In private life":* NEWS: George Cukor, "She Was Consistently Joan Crawford, Star," *N.Y. Times*, 5-22-1977.
384 *"People are always asking me":* My Way of Life, p. 2.
384 *"They fulfilled the idea of what a star is":* Illeana Douglas to SE.
386 *"Look, honey":* UCLA, Bob Thomas papers, Geraldine Brooks interview, box 32, folder 14.

INDEX

NOTE: Page numbers in *italics* refer to photos throughout text. Page numbers in *italics* and followed by *P* refer to photos in insert (examples: *1P, 2P,* etc.). Entries including "JC" refer to Joan Crawford.

Above *Suspicion* (film), *11P*, 165, 176–77
Academy Awards
    Davis and, 292
    JC accepting on behalf of Bancroft, 292
    JC and, 160, 186–88, 236, 372
    Rosher and, 107
    Shearer and, 120
    Wings and, 44
Across to Singapore (film), 55–56
Actors Studio, 331
Adler, Luther, 198
Adler, Stella, 126
Adrian (costume designer)
    background, 89
    on dressing JC, 90–93
    Humoresque, costume design for, 197
    I Live My Life, costume design for, 134
    on JC's divorce from Tone, 140
    leaving MGM for fashion career, 157–58
    Letty Lynton, JC's dress in, 109
    photograph of, *8P*
    physical appearance of, 101
    When Ladies Meet, costume design for, 166
    The Women, costume design for, *9P–10P*, 146, 153–54
Adrian, Iris, 208–9
Agee, James, 186–87, 202
Aherne, Brian, 133–34
Albert, Katherine, 113, 225–26, 280
Aldrich, Robert
    Autumn Leaves and, 257–60
    Hush . . . Hush, Sweet Charlotte and, 294–301
    on JC's alcohol use, 345
    letter to JC following death of Steele, 273–74
    What Ever Happened to Baby Jane? and, 284, 286–93
Allen, Woody, 5
Allied Artists, 219
American International Pictures, 219
Anderson, Anne, 326, 343–46, 350
Anderson, Curtiss, 343–44, 346, 356
Anderson, Maxwell, 110–11
Anderson, Milo, 185

430 - INDEX

Andrews, Dana, 203-4, 269
Angeli, Pier, 239
anti-Semitism, 101
Arden, Eve, *12P*, 190-91, 213, 282-83
Ardmore, Jane Kesner
    ghostwriting *A Portrait of Joan*, 293
    on JC meeting Queen Elizabeth, 268
    on JC's relationship with Christina, 364
    on JC's relationship with Fairbanks, 68
    on JC's relationship with McCabe, 162
    on JC's work ethic, 365
    on lies in *Mommie Dearest*, 379-80
    Porter and, 277
    on rumors of JC's stag film, 69-70
    Thanksgiving with JC, 363
Arletty (actress), 145
Arnold, Edward, 119
Arnold, John, 36, 43
Arzner, Dorothy, 137, 138
Asher, Jerry, 96, 129, 280
Astaire, Fred, 117-19, 145, 201, 233, 308
Asther, Nils, 57, 72, 110
Astor, Mary, 45, 295
Autumn Leaves (film), 257-60
Avedon, Richard, 355
Ayres, Lew, 149

Bacall, Lauren, 244
Bailey, Pearl, 361, 370
Baker, Diane, 276-77, 304-5, 307-8
Bakewell, William, 51
Balanchine, George, 118
Baldwin, James, 356
Ball, Lucille, 316-17
Bancroft, Anne, 294
Bankhead, Tallulah, 84, 122
Bardot, Brigitte, 269
Barefoot in the Park (play), 317-18, 350-51
Barker, Betty

    on JC and Bern, 81
    JC's illness and, 365-67
    JC's letter following husband's death, 366
    on JC's personality, 383
    on JC's relationship with Christina, 364, 379
    as JC's secretary, 247-48
    on lies in *Mommie Dearest*, 376
Barry, Don "Red", 147
Barrymore, Ethel, 205
Barrymore, John, *6P*, 101, 103-5
Barrymore, Lionel, 101, 104-5, 135
Bartlett, Hall, 294
Basinger, Jeanine
    friendship with JC, 342-43, 346-47, 366-67
    interview with JC, 336-37
    JC on Davies, 64
    on JC's personality, 383-84
    on power of JC, 74
    on Shearer, 106
    on *The Unknown*, 48
Bautzer, Greg, 194-95, 205
Beery, Wallace, 101, 103-5
Bell, Arthur, 376
Bell, Monta, 37-38
Benjamin, Richard, 318
Bennett, Constance, 43
Bergen, Polly, 294
Berle, Milton, 309
Bern, Paul, 52, 80-81, 102
Bernhardt, Curtis, 201
Berserk! (film), 321-22
The Best of Everything (film), 275-77
The Big Valley (TV show), 219
Blackglama ad campaign, 355
blacklist, 176, 214, 241, 258
Blair, Mary, 302-3
Blake, Michael, 48

Blake, Robert, 198–99
Blanding, Don, 14
Blanke, Henry, 178
Blanton, Ed, 271
Bloch, Robert, 303
Blyth, Ann, 185, 188, 233, 350
B movie production, 219, 251, 303
Boardman, Eleanor, 37, 38
Bogart, Humphrey, 244
Boleslawski, Richard, 137
Bond, Ward, 242
The Boob (film), 44
Booth, Margaret, 179
Boothe, Clare, 150
Borzage, Frank, 38, 146, 159
Bosley, Tom, 327
Bosworth, Patricia, 337
Bow, Clara, 54, 56
Bradbury, Lane, 285
Braden, Kim, *16P*, 322–24
Brandeis University, Massachusetts, 338
Brandt, Harry, 145
Breen, Joseph, 123–24, 150–52, 154, 156, 181–83
Brian, David, 208, 214
Brice, Fanny, 256
The Bride Wore Red (film), 138
Brinke, Anna "Mamacita", 311, 340–41, 346, 366
Brochu, Jim
    career advice from JC, 312–13
    JC honored at Players Club and, 341–42
    on JC's alcohol use, 321
    on JC's personality, 382–83
    on JC's work ethic, 325
    on lies in *Mommie Dearest*, 379–80
    meeting JC in childhood, 279–80
    visiting JC in New York, 311–13
Brochu, Peter, 279–80
Brooks, Geraldine, 386

Brooks, Louise, 43–44
Brown, Clarence
    The Gorgeous Hussy and, 134
    JC's respect for, 89
    Letty Lynton and, 110
    photograph of, *9P*
    Possessed and, 98–100
    reshoots for *Love on the Run*, 135
    Sadie McKee and, 119
    Tone and, 134
Brown, David, 341–42
Brown, Helen Gurley, 341
Brown, Johnny Mack, 57, 78
Browning, Tod, *3P*, 47
Buckley, William F., 349
Bull, Clarence, 93
Buono, Victor, 291
Burke, Billie, 170
Burke, Paul, 219–20
Burns, David, 312
Butler, Hugo, 258
Butterflies Are Free (play), 351
Byington, Spring, 165

Cabot, Bruce, 159
Caged (film), 210
Cain, James M., 181–83
Campbell, Margaret, 369
Cannes Film Festival, 292–93
Cantor, Eddie, 38
Capra, Frank, 60
Caras, Roger, 305–7
The Caretakers (film), 294
Carey, Philip, 214
Caron, Leslie, 239
Carroll, Harrison, 213
Carroll, John, 159
Carroll, Madeleine, 213
Carson, Jack, 188, 209

Cassin, Anna LeSueur (mother), *1P*, 6, *6P*, 11–18, 72, 247–48, 271
Cassin, Henry (step-father), 9, 13–17, 24
Cassin, Lucille. *see entries at* Crawford, Joan
Cassin Abstract Company, 16
Cassin Airdrome, Lawton, Oklahoma, 13–14, 16
Castle, Terry, 303–5, 307
Castle, William, 303–5, 309–10
censorship, 111, 348–50. *see also* Production Code
Chained (film), 120–21
Chandler, Jeff, 249–51
Chaney, Lon, *3P*, 46–49, 161
Chanslor, Roy, 240–41
Chaplin, Charlie, 53, 64
Chase, Barrie, 308
Chastain, Elizabeth (paternal ancestor), 10
Chatterton, Ruth, 83
Christian Science
    JC and, 16, 125, 139, 174, 352–53, 365
    JC's funeral and, 370
    JC's health issues and, 125, 367, 369
The Circle (film), 38
City of Hope, 313
Civil War, 10–11
Clift, Montgomery, 239
Cliquot (dog), 239–40, 245–46
Cochran, Steve, 164, 210
Coffee, Lenore, 99, 227, 288
Cohen, Herman, 321–22
Cohn, Harry, 89, 359–60
Cole, Jack, 119
Colton, John, 110
Columbia Pictures, 229–30, 251, 307
Complicated Women (LaSalle), 104
Connelly, Marc, 160
Conway, Jack, 89, 130
Coogan, Jackie, 42
Cooper, Gary, 114

Cooper, Jackie, 147–48
Corman, Roger, 219
Cornell, Katharine, 109
Corsaro, Frank, 285
Costello, Dolores, 45
Cotten, Joseph, 298–99
Coward, Noel, 112, 274
Craig's Wife (film), 212
Crawford, Cathy (daughter). *see* LaLonde, Cathy
Crawford, Christina "Tina" (daughter)
    adoption of, 163
    in *Barefoot in the Park* (play), 317–18
    child abuse allegations and, 318, 375–81
    childhood of, 163–64, 191–92, 218, 281–82
    JC's estate and will, 373–75
    marriage to Harvey Medlinsky, 314
    Mommie Dearest, 375–81
    photographs of, *13P*
    relationship with JC, 281–83, 318, 338–39, 364
    in *The Secret Storm*, 318–19
    Steele and, 282, 374
Crawford, Christopher (son)
    adoption of, 163
    arrests and legal trouble of, 271, 273
    childhood of, 191, 216–18, 253
    family of, 283
    JC's estate and will, 373–75
    photographs of, *13P*
    relationship with JC, 338–39, 376–77
    Vietnam War and, 314
Crawford, Cindy (daughter)
    adoption of, 163
    cruise with JC, 279–80
    on lies in *Mommie Dearest*, 378–80
    photograph of, *14P*
    relationship with JC, 314, 380
    on Steele, 253

Crawford, Joan, in films
- *Above Suspicion*, 11P, 165, 176–77
- *Across to Singapore*, 55–56
- *Autumn Leaves*, 257–60
- *Berserk!*, 321–22
- *The Best of Everything*, 275–77
- *The Boob*, 44
- *The Bride Wore Red*, 138
- *The Caretakers*, 294
- *Chained*, 120–21
- *Daisy Kenyon*, 202–4
- *The Damned Don't Cry*, 210–11
- *Dance, Fools, Dance*, 77–78, 100
- *Dancing Lady*, 117–19, 190
- *Della*, 219–20
- *Female on the Beach*, 249–51
- *Flamingo Road*, 208–9
- *Forsaking All Others*, 121–24
- *Four Walls*, 55
- *Goodbye, My Fancy*, 213
- *The Gorgeous Hussy*, 131, 134–35
- *Grand Hotel*, 6P, 81, 101–5
- *Graustark*, 38
- *Harriet Craig*, 212–13
- *Humoresque*, 13P, 157, 196–200, 210–11
- *Hush . . . Hush, Sweet Charlotte* (unfinished), 294–301
- *Ice Follies of 1939*, 148–49
- *I Live My Life*, 133–34
- *I Saw What You Did*, 309
- *It's a Great Feeling*, 209
- *Johnny Guitar*, 237, 240–45
- *Lady of the Night*, 36
- *The Last of Mrs. Cheyney*, 136–37
- *Laughing Sinners*, 78–79, 100
- *Letty Lynton*, 109–10
- *Love on the Run*, 135
- *Mannequin*, 146
- *Mildred Pierce*, 12P, 142, 160, 181–89, 348
- *Montana Moon*, 76
- *No More Ladies*, 129–30
- *Our Blushing Brides*, 76
- *Our Dancing Daughters*, 5P, 57–58, 81
- *Our Modern Maidens*, 73–74
- *Paid*, 76–77
- *Paris*, 45
- *Possessed* (1931), 98–100, 105, 122–23
- *Possessed* (1947), 157, 201–2
- *Pretty Ladies*, 37–38
- *Queen Bee*, 251–52
- *Rain*, 110–12, 348
- *Reunion in France*, 165, 174–76
- *Rose-Marie*, 51–52
- *Sadie McKee*, 119
- *Sally, Irene and Mary*, 3P, 33, 42–44
- *The Shining Hour*, 148
- *Spring Fever*, 50
- *The Story of Esther Costello*, 261, 268–70
- *Straight-Jacket*, 303–7
- *Strange Cargo*, 11P, 158–59
- *Sudden Fear*, 222, 226–29
- *Susan and God*, 158–60, 238–39
- *The Taxi Dancer*, 45–46
- *They All Kissed the Bride*, 169–70
- *This Modern Age*, 97–98, 100
- *This Woman Is Dangerous*, 214–15
- *Today We Live*, 114–15
- *Torch Song*, 232–34
- *Tramp, Tramp, Tramp*, 45
- *Trog*, 16P, 322–26
- *Trouble in Paradise*, 137
- *Twelve Miles Out*, 49
- *The Unknown*, 3P, 47–48
- *Untamed*, 74
- *West Point*, 50–51
- *What Ever Happened to Baby Jane?*, 15P, 284–93
- *When Ladies Meet*, 165–66

Crawford, Joan (*cont.*)
   Winners of the Wilderness, 46
   A Woman's Face, 160–61, 272, 341
   The Women, 9P–10P, 146, 150–57
Crawford, Joan, in TV shows
   The F.B.I., 327
   The General Electric Theater, 219
   Here's Lucy, 316–18
   Hollywood Palace, 308
   Lord Jim, 308
   Marcus Welby, 327
   The Name of the Game, 327
   Night Gallery, 327–30
   Password, 272
   The Revlon Mirror Theater, 219
   Route 66, 220, 272–73
   Royal Bay, 219–20
   The Secret Storm, 318–19
   The Sixth Sense, 332–34
   The Virginian, 220
   The Waltons, 327
   What's My Line, 272
   Zane Grey Theatre, 220
Crawford, Joan, personal life
   alcohol use and, 194–95, 243, 250, 306, 316, 319, 321, 345
   ancestry of, 10–11
   birth and childhood of, 6, 9–10, 13–18
   child abuse allegations and, 226, 318, 375–81
   children and family life of, 163–64, 180, 191–92, 203, 206–7, 216–18, 252–55, 262, 281–83, 314, 356, 380–81
   death and memorial for, 369–72
   depression of, 158
   education of, 16–21
   estate and will of, 372–75, 381
   Fairbanks, marriage and relationship with, 4, 53–54, 56, 59–64, 68, 86–87, 112–14, 141, 189. *see also* Fairbanks, Douglas, Jr. (first husband)
   fears of, 129, 255
   Gable, relationship with, 79, 86, 147, 206, 340–41
   grandchildren of, 283, 360
   health issues of, 296–301, 353, 365–69
   Hollywood, move to, 30–31
   home movies of, 3–5, 64, 163–64
   homes of, 50, 59–60, 66–67, 266–67, 275, 320–21, 344
   McCabe, relationship with, 4–5, 158, 162–64
   My Way of Life, 334–36
   personality of, 15, 41–42, 63, 84, 97, 128–29, 131–33, 139–40, 234–37, 342–43, 382–84
   philanthropy and generosity of, 128–29, 138, 169–70, 200–201, 233–34, 248, 348, 352, 372–73
   photographs of, 1P, 4P–7P, 6, 11P, 13P–14P, 16P
   physical appearance of, 15, 20–22, 39, 41, 90–92, 191, 212, 237, 246–47, 311–12, 361
   A Portrait of Joan, 4, 162–63, 293
   religion and. *see* Christian Science
   sex, attitude toward, 86–87, 146–48, 210–11, 231–32
   social life of, 120, 125–27, 140, 174, 191, 201, 212–14, 216–17, 225–26, 236, 256–57, 267–68, 314–15, 332, 342, 345–46
   stage fright of, 124, 187, 351
   Steele, marriage and relationship with, 252–55, 261–62, 265–67, 273–75. *see also* Steele, Alfred Nu (fourth husband)

Terry, marriage and relationship with, 171–72, 192–93. *see also* Terry, Phillip (third husband)
Tone, marriage and relationship with, 4, 113–14, 124, 126–28, 136, 140–41, 245, 293–94, 314–16. *see also* Tone, Franchot (second husband)
withdrawal from society, 361–64
Crawford, Joan, professional life
Academy Award won by, 160, 186–88, 236, 372
acting methods and style of, 46–49, 69, 87–89, 104–6, 134, 166, 230, 265, 357–60
age and keeping up with changes in entertainment industry, 219–21, 230–32, 235–38, 246–47, 268, 317, 325
Cannes Film Festival and, 292–93
competitiveness of, 105–7, 118, 120, 152–55, 158–59, 165, 243
as dancer, *2P*, 16, 22–26, 34–35, 40–41
early career with MGM, 26–28, 32–49, 54–55
fan club of, 207–8, 234–35
fashion influence of, 89–93, 109
in films. *see* Crawford, Joan, in films
income and bonuses at MGM, 50, 74–75, 77, 78, 130, 145–46, 167
income and bonuses at Warner Bros., 193, 215
income from other movies and TV shows, 229, 275, 286, 294, 304, 307, 322, 327
income from Pepsi-Cola, 277
joining Warner Bros., 177–84
leaving MGM, 148, 176–77
leaving movie career for corporate wife role, 255–57, 266
leaving Warner Bros., 215

legacy of, 108, 382–86
movie rights, purchase of, 240–41
movie star, becoming, 56–59
on movies vs. TV shows, acting in, 237–38
name change of, 32–34
Pepsi-Cola company and, *14P*, 255, 261–62, 277–78, 295, 302–3, 352
photographs of, *2P–3P, 5P–6P, 8P–16P, 142, 222*
publicity and fans, managing, 56–57, 68–69, 71, 82, 93–97, 135–36, 168–69, 207–8, 234–35, 256, 270–71, 354–55, 358
in radio shows, 124, 128, 130
retirement from acting, 334
retirement from Pepsi, 352
stag film rumors about, 69–70, 262–65
in TV shows. *see* Crawford, Joan, in TV shows
voice lessons for, 130, 149
Wampas Baby Star award for, 45
Woman of the Year award, City of Hope, 313
work ethic of, 56–58, 68, 96–97, 112, 148, 185, 237, 325, 332–33, 365
Cregar, Laird, 268
Crocker, Harry, 64
Cromwell, John, 210
Crosby, Bing, 308
Crowther, Bosley, 186
Cudahy, Mike, 41–42
Cukor, George
friendship with JC, 39, 161–62, 347–49
JC's letter following death of Steele, 274
on JC's personality, 383–84
JC's respect for, 89
memorial for JC, 371–72
photograph of, *9P*
retakes for *No More Ladies*, 129–30

Cukor, George (*cont.*)
   Susan and God and, 159–60
   A Woman's Face and, 161, 272
   The Women and, 9P, 150, 152–54, 156–57
Curse of the Demon (film), 269
Curtiz, Michael, *12P*, 182, 184–85, 193, 208–9

Daisy Kenyon (film), 202–4
Damita, Lili, 85
The Damned Don't Cry (film), 210–11
Dance, Fools, Dance (film), 77–78, 100
Dancing Lady (film), 117–19, 190
Daniels, William, 104
Dassin, Jules, 174–76
Daugherty, Herschel, *12P*
Davies, Marion, 64–65, 274
Davis, Bette
   Cannes Film Festival and, 292–93
   Hollywood Canteen and, 172–73
   in *Hush . . . Hush, Sweet Charlotte*, 294–301
   JC and, 201, 324, 355, 358–59
   on JC's death, 370
   motivation for acting, 132
   in *The Night of the Iguana*, 284–86
   Jack Warner and, 179
   in *What Ever Happened to Baby Jane?*, 284–93
Day, Doris, 174, 209
Dee, Sandra, 262
DeFore, Don, 164
Della (film), 219–20
Del Rio, Dolores, 45
DeMarco, Tony, 148
DeMille, Cecil B., 89–90
Dempsey, Michael, 48
Denby, David, 188
Dern, Bruce, 300
Desmond, Norma, 97
Dietrich, Marlene, 145

Disney (company), 302
Disney, Walt, 302
Dors, Diana, 322
Double Indemnity (film), 182
Douglas, Helen Gahagan, 126, 307
Douglas, Illeana, 377–78, 384–86
Douglas, Melvyn, 126, 134, 161, 170, 307–8
drive-in movies, 219, 325
Drury, Allen, 315
Dunaway, Faye, 381
Durante, Jimmy, 313

Eagels, Jeanne, 38, 110–11
The Easiest Way (film), 78
Eddy, Mary Baker, 174
Edwards, Cliff, 77
Ekberg, Anita, 268
Elizabeth II (queen of England), *14P*, 268–69
Elizabeth the Queen (radio broadcast), 130
Ellis, Paul, 32
Esmond, Jill, 84–86, 112, 172
Eunson, Dale, 225–26
Evans, Joan, 225–26
Evans, Robert, 276

Fairbanks, Anna Beth (mother-in-law), 68, 79
Fairbanks, Douglas, Jr. (first husband)
   acting career, 52, 73
   letter to JC following death of Steele, 274
   on lies in *Mommie Dearest*, 377
   marriage and relationship with JC, 4, 53–54, 56, 59–64, 68, 86–87, 112–14, 141, 189
   Olivier, friendship with, 84–85
   photographs, *5P*
   WWII and, 189
Fairbanks, Douglas, Sr. (father-in-law), 52–53, 59, 61–65, 113
Fairbanks, Sylvia Ashley, 206

fan club for JC, 207–8, 234–35
fan magazines, 57, 95–96, 113, 246
fashion, 89–93, 109
Faulkner, William, 114, 182
Fay, Frank, 60
The F.B.I. (TV show), 327
Federal Bureau of Investigation (FBI), 262–65
Feist, Felix, 214
Female on the Beach (film), 249–51
Ferncliff Cemetery, Hartsdale, New York, 370
film noir, 183, 202, 229
Fine, Sylvia, 283
Fink, Hymie, 96
Fitzgerald, F. Scott, 56–57, 120–21, 151
Fitzmaurice, George, 137
Flamingo Road (film), 208–9
Flynn, Errol, 55, 209
Folsey, George, 96, 107–8
Fonda, Henry, 202–4
Fontanne, Lynn, 310–11
Ford, Glenn, 170
Ford, John, 173
Ford, Mary, 40, 173
Forsaking All Others (film), 121–24
Four Walls (film), 55
Foy, Brian, 178–79
Francis, Freddie, 323, 325–26
Frankenstein (film), 85
Frederick, Pauline, 35, 97–98
Free French Relief Committee, 173
A Free Soul (film), 120
From Here to Eternity (film), 229–30
The Fugitive Kind (film), 167–68

Gable, Clark
    acting career, 77–79, 86
    in *Chained*, 120
    in *Dancing Lady*, 117
    in *Forsaking All Others*, 121

    in *Gone with the Wind*, 148
    in *Idiot's Delight*, 158–59
    JC and, 78–79, 86–87, 147, 206, 340–41
    in *Love on the Run*, 135
    marriage to Carole Lombard, 170
    Niven and, 201
    in *Possessed*, 98–99
    stage fright of, 124
    in *Strange Cargo*, 11P, 158–59
Galen, Frank, 252
Garbo, Greta
    on Adrian's costume designs, 157–58
    as box-office poison, 145
    John Gilbert, relationship with, 49, 85–86
    in *Grand Hotel*, 101, 103–5
    income, 78
    in *Queen Christina*, 85–86
    in *Two-Faced Woman*, 157
Garfield, John, 13P, 172, 196–200, 215, 281
Garfield, Julie, 197–98, 215
Garfield, Robbie, 198
Gargan, William, 111
Garland, Judy, 158, 309, 326
Garson, Greer, 158, 165–66, 176
Geddes, Barbara Bel, 207
Geeson, Judy, 324
The General Electric Theater (TV show), 219
Gibbons, Cedric, 32, 43, 57
Gilbert, Jack, 42
Gilbert, John
    career decline, 72–73, 78, 103
    in *Four Walls*, 55
    Garbo, affair with, 85–86
    in *The Hollywood Revue of 1929*, 72
    in *Man, Woman and Sin*, 38
    in *Queen Christina*, 86
    in *Twelve Miles Out*, 49
Gillum, Don, 34
Glyn, Elinor, 42

438 - INDEX

Goddard, Paulette, 153–54, 156
Gold, Zachary, 196
Golden Boy (film), 198
Goldwyn Pictures, 225. *see also* MGM Studios
Gone with the Wind (film), 148, 150
Gooch, Garvene, 15
Goodbye, My Fancy (film), 213
Gorcey, Leo, 146
Gordon, Gale, 316
Gordon, Ruth, 271
The Gorgeous Hussy (film), 131, 134–35
Gough, Michael, 324
Goulding, Edmund, 42–45, 51–52, 89, 102–4
Grahame, Gloria, 228–29
Grand Hotel (film), 6P, 81, 101–5
Granlund, Nils, 26–27
Grant, Cary, 170–71, 230–31
Graustark (film), 38
Great Day! (film), 76
Great Depression, 101, 108
The Great Dictator (film), 28
Green, Lorne, 258
Green, Paul, 315
Greenburg, Adrian Adolph. *see* Adrian
Greenstreet, Sydney, 208
Grey, Virginia, 362–63
Griffith, Corinne, 83
Group Theatre, 115–16, 124, 127, 140, 197
Guilaroff, Sydney, 79–80
Gutner, Howard, 90, 106

Haines, William "Billy"
    acting career, 67
    on Davies, 64–65
    death of, 339–40
    decorating JC's homes, 66–67, 266–67
    defense of JC's character, 84, 235–37
    friendship with JC, 39–40

    health issues of, 331
    interior decorating career of, 66–67
    JC leaving movie industry and, 256–57
    on JC's children and family life, 193, 207
    on JC's dancing, 233
    on JC's late career with MGM, 166
    on JC's marriage to Fairbanks, 71
    on JC's *My Way of Life*, 335
    Porter and, 277
    voice lessons for, 72
    in *West Point*, 50–51
    on young actors, 246
Haller, Ernest, 185, 199
Hamilton, Neil, 78
Harbach, William, 308–9
Hardwicke, Cedric, 174
Harlow, Jean, 107, 118, 127
Harriet Craig (film), 212–13
Harrison, Rex, 201
Hartman, David, 368
de Havilland, Olivia, 179, 298–300, 367
Hawks, Howard, 114–15
Hayden, Sterling, 242, 244, 245
Hayes, Helen, 120, 216–17, 280
Hays, Will, 124
Hayward, Brooke, 319–20
Hayward, Leland, 319–20
Haywire (Hayward), 319–20
Hayworth, Rita, 95, 159
Head, Edith, 91
Hearst, William Randolph, 64–65
Hecht, Ben, 243
Heflin, Van, 202
Heller, Lukas, 285
Hendrickson, Floyd, 75
Hepburn, Audrey, 239
Hepburn, Katharine, 145
Here's Lucy (TV show), 316–17
Heyman, Mel, 136

Hill, Walter, 257
Hillman, James, 230
Hinsdell, Oliver, 72
Hirschfeld, Al, 279–80
Hixton, J. S., 15
Hollywood, California
    as aspirational goal, 29–30
    blacklist and, 176, 214, 241, 258
    JC's move to, 30–31
    nightlife in, 40–41
Hollywood Canteen, 172–73, 180
Hollywood Palace (TV show), 308
Hollywood Regency style, 66
The Hollywood Revue of 1929, 72–73
homophobia, 101
Hoover, J. Edgar, 70, 264–65
Hopkins, Miriam, 168
Hopper, Hedda
    interview with JC, 237
    on JC's driving adventures, 240
    on JC's marriage to Steele, 269
    on JC's mother, 271–72
    on JC's relationship with Bautzer, 195
    on JC's relationship with McCabe, 5
    predicting Academy Award for JC, 186, 187
Hough, Henry (step-father), 16–17. *see also* Cassin, Henry
House Committee on Un-American Activities, 215
Howe, James Wong, 185
Hubbard, Lucien, 51–52
Humoresque (film), *13P*, 157, 196–200, 210–11
Hunter, Ross, 249, 268
Hurrell, George, 93–95
Hurst, Fannie, 196
Hush . . . Hush, Sweet Charlotte (film), 294–301
Hussey, Ruth, 159
Huston, Walter, 111–12

Hutton, Barbara, 171
Hyman, Bernard, 130, 175
Hyman, Eliot, 286–87

Ice Follies of 1939 (film), 148–49
Idiot's Delight (film), 158–59
I Live My Life (film), 133–34
Ingram, Rex, 55
Innocent Eyes (musical), 24–26
Ireland, John, 251–52, 310
I Saw What You Did (film), 309
Isherwood, Christopher, 160
It's a Great Feeling (film), 209
"It's a Small World" at World's Fair (1964), 302–3

Jevne, Jack, 258
Joan Crawford fan club, 207–8, 234–35
Johnes, Carl, 338–39, 350, 368
Johnny Guitar (film), 237, 240–45
Johnson, Sylvester (grandfather), 12, 13
Johnson, William (maternal ancestor), 11
Jones, James, 229
Joy, Jason, 123
Jurow, Martin, 183–84

Kandel, Aben, 321
Kanin, Garson, 271
Kaufman, Joseph, 226–27, 229
Kaye, Danny, 283
Kazan, Elia, 115–16, 127, 140, 227, 285
Keane, Margaret, 276, 346
Kelly, Gene, 268
Kelly, Grace, 276
Kenwith, Herbert, 317
Kerr, Deborah, 230
Kerry, Norman, *3P*
Kibbee, Guy, 111
Kingsley, Sidney, 124

440 · INDEX

Knight, Goodwin, 313
Kobal, John, 310
Korda, Michael, 334–35, 368
Koverman, Ida, 179
Kruger, Otto, 120
Kyser, Kay, 173

labor unions, 79–80, 190
La Cava, Gregory, 150
Ladd, David, 333–34
Lady of the Night (film), 36
LaLonde, Casey (grandson)
    on home movies of JC, 3–5
    on JC and Christian Science, 353
    on JC's estate and will, 373
    on JC's illness, 368
    on lies in *Mommie Dearest*, 378–79
    relationship with JC, 360–61
    on Steele, 255
LaLonde, Cathy Crawford (daughter)
    adoption of, 163
    cruise with JC, 279–80
    JC's estate and will, 373–74
    on lies in *Mommie Dearest*, 378–79
    marriage to Jerome LaLonde, 314
    photograph of, *14P*
    relationship with JC, 314, 360, 380
LaLonde, Jerome (son-in-law), 314
Lamarr, Hedy, 158, 349
Lamarr, Sylvia, 164
Lancaster, Burt, 229–30, 245
Landi, Elissa, 85
Lane, Burton, 118
Lang, Charles, Jr., 229, 259–60
Lang, Jennings, 242
Langdon, Harry, 45
Lange, Hope, 276
LaSalle, Mick, 104–5, 383
The Last of Mrs. Cheyney (film), 136–37

Laughing Sinners (film), 78–79, 100
Lawrence, Gertrude, 159
Lean, David, 109
Lederer, Charlie, 64
Lee, Anna, 290
Lee, Sammy, 118
Leigh, Vivien, 172
Leonard, Robert Z., 165–66
Lester, Eugene, 289
LeSueur, David (paternal ancestor), 10
LeSueur, Hal (brother)
    birth and childhood, 9–10, 13–15
    death, 294
    JC and, 247–49
    JC's financial support of, 18
    move to Hollywood, 72
    photographs of, *6*, *6P*
LeSueur, James (grandfather), 10
LeSueur, Lucille Fay. *see entries at* Crawford, Joan
LeSueur, Thomas (father), 9–13, 247–48
Letty Lynton (film), 109–10
Levee, Mike, 113
Levine, Joseph L., 284, 286
Levy, Phyllis, 194
Lewis, Jerry, 231
Lewton, Val, 181
Lisbon (film), 242–43
"The Little Girl Across the Street" (Blanding), 14
Loew, Marcus, 27, 30–31, 42
Lombard, Carole, 41, 79, 170
Longstreet, Stephen, 179
Loos, Anita, 151, 177, 179
Lord Jim (TV show), 308
Louis, Jean, 212, 258
Louis B. Mayer Productions, 31–32. *see also* MGM Studios
Lovejoy, Frank, 213

INDEX · 441

Love on the Run (film), 135
Lovett, Josephine, 57
Loy, Myrna
   in *Barefoot in the Park* (play), 317
   friendship with JC, 38, 81, 343, 363, 368
   on JC's memory for names and dates, 350
   on lies in *Mommie Dearest*, 378
   at memorial service for JC, 371
   in *Pretty Ladies*, 38
Lubitsch, Ernst, 137, 150
Lunt, Alfred, 310–11
Lusk, Norbert, 96

Maas, Fredericka Sagor, 42, 57
MacArthur, James, 216–17
MacDonald, Jeanette, 80
MacDougall, Ranald, 182, 185, 201, 249, 252
MacMurray, Fred, 173, 176
Maddow, Ben, 241, 243
Maharis, George, 273
Mahin, John Lee, 242
Make-Up Artists and Hair Stylists Guild, 79–80
Mamacita. *see* Brinke, Anna
Man, Woman and Sin (film), 38
Mankiewicz, Joseph L.
   Forsaking All Others written by, 121
   on JC, 131–33, 354
   on JC's family life, 217
   JC's radio broadcasts and, 128
   on JC's relationship with Steele, 275
   on JC's work ethic, 148
   as producer for JC, 130–31
   Reunion in France and, 176
   on *Strange Cargo*, 159
   on Tone, 135
Mannequin (film), 146

Manners, Dorothy, 96, 139–40, 332
Mannix, Eddie, 150, 158
Mansfield, Irving, 368
Mansfield, Jayne, 322
March, Fredric, 106, 159, 238–39
Marcus Welby (TV show), 327
Margaret, Princess (Countess of Snowdon), 268
Marie Antoinette (film), 106
Marsh, Oliver, 107, 152
Marshall, Herbert, 165
Martinelli, Enzo, 333
Marx, Sam, 31–32, 78
Massey, Raymond, 201–2
Maugham, Somerset, 110
Mayer, Louis B.
   on actors having children, 138
   appointing Mankiewicz as JC's producer, 130–31
   on costume design for *The Women*, 153–54
   Dancing Lady and, 118
   Dassin and, 174–75
   Davies and, 64
   Forsaking All Others and, 123
   Grand Hotel and, 103
   Haines and, 67, 339
   JC and production line of, 42
   JC leaving MGM and, 177
   JC on, 56, 355
   Laughing Sinners and, 78
   leaving MGM, 232
   Louis B. Mayer Productions and, 31–32
   moral standards of, 348–49
   perks for actors, 50
   Production Code and, 123, 150
   renewing talent pool for MGM, 158
   Reunion in France and, 174–75
   rules for actresses, 88–89, 93

Mayer, Louis B. (*cont.*)
   rumors of JC's stag film and, 70
   shutting down *Great Day!* at JC's request, 76
   unions and, 80
   women employed at MGM and, 179
MCA talent agency, 181, 220, 241–42, 259, 282
McCabe, Charles, 4–5, 158, 162–64
McCambridge, Mercedes, 242–44, 245
McCarey, Leo, 216
McCarthy, Neil, 171
McConnell, Daisy (sister), 12
McConnell, Edgar, 11–12
McCoy, Tim, 46, 55
McGuinness, James Kevin, 181
McNally, James, 374
Medlinsky, Harvey, 314
Melton, Ruth Clifford, 15
Memory Lane (film), 39
Men in White (play), 124
Meredith, Burgess, 315
Merrick, James, 96
Mertz, Selma and Marty, 346, 365, 368–69
Metro Pictures, 30–31. *see also* MGM Studios
MGM Studios
   biography of JC, 9
   creation of, 30–31
   ethos and style of, 88–89
   Great Depression and, 101, 108
   Haines and, 67
   JC leaving for Warner Bros., 148, 176–77
   JC's early career with, 26–28, 30–49, 54–55
   JC's return to, 232–33
   Letty Lynton lawsuit, 110
   mortgage guarantees of, 50
   multiple stars in movies of, 101–2
   name change contest for JC, 32–34
   renewing talent pool for, 158, 167
   rumors of JC's stag film and, 70
   shift away from silent films, 72–73
   star system at, 130–31
Mildred Pierce (film), *12P*, *142*, 160, 181–89, 348
Milestone, Lewis, 110–11
Milland, Ray, 243
Miller, Ann, 349
Miller, David, 226–29, 268–70
Mines, Harry, 171, 295
Mistinguett, 24–25
Mitchell, John, 206
Molnár, Ferenc, 138
Mommie Dearest (C. Crawford), 375–81
Mommie Dearest (film), 381
Monroe, Marilyn, 55, 95, 231–32, 245, 268
Montana Moon (film), 76
Montgomery, Robert
   in *Forsaking All Others*, 121, 123
   JC meeting, 74
   in *The Last of Mrs. Cheyney*, 137
   in *Letty Lynton*, 110
   Olivier and Fairbanks, friendships with, 85
   in *Our Blushing Brides* with JC, 76
Monty, Gloria, 318–19
Moore, Colleen, 56–57
Moore, Tom, 38
Moral Rearmament, 159
Mordden, Ethan, 105
Morgan, Dennis, 193, 209, 214
Morris, John, 234
Motion Picture Home, 373
movie theaters
   attendance declines in, 176, 214, 229
   block-booking, 145
   drive-in movies, 219, 325

Loew's theaters and MGM, 30–31, 42
silent movies, 51, 55, 72–73, 74, 103
Muhl, Edward, 249–50
Muir, Jean, 331
Mulvey, Kay, 107
Murfin, Jane, 151
Murray, James, 51–52
Murray, Mae, 37
Mussolini, Vittorio, 126
Myers, Carmel, 371
My Way of Life (Crawford), 334–36

Nagel, Conrad, 38, 73
The Name of the Game (TV show), 327
Neal, Patricia, 326
Neely, Edgar, 51
Negri, Pola, 85
Negulesco, Jean, 199–200, 276
Nichols, L. B., 263
Night Gallery (TV show), 327–30
The Night of the Iguana (play), 284–86
The Night Walker (film), 309
Niven, David, 200–201, 219
No More Ladies (film), 129–30
None but the Lonely Heart (film), 231
Notorious (film), 231
Novarro, Ramon, 55–56
Novello, Ivor, 112
Nugent, Frank, 156

Oakie, Jack, 24–26, 28, 173, 347
Oberon, Merle, 206
O'Brien, Sheila, 91–92, 217, 247–48, 265
O'Connor, Donald, 275
Odets, Clifford, 196, 197
Old Clothes (film), 42
Olivier, Laurence, 84–86, 112, 172
Olivier, Tarquin, 172
Olson, Nancy, 218

O'Neal, Patrick, 285
O'Neil, Sally, 43
O'Neill, Robert, 333
The Only Thing (film), 42
Opera House, Lawton, Oklahoma, 13
Orry-Kelly (costume designer), 256–57
Oscars. *See* Academy Awards
Oshatz, Bernice, 369
O'Shea, Michael Sean, 352
Our Blushing Brides (film), 76
Our Dancing Daughters (film), 5P, 57–58, 81
Our Modern Maidens (film), 73–74

Page, Anita, 57–58, 76
Paid (film), 76–77
Palance, Jack, 227–29
Palmer, Betsy, 252
Panic in the Streets (film), 227
Papp, Joe, 352
Paris (film), 45
Park, Art, 220, 259
Parker, Eleanor, 210
Parker, Suzy, 276
Parsons, Louella, 113, 140, 171, 193, 275
The Passing Show of 1924 (musical), 2P, 26
Password (TV show), 272
Paul, Elliot, 160
Peck, Sy, 337
Pepsi-Cola
"It's a Small World" at World's Fair of 1964, 302–3
JC on board of directors for, 277–78
JC's publicity for, 14P, 255, 261–62, 295
JC's retirement from, 352
redecorating loan for Steele and JC, 266–67
Perkins, Anthony, 262
Perry, Frank, 381
Pevney, Joseph, 250–51

Pickford, Mary (step-mother-in-law), 52, 59, 61–64, 113
Pitts, Zasu, 38
Planck, Robert, 108
Players Club, 334
pornography, 349–50
Porter, Cole, 277
A Portrait of Joan (Crawford), 4, 162–63, 293
Possessed (film, 1931), 98–100, 105, 122–23
Possessed (film, 1947), 157, 201–2
The Postman Always Rings Twice (play), 124
Powell, Dick, 219
Powell, Eleanor, 119
Powell, William, 137
Preminger, Otto, 203
Pretty Ladies (film), 37–38
Prevost, Marie, 77
Price, Vincent, 125–26, 322, 367
Princess (dog), 340, 365–66, 368
Production Code
　clothing forbidden by, 76
　Forsaking All Others and, 122–24
　Mildred Pierce and, 181–83
　Possessed (1931) and, 122
　The Women and, 150–52, 154, 156
Prohibition, 40

Queen Bee (film), 251–52
Queen Christina (film), 85–86
Quo Vadis (film), 251–52

Rackmil, Milton, 249
Rain (film), 110–12, 348
Rains, Bob, 250, 274, 345, 363
Rand, Sally, 14–15
Rapf, Harry, 26–27, 31–36, 122, 206
Rapf, Maurice, 35–36
Rathbone, Basil, 176
Rawlins, Lester, 341

Ray, Nicholas, 241–45
Raymond, Gene, 119
Reckless (film), 127
Reilly, Jean Burt, 179
Republic Pictures, 240–46
Reunion in France (film), 165, 174–76
The Revlon Mirror Theater (TV show), 219
Richman, Harry, 26–27
Robertson, Cliff, 258
Robson, May, 110
Rockefeller, Nelson, 293
Rogers, Ginger, 119, 174
Rogers, Henry, 70, 186, 187
Rogers, Peter, 355
Rogers, Rosalind, 216–18, 255
Rogers, Will, 38
Romero, Cesar, 39, 255, 273, 280–81
Roos, Bo, 205–6
Roseanna McCoy (film), 225
Rose-Marie (film), 51–52
Rosher, Charles, 78, 107
Route 66 (TV show), 220, 272–73
Rouverol, Aurania, 77
Rouverol, Jean, 258
Royal Bay (TV show), 219–20
Rule, Janice, 213
Rushmore, Howard, 262–64
Russell, Rosalind, 151, 153, 155–56, 212, 362
Ruttenberg, Joe, 152, 165

Sadie McKee (film), 119
Sadie Thompson (film), 110
Sally, Irene and Mary (film), 3P, 33, 42–44
Saville, Victor, 160
Scaramouche (film), 55
Schary, Dore, 232, 233
Schenck, Joe, 110
Schenck, Nick, 126, 177
Schulberg, Budd, 117

Science and Health (Eddy), 174
Scott, Zachary, 188, 208
Seastrom, Victor, 32
Sebastian, Dorothy, 76
The Secret Storm (TV show), 318–19
Seitz, John, 55
Seltzer, Walter, 72, 168–71
Selznick, David O., 117–18, 134, 148–50
Serling, Rod, 327
Shane (film), 227
Shaw, Irwin, 315
Shearer, Norma
    acting style, 105–6
    hairdresser for, 80
    Hurrell photographing, 95
    in *Idiot's Delight*, 158–59
    income, 78
    JC and, 46, 105–6, 120, 359
    in *Lady of the Night*, 36
    in *The Last of Mrs. Cheyney*, 136
    in *Pretty Ladies*, 38
    retiring from acting, 106–7, 165
    in *The Women*, 9P–10P, 150–53, 155
    on young JC, 37
Sheldon, Willard, 238
Sherman, Hedda, 211, 213–14
Sherman, Vincent, 97, 210–14, 288
Sherry, Edna, 226
Shields, Jimmy, 339–40
The Shining Hour (film), 148
Shurlock, Geoffrey, 181
silent movies, 51, 55, 72–73, 74, 103
Simmons, Jean, 239
Simms, Ginny, 349
Simon, Neil, 317–18
Sinatra, Frank, 268, 309
The Sixth Sense (TV show), 332–34
The Skyrocket (St. Johns), 29–30
Slide, Anthony, 371, 382

Smith, Pete, 32, 34–35, 71–72
Solt, Andrew, 242
Spielberg, Steven, 327–30, 371
Spigelgass, Leonard, 125, 342, 362
Springer, John, 354–55, 362
Springer, June, 354
Spring Fever (film), 50
St. Johns, Adela Rogers
    A Free Soul, 120
    on Gable's sex life, 87
    on JC, 41–42, 61–62
    on JC's sex life, 86
    The Skyrocket, 29–30
Stack, Robert, 294
Stanwyck, Barbara
    friendship with JC, 26, 126–27, 216, 343
    as JC's neighbor, 60
    in *The Night Walker*, 309
    Turney on, 183
    in TV shows, 219–20
Steele, Alfred Nu (fourth husband)
    background, 254, 261
    death, 114, 273–75
    JC's children and, 282, 374
    marriage and relationship with JC, 252–55, 261–62, 265–67
    Pepsi-Cola and, 252, 254, 255, 261, 277
    photograph of, 14P
Steele, Sonny, 247
Steichen, Edward, 93–94
Stein, Jules, 220
Stenn, David, 95
Stephens College, Missouri, 17–21, 61, 71–72, 331
Sterling, Jan, 250
Stern, Isaac, 200
Stevens, George, 227
Stevens, Michael, 348
Stevens, Ruby. *see* Stanwyck, Barbara

Stewart, Donald Ogden, 160
Stewart, James, 149
Stone, Lewis, 103
The Story of Esther Costello (film), 261, 268–70
Straight-Jacket (film), 303–7
Strange Cargo (film), *11P*, 158–59
Strasberg, Lee, 197–98, 331
Strickling, Howard
    on interview strategies, 95–96
    on JC and Mayer, 88
    on JC and sex, 86–87
    at JC's funeral, 371
    on JC's marriage to Fairbanks, 70
    on name change contest for JC, 33
    photo shoot for *The Women* and, 155
Stromberg, Hunt, 150–51, 154, 156
Sudden Fear (film), *222*, 226–29
Sullavan, Margaret, 148, 164, 319–20
Sullivan, Barry, 251–52, 327, 328–30, 351
Susan and God (film), 158–60, 238–39
Swanson, Christina, 15
Swanson, Gloria, 83, 110–11, 351
Swanson, H. N., 370–71
Swope, Herbert, Jr., 68, 86

Talmadge, Constance, 57
Talmadge, Norma, 38
Taradash, Daniel, 229
The Taxi Dancer (film), 45–46
Taylor, Elizabeth, 234, 384–85
Taylor, Robert, 165–66
television. *see also* Crawford, Joan, in TV shows; *individual TV shows*
    decline in movie theater attendance and, 214
    JC introducing movie series on, 348
    movie stars shifting to roles in, 219
Temple, Shirley, 191

Terry, Phillip (third husband)
    background, 171
    children and family life, 180, 191
    letter to JC following death of Steele, 274
    marriage and relationship with JC, 171–72, 192–93
    photograph of, *11P*
Thalberg, Irving
    Davies and, 64
    death of, 151
    Gable and, 78
    Grand Hotel and, 101–3
    health issues, 31
    JC and production line of, 42
    JC's career and, 42, 89, 153
    Louis B. Mayer Productions and, 31–32
    McCoy and, 46
    physical appearance of, 37, 101
    Production Code and, 122–23
    Shearer and, 105–6
    social interactions with JC, 120
    on talking vs. silent films, 103
    unions and, 80
Thau, Benny, 145, 232
Theatre Guild, 124, 167–68
They All Kissed the Bride (film), 169–70
This Modern Age (film), 97–98, 100
This Woman Is Dangerous (film), 214–15
Thomas, Maxine, 107, 128–29
Thorpe, Richard, 89, 176
Today We Live (film), 114–15
Tolson, Clyde, 263
Tone, Franchot (second husband)
    background, 115–16
    in *The Bride Wore Red*, 138
    death of, 314–16
    early acting career, 115–17
    in *The Gorgeous Hussy*, 134
    health issues of, 314–15

influence on JC's acting, 265
on JC, 84
in *Love on the Run*, 135
marriage and relationship with JC, 4, 113–14, 124, 126–28, 136, 140–41, 245
in *No More Ladies*, 129–30
photographs of, *7P*, *16P*
post-divorce relationship with JC, 293–94, 313–14
in *Sadie McKee*, 119
in *Today We Live*, 114–15
Tone, Pat, 127, 314–16, 377
Torch Song (film), 232–34
Tornabene, Lyn, 340–41
Tourneur, Jacques, 269
Tracy, Spencer, *7P*, 128, 133, 146, 147, 173
Tramp, Tramp, Tramp (film), 45
Trevor, Claire, 313
Trilling, Steve, 196, 212
Trog (film), *16P*, 322–26
Trotti, Lamar, 122
Trouble in Paradise (film), 137
Trucolor, 244
Truffaut, François, 244–45
Turner, Lana, 158, 268
Turney, Catherine, 178, 182–83, 192, 376
Twelve Miles Out (film), 49
20th Century-Fox, 202–4
Two-Faced Woman (film), 157
"Two-Faced Woman" (song), 234

UNICEF, 302
unions, 79–80, 190
United Artists (UA), 110–11
Universal Pictures
Dassin and, 176
JC in movies of, 249–50, 309
JC in TV shows of, 220, 238, 327–30, 332
Unkefer, Linn, 287, 289

The Unknown (film), *3P*, 47–48
Untamed (film), 74

Van Druten, John, 52
Van Dyke, W. S., 46, 89, 99, 121–24, 135
Variety, JC's death anniversary memorial in, 381
Varney, Carleton, 320–21, 344
Varsi, Diane, 262
Veidt, Conrad, 161, 176
Veiller, Baynard, 76
Ventura, Michael, 230–31
Vidal, Gore, 125
Viner, Mort, 284
The Virginian (TV show), 220

Wagner, Robert, 216, 237, 327
Wald, Jerry
  The Best of Everything and, 275–76
  Caged and, 210
  Flamingo Road and, 208
  Humoresque and, 196–97, 199
  JC's career and, 148
  Mildred Pierce and, 182–87
  Queen Bee and, 251
Walker, Alexander, 99
Walker, Joe, 170
Walker, Nancy, 267–68
Wallis, Hal, 178, 186
Walters, Charles, 232–35
The Waltons (TV show), 327
Wampas Baby Stars, 45
Wanger, Walter, 43–44
Warhol, Andy, 374
Warner, Harry, 178
Warner, Jack
  JC and, 180, 183–84, 206–7, 213–14, 355
  philosophy of Warner Bros. and, 178–79
  salary of, 193

Warner Bros.
    employee and actor discontent at, 179
    JC leaving MGM for, 148, 176–77
    labor strike, 190
    philosophy of, 178–79
Warrick, Ruth, 203–4
Wasserman, Lew, 181, 183, 220, 241–42, 328
Waterbury, Ruth, 280
Waxman, Franz, 148
Wayne, John, 175, 205–6, 313
Weatherly, Kirby, 225–26
Weiss, Milton, 135–36
Welles, Orson, 65, 303
Wellman, William, 44
Wesleyan University, Connecticut, 336–37
West, Brooks, 191
West, Doug, 282–83
Westerns, 46, 237, 240–45
West Point (film), 50–51
We've Had a Hundred Years of Psychotherapy and the World's Getting Worse (Hillman & Ventura), 230–31
Whale, James, 85
"What Becomes a Legend Most" (ad series for Blackglama), 355
What Ever Happened to Baby Jane? (film), 15P, 284–93
What's My Line (TV show), 272
When Ladies Meet (film), 165–66
Widmark, Richard, 227
Wilder, Billy, 182
Wilding, Michael, 233–34
Williams, Tennessee, 93, 167–68, 284–86
Willinger, Laszlo, 155–56

Wilson, Carey, 35
Wilson, Earl, 245
Winchell, Walter, 5
Winkler, Jill, 239
Winners of the Wilderness (film), 46
Winters, Shelley, 286
Within the Law (play), 76
Wolper, David, 313
A Woman's Face (film), 160–61, 272, 341
The Women (film), 9P–10P, 146, 150–57
Wood, James, 19–20, 71–72
Woolf brothers, 269–70
World's Fair (1964), 302
World War II, 172–73, 180, 189, 215
Wray, Fay, 45
Wuthering Heights (film), 86
Wyler, William, 225

Yates, Herbert, 243
Yeck, Joanne, 182
The Yellow Ticket (film), 85
Yordan, Philip, 241–43
Youmans, Vincent, 76
Young, Betty, 139
Young, Ernie, 23–25
Young, Loretta, 40–41, 219, 267, 367
Young, Polly Ann, 40–41
Young, Robert, 114, 124, 138–39, 213
Young, Roland, 170, 174
Young Woodley (play), 52–53

Zane Grey Theatre (TV show), 220
Zanuck, Darryl, 89, 178, 202–4
Zugsmith, Albert, 249–51

PHOTO CREDITS

INSERT

1. Casey LaLonde Collection
2. Casey LaLonde Collection
3. Shubert Archive
4. Casey LaLonde Collection
5. Scott Eyman collection
6. Michael Blake Collection
7. Scott Eyman collection
8. Scott Eyman Collection
9. Casey LaLonde Collection
10. Casey LaLonde Collection
11. Casey LaLonde Collection
12. Pascal Tone Collection
13. Casey LaLonde Collection
14. Scott Eyman Collection
15. Scott Eyman Collection
16. Scott Eyman Collection
17. Scott Eyman Collection
18. Casey LaLonde Collection
19. Casey LaLonde Collection
20. Casey LaLonde Collection
21. Alan Rode Collection
22. Casey LaLonde Collection
23. Casey LaLonde Collection
24. Casey LaLonde Collection
25. Casey LaLonde Collection
26. Scott Eyman Collection
27. Pascal Tone Collection
28. Leonard Maltin Collection

INTERIOR

iv. Casey LaLonde Collection
6. Casey LaLonde Collection
142. Alan Rode Collection
222. Casey LaLonde Collection

"Eyman has emerged as one of the most distinguished and reliable of popular film historians."

—*The Washington Post Book World*

Available wherever books are sold or at SimonandSchuster.com

SIMON & SCHUSTER